THE
SEVENTY
GREAT
BATTLES
IN
HISTORY

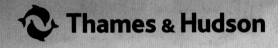

THE SEVENTY GREAT BATTLES IN HISTORY

EDITED BY JEREMY BLACK

Contents

Design: Thomas Keenes

First published in 2005 in hardcover in the United States of America by Thames & Hudson Inc., 500 Fifth Avenue, New York, New York 10110

thamesandhudsonusa.com

Library of Congress Catalog Card Number 2004195113
ISBN-13: 978-0-500-25125-6
ISBN-10: 0-500-25125-8

Printed and bound in China

Hoplite soldiers led the Greeks to victory at Marathon, 490 BC.

Ancient World

Half-title *Red Army soldiers go on the attack during Operation Bagration, the Soviet summer offensive of 1944.*

Title page *The battle of Waterloo, 18 June 1815.*

Mughal army at the first battle of Panipat, 1526.

Medieval World

At Crécy, 1346, English archers then knights slaughtered the French.

Sixteenth Century

Seventeenth Century

Prince Eugene defeats the Turks at the battle of Belgrade, 1717.

Relief of the siege of Vienna, 1683.

Eighteenth Century

US Sherman tank entering St Lô in the Battle for Normandy, 1944.

Nineteenth Century

The battle of Trafalgar, 1805.

Modern Times

Contributors

Jeremy Black is Professor of History at the University of Exeter. Born in London, he was educated in Cambridge and Oxford before teaching at the University of Durham. He received an MBE in 2000 for services to stamp design. Professor Black has appeared frequently on television and radio, and has lectured in the USA, Canada, Australia, New Zealand, Japan, Denmark, Germany, Italy, Spain and France. His many books include *War: Past, Present and Future* (2000), *World War Two* (2003) and *Rethinking Military History* (2004). **33, 35, 39, 40, 41, 42**

Gábor Ágoston is Associate Professor in the Department of History, Georgetown University, Washington, DC, where he teaches courses on the Ottoman Empire and the Middle East. His research interests include Ottoman history, early modern Islamic and European warfare and the comparative study of the Ottoman, Habsburg and Russian empires. His most recent publication is *Guns for the Sultan: Military Power and the Weapons Industry in the Ottoman Empire* (2005). **18, 20, 26, 27, 34, 37**

Charles R. Bowlus is Professor Emeritus of History at the University of Arkansas at Little Rock and has published more than forty articles in English and German on Medieval Central European History. His most important book is *Franks, Moravians and Magyars. The Struggle for the Middle Danube* (1995). His most recent study is *August 955. The Battle of Lechfeld and the End of the Age of Migrations in the West* (in press 2005). **10**

John Buckley is Senior Lecturer in War Studies at the University of Wolverhampton, UK. He has published widely on many aspects of military history but specializes in air power, the interwar era and World War II. His publications include *Air Power in the Age of Total War* (1999) and *British Armour in the Normandy Campaign 1944* (2004). **59, 63, 66**

Bruce Coleman is a member of the Department of History at the University of Exeter. His work on 19th-century British history includes *The Idea of the City* (1973) and *Conservatism and the Conservative Party* (1988). **49, 53**

Philip de Souza is Lecturer in Classics at University College Dublin, specializing in Greek and Roman history. He is the author of *Piracy in the Graeco-Roman World* (1999), *Seafaring and Civilization: Maritime Perspectives on World History* (2001), *The Peloponnesian War 431–404 BC* (2002) and *The Greek and Persian Wars 499–386 BC* (2003). **2, 6**

Michael Duffy is a Reader in British History and Director of the Centre for Maritime Historical Studies at the University of Exeter. He is also Vice President of the Navy Records Society. His recent publications include *The Glorious First of June: A Naval Battle and its Aftermath* (2002), *The Naval Miscellany* vol. 6 (2003) and articles on the battle of Trafalgar in *Mariner's Mirror* and *Journal for Maritime Research* (2005). **44**

Bruce A. Elleman is an Associate Professor in the Maritime History Department of the US Naval War College, focusing on Chinese naval, military and diplomatic history. Recent books include *Modern Chinese Warfare, 1795–1989* (2001), *Wilson and China: A Revised History of the 1919 Shandong Question* (2002), and *Naval Mutinies of the Twentieth Century: An International Perspective,* edited with Christopher Bell (2003). He is currently working on both a China history textbook and an edited book on naval blockades with S. C. M. Paine, as well as a naval history of China. **67**

Charles J. Esdaile has a Personal Chair at the School of History in the University of Liverpool. A leading expert on the Napoleonic Wars and, in particular, Napoleonic Spain, he is the author of many books and articles on the period including *The Wars of Napoleon* (1995), *The Peninsular War: A New History* (2002) and *Fighting Napoleon: Guerrillas, Bandits and Adventurers in Spain, 1808–1814* (2004). **46**

John France is Professor of Medieval History at the University of Swansea, whose special fields of interest are crusading history and medieval warfare. His *Victory in the East* (1994) is a study of the military history of the First Crusade, while *Western Warfare in the Age of the Crusades 1000–1300* (1999) analyzes the development of European war as a whole. His latest book, *The Expansion of Catholic Christendom, 1000–1714* (2005) brings together the themes of warfare and crusading. **9, 11, 12, 13, 14**

Jan Glete is Professor of History at Stockholm University. Among his recent publications are *Navies and Nations: Warships, Navies and State Building in Europe and America, 1500–1860* (1993), *Warfare at Sea 1500–1650: Maritime Conflicts and the Transformation of Europe* (2000) and *War and the State in Early Modern Europe: Spain, the Dutch Republic and Sweden as Fiscal-Military States, 1500–1650* (2002). **28**

David A. Graff is Associate Professor of History at Kansas State University. He is the author of *Medieval Chinese Warfare, 300–900* (2002) and co-editor of *A Military History of China* (2002). **4**

Ross Hassig is an historical anthropologist specializing in Precolumbian and colonial Mexico. His publications include *Trade, Tribute, and Transportation: The Sixteenth-Century Political Economy of the Valley of Mexico* (1985), *Aztec Warfare: Imperial Expansion and Political Control* (1988), *War and Society in Ancient Mesoamerica* (1992), *Mexico and the Spanish Conquest* (1994) and *Time, History, and Belief in Aztec and Colonial Mexico* (2001). **23**

Harald Kleinschmidt is Professor of the History of International Relations at the University of Tsukuba, and Professor of European Studies at the University of Tokyo. Among his many publications are *Geschichte der internationalen Beziehungen* (1998), *The Nemesis of Power* (2000), *Understanding the Middle Ages* (2000, reissue 2003), *Menschen in Bewegung* (2002), *Fernweh und Grossmachtsucht. Ostasien im europaischen Weltbild der Renaissance* (2003), *People on the Move* (2003) and *Charles V. The World Emperor* (2004). **15, 29**

Peter Lorge teaches Chinese history and film at Vanderbilt University. He specializes in the military and political history of 10th- and 11th-century China, and is the author of *War and Politics in Early Modern China, 900–1795* (2005). His next project is a history of the effects of gunpowder on Asian warfare and society. **32**

Philip Matyszak studied ancient history at Oxford University where he received his doctorate on the senate of the Late Roman Republic. He currently works as a computer systems administrator in

Cambridge and as an author. His publications include *Chronicle of the Roman Republic* (2003), *The Enemies of Rome* (2004) and *The Sons of Caesar* (forthcoming). **1, 3, 5, 7, 8**

Charles Messenger served in the Royal Tank Regiment for 20 years before becoming a full-time military historian and defence analyst. He has written numerous books, mainly on 20th-century warfare, and among his recent publications are *The D-Day Atlas* (2004) and *Call to Arms* (2005), an in-depth study of the British Army 1914–18. **60, 61, 64, 65**

Michael Neiberg is Professor of History at the United States Air Force Academy. His recent books include *Warfare and Society in Europe, 1898 to the Present* (2003) and *Fighting the Great War: A Global History* (2005). **47, 52, 55, 57**

Gervase Phillips is Principal Lecturer in History at Manchester Metropolitan University. He is the author of *The Anglo-Scots Wars 1513–1550* (1999) and has contributed articles to academic journals including *The Journal of Military History*, *War and Society*, *War in History*, *The Scottish Historical Review* and *Technology and Culture*. **21, 22, 24, 25**

Michael Prestwich is Professor of History at the University of Durham. His research interests centre on 13th- and 14th-century England. His books include *The Three Edwards* (1980), *Edward I* (1988), *Armies and Warfare in the Middle Ages: The English Experience* (1996) and *Plantagenet England 1225–1360* (2005). **16, 17, 19**

Brian Holden Reid is Professor of American History and Military Institutions and Head of the Department of War Studies at King's College, London. He has written extensively on American history in the mid-19th century, and his books

include *The Origins of the American Civil War* (1996), *The American Civil War and the Wars of the Industrial Revolution* (1999) and *Robert E. Lee: Icon for a Nation* (2005). He is an elected Trustee of the US Society for Military History. **48, 50**

Lawrence Sondhaus is Professor of History at the University of Indianapolis, where he also serves as Director of the Institute for the Study of War and Diplomacy. His latest books are *Navies of Europe, 1815–2002* (2002) and *Navies in Modern World History* (2004). **54, 56, 62**

Tim Travers is Professor Emeritus at the University of Calgary. He is the author of three books on World War I: *The Killing Ground* (1987), *How the War Was Won* (1992) and *Gallipoli 1915* (2001); and is co-author of *World History of Warfare* (2002). Currently he is writing a history of piracy. **58**

Spencer T. Tucker retired in 2003 after 36 years of university teaching, the last six as holder of the John Biggs Chair in Military History at the Virginia Military Institute. He is currently Senior Fellow in Military History for ABC-CLIO Publishing, and is the author or editor of two dozen books of military and naval history, most recently the five-volume *Encyclopedia of World War II* (2004) and *Stephen Decatur: A Life Most Bold and Daring* (2004). **51, 68, 69, 70**

Peter Wilson is Professor of Early Modern History at the University of Sunderland. His recent books include *Absolutism in Central Europe* (2000) and *From Reich to Revolution: German History 1558–1806* (2004). He is currently writing a history of the Thirty Years War. **30, 31, 36, 38, 43, 45**

40 Quebec

51 Gettysburg

41 Saratoga

50 Antietam

42 Yorktown

63 Battle of the Atlantic

27 Lepa

44 Trafalgar

48 Mexico City

2 Salamis

23 Tenochtitlan

47 Ayacucho

60 Battle for Moscow

61 Stalingrad

49 Inkerman

18 Ankara

12 Manzikert

1 Marathon

3 Gaugamela

70 The Iraq War

13 Hattin

53 Omdurman

25 Panipat

39 Plassey

32 Shanhaiguan

66 The American Air Attack on Japan

67 Huai-Hai

15 Hakata Bay

29 Sekigahara

54 Tsushima

5 Gaixia

68 Dien Bien Phu

69 The Tet Offensive

62 Midway

16 Bannockburn

22 Flodden

56 Jutland

65 Operation Bagration

55 Tannenberg

21 Bosworth

33 Naseby

7 Teutoburg Forest

30 Breitenfeld

59 Battle of Britain

14 Liegnitz

28 The Armada

11 Hastings

36 Poltava

19 Agincourt

46 Waterloo

35 Blenheim

52 Sadowa

45 Leipzig

17 Crécy

38 Rossbach

64 Battle for Normandy

57 Verdun

26 Mohács

43 Jemappes

10 Lechfeld

58 The Western Front

34 Vienna

31 Nördlingen

9 Poitiers

24 Pavia

4 Cannae

37 Belgrade

20 The Fall of Constantinople

6 Actium

8 Adrianople

Introduction

In this collection, distinguished scholars seek to give shape to the chaos of war at its climactic moments. The book covers land and sea battles, as well as sieges and campaigns in the air. Our range is global. We include not only the major and familiar battles such as Waterloo (1815) and Stalingrad (1942), but also less well-known but still very important battles. These include Hakata Bay (1281), in which a Mongol invasion force based in China was defeated when it sought to invade Japan. This ensured that Japan, unlike Korea, would remain outside the orbit of the Chinese (then ruled by the Mongols), and thus that it would follow a different course. Sekigahara (1600), another battle included in this collection, was crucial in the consolidation of Japan at the close of the protracted civil warfare of the 16th century. This helped ensure in the long term that a united Japan would be in a position to retain its independence from Western control, whereas more divided areas found it difficult to do so. Another neglected battle, Panipat (1526) in India, led to the Mughal ascendancy of Hindustan, and thus created the basic political unit in South Asia for two centuries.

In discussing the nature of battle from ancient times to the present – its causes, courses and consequences – the contributors are reminding us not only that fighting is the crucial element of military history, but also that battle has been far from constant in character. Fighting is not some result of the corruption of humankind by society: it is integral to human society. From the outset, humans competed with other animals, and fed and protected themselves as a result of these struggles. Yet, even the facts of death and mutilation have meant very different things to people in contrasting cultures. From the physical immediacy of the hand-to-hand warfare between Greeks and Persians at Marathon (490 BC) to the distancing of death in much (but by no means all) modern warfare, we are also reminded of the very different ways fighting has occurred.

Difference extends to the frequency of battle. In terms of large-scale engagements for which reliable sources exist, battle has not been spread evenly across the world. Instead, particular areas and cultures have engaged in battle, while for others, such as the Aborigines of Australia, conflict was on a smaller scale and is difficult to recover from the available sources.

Armoured horsemen, such as this Turkish example of the 15th century, were prominent in late medieval warfare in western and central Asia.

Choice of battles

Any selection of battles of course involves debate, and part of the interest of reading this book is deciding how you would have chosen differently. We have been guided by a number of factors, among which reliable sources is very significant: for certain important battles, there are no such sources. We have also sought to use the selection to indicate changes in the nature of war – some of these changes can be presented as developments in the art of war. Certainly, the greater complexity that stemmed in the 19th century from needing to respond to rail-borne troops and, in the 20th century from mechanized, aerial and submarine warfare, created problems for commanders. We have also sought to con-

sider key battles that determined the fate of people and affected the distribution of power, for example Quebec (1759), which ensured that French power and culture would not dominate North America. The drama of these clashes varied greatly, but all of them were crucial events in history.

It is more difficult to assess what happened on a battlefield than is generally appreciated. When several sources exist, the need to reconcile them suggests the problems (of omission) facing scholars when they have only one source upon which to rely. When it is possible to move from a single source to consider several, there is a welcome deepening of understanding. This underlines the drawback of work that seeks to rely on a limited

The defeat of the Spanish Armada in 1588 was one of the most crucial naval battles in history, leading ultimately to English ascendancy at sea.

13

The so-called 'Battle of the Nations' at Leipzig, 14–19 October 1813, marked the beginning of the collapse of the Napoleonic empire since it led to the expulsion of French forces from Germany.

range of material, a point made by Hans Delbrück (1848–1929), a key figure in the development of German military history, who emphasized the value of the critical examination of sources. This is also true for more recent battles. A paper on the tank strength of German armoured divisions in 1942–43 produced for the official British histories of World War II argued that casualties and fluctuating replenishment priorities were important factors in variations and commented:

'It shows how misleading formal establishments can be compared with the actual – and fluctuating – establishment of a division, and illustrates the importance of keeping this factor in mind. It doubtless applies to all armies at one time or another in their war careers.'

Brigadier C. J. C. Molony added, 'I am apt to turn a rather jaundiced eye on strength returns – perhaps because of vague memories of conjuring

rabbits out of hats, as an adjutant a long time ago!' Tank strength was a particular issue because, as Captain Basil Liddell Hart pointed out, 'To deduce correct lessons it is necessary, above all, to determine the tank strengths on either side in any important operations.' Reconciling sources involved addressing issues such as how best to distinguish those tanks that were fit for action, and also the treatment of light tanks that were only appropriate for reconnaissance duties. This serves to underline some of the problems with explaining what happened. To state that the contributors have done their best is therefore high praise. These scholarly contributions highlight what can be done in throwing light on crucial episodes in world history.

Organization of the book

The book is divided into seven parts, each of

set. As a result, Western forces were deployed at great distances, for example by the British (successfully) to Plassey in India in 1757, and by the Russian fleet (unsuccessfully) to Tsushima in 1905. This was clearly warfare across the world.

This force projection, then, did not necessarily entail success. Instead, the ability to force a path along particular routes and to gain control of individual sites did not mean the subjugation of a society. What was crucial was the willingness to accommodate (even acculturate to) conquerors. This has varied greatly, and will continue to do so, ensuring that battle has to be understood as an aspect of a wider process. For example, the Spanish conquest of the Aztec and Inca empires in 1519–21 (see Tenochtitlan p. 98) and 1531 respectively was followed by the arrival of colonists and their livestock, by Christian proselytization and the destruction of rival religious rituals, by the introduction of Spanish administration structures, and yet, also, by a degree of Spanish acceptance of local elites as well as of local adaptation to the Spaniards.

As will be made clear in this book, each battle, however small, has contributed to the state of today's world and will continue to influence our ever-changing reactions to conflict.

Aerial combat was a key innovation of 20th-century war. During the Battle of Britain, summer 1940, the Spitfire fighter plane proved more than a match for the German Messerschmitts.

which contains discussion of battles that were important to the period and also indicated key aspects of warfare. The organization of the volume – Ancient World, Medieval World, and then a section each for 16th, 17th, 18th, 19th centuries and Modern Times, the last extending to include the Iraq War of 2003 – reflects both the greater frequency of key battles over the last half-millennium and the availability of sources. This greater frequency was in part due to the expansion in power projection stemming not only from the development of oceangoing ships, but also from the willingness to use such vessels in order to create transoceanic maritime empires – a method particularly seen with the western European powers, whose ships first circumnavigated the globe. Philip II of Spain (reigned 1556–98), after whom the Philippines were named, was the ruler of the first empire on which the sun never

Ancient World

German nationalists in the 19th century raised a great statue in 1875 of Arminius, a German tribal leader, wielding the sword of vengeance to celebrate his victory in AD 9 over the Romans at Teutoburg Forest. This captured the continued resonance of the great battles of antiquity in the modern world. In 1914, German strategists planned to repeat, at the expense of the French, Hannibal's victory over the Romans at Cannae (216 BC). Greek triumphs over the invading Persians, especially at Marathon and Salamis (490 and 480 BC respectively), are still used to indicate that larger forces could be defeated by those who were more 'civilized', although the depiction of the Persians is often unduly harsh. We also consider other major battles in this opening chapter. Gaixia (203 BC), a key event in the rise of the long-standing Han empire in China, is a reminder that crucial clashes did not occur only in Europe; while Octavian's victory over Mark Antony and Cleopatra at Actium (31 BC) draws attention alongside Salamis to the key role of naval power. It led to Rome's dominance of the eastern Mediterranean.

The battles of antiquity present considerable difficulties for the historian, but new insights have come from a variety of sources. For example, an increase in archaeological evidence makes it possible to cast fresh light on battles such as that between Sparta and the Persian invaders of Greece at Thermopylae, the prelude to the more major engagement at Salamis later in the year. Other insights come from studying weapons and martial equipment. Thus, an assessment of the properties of galleys has proved very important

The heavily armed Greek hoplite infantrymen – seen here in a Corinthian black-figure vase of c. 625 BC – became the standard by which other soldiers were measured in antiquity.

for understanding options and choices at Salamis and Actium. Similarly, understanding of equestrian factors has helped lead to questions about whether chariots charged *en masse* and were therefore really deadly in battle. The net impact of research has been to offer greater depth to knowledge currently stemming from a simple reliance on literary sources. For example, in considering Cannae, it is important to amplify the Classical historian Polybius's account in order to move beyond a schematic depiction of the battle.

The battles of antiquity are frequently discussed in terms of the 'great man' approach of history, with commanders such as Alexander the Great at Gaugamela in 331 BC, Hannibal at Cannae, and Arminius at Teutoburg Forest. This approach frequently overlapped with the literary genre of the epic and with the style of the romance, thus treating battle as theatre. A focus on great men is fascinating and – in each of the cases above – their generalship made a key difference to the battle, but it can ensure that second-rank commanders, or simply those overshadowed by the more flamboyant or apparently noteworthy, are generally neglected. This makes it harder to evaluate command skills, let alone other factors in success. For example, the Romans, like the Han in China, believed in a mass army based on the adult males of the farming population, and this provided huge reserves of manpower. The Romans used these against Carthage and also in the conquest of Greece.

Alongside warfare with similar regular forces, the armies of the more settled states found themselves in conflict with nomadic forces. Thus, after the Han gained power in China in the civil war, they were challenged by the Xiongnu confederation of nomadic tribes, while the Romans were put under increasing pressure in the late 4th century, with the emperor Valens defeated and killed by the Visigoths at Adrianople in 378. The major series of attacks between AD 250 and 500 known as the 'barbarian' invasions that destroyed or weakened the empires in Eurasia and brought down the western Roman empire was, in fact, another stage in a longstanding series of struggles and complex diplomacy between such empires and tribes. These invasions were also aspects of major migrations. Some of the invasions were mounted by cavalry, which is often held to have become more effective as a result of the stirrup in Central Asia, the region where the horse had first been domesticated. Not all 'barbarians' employed cavalry, but many of the most effective raiders and conquerors were horsemen.

Marathon

1

Date: August 490 BC Location: Attica, Greece

At Marathon we stood alone against Persia. And our courage in that mighty endeavour defeated the men of 46 nations.

(THE ATHENIANS CLAIM THE PLACE OF HONOUR AT PLATAEA) HERODOTUS 9.27

Marathon was a battle of opposites. A tiny democratic city-state opposed a despotic empire hundreds of times its size. One army was almost entirely composed of armoured infantrymen, the other of horsemen and archers. This clash of cultures was profoundly to affect the subsequent development of Western civilization.

For the city-state was Athens, where a functioning democracy had been created just two decades previously. The previous ruler of Athens, Hippias, had fled to the court of Darius I (521–486 BC), king of Persia, whose empire stretched from the Aegean Sea to the banks of the Indus. Until they were conquered by Persia, the Greek colonies in Asia Minor had been independent. Unsurprisingly, they felt a greater affinity with their former homeland of Greece than with their ruler thousands of miles away in Persia. The Greeks of Asia Minor rebelled against the Persians, and were assisted by Athenian soldiers who captured and burned Sardis, the capital of Lydia, in 498. Herodotus the historian tells us:

'Darius enquired who these Athenians were, and on being told … he prayed "Grant to me, God, that I might punish them", and he set a slave to tell him three times as he sat down to dinner "Master, remember the Athenians".'

Preparations for battle

Accordingly, after crushing the rebellion in Asia Minor, in 490 BC a Persian invasion force landed at

Right *Persian infantrymen shown on a polychrome brick-faced wall in the royal palace at Susa (Iran). Their principal weapon was the bow, which they used with deadly effect.*

Marathon, some 32 km (20 miles) east of Athens. Modern research has moved the date of this landing to August from the traditional date in early September. The size of the invading force is uncertain, with some estimates as high as 100,000 men. Probably there were about 20,000 men, including oarsmen and cavalry. Marathon was chosen because it was sufficiently far from Athens for an orderly disembarkation, and because the flat ground suited the Persian cavalry, which outmatched the Greek horse.

Hippias, the former tyrant of Athens, accompanied the invaders. It was hoped that his presence might inspire a coup by the conservative aristocrats of Athens and bring about a bloodless surrender.

The rest of Greece was cowed into neutrality. Even the Spartans, the foremost military power in Greece, discovered a number of pressing religious rituals which would keep them occupied for the duration of the crisis. Only Plataea, a tiny

Right *Most of the Greek soldiers at Marathon were hoplites, their large circular shields offering protection and support to soldiers on their left. Bronze statue.*

Below *In the initial stage of the battle on the plain of Marathon the Athenian centre moved forward first, catching the Persians by surprise.*

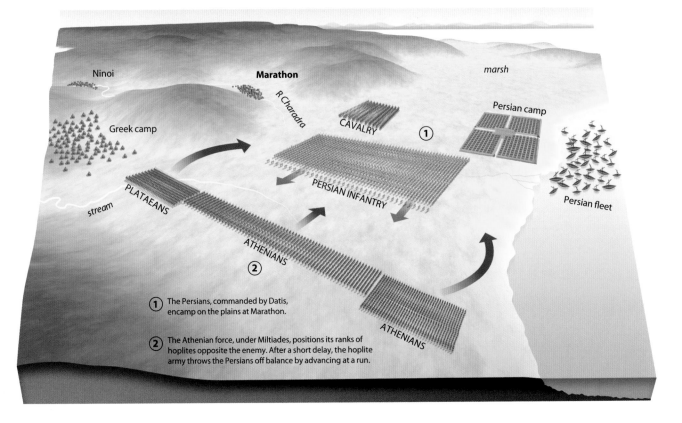

Ninoi

Marathon

marsh

Greek camp

R Charadra

CAVALRY

Persian camp

①

PERSIAN INFANTRY

PLATAEANS

stream

ATHENIANS

②

Persian fleet

ATHENIANS

① The Persians, commanded by Datis, encamp on the plains at Marathon.

② The Athenian force, under Miltiades, positions its ranks of hoplites opposite the enemy. After a short delay, the hoplite army throws the Persians off balance by advancing at a run.

dependency of Athens, sent reinforcements to the Athenian force which mustered before the plain of Marathon, in an area called Vrana between the hills and the sea.

The Athenians had about 7,200 men. They were mostly hoplites, a term which comes from the *hoplon*, the large circular shield which they carried. Each shield also offered support to the soldier on the shield bearer's left, allowing this man to use his protected right arm to stab at the enemy with his principal weapon – the long spear.

The Persian infantry preferred the bow, and were fearsomely adept with it. They fired from behind large wicker shields which protected them from enemy bowfire, but were of doubtful value against attacking infantry.

Miltiades, the Athenian leader, knew his enemy, for he had once served in the Persian army. Now he had to convince a board of ten fellow generals that his plan of attack would succeed. Each general commanded for one day in turn and, though they ceded that command to Miltiades, he still waited until his allotted day before ordering the attack.

This delay was probably for military rather than political reasons. To neutralize the superior Persian cavalry the Athenians might have needed to bring up *abatis*, spiky wooden defences, to guard their flanks. Or they might have waited for the Persian cavalry to consume their available supplies and be forced to go foraging. Or Datis, the Persian commander, might have broken the deadlock by ordering a march on Athens.

The Athenians deployed most of their strength on the wings, perhaps to buffer a cavalry thrust, or so that they could extend their line to counter a Persian envelopment. This left the centre dangerously weak, especially as the toughest of the Persian troops were deployed against it.

The engagement

To minimize their exposure to enemy bowfire, the Athenians did something unprecedented for a

Below *In the battle's final stages, although the Persians had broken through in the centre, on the wings the Athenians wheeled inwards, crushing the enemy and forcing the Persians to flee.*

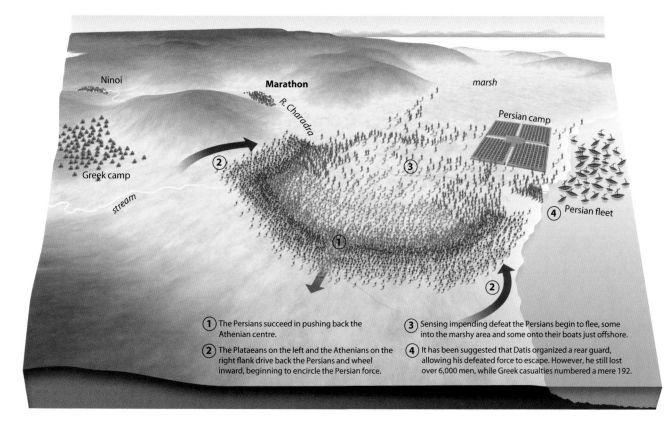

Ninoi

Marathon

marsh

R. Charadra

Persian camp

Greek camp

stream

Persian fleet

① The Persians succeed in pushing back the Athenian centre.

② The Plataeans on the left and the Athenians on the right flank drive back the Persians and wheel inward, beginning to encircle the Persian force.

③ Sensing impending defeat the Persians begin to flee, some into the marshy area and some onto their boats just offshore.

④ It has been suggested that Datis organized a rear guard, allowing his defeated force to escape. However, he still lost over 6,000 men, while Greek casualties numbered a mere 192.

hoplite army: they charged down the slight downhill slope at a run. The startled Persians misjudged the speed of the Athenian advance, and many of their arrows sped over the hoplites' heads and landed harmlessly behind them.

Though caught off balance, the Persians were tough and resilient fighters. They broke the Athenian centre and drove through towards Athens. But the hoplite force destroyed the wings, and rolled them up in disorder before turning on the Persian regulars who had broken their centre. The fight boiled through the Persian camp as the Persians struggled to regain their ships, with those who failed being driven into the marshes behind the camp.

The Athenians captured only six ships – perhaps because the Persian cavalry belatedly reappeared. Nevertheless, it was a stunning victory. Over 6,000 Persians lay dead for the loss of 192 on the Athenian side.

But there was no time for self-congratulation. The Persian fleet then started heading down the coast to where Athens lay undefended. In the subsequent race between the army on land and the army at sea the Athenians were again victorious. On seeing the Athenian army mustered to oppose their landing, the Persians hesitated briefly, then sailed away.

Above right Attic red-figure pelike showing fighting between Greek infantry and a Persian cavalryman.

Below Ancient Greek funerary tumulus at Marathon today.

Outcome

Without a Greek victory at Marathon, Athens might never have produced Sophocles, Herodotus, Socrates, Plato or Aristotle. The world might never have known Euclid, Pericles or Demosthenes – in short, the cultural heritage of Western civilization would have been profoundly altered.

Nor would a young runner called Phaedippides have brought news of the victory to Athens. Phaedippides had earlier gone to Sparta asking for help, and now his heart gave way under the strain of his exertions. But a run of 41 km (26 miles) is still named after the battle from which he came – a marathon.

COMBATANTS

Greeks
- 10,000 men, of which 7,200 were Athenian hoplite infantrymen
- Commanded by Miltiades and Callimachus
- 192 dead

Persians
- 25,000 men
- Commanded by Datis
- 6,400 dead (according to the Greeks)

Salamis

2

Date: September 480 BC   Location: between Attica and the Peloponnese, Greece

At first the Persian line withstood the attack; but quickly
The channel was crowded with our ships, and they
Could not aid each other. Soon their armoured prows
Were crashing into friendly hulls and shearing off the
Banks of oars, while the Greek ships skilfully circled
Round them and attacked from all sides.
AESCHYLUS, *THE PERSIANS*, LINES 412–18

In 480 BC the Persians again invaded Greece, King Xerxes leading a huge army across from Anatolia, shadowed by a fleet of about 1,200 warships. Many of the southern Greek city-states banded together under Spartan leadership to resist him by land and sea. Coordinated attempts to block the advance of his army in the narrow pass of Thermopylae and hold up his fleet at Artemision failed when the Greek land forces were outflanked and forced to withdraw. A small Spartan and Thespiaean rearguard resisted heroically, but was overwhelmed.

The combined Greek fleet moved to the island of Salamis, abandoning the cities of Thebes and Athens to the enemy. A prophecy urging the Athenians to put their faith in a wooden wall caused some of them to fortify their Acropolis with timber, but the majority agreed with the elected general Themistocles that their best hope lay in the city's 200 wooden, trireme warships, the largest contingent in the Greek fleet. After the evacuation of the Athenians to Salamis had been completed, the Greek fleet assembled in the bay on the eastern side of the island.

When the news came that the Acropolis of Athens had been occupied, the Spartan commander Eurybiades ordered his captains to withdraw under cover of darkness to a more defensible position on the Isthmus of Corinth, but he changed his mind later that night and the Greeks sailed out to confront the Persians the

Fifth-century BC lapis lazuli head of a young Persian prince, possibly representing Xerxes I, son of Darius I.

next morning. Herodotus claims that Themistocles sent a secret message to warn Xerxes that the Greeks were about to withdraw, causing him to send ships around Salamis to cut off the Greeks' retreat and forcing Eurybiades to risk a battle.

This story is a highly dubious one, assuming as it does that King Xerxes and his commanders would trust such a message, and that Themistocles would have thought it advantageous to provoke a Persian attack. It is more likely that the Persians planned to surround the Greeks, as they had attempted once before at Artemision. Their aim would have been to drive the Greek ships northwards and westwards out of the narrow

23

channel between Salamis and the mainland, into the open waters of the Bay of Eleusis, and attack them from two sides. For this purpose Xerxes despatched 200 Egyptian ships in the early evening to sail right round Salamis and come at the Greeks from the direction of Eleusis. He also sent a flotilla to cruise the waters around the southern end of the island, while his main fleet (around 600 ships) moved into position at the eastern approaches to the narrow straits, ready to advance at dawn.

The Greeks were made aware of these manoeuvres by Aristeides, an exiled Athenian politician who had returned to join in the fight against the Persians and had probably been sent on a scouting mission to determine whether the escape route to the west was clear. His news was greeted with dismay in the Greek camp, but the commanders resolved to sail out at dawn and take the Persians on in the narrows between Salamis and the mainland, hoping that the superior numbers of the enemy would count for less in such confined spaces.

The battle

In eager anticipation of a magnificent victory, King Xerxes positioned himself opposite Salamis with a good view of the small island of Psyttaleia, where a detachment of Persian troops had been landed during the night. But instead of witnessing his fleet's final triumph over the Greeks, Xerxes saw a naval disaster unfold before his very eyes. The various ethnic contingents of the Persian fleet were lined up several rows deep across the narrow channel with the Phoenicians on the right wing, nearest to Xerxes's position, and the Ionians on the left, nearest to Salamis. As they moved further into the channel their ships became so compacted and confused that they found it impossible to keep in formation. The crews were tired and to make matters worse a strong swell developed, making it even harder for the ships to make headway. Themistocles had anticipated this and seems to have persuaded the other Greek

A Roman copy of a portrait bust of Themistocles from Ostia, possibly based on a 5th-century BC original from Athens.

commanders to delay engaging the Persians until they were clearly in disorder. With the Athenian ships leading, the Greeks rowed out from the shore and turned towards the enemy. On a given signal their fresh crews surged forward and broke through the Persian lines to ram individual ships as they struggled to manoeuvre.

The Persians would have been expecting the Greeks to flee before their superior force, according to the plan worked out the previous day. But, like all ancient battles, once the action had started it was impossible to keep to a specific plan, and the captains of the individual ships were forced to make decisions on the spot. The main decision made by many of Xerxes's captains was to turn away from the attacking Greeks, causing confusion as they encountered more of their own ships trying to advance. In the resulting

chaos the Greek captains urged on their much fresher crews and pressed the attack with great success.

It is impossible to describe the full course of the battle in detail. Our main source, the writer Herodotus, offers only a series of anecdotes about various groups of combatants. It was claimed that 70 Corinthian ships under Adeimantos turned and fled towards the Bay of Eleusis. It is likely that this supposed cowardly northward retreat, which Herodotus presents as an Athenian slander against the Corinthians, may have been a deliberate move to engage the Egyptian squadron and prevent it from attacking the Greek rear. The Corinthians maintained that their ships did not encounter the Egyptians but returned to the battle and acquitted themselves as well as any of the Greeks. One of the most colourful anecdotes concerns Artemisia, the ruler of Herodotus's home city Halicarnassus, which was subject to the Persians. She was in command of her own ship and in the front line of the Persian fleet. When an Athenian trireme bore down on her she tried to escape, but found her path blocked by other Persian ships. In desperation she ordered her helmsman to ram one of them, which sank with the loss of all its crew. The pursuing Athenian captain assumed that Artemisia's ship was on his side and changed course towards another Persian vessel. Xerxes and his advisors saw the incident and recognized Artemisia's ship by its ensign, but their belief that she had sunk a Greek trireme then earned her the king's admiration. Xerxes is also said to have remarked at this point, 'My men have acted like women and my women like men.'

A watercolour of the sea battle of Salamis. This imaginative reconstruction vividly conveys the chaotic nature of the battle in the straits.

Yet another victory for the Greeks as the Persian fleet is routed and defeated by nightfall.

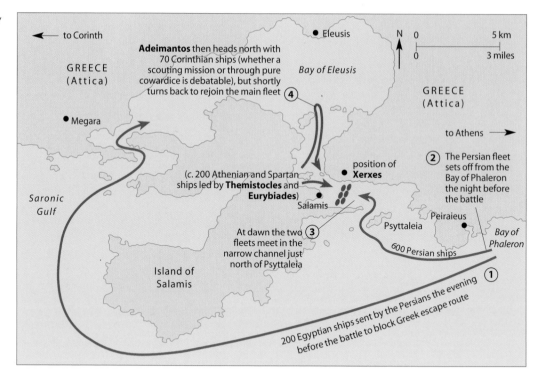

Another story concerns the Persian soldiers on the island of Psyttaleia. They were placed there in anticipation of the bulk of the Greek fleet being driven north and westwards away from the island. Instead they were isolated from their own ships and left vulnerable to attack from the nearby shores of Salamis. Right before Xerxes's eyes his elite troops, including three of his own nephews, were slaughtered by the Athenians.

Along the coast of Salamis, other Persians who managed to get ashore from their foundering ships were killed or captured. Towards the end of the day the Persian fleet retreated in confusion to the Bay of Phaleron, having lost more than 200 ships and having failed in its objective of forcing the Greeks away from Salamis. The Greeks had lost only about 40 ships and sent the enemy back to their anchorage in disarray.

COMBATANTS

Greeks

• Over 300 ships

• Commanded by Eurybiades (Spartan), Themistocles (Athenian), Adeimantos (Corinthian)

• 40 ships lost

Persians

• *c.* 800 ships

• Commanded by King Xerxes

• Over 200 ships lost

Aftermath

Xerxes took the remains of his fleet and much of his army back to Anatolia, leaving his general Mardonius with a substantial army in central Greece. The following year a Greek army led by the Spartan king Pausanias defeated them at Plataea, north of Athens, effectively freeing mainland Greece from the threat of Persian domination. Themistocles was honoured by the Spartans for his part in the victory, but his own countrymen seem to have turned against him, eventually forcing him to take refuge with the Persians. Xerxes's son Artaxerxes I made him governor of Magnesia on the Maeander River, where he died around 459 BC.

Gaugamela

Date: 1 October 331 BC   Location: Mesopotamia (modern Iraq)

Alexander said that Darius had relieved any anxiety he might have had by
bringing his massed forces together so that in one day everything could be decided,
and they would be spared a long period of difficulty and danger.
DIODORUS SICULUS, *BIBLIOTHECA HISTORIA*, 17.56.1

On 1 October 331 BC two armies met in Mesopotamia to decide the fate of an empire. The larger by far of these armies was commanded by Darius III, king of kings, and master of all between the Euphrates and Afghanistan. Once, his domains had reached the Mediterranean, but these lands had been conquered by the invading Macedonians of Alexander the Great. Darius had offered Alexander a huge bribe in a desperate effort to secure peace. Parmenio, one of Alexander's generals, had commented, 'I would take it if I were you,' and Alexander had replied sharply, 'Yes, I would, if I were *you*.'

His offer rejected, Darius collected a massive army of about a quarter of a million men, including Scythians from the shores of the Black Sea and Bactrians from the foothills of the Himalayas. He also recruited 6,000 Greek mercenaries as a personal bodyguard.

Darius chose his battlefield carefully. At Issus in 333 BC the terrain had not allowed him to use his superior numbers. This time, he chose the plain of Gaugamela, near Irbil in modern Iraq. (The Greek historian Plutarch says that Gaugamela meant 'camel's home', being named after the beast that had once taken a refugee king to safety there.)

Darius's cavalry ranged from horse archers to armoured cataphracts, and was his main striking force. The wide plain gave his cavalry a good chance of overwhelming Alexander's horse. Though the latter were superior in quality, they numbered 7,000 against Darius's 40,000. The Macedonian cavalry wore body armour and

Persian guards of the king in fluted hats. They held the centre of the Persian infantry line at Gaugamela. The elite Persian infantry were known as the 'Immortals'. The ceremonial dress here was probably replaced with more practical clothing on the battlefield. As well as spears with a 'pomegranate' counter-weight, like most Persian infantrymen they also carried bows.

helmets, but probably fought shieldless, needing both hands to control their long cornel-wood spears (called *sarissae*). The cavalry who fought alongside Alexander were called the 'Companions'.

The historian Arrian puts the Macedonian

infantry at some 40,000 men, a fraction of Darius's host. But the Persian foot were mostly poorly armed and almost untrained, whereas Alexander was leading hardened veterans accustomed to victory. Some Macedonians were conventionally armed *hypaspists* (shield-bearers), but the backbone of the infantry were *phalangites*. These fought in ranks up to eight deep, yet every man could bring his immensely long pike to bear. When lowered, these pikes presented the enemy with a hedge of spearpoints. This 'phalanx' was formidable only if it retained its formation. If disordered, it could be overwhelmed and, to do this, Darius had scythed chariots.

These chariots had two weaknesses. They were vulnerable to cavalry and they required the smoothest of terrain, since their huge scythes made any loss of formation catastrophic. Darius relied on his cavalry to protect his chariots, and on the battlefield he carefully prepared a number of obstacle-free runs to take the chariots into the heart of Alexander's infantry. There may have been a few elephants to follow up the chariots, and after the cavalry had broken up the phalanx yet further, the Persian infantry would finish the job with sheer weight of numbers.

Below Darius chose a battlefield in which he hoped his chariots would disrupt the Macedonian infantry, allowing his huge superiority in numbers to swamp the invaders before they could rally. Alexander countered by refusing to attack his enemy head-on, and moving his force ever further to the flank as the two sides closed in.

On the battlefield

Alexander was soon on his way. He had taken an eclipse of the moon earlier in the month as a sign presaging victory. Establishing his main camp by the River Boulemus, he pushed on with his men carrying only battle gear and a few days' supplies.

The Macedonians reached Gaugamela in the early afternoon of 30 September and discovered the king's army drawn up, with its battle front extending kilometres across the plain. Alexander wanted to rush immediately into battle, but Parmenio urged restraint. This probably saved the

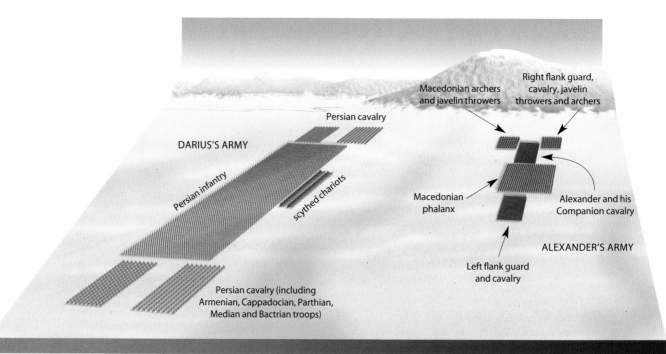

Persian cavalry

DARIUS'S ARMY

Persian infantry

scythed chariots

Persian cavalry (including Armenian, Cappadocian, Parthian, Median and Bactrian troops)

Macedonian archers and javelin throwers

Right flank guard, cavalry, javelin throwers and archers

Macedonian phalanx

Alexander and his Companion cavalry

ALEXANDER'S ARMY

Left flank guard and cavalry

Left *Part of a Macedonian phalanx in battle array. The main function of Alexander's phalanx was to pin the enemy forces until the cavalry could exploit any weaknesses in the enemy's line.*

Below *The angled Macedonian advance made Darius launch his chariots early, and his cavalry force had to gallop from the distant right flank before they could engage. By this time, Alexander had already hit the opposite flank, and was cutting through towards the centre and Darius himself.*

army, since Alexander then took the time to scout and discovered the chariot runs of Darius's trap.

But Alexander refused to countenance Parmenio's idea of fighting at night, when darkness would mitigate the Persian advantage of numbers. 'I will not steal victory', declared Alexander haughtily. This forced Darius to keep his troops standing to all night just in case, while the Macedonians gained a night's rest.

At dawn, Alexander's army formed up with parade-ground precision, slightly to the left of the Persian centre where Darius was stationed. They advanced, but obliquely and towards the Persians' left. This crabwise attack took them away from Darius's chariot runs and forced the Persian king to extend the left wing of his army.

Darius had to launch his chariots earlier than planned. As they closed in, the chariots were met by javelins and arrows. When the remnants reached the phalanx, the files opened smoothly and they passed harmlessly through.

As Darius had planned, the phalanx was now vulnerable. But his chariots had attacked too soon, and the cavalry intended to exploit the

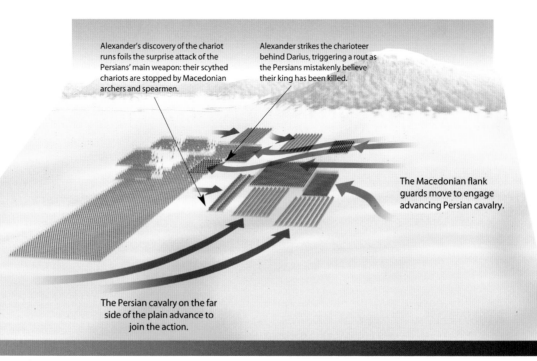

Alexander's discovery of the chariot runs foils the surprise attack of the Persians' main weapon: their scythed chariots are stopped by Macedonian archers and spearmen.

Alexander strikes the charioteer behind Darius, triggering a rout as the Persians mistakenly believe their king has been killed.

The Macedonian flank guards move to engage advancing Persian cavalry.

The Persian cavalry on the far side of the plain advance to join the action.

opening of the phalanx was blocked by a counter-attack from Alexander's lancers. Hastily Darius ordered the cavalry on the right wing to join the battle, but these had considerable ground to cover before they reached the Macedonian left, commanded by Parmenio.

Alexander joined the battle personally, leading his Companions against the left wing of the Persian infantry. According to Plutarch, 'The barbarians were starting to scatter. Alexander followed up strongly, driving the enemy into the midst of the battle, and to where Darius was commanding at the centre of his line.'

The battle was finely balanced. Darius's chariots had failed, but his cavalry was pressing back the lancers. On the right flank, the Persian cavalry had struck the Macedonian left, which was fraying fast. If the cavalry could get among the phalangites and disorder them, Darius could smother the remnants with his infantry.

What had been a generals' battle broke into a confused mêlée. The cavalry had created huge clouds of dust, blinding everyone from all but their own corner of the field. Alexander was too busy with his style of hands-on leadership to see the whole picture, while Darius was hampered by the bulk and inexperience of his army.

Darius against Alexander

Consequently, when the Persian cavalry broke through the Macedonian left, they believed that victory was imminent and charged on to take Alexander's camp. Meanwhile the Macedonian right hit the left flank of the Persian army, following Alexander who was intent on reaching Darius. As with chess, if the king was taken the game was won. The Sicilian historian Diodorus Siculus believed that Darius fought well:

'The Persian king met the Macedonian attack on his chariot, raining javelins on his enemies, with his bodyguard at his back. As the two kings closed the range between them, a javelin hurled by Alexander missed Darius, but impaled the chariot driver standing behind him, knocking him off the chariot. A shout went up at this from the Persians around Darius, and those further away from the scene thought their king had been brought down. These

people were the first to flee, and then those beside them, and so on until the entire Persian army disintegrated. With the enemy now on both flanks, the king became worried. He drew back, and this was the signal for a general rout.'

Alexander's biographers – Arrian, Curtius Rufus and Plutarch – have Darius fleeing at the mere sight of Alexander, but these accounts are not contemporary. A laconic account from a Babylonian astronomical calendar supports Diodorus's suggestion that Darius's army deserted *him* rather than vice versa.

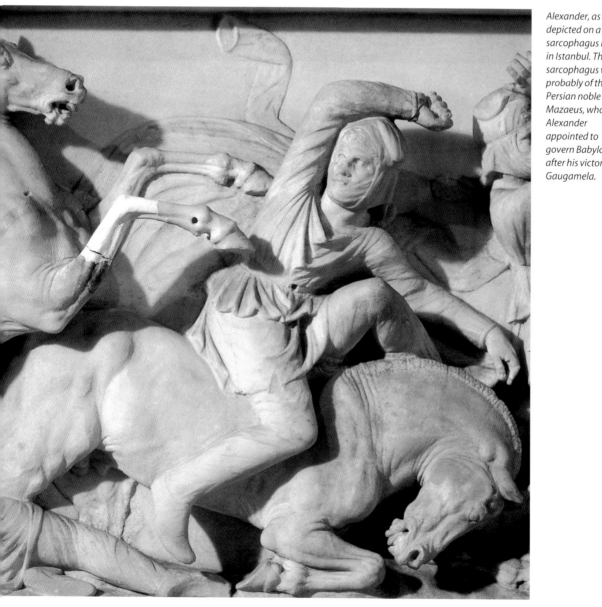

Alexander, as depicted on a sarcophagus now in Istanbul. The sarcophagus was probably of the Persian noble Mazaeus, whom Alexander appointed to govern Babylon after his victory at Gaugamela.

Aftermath

News of Alexander's success was slow to reach the Macedonian left, where Parmenio was having a torrid time. He had swung his reserves about to cover the rear of the army, and was almost surrounded on three sides. Receiving Parmenio's call for help, Alexander promptly rushed to the rescue. But by the time he reached Parmenio's side, a spirited charge by the Thessalian cavalry, combined with bad news from the rest of the battlefield, had already caused the Persians to retreat.

Alexander led a brutal chase towards the city of Arbela, slaying tens of thousands of fleeing Persians. He was haunted by the thought that Darius would raise another army with these men and that he would have to fight again. But in fact Darius was later assassinated by Bessus, the general who had commanded the left wing of the Persian army here at Gaugamela.

With the death of his rival, Alexander became undisputed lord of the Persian empire, and Greek influence stretched from its ancient homeland almost to the Himalayas.

Cannae

Date: 2 August 216 BC Location: modern Cannosa, southeast Italy

On the next day, when he had command, Varro did as expected and,
without consulting his colleague in any way at all, ordered the men to prepare for battle.
He then drew up the legions and marched them across the river. Paullus followed, despite
his deep disquiet at what was being done.
(THE ROMAN COMMANDERS BEFORE CANNAE, 216 BC) LIVY 22.45

Right *The Capua bust, presumed to be of Hannibal. The Romans imagined Hannibal to be vindictive and inhumanly cruel, qualities which this artist has captured well.*

The Second Punic War (218–202 BC) is sometimes, quite justifiably, called 'Hannibal's War'. Hannibal's desire to avenge the defeat of Carthage in the First Punic War (264–241 BC) inspired him to gather an army in Spain and, in one of the most famous marches in history, take that army over the Alps into Italy.

This invasion had a political as well as a military objective. Hannibal hoped that once his army was on Italian soil the peoples of Italy would rise against Rome. This was realistic, for the Samnites of central Italy had only recently been conquered. Many Greek cities in the south, such as Naples and Taranto, chafed under Roman rule, and the Gauls of northern Italy were both unconquered and hostile.

Though the Gauls flocked enthusiastically to Hannibal's banner, the rest of Italy remained unconvinced. Hannibal defeated the Romans at Trebbia in 218, and again crushingly at Lake Trasimene in 217, but there was no general uprising against Rome.

In 216 Hannibal tried again, capturing Roman stores at Cannae (modern Cannosa) and positioning his army across the Roman supply lines, from where he dared them to dislodge him. Hannibal felt it necessary to resort to this because Fabius Maximus ('the Delayer') had adopted the tactic of stalking Hannibal's army – never offering battle, but never drawing off to allow the Carthaginians to forage unhindered.

However, unknown to Hannibal, Roman policy had changed. Rome had resolved to destroy him

once and for all and had mustered 16 legions, together with supporting auxiliaries and cavalry. This represented 80,000 infantry and a further 6,000 cavalry. To put this into perspective, 300 years later when Rome's power stretched from Britain to Mesopotamia, the empire had in total about 25 legions.

The antagonists

To add to Hannibal's problems, the Roman legion was beyond doubt the finest fighting force in antiquity. At this time the legionaries fought in chain mail and carried slightly oval shields. Their main weapons were a heavy throwing spear, the *pilum*, and a deadly short sword called the *gladius*. The legionaries fought in close formation, almost shoulder-to-shoulder, stabbing underarm with their *gladii*. Most of their opponents fought with longer swords and needed a greater frontage so as to slash effectively. This almost guaranteed the legionaries local superiority on the battlefield, no matter what the overall odds, since the Romans could put three men against their enemies' two.

Hannibal commanded a rag-bag of nationalities. He had Lusitanians and Celtiberians from Spain, Gauls from the Alpine passes, recruits from Italy itself, a hard core of Libyan infantrymen, and cavalry from Numidia in north Africa. It is a testament to Hannibal's quality as a leader that in all the years he was in Italy the different components of his army remained well disciplined and completely under control. Only soldiers with complete faith in their commander could have carried out Hannibal's plan at Cannae.

Hannibal could guess that Rome's formidable infantry would drive straight at his line, confidently expecting to break it. Livy's reports of disagreements between the Roman consuls about this tactic are probably to shift blame from the patrician consul Aemilius Paullus. The other consul was the plebeian Terentius Varro. Normally each Roman consul commanded his own army, for the consulship was the top political and military position in Rome. But so huge was this Roman army that both consuls were present, and commanding on alternate days.

The day of battle

At Cannae on the morning of 2 August 216 BC, Aemilius Paullus led the cavalry on the Roman right, facing the Spanish and Gallic heavy cavalry between the River Aufidius (the modern Ofanto) and the left flank of Hannibal's infantry. On Hannibal's other flank was the Numidian cavalry under Maharbal, a dashing commander with a string of successful engagements to his name.

Hannibal and his brother Mago commanded the centre where the main blow would fall, and

where total precision was required. Perhaps the most reliable of Hannibal's troops were the Libyans, who wore mostly Roman armour won in earlier victories, and were an obvious choice to take the first shock of the Roman charge. But instead Hannibal placed his Gallic and Spanish troops in the centre, with the Libyans in two solid blocks on right and left behind the front line.

The battle began with Hannibal's heavy cavalry breaking the Roman horse of Paullus with a savage charge. This would not have surprised the Romans. Hannibal's superiority in cavalry had been known ever since an action at the River Ticinus near Pavia in 218, when the Roman commander Publius Scipio (father of the great general Scipio Africanus) had been wounded.

So while Terentius Varro led his cavalry against Maharbal's Numidian horse, Paullus abandoned his routed troops and rejoined the main body of the army as it crashed into the Carthaginian line. This bowed under the impact, starting slowly to give way. Polybius tells us:

'Paullus threw himself into where the fighting was fiercest in the centre of the line, smiting the enemy and urging on his men. Hannibal, who had been in that place since the start of the battle, was doing exactly the same.'

Part of the relief of Domitius Ahenobarbus showing soldiers wearing chain mail and with shields. Note that these shields were longer and more oval than legionary shields in the empire. In the legions the armour (lorica hamata) was eventually replaced by the better-known 'lobster plate' armour (lorica segmentata), but it continued in use among the auxiliaries.

For Hannibal it was crucial that his centre gave ground without breaking. In ancient warfare, most casualties were suffered when a battle line broke and the routers were cut down. When a line did break, those with the best chance of survival were those who ran first, so morale and discipline were essential in holding a line under pressure and going backwards. The Gauls and Spaniards, despite their reputation for indiscipline, did exactly as Hannibal required.

Behind the Romans, developments became ominous. The Carthaginian heavy cavalry rallied from its pursuit of the Roman horse, and rode across the back of the battle line to fall on Varro's cavalry. Attacked from two sides, the Roman cavalry bolted, leaving thousands of Carthaginian cavalry unchecked behind the Roman infantry.

The Roman commanders still felt that victory was close. The Carthaginian centre was buckling. Roman reserves poured into the breach, bending their battle line into a blunted V. At the point of the V the Gauls and Spaniards were at their last gasp. But on each side were the Libyan infantry, and before the Romans could reorganize, these Libyans turned and fell on the Roman flanks. At that moment, the Carthaginian cavalry attacked the rear of the Roman battle line.

Massacre

It was a classic envelopment manoeuvre. The Romans were surrounded, disordered and hampered by their own numbers. Experienced infantry might conceivably have fought their way out of the trap, but many of the Roman legionaries were new recruits, fighting their very first battle. Though in a hopeless situation, they

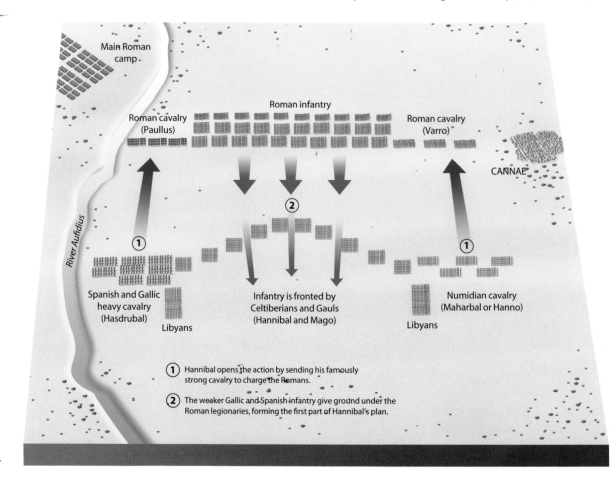

Main Roman camp

Roman infantry

Roman cavalry (Paullus)

Roman cavalry (Varro)

CANNAE

River Aufidius

Spanish and Gallic heavy cavalry (Hasdrubal)

Libyans

Infantry is fronted by Celtiberians and Gauls (Hannibal and Mago)

Libyans

Numidian cavalry (Maharbal or Hanno)

① Hannibal opens the action by sending his famously strong cavalry to charge the Romans.

② The weaker Gallic and Spanish infantry give ground under the Roman legionaries, forming the first part of Hannibal's plan.

fought with the stubbornness that was the hallmark of their republic. The slaughter, 'butchery rather than battle' as Livy called it, lasted the entire afternoon.

When the victory was won, the plain of Cannae was a charnel house of some 60,000 corpses (including that of Aemilius Paullus, though Terentius Varro escaped). Hannibal's advisors urged him to march immediately on Rome. But Hannibal's army was exhausted. The Carthaginians had no siege equipment to use against Rome's walls and, in any case, Hannibal expected that such massive defeat would finally force Rome to terms. Or if not, her allies and subjects in Italy would surely now abandon Rome? To Hannibal's objections, the exasperated Maharbal replied, 'No general is completely talented. You, Hannibal, can win battles, but you do not know how to use your victory.'

He was right. Rome neither sued for peace nor lost many of the alliances which she had built as durably as her roads. Rome rallied, and though Hannibal remained in Italy for another 14 years, he never achieved another victory like Cannae or Lake Trasimene. Eventually, Hannibal was recalled to Africa and was defeated at the battle of Zama in 201 BC. Fifty years later, Roman vengeance saw Carthage demolished and salt sown on the foundations to prevent the city ever rising again.

COMBATANTS

Carthaginians
- 50,000 men
- Commanded by Hannibal
- 8,000 dead

Romans
- 86,000 men
- Commanded by Terentius Varro, Aemilius Paullus
- 50,000 dead

Below After driving off the Roman cavalry, the Carthaginian horse swept into the back of the Roman lines. This completed the encirclement begun when the Libyan infantry closed like a vice on the disorganized Romans as they pushed through the middle of the Carthaginian battle line.

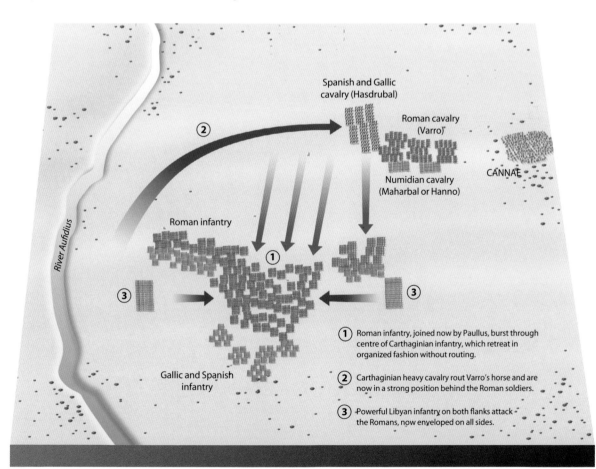

Spanish and Gallic cavalry (Hasdrubal)

Roman cavalry (Varro)

②

Numidian cavalry (Maharbal or Hanno)

CANNAE

River Aufidius

Roman infantry

①

③

③

Gallic and Spanish infantry

① Roman infantry, joined now by Paullus, burst through centre of Carthaginian infantry, which retreat in organized fashion without routing.

② Carthaginian heavy cavalry rout Varro's horse and are now in a strong position behind the Roman soldiers.

③ Powerful Libyan infantry on both flanks attack the Romans, now enveloped on all sides.

Gaixia

Date: 203 BC Location: near modern Guzhen, Anhui province, China

He called his enterprise that of a Hegemon King, intending to manage the world by means of mighty campaigns. After five years, he finally lost his state and died himself at Tung-ch'eng [Dongcheng], yet even then he did not come to his senses and blame himself. What error!
(ABOUT XIANG YU) SIMA QIAN, *THE GRAND SCRIBE'S RECORDS*, C. 100 BC

Right *This painted pottery figurine of a cavalryman, a Western Han burial object, reflects the transition from the use of chariots to the use of cavalry and infantry as the main force in battle.*

Below *Liu Bang pursued Xiang Yu eastwards across the North China Plain to Gaixia, where the Chu army was trapped by the convergence of three other Han forces.*

The battle of Gaixia was the final engagement of the protracted struggle between the rival generals Liu Bang and Xiang Yu for dominance over China, following the collapse of the short-lived Qin dynasty. This encounter marked one of the most significant turning points in Chinese history, when disunity and internal strife gave way to a lasting imperial order.

The contenders

Soon after the death of the First Emperor in 210 BC, the harsh rule of the Qin dynasty was challenged by a series of rebellions. Two men eventually emerged as preeminent among the rebel leaders. The fierce and impetuous Xiang Yu, scion of a line of hereditary generals in the Yangzi valley kingdom of Chu, commanded the most powerful military force and the allegiance of most of the other leaders. But it was the wily Liu Bang, a former Qin functionary of humble birth, whose troops had captured the Qin capital Xianyang (near today's Xian). Xiang Yu assigned kingdoms to eighteen of the rebel leaders, reserving for himself a position as first among equals with the title Hegemon King of Western Chu. He compelled Liu Bang to evacuate the capital region and move his forces southward into the Han River valley where he would assume the title of King of Han. A few months later, in the summer of 206 BC, Liu Bang took advantage of Xiang Yu's distraction elsewhere to reoccupy the territory around Xianyang, precipitating the war between Chu and Han.

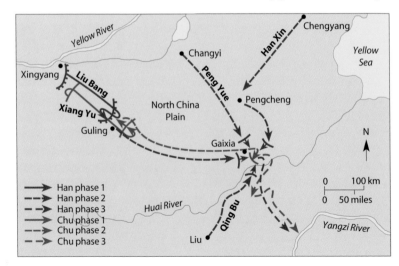

COMBATANTS

Han forces
- *c.* 300,000 soldiers
- Commanded by Liu Bang
- Unknown casualties

Chu forces
- *c.* 100,000 soldiers
- Commanded by Xiang Yu
- *c.* 80,000 dead

The Chu–Han struggle

After securing the highland region around Xianyang, Liu Bang moved east to contest Xiang Yu's rule over the North China Plain. For two and a half years, the two sides battled for control of a series of fortified positions at Xingyang, Chenggao and Gongxian, just south of the Yellow River in today's Henan province. While Xiang Yu focused on attacking these Han positions frontally with his superior forces, Liu Bang sent his best general, Han Xin, to defeat the Hegemon King's allies north of the Yellow River, suborned another key Chu ally in the Yangzi valley, and set his own ally Peng Yue to work harassing the supply lines that stretched eastward to Xiang Yu's home base in the modern provinces of Jiangsu and Anhui. By the autumn of 203 BC, the success of this multi-pronged strategy had left Xiang Yu's main army weakened, dispirited and short of provisions. At this point Xiang Yu reached an agreement to divide the empire with his rival, and withdrew eastward towards his capital at Pengcheng.

The final battle

Liu Bang's advisors now persuaded him to break the agreement and set out in pursuit of the Chu army. Overtaken at Guling, Xiang Yu struck at his pursuers and threw them on the defensive. As armies led by Han Xin, Peng Yue and other Han allies converged on the area, however, the odds against Xiang Yu became overwhelming and his army was encircled at the town of Gaixia, about 32 km (20 miles) east of today's Guzhen, Anhui. There he gave battle with 100,000 men against a combined Han force of 300,000.

The Han army deployed in three echelons, with Han Xin commanding from the centre of the first echelon. The Han general's opening thrust was repulsed, but the Chu counter-attack was stalled by the divisions on his left and right flanks, giving him the opportunity to return to the offensive and defeat the Chu army. Surrounded in his camp at Gaixia and hearing the sound of Chu songs from the Han lines, Xiang Yu believed that his entire kingdom had been overrun. In despair, he broke out of the encirclement with an escort of

800 horsemen and fled southwards, but was soon brought to bay near the north bank of the Yangzi River. There he slit his own throat.

Consequences

The elimination of Xiang Yu cleared the way for Liu Bang to take the imperial throne and establish the Han dynasty. Where Xiang Yu had favoured a loose confederation of autonomous regional kingdoms, Liu Bang and his heirs laboured to construct a more centralized imperial state. The dynasty they created did not fall until AD 220, and the imperial system of government in China survived until AD 1912.

Painted pottery figurines of lightly armoured Western Han infantrymen – burial objects from a 2nd-century BC tomb near Xian. These are representative of the mass infantry armies of Han China.

Actium

Date: 2 September 31 BC   Location: near the island of Levkas, western Greece

On one side Augustus Caesar, high up on the poop, is leading
The Italians into battle, the Senate and People with him...
On the other side with barbaric wealth and motley equipment,
Is Antony, fresh from his triumphs in the East, by the shores of the Indian
Ocean; Egypt, the powers of the Orient and uttermost Bactra
Sail with him; also – a shameful thing – his Egyptian wife.
VIRGIL, *THE AENEID*, VIII, 678–88

Marble portrait head from a statue of Octavian, c. 30–25 BC.
He was the son of Julius Caesar's niece and was adopted by
Caesar in his will.

In 44 BC the assassination of the dictator Julius Caesar sparked off a lengthy series of civil wars that engulfed the whole of the Roman world. By 32 BC it had boiled down to a contest between two powerful Roman aristocrats and their followers. Caesar's heir, Gaius Julius Caesar Octavianus, (known to modern historians as Octavian) faced Caesar's former right-hand man, Marcus Antonius (or Antony as he is usually called). Octavian, based in Italy, dominated the western half of the Roman empire. Antony controlled most of the eastern half of the empire, with the aid of his ally and wife Cleopatra VII, ruler of the Hellenistic kingdom of Egypt. The decisive confrontation between them came in 31 BC on the western coast of Greece.

Achieving naval superiority was essential for both sides in this campaign; without it Octavian could not hope to bring supplies and reinforcements from Italy, or stage a potentially decisive invasion of Egypt. Antony for his part needed to be able to sever Octavian's lines of communication and cross the Adriatic to invade Italy, whilst maintaining his own links with Egypt and the eastern provinces.

The bulk of Antony's army was at Patrai in the Gulf of Corinth, with garrisons at strategic points around the Peloponnese, and naval squadrons dispersed throughout the nearby islands. His fleet was laid up at Actium, at the entrance to the mouth of the Ambracian Gulf, a large bay that was closed by a very narrow channel less than half a mile in width. Early in the spring of 31 BC Octavian managed to establish his army on the northern headland of this channel while his fleet, ably commanded by Marcus Vipsanius Agrippa, defeated Antony's squadrons on the islands and gradually cut off the supply routes to Actium. Antony and Cleopatra brought their army up to the northern headland in an attempt to force Octavian into a decisive battle, while their fleet remained at Actium. There the unhealthy, marshy conditions, poor supplies and dwindling morale encouraged widespread disaffection among their commanders and wholesale desertions by the rowers of their warships.

By midsummer the position had become desperate. Antony's principal admiral, Gaius Sosius, attempted to break out by sea, while Antony led half his army inland, hoping to draw Octavian away from the area in pursuit; he probably intended to link up with Sosius on the eastern coast of Greece. Sosius defeated the squadron of ships that was blockading the entrance to the gulf, but Agrippa brought the rest of the fleet up in pursuit and routed Sosius, forcing him to turn back.

News of this defeat caused Antony to return to his camp, where a debate raged over whether to abandon the fleet altogether and head north for Macedonia, where allies might still be found, or to man as many of the warships as possible with his best soldiers and attempt another break-out by sea. If the latter was successful, Antony could head for Egypt and perhaps assemble another army. Antony was not an experienced naval commander, but the arguments for a sea-fight, advocated also by Cleopatra, were sound. Even if

he did manage to lead his army away intact, by giving up his fleet he would cut himself off from the legions that were still loyal to him in Syria and Cyrenaica.

Preparations for battle

On 2 September Antony burnt his spare ships, mostly troop transports, to deny Octavian their use. He then embarked his best soldiers on the remaining warships, which were fully crewed. The exact strength of each fleet is impossible to establish, but Antony was heavily outnumbered. Octavian had over 400 warships available, while Antony's effective battle fleet, deprived of the ships stationed around the coast and islands, and further reduced by sickness and desertion among his crews, numbered around 230.

Ancient warships were powered by oarsmen seated on up to three levels. The ratings applied to such ships vary from 'twos' to 'sixteens'. They refer not to the number of men pulling each oar, but to the total number of men in each vertical group of oarsmen. Hence a 'five' would have oars

Above left
Green basalt bust probably representing Mark Antony c. 40–30 BC. He married Octavian's sister, but divorced her in 32 BC.

Above right
Marble portrait of Cleopatra VII, c. 50–30 BC. She had a son by Julius Caesar and three children by Antony.

at only three levels, but on the top two levels the oars were each pulled by two men, while the lowest level had one man to each oar.

Right *Roman silver coin minted in 16 BC, showing the god Apollo of Actium making a sacrifice on a platform decorated with the prows and anchors of captured warships. Octavian adopted this version of Apollo as his divine patron.*

Below *Marble relief from Praeneste showing warship, c. 40–30 BC. The ship has two banks of oars and is probably a 'four'.*

The ships in Octavian's fleet ranged from the triremes, rated as 'threes', that carried about 200 soldiers and oarsmen, to 'sixes', that could take in excess of 500 men. They were equipped with rams on their prows, but their principal tactic was to come alongside an enemy vessel, attack it with missile weapons, including small catapults, then grapple and attempt to board.

Antony had similar vessels, plus a few larger ships rated up to 'nines' and 'tens', which were floating fortresses with towers at bow and stern for archers and hundreds of soldiers on their broad decks. His ships were carrying their sails, which was not normal practice in an ancient sea

battles, but Antony's plan was to head out to sea and, as soon as his ships had a favourable wind, to set sails and head south, round the Peloponnese and on to Egypt. In addition to the warships there were numerous merchant vessels which carried few troops and had no rams or catapults, but bore the treasure chests containing Antony and Cleopatra's war funds. It was vital that these ships got away. The squadron of warships detailed to escort them included Cleopatra's own flagship.

The engagement

Octavian's aim was simply to block the exit from the Ambracian Gulf with a double line of warships. Marcus Agrippa commanded the left wing of his fleet, Lucius Arruntius the centre, while Octavian himself was on the right wing in a small,

COMBATANTS

Octavian (Gaius Julius Caesar Octavianus)

• 406 ships

• Commanded by Marcus Vipsanius Agrippa and Lucius Arruntius

• Unknown casualties

Antony (Marcus Antonius) and Cleopatra VII

• 230 ships

• Commanded by Publius Canidius Crassus, Gaius Sosius, Lucius Gellius Publicola and Marcus Octavius

• c. 150 ships destroyed

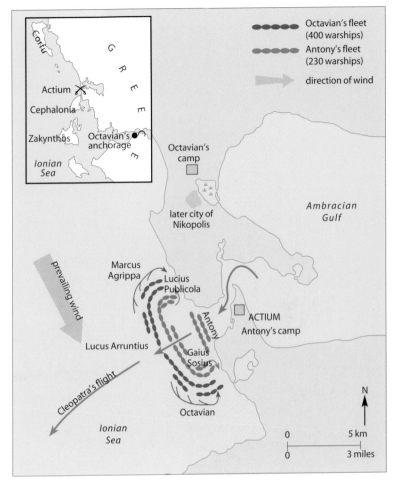

fast 'liburnian' ship. In order to increase the chances of breaking through the enemy lines, Antony ordered the ships on his extreme right and left wings – under the command of Lucius Gellius Publicola and Gaius Sosius respectively – to try to move away from the centre, forcing the enemy to move with them and away from the centre of their own lines. This caused a gap to develop through which it was possible for Cleopatra's squadron to sail with the heavily laden merchant ships.

On the left wing of Octavian's fleet Agrippa's ships defeated Publicola and drove on towards Antony and the third, central squadron under Marcus Octavius. Antony's own flagship had become inextricably bound up with several other vessels in the fierce fighting on the right wing, so he had to transfer to another, smaller ship and follow after Cleopatra's squadron. He was chased by some of Octavian's lightest and fastest vessels. By the time they caught up with him he had transferred again to Cleopatra's flagship and the pursuers were driven off. In all he managed to save about seventy warships.

Aftermath

Octavian created a huge victory monument on the site of his own camp, decorated with rams from captured enemy ships. He also founded a city there which he called Nikopolis (Victory City). Contemporary poets such as Virgil and Horace

hailed the battle of Actium as the beginning of a golden era for Rome. It was not so much the naval defeat as the abandonment of their army that spelled the end for Antony and Cleopatra, and their chances of ever defeating Octavian. Although the army began a northward withdrawal from Actium towards Macedonia, under the command of Publius Canidius Crassus, as soon as Octavian's forces caught up with them the veteran legions stopped and negotiated a change of sides. Their sense of loyalty to Antony was not powerful enough to make them ignore the realities of the situation.

The doomed couple were pursued to Alexandria by Octavian. Both committed suicide rather than submit to the new ruler of the Roman world. Octavian returned to Rome, renamed himself Augustus Caesar and inaugurated the line of Roman emperors that lasted for 500 years.

Publicola and Sosius tried to draw Agrippa's and Octavian's ships away from Antony's centre, thus creating an opening for Cleopatra. Sosius retreated from Octavian, while Publicola's squadron was defeated by Agrippa, who then engaged the centre. Antony struggled to break clear of Arruntius's ships, but Cleopatra sailed through, followed eventually by Antony.

7 Teutoburg Forest

Date: autumn AD 9 Location: Kalkriese, Germany

In the field, the bones of the soldiers lay scattered about, each where he had fallen either standing his ground or trying to flee. There were bits of weapons, and the bones of horses amongst them, and human heads had been nailed to the trunks of the surrounding trees.

TACITUS, *ANNALS*, 1.61

Right *Detail of the iron point of a lance. Some German warriors merely used fire-hardened wooden speartips.*

Below
Reconstruction of palisade. The building of this palisade is indicative of Arminius's careful planning, as was his use of terrain to nullify the superior equipment and training of the Romans.

In the early years of the 1st century AD the emperor Augustus tried to bring Germany under his control. An unconquered Germany was uncomfortably close to Italy, and Augustus may have felt that a defensive line along the Elbe was easier to maintain than the current one along the Rhine.

By AD 9 Germany seemed sufficiently conquered for Augustus to send a governor whose main concern was the Romanization of the province. This was Quintilius Varus, former governor of Syria and husband of Augustus's great-niece.

Varus commanded three legions – the XVII, XVIII and XIX. Also, some of the many tribes of Germany were allied with the Romans. Among the young German aristocrats who served with the Roman legions for military experience was Arminius, son of a chieftain of the Cherusci tribe.

Varus was unaware that the despoiling of his native land had made Arminius a bitter enemy of Rome. From the moment Varus arrived in Germany, Arminius plotted to unite the tribes and bring about the Roman leader's downfall.

These tribes sent to Varus and asked for garrisons to be stationed with them. Varus agreed readily and sent detachments, thus weakening his main force. Finally, in AD 9 Arminius arranged for reports of trouble in a distant part of the province to reach Varus. It was now autumn, and Varus seems to have decided to move his whole camp and deal with the problem on his way to winter quarters. Another German leader, Segestes, pleaded passionately with Varus not to trust Arminius, but he was ignored.

Action

Arminius's guides led the Romans astray. Then the Germans attacked. Initially these attacks were pinpricks – ambuscades which melted at the first sign of serious resistance, and the threat seemed minor. The Romans had armour, equipment and training, while many Germans fought naked. Though some warriors had swords, others had merely a crude spear (the *framea*), sometimes with only a fire-hardened wooden point.

But the Romans were uncomfortable in the dense forest, and were made more miserable by a series of thunderstorms. Near modern Kalkriese,

on the edge of the Wiehen hills north of Osnabrück, Arminius had prepared an ambush. Here, the forest extended almost to the edge of an impenetrable marsh. The Roman army was caught on the narrow stretch of land between the two when the Germans attacked.

The Romans were penned in by a wall at the forest edge. This was part-rampart, but mostly a fence woven with branches between the trees, of a type that the Germans used to stop their cattle from straying. The Romans were probably split into pockets by the first attack and unable to co-ordinate their efforts. In confused skirmishes and a running battle lasting several days, the trapped Romans were steadily worn down.

Outcome

Varus was either killed or fell on his sword. Others followed his example, for the Germans had a grisly way with prisoners. In the end, not one single Roman survived. What we know of the battle is from reconstructions, the first by the Romans themselves, who returned to the scene a few years later. They found places where senior Roman officers had been messily sacrificed, and the bones of the dead scattered where they had fallen.

Gradually the site of the disaster was forgotten. A massive monument to the battle was eventually erected at Hiddesen, south of Detmold. This was some 50 km (31 miles) from the actual site of Teutoburg Forest, which was

Above *Roman face helmet from the Teutoburg Forest battle site.*

Below *The yellow patches of richer archaeological finds suggest that the Romans twice attempted to break through the palisades before their force was broken and the survivors hacked down.*

discovered very recently by Major Tony Clunn, an amateur archaeologist. He found Roman metal artifacts which suggested a battle, and professional archaeologists confirmed that this was the site of the *Varusschlacht* – where Varus's legions had been destroyed.

Arminius's victory ensured that northwest Europe had a Germanic rather than a Latin culture. This in turn profoundly affected subsequent European history, and thus the history of the world.

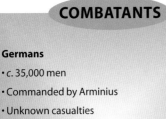

COMBATANTS

Germans
• *c.* 35,000 men
• Commanded by Arminius
• Unknown casualties

Romans
• 20,000 men
• Commanded by Publius Quintilius Varus
• 20,000 dead, plus *c.* 3,000 civilians

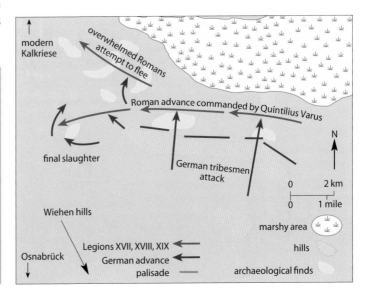

Adrianople

Date: 9 August AD 378 Location: modern Edirne, Turkey

Then the two lines of battle threw themselves against the other. Like the prows
of ships driving into each other, they were tossed back and forth like waves of the sea.
Our left wing had advanced right up to the wagons, and would have pushed on still
further if properly supported. But the rest of the cavalry abandoned them to it.
They were hard pressed by the superior numbers of the enemy, overwhelmed,
and beaten down like the ruins of a great rampart.
AMMIANUS MARCELLINUS 31.12

Despite the stubborn Gothic defence of their hilltop wagon fort, the Romans were confident of victory until the unexpected arrival of a massive Gothic cavalry force.

In AD 376, the eastern Roman emperor Valens gave permission for the Goths to cross the Danube and settle within the Roman empire. The Goths were seeking refuge from the Huns sweeping westward from Central Asia, while the Romans hoped that abandoned areas would be repopulated with taxpaying peasants who could supply their army with recruits. The greed and extortion of the Roman officials in charge of the resettlement instead provoked the Goths into war with the empire.

Two years later, with the Goths still unsubdued, Valens set out to finish the war personally. He took with him about 40,000 veteran infantry, and a mixture of heavy cavalry, horse archers and Arab scouts, making about 20,000 in total.

In early August, Valens found the Goths in Thrace, near the city of Adrianople. Valens was encouraged by reports of victories against the barbarians from Gratian, emperor in the West, and his general Sebastian. Furthermore, his scouts reported far fewer enemy than expected – about 10,000 in all, and these mostly infantry. As if to confirm their weakness, the Gothic leader Fritigern sent to Valens, asking for peace.

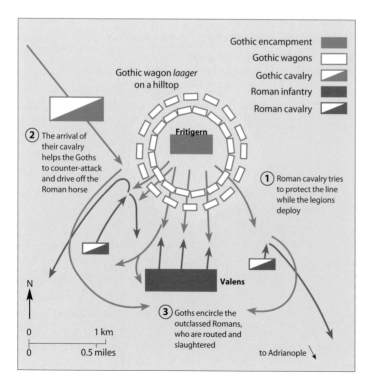

Gothic encampment
Gothic wagons
Gothic cavalry
Roman infantry
Roman cavalry

Gothic wagon *laager* on a hilltop

Fritigern

(2) The arrival of their cavalry helps the Goths to counter-attack and drive off the Roman horse

(1) Roman cavalry tries to protect the line while the legions deploy

Valens

(3) Goths encircle the outclassed Romans, who are routed and slaughtered

N

0   1 km
0   0.5 miles

to Adrianople

COMBATANTS

Goths

• 60,000 men, comprising 50,000 cavalry

• Commanded by Fritigern

• Estimate of 2,000 dead

Romans

• 60,000 men

• Commanded by Emperor Valens

• 40,000 dead, including Valens

Confident of victory, Valens spurned Fritigern's offer. Though Valens's advisors urged him to wait for further reinforcements, the emperor was determined to engage the enemy as soon as possible. On 9 August 378 Valens marched from Adrianople to where the Gothic encampment of wagons, or *laager*, lay on a hilltop several hours' march away. The Goths attempted further negotiations, and set fire to the fields around the hill to further delay the Romans. Finally, the Roman infantry, frustrated by the delay, seem to have taken matters into their own hands and attacked.

This first uncoordinated assault was a failure, but the veteran Romans briskly re-organized and pressed forward again, still confident of victory. At this point in the battle, the reason for the Gothic attempts at delay became suddenly apparent. The Gothic heavy cavalry had been away, whether raiding or foraging is unclear. But now, in a devastating blow to Roman morale, they returned – all 50,000 of them.

The totally outclassed Roman cavalry were swept away in the first charge. The infantry were caught off-balance by the new threat. Their retreat down the hill turned into rout as the Gothic infantry attacked from the wagons even as the cavalry closed in. Ammianus Marcellinus tells us:

'Amidst all the uproar and confusion our infantry were exhausted by exertion and danger, until at last they had neither strength left to fight, nor the will to plan anything; their spears were broken by the fre-quent impacts, so that they resorted to using their swords. These they thrust into the massed ranks of the enemy. They were suicidally brave, since they now had no hope of saving themselves. They were slithering on ground saturated with rivulets of blood, as they tried to sell their lives as dearly as possible….At the last wherever one looked there was nothing but heaps of the slain and lifeless corpses.'

The general Sebastian was killed trying to rally his men. Legend has it that Valens was pursued by Gothic cavalry into a farmhouse and the Goths, not knowing whom they had at their mercy, secured the cottage and burned it and all within. We cannot tell if this is indeed the truth, but certainly Valens perished either in the battle or immediately afterwards.

It was 'the end of all humanity, the end of the world', lamented St Ambrose. Ammianus says that only a third of the army escaped, so Roman casualties were in the order of 40,000 men. It was the greatest Roman military disaster since Cannae (see p. 32), and one from which the empire was never to recover.

Above *The Ludovisi Sarcophagus showing battle between Germans and Romans. The Roman on horseback in the top right corner with the outflung arm has been identified with Hostilian, son of the emperor Decius who died in AD 251.*

Above left *Silver medallion from Trier, showing portrait of Valens from AD 367–75. Valens was the younger brother of the emperor Valentinian I, and a better financial manager than he was a soldier.*

hIC

Medieval World

The most dynamic military forces of this period, in terms of territory and people conquered, were not the feudal cavalry of western Europe – who won in wars within Europe at Hastings (1066), losing at Bannockburn (1314), Crécy (1346) and Agincourt (1415) – but the newly Islamic Arab armies of the 7th century, as well as the 13th-century Mongols. The Arabs conquered Egypt, Syria, Mesopotamia, Persia, North Africa and most of Spain, only to be stopped at Poitiers (732) in western France; the Muslims never again raided as far north. The impact of these Muslim advances can still be felt today.

The Mongols conquered not only China, but also Persia, Mesopotamia and southern Russia. Advancing into eastern Europe, they were victorious at Liegnitz (1241) at the expense of a German-Polish army. The horns of the more numerous Mongol deployment outflanked their opponents, who were hit hard by archers from the flank. The following year, the Mongols turned back in Europe when news arrived that the Great Khan had died. In 1260, another Mongol force captured Aleppo and Damascus in Syria, but was defeated by the more numerous Egyptian-based Mamluks at Ain Jalut, southeast of Nazareth. In Japan, the Mongols were defeated in Hakata Bay (1281). Modelling himself on the Mongols, Timur the Lame (1336–1405, later called Tamerlaine), overran Central Asia, sacked Delhi, captured Damascus and Baghdad and, in 1402, with rumours circulating of his plans for global conquest, smashed the Ottomans at Ankara.

In comparison, the attempts by western Europeans to expand their power were restricted to

In this famous scene from the Bayeux Tapestry, King Harold of England stands mortally wounded, and the battle of Hastings (1066) is lost to the Norman invaders.

Page from the Trier Apocalypse, *8th–9th century, showing early medieval soldiers. Alongside the Roman legacy, rulers were dependent on the retinues of their most prominent vassals (sworn followers). Compared to the Romans, military forces were small, less well trained and frequently 'privatized' expressions of social power, rather than public expressions of state power. Furthermore, as troops were not paid cash, campaigning only really 'worked' if it produced land to distribute or plunder.*

eastern Europe and the Mediterranean and, in the latter, the Crusaders were beaten at Hattin (1187) by another of the Muslim empires: the Kurdish general Saladin (1138–93) took over Egypt, Syria and most of Palestine, while his generals advanced to Yemen and into modern Sudan and Tunisia. If Palestine could not be preserved by the Crusaders, Byzantium – the eastern Roman empire – was also unable to hold its positions. Manzikert (1071) was a spectacular defeat at the hands of the Seljuk Turks, and the process culminated with the fall of Constantinople in 1453. Ottomans had already overrun Greece, Bulgaria and much of Serbia, with crucial victories at Nicopolis (1396) and Varna (1444).

The western Europeans were more successful in holding onto their core areas: the Magyars were defeated at Lechfeld, Germany, in 955, the heavy cavalry of the Germans playing a key role. As was characteristic of western European warfare, this cavalry relied not on archers but on weapons for close combat, principally swords.

Within Europe, the Frankish development of knights, castles and siege techniques enabled those rulers who were able to employ them in some quantity to extend their power, both against domestic opponents and on their frontiers. Infantry also played a major role in

siegecraft and the defence of castles, and also an important part in battle. The significance of infantry was demonstrated at Hastings (1066). Far from being a walkover victory by an advanced military system – Norman cavalry easily defeating English infantry – the battle was a hard-fought struggle between two effective systems, and its outcome was far from certain. Harold chose a strong defensive position on the slopes of a hill, thus offering protection against the Norman cavalry. Eventually, the shield-wall of the English housecarls was disrupted by advances designed to exploit real or feigned retreats by the Normans and, at last, the English position was broken.

Infantry took a more prominent part with the development of pikemen, victorious at Bannockburn (1314), and archers, victorious at Crécy and Agincourt. These conflicts were at once civil wars and battles between proto-nations: Scots fought for and against Edward II of England and Frenchmen for and against Henry V of England, who also claimed the French throne. In such civil wars, political factors played a major role, as seen with the defeat of Richard III at Bosworth (1485). Command skills were also important in battle. At Bannockburn, the English handled their archers very badly while Scottish pikemen on well-chosen ground routed the English cavalry.

Poitiers

9

Date: *c.* 732 Location: midwestern France

With Christ's help he [Charles Martel] overran their tents, following hard after them in the battle to grind them small in their overthrow, and when 'Abd ar-Rahnan perished in the battle he utterly destroyed their armies, scattering them like stubble before the fury of his onslaught; and in the power of Christ he utterly destroyed them.
THE CHRONICLE OF FREDEGAR, C. 732

In this battle Charles Martel, Mayor of the Palace (*c.* 688–741) of the Frankish kingdom, defeated a Muslim army and killed its leader, 'Abd ar-Rahnan al Ghafiqi, governor of Muslim Spain or *al-Andalus*. The Franks were a Germanic people who, under the kings of their Merovingian royal house, had settled between the Rhine and the Loire since the 5th century and dominated the surrounding lands. Warfare amongst the Merovingian rulers had weakened their power, which was then usurped by great nobles calling themselves Mayors of the Palace. The Muslims had seized Spain in 711 in the great tide of Islamic conquest that swept around the Mediterranean after the death of the Prophet in AD 632. Our sources for this period are poor and even the year of the battle is uncertain. Spanish Muslim sources written centuries later indicate 732, but the contemporary Spanish Christian *Chronicle of 754* suggests late 733 or 734, probably in October.

The campaign and context of the battle

Charles Martel was the latest in a sequence of Arnulfing clan members who had managed to seize the position of Mayor of the Palace and impose himself as *de facto* ruler of the Frankish heartlands, relegating the Merovingian Theuderic IV (721–37) to an honorific role. The bitter power struggles during the Arnulfing family's accession had weakened Frankish dominion over peripheral areas which they had traditionally ruled. Duke Eudo held wealthy Aquitaine and was able to defy Charles until 720, when the Spanish

Muslims began raiding across the Pyrenees. In 720/21 Eudo defeated a major Muslim army at the battle of Toulouse, but was unable to prevent Muslim raids on Autun in 725, and the fall of Carcassonne and Nîmes the following year. Eudo tried to exploit differences between the Berber and Arab conquerors of Spain, marrying his daughter to Munnuza, a Berber chief who led a major but unsuccessful rebellion. In retaliation the Arab leader 'Abd ar-Rahnan led a major raid into Aquitaine, probably in 733, which forced Eudo to seek help from Charles.

The battle

Charles gathered a large army, most of which was Frankish, but included Burgundians, and confronted 'Abd ar-Rahnan as he marched north from Poitiers towards Tours.
Both sides estab-

Light cavalry, like this mounted bowman, were an element in Islamic armies, but most of those at Poitiers probably fought on foot like their Frankish enemies.

The Muslim attackers certainly raided the Christian countryside, but if they had achieved a major victory over the Franks it could have opened the way to conquest.

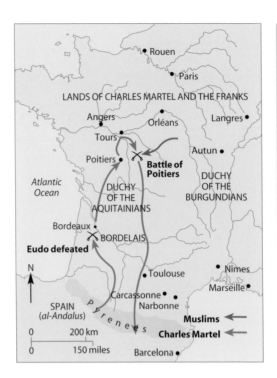

Franks
• Commanded by Charles Martel

Arabs
• Commanded by 'Abd ar-Rahnan (Muslims and Berber army from Spain)

Numbers unknown. Both sides probably fought mainly on foot with substantial numbers of horsemen in the ranks but probably not used in any systematic way. The Franks are said to have stood as if frozen against the enemy assault, but nothing is known of the battle at all for certain. Even the place and year of the battle are contested.

lished fortified camps, but frustratingly we know nothing of how they fought in this first clash between a Muslim force and a major north European power. The quotation from Fredegar's continuation shows the western view, while the *Chronicle of 754* adds little except that the Franks stood firm against the invaders. Frankish armies in this period seem to have centred on well-armed and usually mounted retinues of the Lords fighting on horseback or foot with spear, sword and bow, supported by larger forces of poorly equipped infantry. The late 19th-century German writer Brunner suggested that the Arabs were a largely cavalry army and that Charles owed his victory to the development of heavy cavalry, knights and 'shock' tactics, but modern historians do not believe that these emerged before the early 10th century. While it is certainly true that Arab light cavalry was important in the armies of *al-Andalus*, infantry was also a key element, so the two armies were not radically different.

The significance of the battle

Fredegar suggests that Charles enjoyed a decisive victory but, although 'Abd ar-Rahnan was killed, the Muslim army ravaged systematically on

their retreat to Spain. Moreover, Charles still failed to subdue Aquitaine or the sons of Eudo, and only under Charlemagne (768–814) was Arnulfing rule finally secure in this area. The Muslims never again raided this far north. However, they continued to establish themselves in Provence where their rule was firmly founded upon control of Narbonne and the coastal cities. Charles attacked the area in 737 and again in 739 with little success.

Earlier generations saw the battle of Poitiers as the turning point when Islam was halted and western Christendom saved, a point reinforced by the failure of the last Arab attack on Constantinople in 718. More recently the Arab expedition of 732/733 has been seen as a mere raid that withdrew at the first sign of serious opposition, and the decisive struggle was then fought out in protracted and obscure wars for control of Provence. But the tide of Islamic invasion had always profited from the divisions and weaknesses of their enemies as much as from their own strength. In Provence the Arabs enjoyed the support of Maurontus, Duke of Marseille and an enemy of the Arnulfing house, and an Arab victory at Poitiers could have continued this pattern. It should be remembered that this was a strong Muslim army led by the Muslim governor in person. Charles was merely a struggling war-lord, but in 732 he defeated a Muslim attack whose victory could have had the most serious consequences.

Lechfeld

Date: August 955   Location: near Augsburg, southern Germany

Those who came to the river crossings were pitched into the water by our men manning the ferries, the rest were cut down. Those who did manage to reach the opposite bank were slaughtered by the men who watched the shores.
GERHARD OF AUGSBURG, THE LIFE OF SAINT ULRICH, C. 985

In mid-August 955 the forces of the German king, Otto I, annihilated a huge army of Hungarians (also known as Magyars), who were predatory mounted archers. Their semi-nomadic way of life and military tactics resembled those of Huns, Avars and (later) Mongols. They had settled on the plains of the Carpathian Basin (c. AD 900), whence they launched pillaging expeditions into western Europe. Although Germany and northern Italy suffered most from these depredations, the Magyars' highly mobile forces occasionally reached France, southern Italy and once even Spain, but their catastrophic defeat in 955 ended these incursions. The leaders of the expedition, Bulksu and Lel, were captured and hanged, and most of their men were killed in the fighting.

Date and place of the battle

Because of a reference to St Lawrence Day in the contemporary *Annals of St Gall*, the battle of Lechfeld is dated 10 August. But two reliable contemporaries, the monk Widukind of Corvey and cleric Gerhard of Augsburg, concur with another reference in the *Annals* in recording that the annihilation of the Magyars occurred after numerous skirmishes on the days that followed. This catastrophic defeat therefore could not just have taken place on St Lawrence Day on the Lechfeld, the broad plain of the Lech River, but rather the decisive action must have occurred as the Magyars fled eastwards through Bavaria in the direction of their homeland.

Build-up to the battle

The Hungarians invaded in mid-summer. Taking advantage of insurrections in Germany, they hoped to engage Otto's forces in a decisive battle. The invaders swept through Bavaria south of the Danube, crossed the Lech and pressed on to the Iller River in the neighbouring duchy of Swabia. Then, falling back, they devastated a strip of territory 100 km (60 miles) wide and laid siege to Augsburg, an episcopal centre presided over by Bishop Ulrich. Gerhard, the bishop's hagiographer, describes his heroic defence of the city, a factor in Ulrich's later canonization. Meanwhile, Otto concentrated his forces in Ulm and

Left *Otto I in a contemporary sculpture in Magdeburg.*

Below *Hungarian warrior equipped with composite bow fully strung in a waterproof case.*

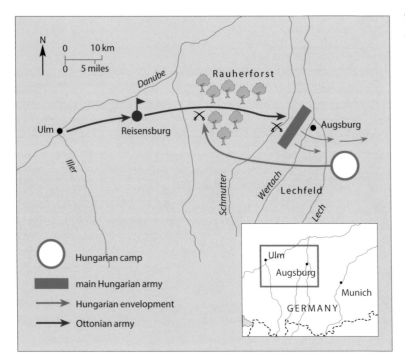

- ⬤ Hungarian camp
- ▬ main Hungarian army
- → Hungarian envelopment
- ➜ Ottonian army

Widukind describes chaotic hand-to-hand combat in which Magyar forces were cut to pieces. Since heavily armed Ottonian cavalry had an advantage fighting in close quarters against light mounted archers, many historians believe Magyar leaders made the fatal mistake of standing their ground against the charge. Gerhard, however, relates the events from a different perspective. Although he stood on the ramparts of Augsburg, he could not see the encounter 8 km (5 miles) west of the city. He heard the clash of arms and then witnessed the Hungarians riding back towards Augsburg in good order. Their movements conveyed the impression that the Magyars were returning to resume the siege. Thus, Gerhard heaved a sigh of relief when these riders bypassed the city, crossed the Lech and entered the broad Bavarian Lechfeld.

Gerhard's description of their flight is consistent with a well-planned feigned retreat to lure Otto's men onto a treeless landscape east of the Lech where their tactics would be most effective. But the German king did not fall for the ruse. He pursued them cautiously for a short distance and returned to Augsburg before dusk. On the following morning (11 August), he dispatched couriers on swift mounts to the men who guarded the fords and ferries at river crossings in eastern Bavaria. It was at these crossings, not on

After their envelopment failed, the Magyars feigned retreat, trying to lure Otto's forces onto the Lechfeld, an optimal landscape for mounted archery. The king did not take the bait.

marched through the wasted landscape west of Augsburg.

After learning of the king's advance, the Magyar leaders lifted the siege and deployed forces to meet the relief column. A wooded region west of Augsburg (Rauherforst) protected the Germans from Magyar archers, whose primary tactic was to rain arrows down on their enemies from a distance, but the wood may also have hindered the German's visibility, for a Hungarian detachment slipped unnoticed behind Otto's troops. After slaughtering a Bohemian contingent guarding the baggage, they attacked two Swabian legions at the end of the column. Disaster was averted, however, when Conrad, the king's son-in-law, launched a vigorous counterattack that drove off the encircling force.

The main battle

Freed from this threat to his rear, Otto deployed his men and launched a frontal assault of heavy cavalry on the primary Hungarian force between him and Augsburg. Two sources describe the ensuing encounter (generally called 'the main battle'). Writing from the standpoint of informants who had participated in the charge,

COMBATANTS

Germans

- 8,000 well-armed men including at least 1,000 heavy cavalry; c. 1,500 defenders of Augsburg; at least 3,000 Bohemian and Bavarian heavy cavalry in fortresses at river crossings

- Commanded by King Otto I

- 3,000 men (3 legions) killed by surprise rear attack; unspecified number in the main battle

Hungarians (Magyars)

- Max. 20,000 mounted archers; 5,000 foot soldiers

- Commanded by 'Horka' Bulksu and Lel

- Few survivors

the Lechfeld, where other forces occupying forts in eastern Bavaria destroyed the Hungarians on the days that followed.

Conclusion

It is difficult to explain the annihilation of this Magyar army of more than 10,000 mounted archers since Otto's relief force numbered only 8,000. Even if the German ruler had defeated the Hungarians on the Lechfeld, under normal circumstances these elusive steppe warriors surely could have fled back to the Carpathian Basin to lick their wounds, rebuilt their strength and raided once again. Centuries later Simon de Keza, a Hungarian chronicler, wrote that Otto had defeated his ancestors 'because it rained'. Indeed, heavy rains on the days following St Lawrence

Day 955 must explain the decisive nature of Otto's victory. Mounted archers do not function well in inclement weather, for their delicate composite-recurve bows come unglued. Moreover, the Danube and its principal tributary, the Inn, rapidly funnel run off from torrential rains (which frequently occur in August) into the narrow landscape between Passau and Vienna. The result is a clogged watershed with murky waters backing up throughout the system, in which the invaders were trapped. It is no wonder that both Gerhard and Widukind stress the difficulties that the Hungarians experienced at river crossings.

Following Lechfeld, Otto restored order in Germany, paving the way for his coronation as Holy Roman Emperor in 962. Thereafter in the West, a German ruler generally held this title.

Unable to hold their ground in the face of a successful charge of heavy cavalry, lightly armoured Magyar steppe warriors release Parthian shots from their composite bows to cover their flight from the field of combat.

Hastings

Date: 14 October 1066   Location: Sussex, England

*So a combat of an unusual kind began, with one side attacking in different ways
and the other standing firm as if fixed to the ground.*
WILLIAM OF POITIERS, *DEEDS OF WILLIAM*, C. 1071

Martial skill was the essence of political leadership in the 11th century, which is why William has here had himself portrayed in the panoply of war on this seal.

This battle between Harold, king of England, and William the Bastard, Duke of Normandy, was the result of a succession crisis in the English realm: Edward the Confessor, king of England 1042–66, had no heir. Edward was the son of Aethelred the Unready, king of England 978–1016, and Emma of the Norman ducal house, and had been raised in exile at the Norman court before his recall to England in 1042. He had brought Normans to England to assist him in its government. Edward feared the power of Godwin of Wessex, a leading English magnate, whom he expelled in 1051, and promised the succession to Duke William, a relative whom he had known as a boy. In the event Godwin organized attacks on England and enjoyed some sympathy amongst the other leaders of English society, so within a year he was restored to power. After his death in 1053 power passed to his eldest son, Harold, who was not only the most powerful man in England but his sister, Edith, was married to King Edward. Another claimant was Harald Hardrada, king of Norway 1047–66, who descended from King Cnut 1016–35, who had ruled England and Scandinavia.

A claimant needed acceptance from the powerful English aristocracy and, though it is possible that some were opposed to his succession, Harold was probably the most acceptable candidate. Moreover, before his death on 5 January 1066, Edward designated Harold as his successor. He was crowned the following day. Both William and Harald Hardrada, who allied with Harold's exiled brother, Tostig, prepared for war.

The campaigns of 1066

Harold mobilized an English fleet and army on the south coast to meet the threat from Normandy where William gathered an army of 7,000 carried by 776 ships, drawing on the resources of all northern France. William was fortunate that a minor on the throne in France and conflict in Anjou had neutralized potential continental enemies. Moreover, skilful diplomacy persuaded the pope to bless his expedition with a papal

banner. Harald of Norway and Tostig and their fleet of 300 ships landed close to York, defeating the northern earls on 20 September at Fulford Gate. Harold's army had disbanded on 8 September for lack of supplies, but he had kept some forces with him and marched north at great speed, about 40 km (25 miles) per day. He surprised the Norse army at Stamford Bridge on 24 September, killing Harald and Tostig.

On the night of 28 September William's army crossed the Channel and created bases, first at Pevensey, then at Hastings. William sought battle because he needed a rapid decision, and provoked Harold by ravaging Sussex. Harold was back in London by early October and, perhaps inspired by his earlier victory, was eager to attack. Although he could have waited for further reinforcements, Harold raced towards Hastings.

The battle

Harold ordered the local levies to join him at the 'hoary apple tree' north of Hastings, and the sources suggest that the turnout was not as great as he had expected. Disloyalty has been one explanation, but it may simply be that Harold hoped to catch William by surprise and the levies were slow to gather. Travelling down the London road, Harold's army deployed on the ridge of what is now called Battle Hill. William's spies spotted his advance and the Norman army gathered at the foot of the hill. The English army rested its flanks on the woods to either side, so William's men faced an uphill charge which slowed both cavalry and infantry. The Norman leader needed a quick victory, but if the English held him off their forces would in time increase – a circumstance which must put in question Harold's haste to fight.

Both sides depended on their elite troops. William's knights and Harold's thegns wore much the same kind of mail armour and used spears and swords, though many of the English preferred battle-axes. There were significant differences between the armies.

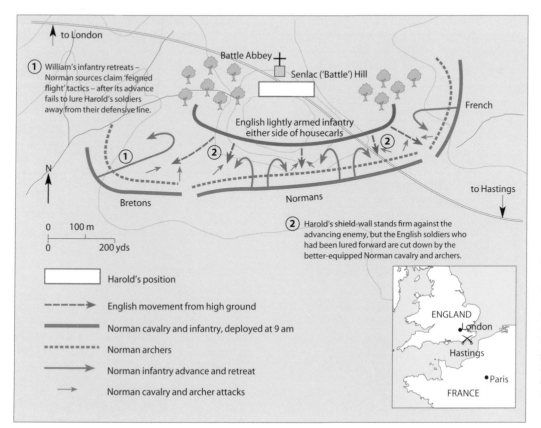

1 William's infantry retreats – Norman sources claim 'feigned flight' tactics – after its advance fails to lure Harold's soldiers away from their defensive line.

English lightly armed infantry either side of housecarls

2 Harold's shield-wall stands firm against the advancing enemy, but the English soldiers who had been lured forward are cut down by the better-equipped Norman cavalry and archers.

to London

Battle Abbey

Senlac ('Battle') Hill

French

N

Bretons

Normans

to Hastings

0   100 m

0   200 yds

☐ Harold's position

- - - → English movement from high ground

━━━ Norman cavalry and infantry, deployed at 9 am

· · · · · Norman archers

→ Norman infantry advance and retreat

→ Norman cavalry and archer attacks

ENGLAND
London
Hastings
Paris
FRANCE

Above *The stirrup seems to have spread to Europe from the steppe lands of Asia, perhaps via the Arab world. Its importance was that it improved the stability of the rider in the saddle and made him a much more formidable warrior.*

Left *Perhaps thwarted in his attempt to surprise the Normans, Harold formed his 'shield-wall' at the top of the steep slope of Senlac Hill with his flanks guarded by woods, so that William had no alternative to a frontal assault.*

Scene from the Bayeux Tapestry. The Anglo-Saxons' shield-wall confronted the Normans who had lost impetus on the steep slope. Elite warriors on both sides wore much the same armour and used similar weapons; but the unprotected archer at far right wields a bow, the poor man's weapon.

The English thegns travelled on horseback, but their tradition to fight on foot was reinforced in this instance by Harold's defensive position; by contrast the Normans had 2,000 cavalry which provided them with mobility. The English elite were supported by lightly-armed local levies of questionable military value, while Duke William had recruited a mass of well-equipped knights and mercenaries. In addition, the English had few archers, perhaps a chance consequence of Harold's rush to battle, while the Normans had gathered many.

Harold created a densely packed 'shield-wall' along the ridge with his thegns to the fore.

William threw forward archers to harass them but, firing uphill, they did little damage. His cavalry and knights on foot were organized in three divisions: Bretons on the left, Normans in the centre, and French on the right. Battle began at about 9 am. A first assault by the Norman infantry was thrown back and William then had to commit his cavalry in support, lest their retreat precipitate a rout. The English right began to pursue the opposing Bretons on the left wing who seem to have fallen into disorder, then a rumour spread that William was dead, but he rallied his men by raising his helmet and galloping along the line of battle. The English who had

English faltered and the final Norman assault gave William victory.

In an age when battles rarely lasted over an hour, both armies at Hastings had persisted all day. Both commanders had imposed a remarkable discipline on their troops and William had shown tactical skill in exploiting his mobility, if we can believe the Norman accounts of 'feigned flights'. But in the end, as so often in battle, chance was decisive: the death of Harold left the English with nothing to fight for.

The significance of the battle

Victory at Hastings did not guarantee command over England, but with no obvious candidate for the kingship the English notables reluctantly accepted William, who was crowned on Christmas Day 1066. He then faced rebellions and it was not until the early 1170s that his reign was secure. Because the battle decided the fate of the English realm it attracted a great deal of attention from contemporary writers and was also the subject of a great embroidery, the Bayeux Tapestry, whose vivid images have impressed themselves onto the public mind. Moreover, unusually, the field of battle has not been built upon since, and we know where the fighting took place because William founded Battle Abbey to commemorate his victory, ordering that its high altar be placed on the very spot where Harold was killed.

advanced were cut off and destroyed.

It is possible that Harold had intended a general advance which was aborted by the death of his brothers who led it. The Norman sources say that this crisis suggested a useful stratagem: feigning flight to draw the English from their defensive line so that they could be killed in the open. This may have been used twice in the course of the day. However, the battle developed into a slogging match in which the shield-wall stood, albeit battered. A random event decided the outcome. As evening gathered and the Normans prepared a final attack, Harold was fatally struck in the eye by a chance arrow, the

Manzikert

Date: 19 August 1071   Location: modern Malazgirt, eastern Turkey

*The Emperor of the Romans was led away, a prisoner, to the enemy camp and
his army was scattered. Those who escaped were but a tiny fraction of the whole.
Of the majority, some were taken captive, the rest massacred.*
MICHAEL PSELLUS, *CHRONOGRAPHIA*, 1018–79

A 10th-century Armenian carving of a Byzantine heavy infantryman. Such men would have been a major element in the Byzantine army. His armour is lamellar, consisting of strips or scales of metal sewn onto a fabric or leather base.

At Manzikert the Seljuk sultan of Baghdad, Alp Arslan (1063–72), decisively defeated the Byzantine emperor Romanus IV Diogenes (1067–71), opened the way for the Turkish domination of Anatolia and ultimately triggered the Byzantine appeal for aid which gave rise to the First Crusade in 1095.

The Turks were a pagan Steppe people who attacked Islam on its northern frontier. As brilliant horse-archers, many were taken into the service of the Caliph of Baghdad and other Muslim potentates. Long contact converted the Turks to Islam. Under the command of the Seljuk family they moved into the Arab world and seized control of the Caliph at Baghdad in 1055. The leading member of the Seljuk family ruled as Shah. Many of the tribes resented Seljuk domination and attacked Byzantium, where their Muslim zeal as new converts provided a religious cloak for their natural raiding ways. In 1057 they sacked Melitene (Malatya), in 1059 Sebasteia (Sivas) and by early 1060 were savaging eastern Anatolia.

This came at a difficult time for the Byzantine empire. Its hold on south Italy was threatened by rebellious Norman mercenaries, while Patzinacks from the Steppe attacked the Balkans. The Macedonian dynasty had died out shortly after the death of Basil II (976–1025) and no dominant emperor emerged who could impose his dynasty. As a result there was bitter rivalry between the great noble families. There were no fewer than thirty rebellions in the period 1028–57, and the frontiers were stripped of troops to put them down. In eastern Anatolia weak central govern-

Byzantine and Arab cavalry. The close-packed ranks of both armies reflects the tactics of close-order battle, in which each man supported his fellows in the fray.

ment gave rise to turbulence as the numerous Armenian and Syrian Christians feared that Constantinople aimed to impose religious unity upon them. The imperial army was a mercenary force and extremely expensive, so military expenditure was cut or expanded at the whim of emperors. Constantine X Doukas (1059–67) was the head of a great noble family and on his deathbed he vested power in his wife to rule on behalf of his son. But the rule of a woman in such difficult times was not acceptable and she married a successful general, Romanus IV Diogenes. The Doukas family regarded him as merely guardian of their succession, but when he produced two sons they began to fear for their position.

The campaign and context of the battle

Romanus's prestige depended on him successfully dealing with the Turks. It was suggested that he reduce to a desert the eastern provinces across which they raided, but he was reluctant to do this. He preferred to force the Shah to curb the raiders by attacking Syria in great military expeditions, as in 1068 and 1069. Alp Arslan was preoccupied in attacking Egypt where a dissident Caliphate had formed a rival centre of power, and had no wish for war with Byzantium. However, when Romanus mounted a great expedition in 1071 he could not ignore the threat. On this occasion a huge Byzantine army, perhaps 40,000–60,000 men, was raised – a mixed force of native levies and mercenaries. Amongst the native units the emperor's Varangian Guard and a few others were of high quality, but the Armenians and Syrians were unwilling soldiers. Amongst the mercenaries there were Frankish, German and Norman heavy cavalry and Turkish light cavalry. During the march the Germans had attacked the emperor in pursuit of claims to wages, while there had been frequent clashes with local Armenians.

The battle

Before Romanus attacked Manzikert, where resistance was weak, he sent his best troops on to Chliat under General Joseph Tarchaniotes. He divided his army in the belief that Alp Arslan was in retreat. In fact the sultan gathered a small but efficient force of Turkish cavalry and surprised Romanus's troops, whose anxieties were

COMBATANTS

Turks

• Almost entirely cavalry, especially mounted archers

• Commanded by Seljuk sultan of Baghdad, Alp Arslan

• Unknown casualties

Byzantines

• 40,000–60,000 men: natives – Varangian Guard, Armenians, Syrians; mercenaries – Frankish, German, Norman heavy cavalry, Turkish light cavalry; elite units mounted; some heavy cavalry

• Commanded by Byzantine emperor Romanus IV Diogenes

• Unknown casualties

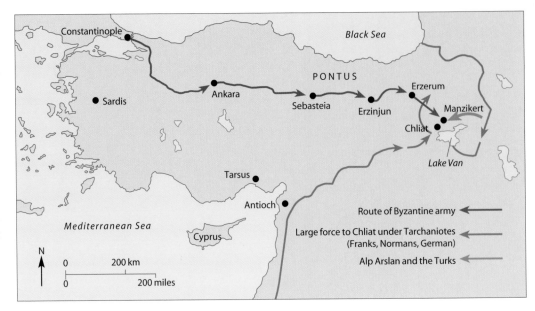

The large Byzantine army intended to strengthen the fortifications of the eastern frontier and to invade Turkish Syria. The wild Turkish tribes who were raiding the empire could probably not have opposed this assault, but Alp Arslan was drawn into the fray by the threat to the Seljuk lands.

Route of Byzantine army ←

Large force to Chliat under Tarchaniotes (Franks, Normans, German) ←

Alp Arslan and the Turks ←

N

0   200 km

0   200 miles

increased by the desertion of many of their own Turkish troops. But Alp Arslan was aware of his weakness and offered to negotiate. Romanus, however, needed a victory to shore up his prestige and knew the Turks were few. Accordingly, he deployed his army with Nicephorus Bryennius on the left, himself in the centre and a leader called Alyattes on the right. Andronicus Doukas commanded the reserve. The army advanced with the cavalry to the fore and the heavily outnumbered Turks retreated.

As evening approached, Romanus gave the order to turn back to the camp, and his division did so in good order. Those more distant from Romanus were uncertain of what was expected of them, and so they believed the story spread by the fleeing Andronicus that the emperor had been defeated. These confusions augmented the tensions within the army and a general flight began, led, we are told, by the Armenians. The astonished Turks slaughtered the fleeing troops while Romanus and his division fought bravely, but ultimately had to surrender. The main force of the Byzantine army at Chliat, including the Franks, Normans and Germans, had simply fled when they heard that Alp Arslan was nearby. The Byzantine defeat illustrates the difficulties of controlling a large army, in this case made worse by its diverse nature and the forces of treachery.

Significance

Although Manzikert was a heavy defeat, it need not have had serious consequences. Alp Arslan freed Romanus in return for tribute and the dismantling of Byzantine fortresses. But the emperor's enemies then blinded him and renounced the treaty, recognizing Michael VII Doukas as emperor. But he was not a strong ruler. The empire divided between feuding families who frequently called in the Turks.

Anatolia was effectively given away to a series of Turkish war lords. Dissident Seljuks ruled the greatest of these principalities, based on Nicaea and Iconium, the Danishmends controlled the area around Erzincan, the Menguchekids around Erzurum, while a Turkish prince held Smyrna and Ephesus. Alexius Comnenus (1081–1118) managed to hold the empire together by an alliance with the other great families. The empire remained rich, but Alexius lacked troops and was thus frustrated in his attempts to reconquer Anatolia. When the great Seljuk sultanate of Baghdad began to break up after 1092 he asked Pope Urban II (1088–99) to help him raise mercenaries, influencing westerners with terrible tales of the sufferings of Christians under the Islamic yoke. This inspired Urban II to launch the First Crusade which would have such consequences for the Byzantine empire.

Hattin

Date: 3–4 July 1187   Location: near Lake Galilee, Damascus

Now I shall tell you about King Guy and his host.... Some people in the host said that if the Christians had pressed on to meet the Saracens, Saladin would have been defeated.
THE OLD FRENCH CONTINUATION OF *THE HISTORY OF WILLIAM OF TYRE*, 1184–97

In 1099 the First Crusade captured Jerusalem and established in the Holy Land the Christian principalities of Edessa and Antioch, and the kingdom of Jerusalem. The county of Tripoli was established a little later. Muslim disunity made this possible, but a series of Muslim leaders sought to unify Islam against these intruders, culminating in the rise of Saladin, who by 1176 ruled both Syria and Egypt, threatening the existence of the Christian enclaves. Their position worsened because the Christian king Amalric I (1162–76) was succeeded by a leper son, Baldwin IV (1174–85), whose reign was punctuated by regencies. The succession now rested with his sister Sibyl, whose husband died in 1177 leaving a child, Baldwin V. Sibyl increased tensions amongst the nobility by marrying a newcomer to the east, Guy of Lusignan. When the child-king died in 1186, Guy and Sibyl seized power, alienating many of the great lords, notably Raymond III of Tripoli who aspired to the throne. Some nobles fled to Antioch, while Raymond was so angry that he agreed a truce with Saladin permitting the Muslims to raid royal territory across his lands.

The campaign and context of the battle

Saladin posed as the champion of Islam, but his attacks on the Franks (Guy and the Christians) had not brought much success. Preoccupied with inter-Muslim politics, he made no effort to breach the truce then in force with Jerusalem, though it is likely that he was preparing to attack when it expired in 1187. Reynald of Châtillon was one of Guy's key supporters, holding the castles of Kerak and Montréal which dominated the route between Egypt and Syria. In late 1186 Reynald seized a rich caravan and refused to make restitution to Saladin for this breach of the truce. With his prestige at stake, Saladin prepared a great army, perhaps some 30,000 strong. This forced Guy and Raymond of Tripoli to consider reconciliation, and the king sent an embassy of important men to Raymond. As they moved north, Raymond agreed to permit a major Muslim force to cross his lands, and on 30 April at the Springs of Cresson they annihilated 150 Hospitallers and

Saladin ravaging the Holy Land, from a manuscript of William of Tyre's history of the crusades. Once Saladin had defeated Guy at Hattin, the whole kingdom, which had been stripped to provide troops for the king, was at his mercy.

Templars (Monk knights) who had unwisely challenged them. This shock brought Raymond to submission, but tensions amongst the barons remained high.

On 1 July Saladin and his great army crossed the Jordan and besieged Raymond's city of Tiberias on Lake Galilee where his wife was trapped. On 2 July Guy and his army were camped at Saffuriyah, 26 km (16 miles) to the west, a strong position with ample water. King Guy had raised the largest army the kingdom had ever fielded. Its core was 1,200 heavily armed knights, supported by numerous light cavalry and nearly 12,000 infantry. To achieve this all city and castle garrisons had been stripped and large numbers of troops raised for cash.

The battle

Saladin's army advanced towards Saffuriyah on 2 July, but Guy refused to accept battle. That night

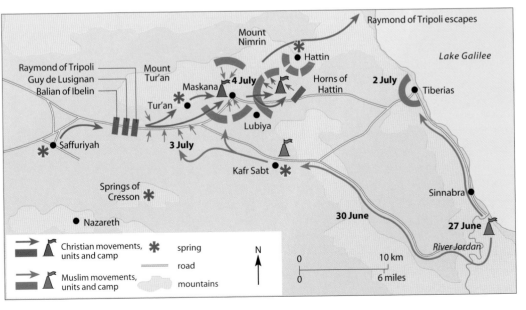

Above The army of Jerusalem customarily carried the 'True Cross' into battle, and both sides saw the moment of its capture at Hattin as decisive in Guy's defeat.

Right Saladin drew Guy into a long march across open territory, which favoured his highly mobile tactics and enabled him to cut the Franks off from crucial water sources.

there was a dramatic and angry council to decide what to do. The accounts given of this by those we think may have known what happened are coloured by the desire of the various Christian factions to distribute blame for the defeat that followed. Two courses of action were suggested: that battle should be given, or that battle should be declined and Tiberias left to its fate. It is not clear who urged what, though many sources suggest that Raymond of Tripoli was in favour of declining battle while his enemies, Reynald of Châtillon and Gerard of Ridefort, Grand Master of the Temple, took the opposite view.

There was a good case for either course of action. The kingdom was anchored by its fortified cities and castles and no attacker could undertake a serious siege as long as a field army existed. Accordingly, as in 1183 when Guy had been in command, the crusaders usually preferred to shadow their enemy so that he could achieve little before the campaigning season ended and his army dissolved, avoiding the risks of battle. Tiberias was a minor city and its fall would achieve little. If Saladin's army did not then disperse it could be lured into challenging the crusaders on grounds of their choosing.

On the other hand, Guy had a huge army and an opportunity to defeat Saladin, and revenge the destruction he had wrought on the kingdom. Moreover, Guy needed the prestige of victory to unite the kingdom. He would have remembered that many who urged avoidance of battle had attacked him for doing just that in 1183 and he would have been fearful of criticism for abandoning the lady of Tiberias. Therefore he decided to lead the army out to battle on 3 July. That he intended to give battle is obvious, but we have no idea where and how he hoped to do this.

The core of Guy's army were the knights, and they were drawn up in three divisions for the march, a vanguard under Raymond of Tripoli, a rearguard commanded by Balian of Ibelin and a centre where Guy marched. They were protected from enemy missile attack by a screen of foot-soldiers marching about them. Saladin's army had its own heavy cavalry and clouds of mounted archers. The crusader army paused on the springs

of Tur'an then resumed its eastward march. Saladin's cavalry surrounded and cut them off from Tur'an, and attacked the rearguard ferociously as they struggled uphill to Maskana. There the army halted for the night, desperately short of water and surrounded by their enemies.

The next morning the Muslims held back until the heat of day sapped the crusaders. We have no dependable account of the fighting on 4 July, but

Saladin's ghulams *(Muslim slave warriors) were heavy cavalry, and their arms and equipment were similar to, but lighter than, those of the Frankish settlers.*

The mail hauberk of this 13th-century crusader has an integral hood and aventail, mail sleeves with mittens, mail chausses and he is being handed a heavy 'closed' helmet. The western warriors in the Holy Land used similar equipment, but the armour was probably less full and less heavy due to the climate.

COMBATANTS

Latins

• *c.* 20,000, including 1,300 knights, at least 13,000 light cavalry and a large infantry force
• Commanded by Guy of Lusignan, king of Jerusalem
• All infantry & majority of knights killed or captured

Muslims

• *c.* 30,000, including infantry occupied at Tiberias and not a major element
• Commanded by Saladin, ruler of Syria and Egypt
• Unknown casualties

it seems that the infantry, their will sapped by the lack of water, deserted the cavalry and took refuge on the hills known as the 'Horns of Hattin'. William of Tyre tells us:

'They left the Springs of Saffuriya to go to the relief of Tiberias. As soon as they had left the water behind, Saladin came before them and ordered his skirmishers to harass them from morning to midday. The heat was so great that they could not go on so as to reach water. The king and all his men were too spread out and did not know what to do. He sent to the Count of Tripoli, who led the vanguard, to ask his advice. The message came back that he should pitch his tent and make camp. The king gladly accepted this bad advice, though when he gave him good advice he would never take it.'

The cavalry, exposed to attack by enemy horse-archers, tried to break the encirclement, but only Raymond of Tripoli and Balian of Ibelin and a few others escaped. After a last desperate attempt to establish a camp on Hattin, Guy surrendered. Saladin's superior numbers had enabled him to hold off the increasingly desperate Christian charges. It seems inconceivable that Guy expected to march 26 km (16 miles) to Tiberias in one day, exposing his army to terrible thirst in an arid countryside. Whatever his plan, it evidently went wrong.

The significance of the battle

Saladin treated Guy with courtesy and most of the noble survivors were ransomed, but he personally decapitated Reynald and ordered a massacre of the Templars and Hospitallers. The remaining survivors were enslaved. Because of the effort Guy had made to raise troops, the cities of Palestine were virtually helpless before Saladin's army. Acre surrendered on 8 July, Sidon on 29 July, Beirut on 6 August and Ascalon on 4 September. Balian of Ibelin held out in Jerusalem, but surrendered on terms on 2 October. This disaster created a wave of crusading fervour in Europe which endured until the Seventh Crusade, 1248–54, led by St Louis of France (1226–70). The kingdom never recovered from the defeat of Hattin, after which it was always dependent on external forces for its very survival.

Liegnitz

Date: 9 April 1241   Location: modern Legnica, Poland

For touching upon the cruelty and cunning of these people, there can be no infamy great enough.… The Tartar chief, with his dinner guests and other cannibals, fed upon their carcasses [of their enemies] as if they were bread and left nothing but the bones for the vultures.…those who were beautiful were not eaten but were suffocated by mobs of ravishers in spite of all their cries and lamentations. Virgins were raped until they died of exhaustion; then their breasts were cut off to be kept as dainties for their chiefs, and their bodies furnished an entertaining banquet for the savages.

MATTHEW PARIS ON THE MONGOLS, *THE ENGLISH HISTORY*, 1200–1259

Liegnitz (Legnica, modern Poland) was witness to a clash of nations in 1241, when the ferocious Mongols forced their way into Europe from the East to wreak revenge on Hungary. They were met by a strong coalition of Polish-German armies.

The contestants

The steppe of Central Asia had always been dominated by nomad tribes whose way of life depended on pastoral farming and hunting. This lifestyle in a harsh environment made them excellent soldiers and ferocious raiders of their settled neighbours on the edges of the great plains. From time to time federations arose which made a much greater impression, such as those which threatened China and forced the building of the Great Wall. Europe felt the impact of the Huns in the 5th century, the Avars in the 6th century and the Hungarians in the 10th century. Amongst the tribes to the north of China there was born about 1162 a leader of genius, Temüjin (died 1227), who welded the peoples of the steppe into a great political power. By 1206, as

The terror inspired by the Mongol attack is clearly revealed by Matthew Paris in this sketch of Mongols eating Christians.

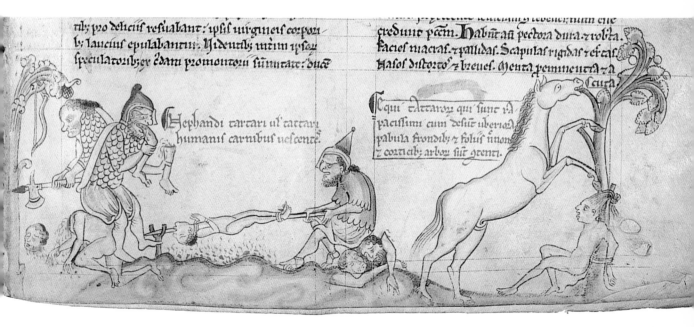

European heavy cavalryman. The heavily armed knights were the most important element in any western army. Man for man they were much better equipped than the Mongols, but they were also relatively few, and the poor discipline of the allied army brought about their defeat.

structure, notably the Turks who were often a major element in their cavalry, and Chinese and others who provided infantry and engineers. Mongol cavalry were poorly armed and mounted on ponies, but each soldier had a whole string of animals so that they could move quickly across the steppe, or sustain concentrated combat over long periods by changing mounts. Individually, Mongol horsemen were inferior to almost all their enemies in the settled lands. To compensate, Mongol generals tried to marshal superior numbers whose discipline enabled them to operate in a concerted manner and to accept heavy casualties. They also recognized the value of terror and deliberately unleashed destruction on enemy lands to frighten their foes. So dreadful was their reputation that Europeans called them Tartars, denizens of *Tartarus* or Hell.

In addition, these steppe horsemen were well aware of the value of careful reconnaissance. The primary weapon of attack was the bow, and special arrows were devised incorporating whistles, fired by the best archer in the group as a guide to the rest. Waves of mounted archers would break up the formations of their enemies before engaging at close quarters. A favourite tactic was to lure the enemy into ambushes by feigned retreat in the certain knowledge that encircling them would undermine morale: this was directly derived from the great encircling movements by which Mongol tribes rounded up game over vast areas to slaughter them for the winter. Horse archers were very poorly armoured, but increasingly Mongol armies incorporated better protected elements of heavy cavalry, sometimes raised from subject peoples, for the close-quarter battle.

Chingis (or Genghis) Khan – 'Universal Ruler' – he dominated all of Mongolia, establishing his capital at Karakoram. He unleashed an astonishing expansion, attacking China where a Mongol dynasty would establish itself by the 1260s. By 1220 Persia was devastated, Kievan Russia was destroyed in 1240 and Baghdad was sacked in 1258.

The Khans imposed upon their lands a sophisticated governmental system, derived from the Chinese and the other peoples whom they conquered. This sustained the army whose organization skilfully disciplined the natural martial skills of the Mongols. The major fighting unit of a Mongol army was the *tümen*, of 10,000 mounted men, subdivided into elements of 1,000, 100 and 10. Iron discipline reinforced the natural habits of cooperative hunting and herding. This was the secret of their success. The Khans incorporated conquered peoples into this

By contrast European battle tactics depended on elite groups of heavy cavalry. Relatively few in number, their shock effect as they closed for close-quarter battle could be very effective, provided that they maintained close formation. However, they tended to lack cohesion, partly because western armies came together only for short periods and partly because the knights were imbued with a spirit of aristocratic individualism. Infantry were also raised for short periods, lacked cohesion and were often treated with contempt by aristocratic commanders.

The campaign and context of the battle

The Mongolian leader Sübedei commanded the assault on Russia which brought Europe into the Mongol view. It may be that the primary purpose of the attack in 1241 was to punish Bela IV (1235–70) of Hungary, who had given shelter to Cuman tribes fleeing before the Mongols, and certainly Hungary was their main focus. Good intelligence would have told the Mongols that no great power would fight them because European affairs were dominated by the bitter conflict between Emperor Frederick II (1212–50) and the papacy. However, the intention of the Mongols to move west was well known by 1240 and this brought together Bela IV, Wenceslas of Bohemia (1230–53), the warring rulers of the four principalities into which Poland had dissolved, and other minor powers. Such a coalition could have successfully resisted the Mongols.

Sübedei had an army of about 150,000, but he sent 30,000 under Baidar and Kadan into Poland while the main force assaulted Hungary. Henry II of Silesia, the most important of the Polish princes, rallied an army 20,000 strong, consisting of the levies on foot and horse of the other Polish princes, volunteers like the Bavarian gold-miners of Silesia, some Templars and Hospitallers, and a formidable force provided by the Order of the Teutonic Knights who saw the Mongols as a grave threat to their position in the Baltic lands. They gathered near Liegnitz in modern Poland and awaited support from Wenceslas.

The battle

Baidar thrust into Poland, burning as he went, lured out and massacred the garrison of Cracow, which was sacked, then advanced towards Breslau where he joined Kadan. Henry of Silesia was awaiting the army of 50,000 Bohemians, but as the Mongols approached he chose to give battle, not realizing that Wenceslas was only a day's march away. Accounts of the battle are confused. It seems that Henry divided his army into four divisions: the Bavarian gold-miners and

other peasants; the forces of Greater Poland; the forces of another Polish principality, Oppeln, with the Teutonic Knights; and his own Silesian troops and mercenaries perhaps numbering 10,000.

The Mongols seem to have attacked by surprise, disordering the Silesians and drawing the allied troops into an ambush. Duke Henry, seeing what he thought was a small enemy army, sent his cavalry forward against their centre, but the wings of the Mongol army now revealed themselves and swept around the attacking knights, separating them from the rest of their army. Accounts refer to the Mongols using smoke to confuse the westerners and this may be true, since gunpowder was known to the Mongols from China. Duke Henry was killed in the rout of his army and most of his troops were slaughtered. The Mongols cut off ears to count enemy dead and after Liegnitz are said to have sent home nine bags full of this gory evidence.

Mongol horseman. The Mongols rode small horses and their armour, probably lamellar (strips of metal or bamboo sewn onto fabric or leather) was correspondingly lighter. However, as mounted bowmen they could weaken their enemies at a distance and then were sufficiently protected to close with them in the final fight.

Significance of the battle

The thrust into Poland had been a diversion which worked beyond all expectation. On 11 April 1241 Sübedei's main army destroyed the Hungarian army at Mohi. Europe feared further disasters, but to their surprise the Mongols went home. Ultimately this was due to the death of the Khan Ögödei (1227–41) which precipitated a struggle for succession at Karakoram. However, they did not then give up control of Russia. It is likely, therefore, that their retreat was due to heavy casualties in the two battles, difficulties in feeding their vast numbers of horses and to a sense that they had achieved their real purpose, the punishment of Bela.

The Mongols never really returned, becoming more and more preoccupied with the conquest of China and the assault on the Muslim Middle East. To assist this latter enterprise they opened diplomatic negotiations with Christian Europe, a situation that may well have dissuaded them from renewing their attack. Gradually Europe recognized that the Mongols offered opportunities as well as terrors and, while nothing came of suggested alliances against Islam, the peace which the Great Khans imposed upon Central Asia attracted traders like Marco Polo, who extended European knowledge of the world.

COMBATANTS

Europeans

- 20,000 mostly Polish and German forces, with a few French; heavy cavalry, knights and numerous infantry
- Commanded by Duke Henry II, Count of Silesia
- Casualties in the thousands

Mongols

- 30,000 light horsemen, mostly archers
- Sübedei in overall command, and the forces led by Baidar and Kadan
- Unknown casualties

Liegnitz was essentially a sideshow. Sübedei's main purpose was to invade Hungary, and the task of Baidar and Kadan was to ravage Poland, thus drawing off substantial forces from reinforcing the Hungarians. The presence of Henry of Silesia at Liegnitz and the movement of the Bohemians to support him testify to the success of this feint, even before battle was joined, because only two days after Liegnitz, on 11 April, Sübedei destroyed the Hungarians at Mohi.

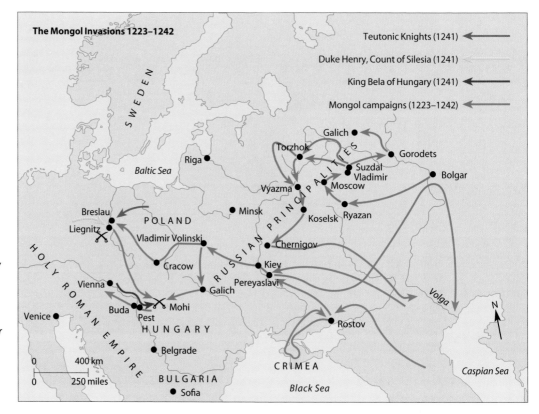

The Mongol Invasions 1223–1242

Teutonic Knights (1241)
Duke Henry, Count of Silesia (1241)
King Bela of Hungary (1241)
Mongol campaigns (1223–1242)

Hakata Bay

15

Date: 14–15 August 1281   Location: northern Kyushu, Japan

When tidings of its riches were brought to the Great Khan [Kubilai]…
he declared his resolve to conquer the island.
MARCO POLO, *IL MILIONE*, C. 1295

Mongol warriors reached Beijing in 1215, thereafter establishing themselves as rulers over China under the name of the Yuan dynasty. Kubilai Khan, the head of the dynasty, occupied the Chinese imperial throne from 1260 until his death in 1294. Mongol expansion was not restricted to the Eurasian mainland, as Kubilai Khan and his warriors pushed into the Pacific Ocean to include Japan in their realm. The Japanese archipelago was known to Chinese as a group of eastern islands in the area 'where the sun rises'. This name denoted remoteness from the point of view of Chinese centralism, and indicated the tributary status of the archipelago's inhabitants. Kubilai did not allow his warriors to be discouraged by the perception that the Japanese islands were difficult to approach. He used diplomacy at first to urge the Japanese rulers to surrender voluntarily to Mongol authority, sending five missions between 1268 and 1273. But once the diplomatic efforts proved fruitless and some of Kubilai's emissaries were killed in Japan, he showed determination to use force.

Invasion

Kubilai dispatched some 25,000 Mongol warriors to Korea (Kôryu) and pressurized its subservient emperor to recruit an army of some 15,000 men from among Korean farmers and to supply a fleet of about 900 vessels capable of transporting the men, horses and artillery to Kyushu, the westernmost of the large Japanese islands. In November 1274 the fleet set sail for Japan. After the core of the troops had landed on Kyushu, however, not only did the fleet encounter resistance from the warriors of northern Kyushu, but a storm

Below *An example of tetsuhau, the world's oldest anti-personnel explosive, excavated from a ship wrecked during the battle.*

Left *The Japanese warrior Takezaki Suenaga attacks Mongol bowmen, though his horse is wounded. A bomb explodes in the air at centre.*

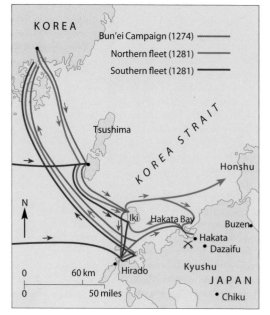

The attempted invasions of Japan, 1274 and 1281.

KOREA

Bun'ei Campaign (1274) ———
Northern fleet (1281) ———
Southern fleet (1281) ———

Tsushima

KOREA STRAIT

Honshu

N

Iki Hakata Bay
Buzen
Hakata
Dazaifu
Hirado Kyushu
JAPAN
Chiku

0   60 km
0   50 miles

COMBATANTS

Japanese
· Details unknown

Mongols
· *c.* 170,000 men (including Korean and Chinese auxiliaries) on 4,500 ships
· Commanded by Kubilai Khan
· *c.* 140,000 dead

then wrought havoc among the ships, many of which sank. The expedition lost approximately 13,200 men, but Kubilai was determined to try again. By 1281, after the failure of subsequent Mongol diplomatic missions, he assembled even larger fleets ready for a further expedition.

This time, Kubilai Khan could not merely rely on Korean auxiliaries, but had to recruit a large contingent of men from southern China (Fukien). The so-called Northern Fleet, composed of about 70,000 Mongol and Korean warriors on about 1,000 vessels, set sail in the spring of 1281 while the Southern Fleet, comprising 3,500 ships and 100,000 men, was not yet ready. The Northern Fleet began landing, again in northern Kyushu, on 23 June 1281, and details of their movements between then and August of the same year remain obscure. But it does seem that the invasion was aimed at rolling up Japanese coastal defences from inland rather than attacking directly from the sea, as Japanese warriors in Kyushu had stepped up their defence efforts after 1274. The archipelago was then under the rule of elite warriors whose leaders had established their headquarters in the provincial town of Kamakura, near modern Tokyo, over 1,000 km (621 miles) away from the war zone. The Kamakura rulers were aware of the strategic vulnerability of north-

ern Kyushu, the traditional hub of Japan's relations with the continent, so dispatched men to guard and fortify ports of perceived military significance, and built coastguard flotillas.

The centrepiece of a long line of defence was the port town in Hakata Bay on the northern coast of Kyushu. The line proved strong enough to hold the invaders in check until mid-August, allowing Japanese small vessels to penetrate the ranks of the now-combined Northern and Southern Fleets and destroy some vessels. While neither side appears to have made any leeway, another storm arrived from the north during the night of 14/15 August 1281, pushing the Mongol fleet, jammed and disorderly, into Hakata Bay. Apparently, some 12,000 Korean and probably 30,000 Mongol warriors were killed, while the Southern Fleet lost most of its 100,000 men.

Outcome
Disastrous as this second expedition had been, Kubilai Khan gave orders for the construction of another fleet, but a rebellion in 1286 forced him to postpone building. Kubilai's successor Timur eventually abandoned the plan. Even though the Kamakura warriors soon afterwards plunged into domestic warfare – to last intermittently into the early 17th century – no further invasion of Japan was attempted until the 19th century. As the Yuan dynasty was replaced by the Ming dynasty in 1344, the new imperial government reverted to a less war-prone foreign policy towards its eastern neighbours. In the 14th century, friendly diplomatic relations between Japan and China prevailed and the bilateral trade grew.

Bannockburn

Date: 23–24 June 1314   Location: near Stirling, Scotland

*O famous race unconquered through the ages, why do you,
who used to conquer knights, flee from mere footmen?*
VITA EDWARDI SECUNDI, 1326

The Wars of Independence between England and Scotland began in 1296. Initially the English were successful, with the sack of Berwick, the defeat of the Scots at Dunbar, and the removal from the throne of John Balliol. English defeat at Stirling Bridge in 1297 was countered by Edward I's triumph at Falkirk in the following year. By 1304, Scotland was conquered. Then, in 1306, Robert Bruce seized the Scottish throne, and the war reopened.

Edward II, who came to the throne in 1307, was incapable of providing the determined leadership that his father had exercised. The English position became increasingly difficult. One of the most important of the castles in English hands was Stirling, which commanded the route northwards into the Highlands. In the spring of 1314 it was besieged by King Robert's brother Edward. An agreement was reached that if no relieving force had arrived by midsummer, then the castle would be surrendered to the Scots (it was long thought that this agreement was made in 1313, but this is now acknowledged to have been a mistake by Bruce's biographer, John Barbour).

The English could not ignore this challenge. Military preparations were already underway; the news from Stirling galvanized Edward II into action. His force was substantial. A feudal summons had been issued, a signal that this was to be a major campaign, on a similar scale to those conducted by Edward I in Scotland. The army probably numbered some 2,000 cavalry and 15,000 infantry, many of whom would have been longbowmen. Edward and his advisers were well aware of the terrain where the Scots were likely to

challenge them, and orders went out that the troops should prepare for an enemy established in the boggy ground near the River Forth.

There is little evidence about the composition of the Scottish army. Probably it numbered between 7,000 and 10,000 men, of whom no more than about 500 would have been mounted. The Scottish cavalry were not equipped in the same way as the heavily armoured English knights; they would have been light horsemen, good for skirmishing and reconnaissance, but not suitable for charging enemy lines. The infantry would have had axes, swords and pikes, with few bowmen among them.

The battle

The account of the battle by John Barbour, Robert Bruce's biographer, written much later in the 14th century, suggests that the English advanced on Stirling in ten divisions, or battles, but this is unlikely. The precedents of other English armies, such as those of 1298 and 1300, suggest that there would have been no more than four battles at the most. The Scots were probably in three divisions, prepared to fight in 'schiltroms', strong defensive circles of men, bristling with pikes.

The battle was unusual in that it was fought over two days; most medieval conflicts were short-lived, lasting only a few hours. On 23 June two English cavalry formations advanced. The vanguard under the earls of Gloucester and Hereford encountered a body of Scots. Among them was none other than Bruce himself, and the celebrated single combat took place between him and Henry de Bohun, Hereford's nephew. Bohun

A statue of Robert Bruce was added to the Edinburgh castle entrance in 1929. It shows how he was envisaged by a much later generation.

attempted to charge Bruce, and when the two passed side-by-side, the Scottish king split Bohun's head with his axe. Fighting between the two sides followed. This relatively minor engagement showed that the English cavalry were far from invulnerable. The other English cavalry force, under Robert Clifford, advanced on the opposite flank. They came up against a schiltrom commanded by Thomas Randolf, Earl of Moray. Clifford and his men withdrew in confusion, unable to break the Scottish formation.

In the night, English forces crossed the stream known as the Bannock Burn and established their position in a plain beyond it. Alexander Seton, a Scottish knight in Edward II's service, deserted the English camp and went to tell Bruce of the low morale of the English and to encourage him to attack. The Scots duly advanced out of the woods of the New Park early the next morning, encouraged by inspirational words from their king. The English archers should have been able to counter the Scots advance, but they were neutralized by a

Above An early 14th-century memorial brass (of Roger de Trumpington), showing armour largely of mail, typical of what English knights wore at Bannockburn.

Right This page from the early 14th-century Holkham Picture Bible Book shows knightly warfare in the upper panel, while common soldiers fight below.

Scots cavalry charge led by Sir Robert Keith.

The English response to the Scots advance was a charge by the Earl of Gloucester. The earl was a young man, whose career up to this point had been marked by sense and moderation, but who now squabbled with the Earl of Hereford over which one had the right to lead the vanguard into battle. He had also argued with the king that battle should be postponed; Edward accused him of cowardice. This, perhaps, goaded Gloucester into his fatal charge. Few accompanied him, and once he reached the Scottish lines he was soon surrounded and killed.

The fight soon became general, and gradually the English were pushed back and ground down by the Scots in their schiltroms. The cavalry was hemmed in and surrounded, and as the English pulled back, so they found it increasingly impossible to manoeuvre. The fighting was horrific. As Barbour put it, 'There was such a din of blows as weapons struck on armour, and a great breaking of spears, and such pushing and thrusting, such snarling and groaning.' The English were unable to hold their formations, and broke ranks.

As it became clear that the English had lost, those with Edward II decided that he must be led away from the disaster. When Edward was safe, one knight, Giles de Argentine, heroically declared that he was not accustomed to flee, and turned round to make one final charge into the ranks of the Scots, only to die on their spears.

Conclusion
Although the accounts of the battle are not all consistent one with another, the reasons for the Scottish triumph are plain. The Scots had been able to establish a strong position on ground which favoured them. They had a charismatic leader, and a well-thought-out plan of action. The English lacked any coherence in command. Chivalrous actions such as those by the Earl of Gloucester and Giles de Argentine proved to be suicidal. The defeat opened the north of England to vicious Scottish raids. It was not until 1332 and 1333, with English victories at Dupplin Moor and Halidon Hill, that the course of the war was once again reversed.

COMBATANTS

Scots
- Unknown numbers, perhaps 7,000–10,000, including *c.* 500 light horsemen; infantry with axes, swords and bowmen
- Commanded by Robert Bruce
- Unknown casualties

English
- Perhaps 15,000–20,000, including 2,000 cavalry and 15,000 infantry
- Commanded by King Edward II; Earl of Gloucester; Earl of Hereford; Earl of Pembroke
- Unknown casualties

Bannockburn was fought in boggy terrain close to the River Forth over two days. The exact site is impossible to determine; that shown is the most probable.

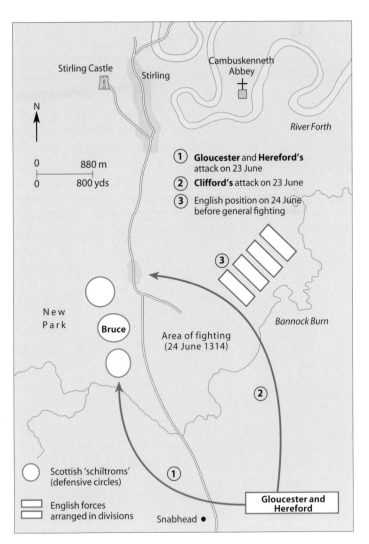

Crécy

Date: 25–26 August 1346   Location: Picardie, northwestern France

The archers shot so marvellously that when the horses felt the barbed arrows some would not go forwards. Some would leap into the air as if maddened, some bucked horribly, and others turned their rumps towards the enemy, regardless of their masters, because of the arrows they felt.

(ABOUT THE FRENCH CAVALRY) JEAN LE BEL, *TRUE CHRONICLES*, C. 1352

The Hundred Years War between England and France began in 1337. The initial phase saw the English construct a grand alliance of princes in the Low Countries. When in 1339 they and their allies confronted the French, neither side had sufficient stomach for battle and none took place. The conflict appeared indecisive and inconclusive until 1346, when the course of the Hundred Years War was transformed by an extraordinary campaign led by Edward III, which culminated in the first great battle of the war – Crécy.

The English had landed, quite unexpectedly, in western Normandy on July 12 1346. This was probably deliberate, but it may be that contrary winds meant that the fleet could not make its intended voyage south to Gascony. Resistance was ineffective; even the city of Caen fell with sur-

prising ease to the English, who relished the plunder they took there. The plan was to continue to march northwards, but the River Seine presented a major obstacle. The French destroyed the bridges, and Edward's army was forced to march upstream, until it approached Paris. Challenges to fight Philip VI of France came to nothing. At Poissy, the English were able to repair the bridge, and marched rapidly northwards. The next obstacle was the Somme, which the army forded at Blanquetaque, aided by local knowledge. At Crécy, Edward III halted and prepared to fight. Crécy lay in the county of Ponthieu, an English possession since 1279 but currently occupied by the French. There was a moral advantage in fighting on what might be regarded as home ground. More importantly, the ridge that lay between the villages of Crécy and Wadicourt pro-

The longbow, with its rapid rate of shooting, was a decisive weapon at Crécy. Volleys of arrows would terrify men and horses alike. These English archers are shown with their quivers, each of which would hold two dozen arrows.

vided an ideal site for the English to establish a strong defensive position. The valley below was defined by a steep bank on the opposite side, making it hard for the French to manoeuvre. The bank partially enclosed what would become a savage killing ground.

Did Edward deliberately seek out battle with the French, or was he placed in a position by them in which he had no option other than to fight, caught in a trap? This has been much debated. English royal propaganda was clear; Edward wanted to fight his rival Philip in battle. However, he could have faced Philip at an earlier stage in the campaign, and surely he need not have avoided the French by crossing the Seine at Poissy, then making his way northwards at some speed? Certainty is not possible, but it is hard to dismiss the contemporary evidence that Edward wanted to fight the French. There was no better way to prove his case that he was the rightful king of France, by inheritance through his mother Isabella of France.

The battle

The size of the English army is not known for sure, but it probably numbered about 15,000, of whom almost 3,000 were knights and men-at-arms. This was a paid force, in which many served their lords in accordance with formal indentures, or contracts, previously agreed upon. Chroniclers' descriptions of the way in which the English drew up this army for battle are not consistent one with another. There was a circular formation of carts at the rear, defending the baggage. It was probably here that they had a small number of guns, ineffective but noisy. There were three main divisions in the army, but whether they were drawn up one behind the other, or along a long front, is not so clear. The Prince of Wales, with the earls of Northampton and Warwick, commanded the first division, the king himself the second, and probably the earls of Arundel and Huntingdon, with others, the third. The English knights and men-at-arms dismounted to fight, as they had learned to do in the Scottish wars. There has been much argument about the archers, described by the chronicler Froissart as drawn up *en herse*, proba-

bly meaning triangular formations. They flanked the main English force, and were ideally positioned to cause havoc as the French advanced on 25 August.

The French forces were undoubtedly far more numerous than those of the English, but they were infinitely less well led. There was much confusion among the French, and argument as to whether to wait to fight on the following day. Finally rashness overcame wisdom. The French flew their celebrated war banner, the Oriflamme,

An imaginary scene, in which the young Edward III receives his shield, showing three leopards, from St George. Both figures bear aillettes, rectangular shoulder-pieces displaying their arms.

and orders were issued on both sides that no quarter was to be given.

Genoese crossbowmen were sent forward; they did not even have all their equipment since there had not been time to unpack it. In particular, they lacked their large shields, or *pavises*. According to later accounts, their bowstrings became damp in a rainstorm, rendering their weapons less effective. The English longbows, on the other hand, could not have been more potent. The Genoese were savaged, and forced back, only to be cut down by French cavalry as they advanced.

Accounts of the battle as it proceeded are inevitably confused and contradictory. It appears to have consisted of repeated French attacks on the English lines of dismounted men-at-arms. Perhaps at one point the French even forced Edward III's men back to the defensive encampment in the rear. The division of Edward, Prince of Wales, bore the brunt of the fighting, and twice the prince was brought to his knees as the French attacked. Froissart famously told the story of how the king refused to send assistance, saying that the boy should be allowed to win his spurs. The other celebrated incident came in the closing stages of the battle, when the blind king of Bohemia, John of Luxembourg, demanded that he be led into the fighting so that he could strike one blow with his sword. His men tied their horses together in a ring, and the following morning John was found dying, and his men dead. French casualties in the battle were very heavy. Many were killed in the sheer crush of men on the battlefield, suffocated in their armour as men piled up over them. It was claimed that a total of nine princes, 1,200 knights, and 15,000–16,000 others were lost. Few were taken prisoner; German troops fighting for Edward III complained at the loss of potential ransoms.

The battle had begun late in the afternoon, and by the time it was over, it was dark. There was,

Right *The Pembridge helm, an English helmet of the later 14th century. This type was increasingly used for tournament more than battle, where helmets with movable visors were preferred.*

Below *At Crécy the English had a clear tactical advantage, for their position was on a slope overlooking a wide valley.*

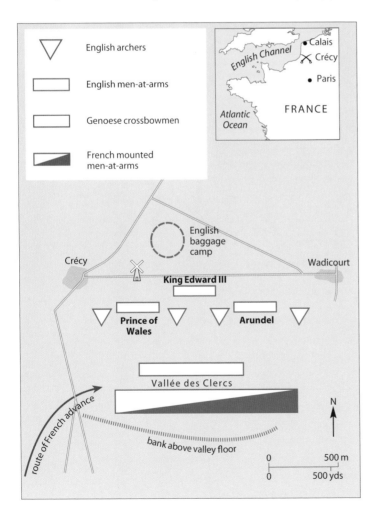

English archers

English men-at-arms

Genoese crossbowmen

French mounted men-at-arms

English Channel
Calais
Crécy
Paris
FRANCE
Atlantic Ocean

English baggage camp
Crécy
Wadicourt
King Edward III
Prince of Wales
Arundel
Vallée des Clercs
route of French advance
bank above valley floor
N
0   500 m
0   500 yds

COMBATANTS

English
- *c.* 15,000 men
- Commanded by King Edward III; Edward, Prince of Wales; Thomas Hatfield, Bishop of Durham
- estimated at fewer than 100

French
- At least 30,000 men
- Commanded by Philip VI; John, king of Bohemia; Charles, Count of Alençon
- 1,542 men-at-arms (by one estimate) and an unknown number of infantry

The English, on the left, in battle against the French on the right. The French king is shown prominently, with his insignia of the fleur-de-lys, as is the English royal banner bearing the three leopards.

therefore, no extensive rout and pursuit, though fighting did reach as far as Watteglise, some way to the northwest of Wadicourt. On the next day there was some alarm at the possibility of further French troops renewing the fight, but they turned out to be peasant militiamen, belatedly making their way to the battlefield. The English massacred them in a final cruel blow.

Summary

The reasons for the English triumph were several. The English chose their position well. The longbow was important: a skilled archer could shoot three or four times as quickly as a crossbowman, and horses were soon maddened by the arrows that came on them in massive storms. The tactics whereby the knights and men-at-arms fought on foot had been developed in Edward III's Scottish wars, and again proved highly effective. Intangible factors, such as the quality of the king's leadership, undoubtedly had their part to play. As for the French, their Genoese crossbowmen were no match for the English archers. French tactics had not been developed to take account of the way in which the English fought. Philip VI may have fought bravely, but he did not have the charisma as a leader that Edward III possessed. Uncertainty among the French commanders at the start of the battle was followed by confusion during the course of it.

The battle of Crécy did not win the war for the English, but had Edward been defeated, it would surely have marked the end of his ambitions in France. As it was, it enabled the English army to move on to Calais, which was captured in the next year. The victory led to the foundation of the Order of the Garter. In many ways it was the foundation of Edward III's fame.

18 Ankara

Date: 28 July 1402   Location: capital of modern Turkey

He [Timur] reached Angora [Ankara] early in July, and on the 20th [in fact, on the 28th] of that month the fateful battle was fought. At Angora the Ottoman Turks were totally defeated by Timur's Tatars, and [the Ottoman sultan] Bayazid, a captive, is said to have been carried eastward with his conqueror in an iron cage. Bayazid died miserably in March 1403, and Constantinople for the next half century was thus spared to Christendom.

RUY GONZALES DE CLAVIJO, *EMBASSY TO TAMERLANE*, 1403–06

The early 1400s were especially eventful in the history of Eurasia and the Middle East due largely to the rise and conquests of Timur the Lame (floruit 1370–1405), known in western literature as Tamerlane. By 1370, Timur, a skilful and cruel military leader of Mongol descent from Transoxania (modern Uzbekistan), who was Turkish in speech and Muslim by religion, had established himself as the undisputed ruler of this area. From his capital in Samarkand his army, dominated by expert Chaghatay nomad cavalry archers, overran the territories of the Golden Horde, northern India, Persia, Syria and eastern Anatolia. When, in the late 1390s, the Ottoman sultan Bayezid I (1389–1402) extended his rule over eastern Anatolia, the clash between the two rulers became unavoidable. Smaller local lords in eastern Anatolia tried to manoeuvre between the two great rulers. They sought and found refuge with either Bayezid or Timur, giving ample pretext to both conquerors to attack the other.

After Timur had invaded Syria and Iraq and

A war elephant from Rashid al-Din's History, early 14th-century Iran. Timur's army is said to have had some 30 war elephants.

sacked Aleppo, Damascus and Baghdad in 1400 and 1401, he spent the winter of 1401 in Karabagh in the Caucasus. In early summer 1402 he left his winter headquarters and marched into Asia Minor via Erzurum and Erzincan to recapture the disputed fortress of Kemah, which controlled the upper Euphrates and had recently been seized by Bayezid from Taharten, lord of Erzincan. The fortress fell within ten days and was restored to its former lord. From here Timur continued to Sivas, where he met the Ottoman envoys.

Timur demanded the surrender of Ahmed Jalair, the fugitive sultan of Baghdad, and of Kara Yusuf, the ruler of the Karakoyunlu (Black Sheep) Türkmens of Azerbaijan, who had both found refuge with the Ottomans. But the sultan's envoys informed Timur that Bayezid would not accept these demands and, since diplomacy failed, Timur continued his march into Anatolia.

From Sivas Timur's army advanced to Ankara following the River Kızılırmak. Having refreshed his tired army with the products and fruits of the well-tilled country, Timur laid siege to Ankara. The siege was lifted when scouts brought news of the approaching Ottoman army, which arrived 'perishing with distress and murdered by thirst', after a long march.

The battle

The action took place at Çubukovası (Çubuk Plain), northeast of Ankara, on Friday 28 July 1402. Figures regarding the size of the opposing armies vary greatly from several hundred thousand to the imaginary 1.6 million. Reliable modern estimates put the number of Timur's and Bayezid's armies at 140,000 and 85,000 men respectively. Ottoman sources underline that Bayezid's army had been exhausted by the long forced march from Bursa to Sivas and Tokat and back to Ankara in the pursuit of the enemy.

Apart from their numerical inferiority and exhaustion, another factor that significantly weakened the Ottomans was their lack of fresh water resources, a major drawback in the hot Anatolian summer. Most accounts agree that Timur destroyed the wells situated around Ankara. Modern scholarship has suggested that

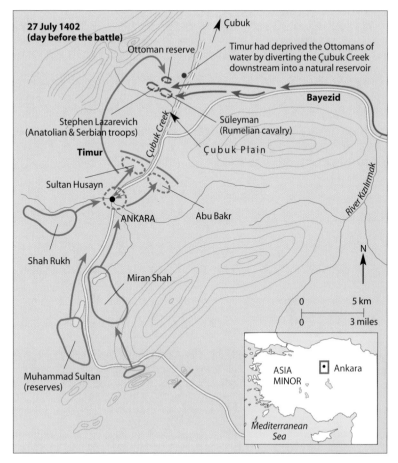

Timur had also diverted the Çubuk Creek that flowed on the Çubuk Plain by constructing a diversion dam and an off-stream reservoir south of the town of Çubuk, denying drinking water to the Ottoman fighting forces and their horses on 28 July.

Battle started in the morning at around 9 am and lasted until late evening. The vanguards of Timur's army were commanded by Timur's grandsons: princes Abu Bakr and Sultan Husayn on the right and left wings respectively. Behind them stood the main army whose right and left wings were under the orders of Timur's sons, princes Miran Shah and Shah Rukh. Timur, the Lord of the Fortunate Conjunction, led the centre, supported by reserves under the command of Prince Muhammad Sultan, another of Timur's grandsons.

The provincial cavalry from Rumelia on the left wing of the opposing Ottoman army was under

Although Timur reached Ankara from the south and Bayezid came from the north, they changed positions the night before the battle. This plan shows an older, more traditional reconstruction of the battle based on Alexandrescu-Dresca's 1977 map, which is now generally agreed to show an unrealistically large force led by Timur.

The capture of Beyazid I by Timur, Mughal miniature. Sultan Bayezid died in Timur's captivity on 8 March 1403 near Akşehir.

Turco-Mongols (Tartars)

- 140,000 men
- Commanded by Timur the Lame (or Tamerlane), ruler of Transoxania and founder of the Timurid empire
- 15,000–40,000 killed and wounded

Ottomans

- 85,000 men
- Commanded by Bayezid I, Ottoman sultan (1389–1402)
- 15,000–40,000 killed and wounded

the sultan's fate was sealed. Abandoned by his sons, Süleyman and Mehmed, he fought bravely with his janissaries and Serbian vassals, until he was defeated and captured. Bayezid I, known as Thunderbolt for his swift conquests, died in Timur's captivity in March 1403.

Significance

As in Syria and Iraq, plundering Tartar hordes brought devastation and horror to Asia Minor. Territories in eastern Anatolia, recently seized by Bayezid, were restored to their former lords by the victor. Over the remaining Ottoman realms a bitter fight started among the sultan's sons. A decade of interregnum and fratricide almost led to the downfall of the sultanate. Fortunately for the Ottomans, however, basic institutions of state had already taken root and large segments of Ottoman society had vested interests in restoring the power of the House of Osman. In 1453, the Ottoman troops were again at the gates of Constantinople (see p. 85). The Aragonese ambassador, Ruy Gonzales de Clavijo, travelled through Byzantium and Asia Minor a year after the battle on his way to Timur's capital, Samarkand (see opening quote). Although he got the date of the battle wrong, and was one of those contemporaries to spread the legend of the 'iron cage' (as in the picture above), his summary as to the significance of the battle is perfect: it gave Byzantium a half-century reprieve.

the orders of Prince Süleyman, Bayezid's eldest son. The Anatolian troops along with some 20,000 Serbian cavalry stood on the right, commanded by Stephen Lazarevich of Serbia, the sultan's brother-in-law and vassal. Some 5,000 janissaries, the sultan's professional foot soldiers, stood in the centre along with the infantry azabs and were under the command of Bayezid and three of his sons, princes Musa, Mustafa and Isa. The mounted forces of the sultan's standing army formed the centre of the second row, flanked by Tartar and Serbian vassals on the left and right wings, respectively. The Ottoman reserve consisted of cavalry from Sivas, Tokat and Amasya.

Despite all their disadvantages, the Ottomans fought successfully for a while. When, however, the Kara (Black) Tartars on the Ottoman left wing, in treacherous agreement with Timur, attacked the Ottomans' back, and when the cavalrymen from the recently subjugated emirates deserted,

Agincourt

Date: 25 October 1415   Location: near Arras, Nord-Pas-de-Calais, France

*The cloud of arrows flew again from all directions, and iron sounded
on iron, while volleys of arrows struck helmets, plates and cuirasses.
Many of the French fell, pierced with arrows, here fifty, there sixty.*
THOMAS OF ELMHAM, *LIBER METRICUS DE HENRICI QUINTO, C*. 1418

Henry V's famous victory at Agincourt was the last great English triumph of the Hundred Years War. It was a battle won against all the odds, by a small tired army, and it paved the way for the English conquest of Normandy. The success of 'We few, we happy few, we band of brothers' on St Crispin's Day inspired Shakespeare's great patriotic play about Henry.

Background

The failure of a diplomatic mission to France early in 1415 provided Henry V with reason for resorting to arms. Preparations began as early as February; the fleet sailed in August, transporting an army which was some 12,000 strong. The objective was Harfleur, a port whose capture would open up Normandy to the English. Once it was in his hands, Henry could then engage in a war not of raids, like Edward III's campaigns, but of conquest. The army was well equipped with guns and more traditional siege engines, but despite this, the defences delayed the English for over a month. In addition, the army was severely affected by dysentery in the course of the siege. A major campaign to follow up the success at Harfleur would have been impossible, but instead of sailing home directly, it was decided that it would be better to march to Calais, and take the shortest sea-crossing. This had the added advantage of enabling the king to make a show of force, though it seems unlikely that he was aiming at a major confrontation with the French.

A portrait of Henry V, from the Royal Collection.

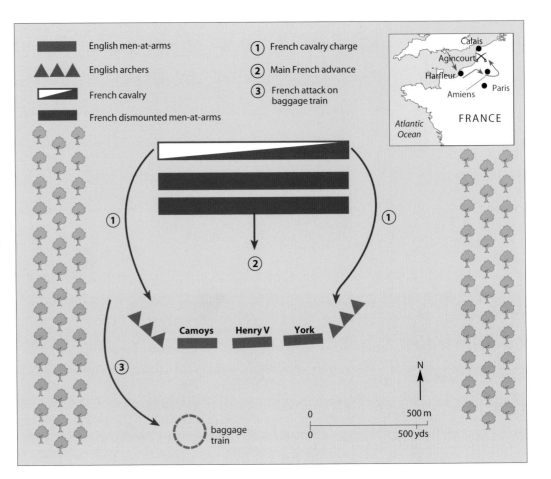

Right *The battlefield at Agincourt was defined by the woods on either side, which limited the French scope for manoeuvre very considerably, so that they were unable to take advantage of their superior numbers.*

Below *The English archers with their longbows played a decisive role at Agincourt. This is a modern reconstruction of the way they were dressed and equipped.*

- English men-at-arms
- English archers
- French cavalry
- French dismounted men-at-arms

(1) French cavalry charge
(2) Main French advance
(3) French attack on baggage train

Calais
Agincourt
Harfleur
Amiens
Paris
Atlantic Ocean
FRANCE

Camoys Henry V York

(1) (2) (3)

baggage train

N

0   500 m
0   500 yds

Henry and his army crossed the Somme with some difficulty, for the ford that had been used by Edward III in 1346 (see Crécy p. 74) was now held by French forces, and they had to move further upstream. The army was exhausted, with many men still ill with dysentery. Near the village of Agincourt the French blocked Henry's route northwards. The two armies manoeuvred within sight of each other on 24 October, the English taking care not to be surrounded. Walter Hungerford told the king that he would be glad of 10,000 additional archers. Henry rebuked him: 'Do you not believe that the Almighty, with these His humble few, is able to overcome the opposing arrogance of the French?' Henry's forces spent the night in silence, while the French caroused, confident in victory. The next morning the French drew up their forces in battle array.

The battle

The English army was perhaps some 8,000 strong; the French was very much larger, though the sources do not allow a definitive figure to be given: 20,000 is a conservative estimate. The battlefield was level; the only advantage that the English possessed was that it was hemmed in on either side by woods. English men-at-arms, dismounted, formed a line across the field. The vanguard was placed on the right, the rearguard to the left. How the English archers were arrayed is not quite clear. One account says that they formed wedges between the three 'battles' or divisions, another that groups of archers were intermingled with the men-at-arms. It is likely that the majority were placed on the wings. As well as their bows, they were equipped with stakes (prepared in advance) to block French cavalry attacks. The French were arranged in three 'battles', one behind the other. Like the

COMBATANTS

English

- *c.* 8,000 men
- Commanded by King Henry V; Edward Duke of York led the vanguard, and Thomas Lord Camoys the rearguard
- Fewer than 1,000 casualties, including the dukes of York and Suffolk

French

- *c.* 20,000 men
- Commanded by Marshal Boucicaut, the Constable Charles d'Albret, the dukes of Orléans, Bourbon and Alençon
- 5,000–10,000 casualties

A filmed reconstruction of English cavalry charging at Agincourt, the work of the Royal Armouries.

English, most of them were dismounted, with the cavalry forces in the rear.

As so often in medieval battles, there was a long period of a face-off, with neither side prepared to advance. It was not until evening that Henry V took the bold step of ordering his men to advance. This was contrary to all past English experience, which taught that they should maintain a strong defensive line. The English did not advance far, but it was sufficient to spur the French into attacking. The French tried but failed to break the formations of English archers with cavalry charges on the flanks. The French knights were forced back against their own lines of dismounted men. The hail of arrows did a great deal of damage and the mêlée then developed. The English were pushed back some way.

Henry himself was in the thick of things; one Frenchman came so close to him that he was able to make a hole in the king's helmet, and knock the crown off it. When his brother, Humphrey of Gloucester, was wounded, Henry stood over him to protect him. As the battle progressed, the press from behind forced the French forward, onto the bodies of those killed in the initial fighting. More and more piled up one on another and horrific heaps of dead men marked the battlefield. English archers, their bows abandoned, slaughtered the French with knives, daggers, and anything else that came to hand.

In the closing stages of the fight, there was a sudden fear that the French rearguard was about to attack. Henry decided that the many prisoners taken during the fighting should be killed, for to leave them alive was too risky. It is not clear how many were in fact executed by the archers appointed to undertake this grim task. This may appear unchivalrous, but although there were certainly those on the battlefield who opposed Henry's decision, he was not criticized for it, even by French chroniclers. In the event, the renewed attack did not materialize and the English were left victorious.

The battle was bloody. Casualties, among the French, were extremely high, with most contemporary estimates putting the number killed at between 5,000 and 10,000. Among the English, there were two notable deaths, those of the dukes of York and Suffolk. Many of those who died were suffocated, as huge piles of dead and dying men built up and men pressed forward in the fight.

An interesting feature of Agincourt is that the plan of battle which the French had drawn up in advance survives. There was to be a large vanguard, and a second substantial cavalry battle. Two wings of infantry would be on the flanks, with archers in front. A further cavalry battle was to be kept in reserve, and used against the English archers. A final, smaller cavalry force was deputed

A 15th-century manuscript illustration of the battle of Agincourt, showing the English forces on the right. Although Shakespeare omits the longbowmen completely from his account of the battle in Henry V, here their crucial part in the English victory is acknowledged by their prominence.

to attack the English baggage train. In the event, the plan could not be fully carried out, with the exception of the final element. The terrain was not suitable for it, and it did not provide for the way in which the English archers were able to hold off cavalry attacks, partly by means of the stakes they planted.

Summary

There are many reasons for the English victory. The relatively narrow battlefield countered the French advantage in numbers. Heavy rain the night before the fight meant that the ground was soon churned to mud, making it very hard for the French cavalry. English archery was a very significant factor; the longbow was a decisive weapon. Henry V's powers of leadership contrasted with the incoherent French command structure. The

mentally unstable French king, Charles VI, was not capable of leading the army. There was no one individual who had the prestige to take command, and the collective leadership of the Marshal, the Constable and the young royal princes was ineffective.

Agincourt, like so many battles, did not win the war. Victory for the French, however, would have meant that the English lost the war much sooner than they did. Not only that, but Henry V's kingship would have been thoroughly discredited. As it was, the English victory paved the way for him to invade and conquer Normandy. The duchy's capital, Rouen, fell early in 1419, and peace negotiations led to the marriage of Henry to Katherine, daughter of Charles VI of France. The war continued until the final expulsion of the English from France in 1453.

The Fall of Constantinople 20

Date: April–May 1453   Location: Istanbul, modern Turkey

Either I shall take this city, or the city will take me, dead or alive….If you will admit defeat and withdraw in peace…we shall be friends. If you persist in denying me peaceful entry into the city, I shall force my way in and I shall slay you and all your nobles; and I shall slaughter all the survivors and allow my troops to plunder at will. The city is all I want, even if it is empty.
SULTAN MEHMED II TO EMPEROR CONSTANTINE XI

In 1451, at the time of 19-year-old Mehmed II's second accession to the Ottoman throne, the Ottomans controlled most of the Balkans, except for Serbia, Bosnia and the Morea, while in Asia Minor the Antalya-Akşehir-Kayseri-Trabzon line marked their eastern borders (for the principality of Karaman had not been conquered). The conciliatory policy of previous decades was over and the new sultan revived the old Ottoman warrior tradition. His first target was Constantinople, seat of the thousand-year-old empire of the Romans, known as the Byzantine empire. Constantinople not only separated the sultan's European and Asian provinces, but its emperor also played a crucial role in inciting anti-Ottoman crusades and rebellions in the Balkans and Anatolia. Emperor Constantine Palaiologos (1448–53) unnecessarily provoked the sultan by asking him to double the amount paid annually by the Ottomans for Orhan, a pretender to the Ottoman throne who had been kept in Byzantine custody in Constantinople.

Preparations for the siege and the defence

To forestall potential attacks by the Ottomans' traditional enemies during the planned siege, the sultan renewed the peace treaty with Hungary, led a military campaign against the powerful Turkic emirate of Karaman in Asia Minor, and sent an expeditionary army into the Peloponnese against the emperor's two brothers, despots Thomas and Demetrios. To assume control over

the straits, Mehmed had a fortress built at the narrowest point of the Bosporus. Rumeli Hisarı or the 'European castle' stood opposite the old or Anatolian castle that had been erected by Bayezid I (1389–1402) during the first Ottoman siege of Constantinople. With their cannons deployed on the walls of the two castles, the Ottomans effectively sealed off Byzantium, depriving it of reinforcements and supplies.

As part of the military preparations, some 16 large and 60 light galleys, 20 horse-ships and several smaller vessels were constructed in the Ottoman arsenal of Gallipoli. The sultan's army of 80,000 to 100,000 men was assembled in Edirne, the Ottoman capital. In the Edirne foundry some 60 new guns of various calibres were cast. Some of them threw shots of 240, 300 and 360 kg (530–793 lb). The largest bombard that the Hungarian master Orban made for the sultan fired, according to the somewhat contradictory testimonies of contemporaries, stone balls of 400 to 600 kg (800–1,322 lb). It was transported to Constantinople by 60 oxen.

The emperor did all that he could to prepare for the siege. Envoys were sent to Venice, Genoa, the Pope, the Western emperor, the kings of Hungary and Aragon, with the message that, unless immediate military help was provided, the days of Constantinople were numbered. The response was unimpressive. Some Italians, embarrassed at their government's impotence, came as volunteers. The most famous of them

Heavily repainted in the 19th century, this portrait of Sultan Mehmed II has been attributed to Gentile Bellini and is dated to 1480. Mehmed II, a true renaissance ruler, wanted to make Constantinople the most powerful and magnificent city in the Eastern world.

Opposite The Siege of Constantinople *from Bertrandon de la Broquière's manuscript* Le Voyage d'Outremer *(c. 1455). Ottoman military superiority and Mehmed II's careful planning and ingenuity proved crucial in the conquest of the city.*

Right *Mehmed II's cannons breached the city's thousand-year-old walls. Here, the land walls of Istanbul as they appear today.*

Below *By 23 April the Ottomans had transported 70 ships over land from the Bosporus to the Golden Horn. Then on 29 May Mehmed's final assault began.*

was Giovanni Giustiniani Longo, a celebrated Genoese expert in siege warfare, who arrived with 700 soldiers. The Venetian colony in Constantinople and many citizens in Pera, opposite Constantinople, also stayed, as did Orhan, the Ottoman pretender with his Turks. All in all, the emperor had some 8,000 Greeks and 2,000 foreigners at his disposal along with some 30,000 to 40,000 civilians who rendered valuable service by repairing the 18-mile-long walls of the city before and during the siege.

From the south and east, Constantinople was protected by the Sea of Marmara, whereas the Golden Horn guarded the city's northern side. On 2 April, in order to deny the Ottoman fleet access into the Golden Horn, the Byzantines stretched a boom across the entrance to the harbour. That very same day, the advance forces of the sultan appeared near the city's western landward walls.

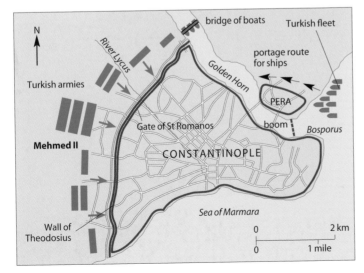

The siege

On 5 April Sultan Mehmed arrived with the rest of his troops and erected his tent opposite the Gate of Saint Romanos. On the sultan's left, all the way to the Golden Horn, were the European troops, commanded by Karaca Pasha. The Anatolian forces, under the command of Ishak Pasha, camped to the sultan's right all the way to the shore of the Sea of Marmara.

In the first weeks, 'onslaughts, attacks, bombardment and general warfare were continuous', but the city stood firm. Ottoman shipboard artillery was ineffective against the tall Christian galleys in the harbour. Sultan Mehmed, a keen student of contemporaneous military technology, urged his cannon-makers to make a different type of cannon which could fire its shot 'to a great height, so that when it came down it would hit the ship'. Designed by the sultan, this new weapon – soon to be known as mortar – sank a Christian ship in the harbour.

On the morning of 23 April, the Byzantines noticed with terror that some 70 to 80 smaller Ottoman ships had been lowered into the Golden Horn. Using sheep and ox tallow as lubricants, the Ottomans transported their smaller ships from the Bosporus on rollers either along the longer (12 to 13-km or 8-mile) land route that connected the Double Columns (Beşıktaş-Kabataş) with Eyüb, or along the usually accepted shorter (2 to 3-km or 1.8-mile) Tophane-Taksım-Kasımpaşa route. Sultan Mehmed's ingenious manoeuvre was a serious blow for the Byzantines, who were now forced to allocate men and resources to defend the walls along the Golden Horn.

Ottoman assaults and bombardment continued. Food supplies and ammunition in the city were running short. When it was learned that neither relief forces nor the promised Venetian armada would arrive, the defenders lost hope and felt abandoned. The sultan's messengers urged the citizens to surrender or face slaughter and slavery. Peculiar natural phenomena preceding the fall of the city had major psychological effects on both sides. Modern historians explain the lunar eclipse, the unseasonably chilly weather, the violent thunderstorm and thick fog, and the

infernal lights upon the roof of the church of the Holy Wisdom with the massive volcanic explosion that wiped out the South Pacific island of Kuwae and spread enormous clouds of volcanic ash throughout the upper atmosphere worldwide. Unaware of such explanations, Constantinople's desperate defenders took these natural occurrences as signs of divine displeasure and omens that foretold the looming fall of their city. To the besiegers, though, these were signs of hope and of imminent victory.

On 29 May, shortly after midnight, the last assault began. While the Ottoman shipboard artillery bombarded the walls along the Sea of Marmara and the Golden Horn, the army attacked the city's landward walls. The sultan first sent his irregulars and volunteers against the walls, but the defenders, commanded by Giustiniani and the emperor, drove them back. These were followed by more experienced and disciplined Ottoman troops, who attacked 'like lions', but they too were forced to withdraw. At the break of dawn, Mehmed ordered his elite janissaries against the walls. In the midst of this fight, Giustiniani was badly wounded by an arrow or musket

shot, and was taken to a Genoese ship in the harbour. Not seeing their general, Giustiniani's men lost their spirit. The janissaries took advantage of the defenders' confusion and several of them forced their way through the breaches, now opened by the constant bombardment. Last seen near the Gate of Saint Romanos, Constantine Palaiologos, the last emperor of the Romans, died as a common soldier, fighting the enemy. Sultan Mehmed entered the city on horseback through the very same gate, known to the Ottomans as Topkapı. The sultan granted a three-day plunder to his troops. After the plunder, however, Mehmed entrusted the newly appointed Ottoman governor of Constantinople with the reconstruction and repopulation of the city.

Significance

The Ottoman conquest of Constantinople brought military, geopolitical and economic rewards, as well as political and psychological prestige in both the Muslim and Christian worlds. It eliminated a hostile wedge that had separated the sultan's provinces, and gave the Ottomans an ideal logistical centre for further campaigns and a commanding position over the trade routes between Asia and Europe, the Black Sea and the Mediterranean. Possession of the city enabled the Ottomans to cement their rule in southeastern Europe and Asia Minor and to create the strongest contiguous empire in the area.

Janissaries of the Ottoman army on parade. These were the elite warriors of Mehmed's army and took part in the final assault. The symbols on their hats denoted their positions and tasks within the army.

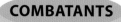

COMBATANTS

Ottomans

• 80,000–100,000 men

• Commanded by Sultan Mehmed II

• No credible estimates of casualties

Byzantines

• 10,000 soldiers and 40,000 civilians

• Commanded by Emperor Constantine Palaiologos XI and Giovanni Giustiniani Longo of Genoa

• No credible estimates of casualties

Bosworth

Date: 22 August 1485 Location: Leicestershire, England

He said, 'Give me my battle-axe in my hand,
Set the crown of England on my head so high!
For by him that shaped both sea and land,
King of England this day will I die!'
ANONYMOUS, *THE BALLAD OF BOSWORTH FIELD*, C. 1490

Richard III had seized the English throne on the death of his brother, Edward IV, in 1483. He had fended off one rebellion, led by the Duke of Buckingham, before the emergence of the next challenge – Henry Tudor, Earl of Richmond. Tudor was an exile in Brittany. Through his mother, Margaret Beaufort, he claimed a tenuous Lancastrian lineage. His betrothal to Edward IV's eldest daughter, Elizabeth, also won over disaffected Yorkists to his cause.

On 7 August 1485, Henry landed in Pembrokeshire ready to make his bid for the crown. A Welshman by birth, he was able to attract much local support as he marched through mid-Wales. On crossing the border into England, he was joined by about 500 men under Sir Gilbert Talbot. Whilst Henry's stepfather, Lord Thomas Stanley, refused to commit himself to either side, his more impulsive brother, Sir William Stanley, may have encouraged the pretender. Together, the Stanleys controlled the military manpower of Lancashire, Cheshire and much of north Wales. Their forces shadowed the rival armies, a disconcerting presence for king and would-be king alike. Richard had called upon his own supporters, mainly from northern England, to muster their retinues in all haste, and his army assembled in the Midlands in a matter of days. On the eve of battle he commanded some 8,000–10,000 men, perhaps twice the number fielded by Henry.

The battle

There is much mystery surrounding the battle of

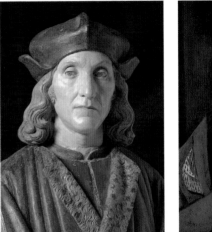

Bosworth, even regarding its precise location. The topography of the battle and the dispositions of the troops thus also remain the subject of debate. The rival armies probably deployed on the plain southwest of Ambion Hill, near to Market Bosworth, in Leicestershire. Henry's army appears to have been formed around a core of French mercenaries, armed predominantly with pikes and halberds. Henry's Welsh and English troops would have been armed with bows, bills and spears. He also had some cannon, probably taken from the garrison of Lichfield. The 28-year-old Henry was not an experienced soldier, but could count on wise counsel from John de Vere, Earl of Oxford, and the French captain Philibert de Chandée. In contrast, Richard III was a proven commander, a veteran of fighting in England and Scotland, and familiar with continental methods,

Above left
A 16th-century Florentine bust of the victor of Bosworth, Henry VII.

Above *Richard III portrayed in a Tudor portrait (c.1533–43) as a defeated usurper with shivered sword. His reputation remains contested, but, usurper or not, he lived his last few moments like an English king and died refusing to yield his crown.*

having served alongside the Burgundian army during the abortive 1475 campaign in France. He led a large and well-balanced army. His infantry, for the most part longbowmen and billmen, were supported by some artillery and a strong force of mounted men-at-arms.

On the morning of the battle, 22 August, all the odds seemed in Richard's favour. For him, the day would be a chance to establish the legitimacy of his kingship through victory. For this reason he fought most conspicuously as a king: a gold crown was fixed to his helmet and he wore a loose-fitting robe displaying the royal coat of arms over his armour. Acting in accordance with established military wisdom, he divided his army into three 'battles'. The vanguard, perhaps 1,200 strong, was led by the Duke of Norfolk; the main battle, of 2,000–3,000 men, by Richard himself; and the rearguard, of a similar size, by the Earl of Northumberland. Henry seems to have concentrated his smaller army into a single main battle. He had met, once again, with the Stanleys on 21

August but had not secured a firm pledge of their intentions. They now took up a position on Richard's left flank.

Faced with a numerically superior enemy, Henry needed to gain some tactical advantage. As the engagement opened, Oxford led Henry's main battle in a sweeping flank march, onto the right of Norfolk's vanguard. With these two bodies of men locked in a savage combat, Richard might have moved his main battle in support of Norfolk. Instead, he seized upon a momentary opportunity to deliver a decisive stroke elsewhere on the field. Henry and his bodyguard had become separated from the mass of their troops and Richard had seen them. Striking his horse with his spurs, Richard and his men-at-arms charged. Thundering over the ground, they seemed an irresistible force. Henry's standard bearer, William Brandon, was transfixed on Richard's lance. A ferocious struggle around the toppled banner ensued. Sir John Cheney courageously threw himself in Richard's path, but was knocked to the ground.

Although the precise location of Bosworth Field, and the dispositions of the rival armies, remain much contested, it seems most likely that the action took place in the rolling Leicestershire countryside, south-west of Ambion Hill.

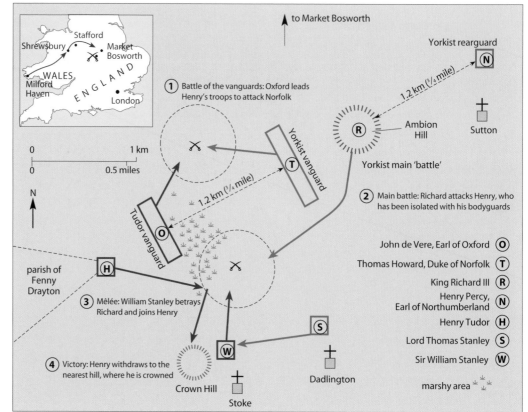

Richard can only have been yards from his rival when a fresh onslaught convulsed the mêlée.

Sir William Stanley had joined the battle, charging Richard and his isolated body of men-at-arms. Unhorsed, the king was urged to flee as his dwindling band of followers was hacked down around him. Screaming his defiance and cursing traitors and rebels, he refused to run and was 'killed fighting manfully in the press of his enemies'. Many in his vanguard suffered a similar fate. As Oxford pressed forward, Norfolk was killed and his command scattered. Northumberland's rearguard, though, either through treason or in the confusion of battle, neither struck nor received a single blow before withdrawing from the fray. Henry was victorious.

Bill, sword and poleaxe clash as modern re-enactors strive to capture the ferocity of 15th-century infantry combat. Richard, although small in stature, was a strong and skilful warrior and fought his way through such a mêlée to within yards of Henry Tudor.

COMBATANTS

Yorkists

- 8,000–10,000 men
- Commanded by King Richard III; Thomas Howard, Duke of Norfolk; Henry Percy, Earl of Northumberland
- 900 casualties

Tudors

- Tudor army: 5,000; the Stanley contingent: 3,000
- Commanded by Henry Tudor, Earl of Richmond; John de Vere, Earl of Oxford; Philibert de Chandée; Sir William Stanley
- 100 casualties

Tudor England

Although traditionally seen as marking the end of the medieval period, Bosworth had little impact on the lives of most people in England and Wales. Even the new dynasty was not wholly secure. Henry VII, as he was crowned, would defeat one Yorkist pretender at Stoke-by-Newark in 1487, another claimant accompanying a brief Scottish foray into northern England in 1496. Yet in retrospect, Bosworth assumed an immense historical significance. The establishment of the Tudor dynasty seemed to mark a new beginning after 30 years of strife and instability. So, as Henry visited imprisonment, execution or exile upon potential rivals for the throne, he fostered, too, the legend of Bosworth: of anarchy conquered by order, of a usurper overcome by nemesis.

Sixteenth Century

Major drives for expansion led to, and were secured by, key battles. Tenochtitlan (1521) ensured the Spanish conquest of Aztec-ruled Mexico, Panipat (1526) the Mughal conquest of Hindustan, and Mohács (1526) the Ottoman overrunning of Hungary. In contrast, defeat at Lepanto (1571) helped stop the impetus of Ottoman advance in the Mediterranean. Other battles, such as Flodden (1513), Pavia (1525) and the defeat of the Armada (1588), were more clearly within military systems and cultural areas, in these cases the western European military system. Pavia was an important step in the use of firearms, against both pikemen and cavalry, although it is also necessary to make due allowance for Spanish effectiveness in the small-unit engagements they sought, and to emphasize the role of generalship. At Flodden, cannon played a role, but the key elements in the English army were archers and billmen, not arquebusiers and pikemen. The more mobile billmen proved more effective than the Scottish pikemen. Mobility was also important in the Armada's defeat. The Spanish warships relied on a tight formation and lacked the flexibility to take advantage of more fluid fighting conditions.

In all these battles, firepower played a role. Gunpowder weaponry had developed first in China, where the correct formula for manufacturing gunpowder was discovered in the 9th century, and where effective metal-barrelled weapons were produced in the 12th century. By the beginning of the 16th century, restrictions on the use of gunpowder weaponry had been overcome in a number of important areas, especially

Massacre of the Aztec nobility, 23 May 1520. The destruction of the leadership was vital to Spanish success in Mexico, and accomplished by war, massacre and the effect of smallpox.

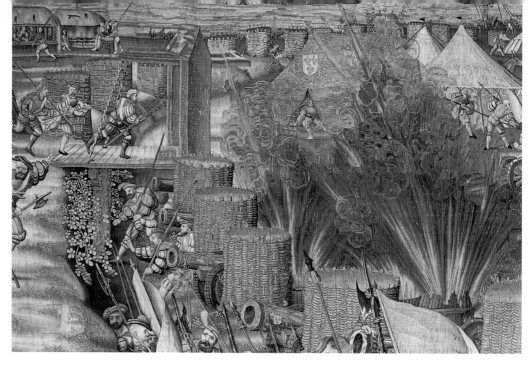

A tapestry showing the munitions store exploding in the French camp at Pavia. The battle was decided by the combination of pikemen and arquebusiers fighting in the open, rather than depending on field fortifications.

thanks to the development of the arquebus, and it was to spread during the century. The Ottomans, victors at Mohács, for example, had made the transition from the traditional Central Asian nomadic force of archers on horseback, to a more mixed force including elite infantry equipped with firearms and cannon.

In many cases, decisive victories in this period reflected a technological gap in weaponry, specifically the role of cannon at sea, and the advantage on land that firearms offered over cutting and thrusting weapons. Firearms could also help relatively small forces defeat far more numerous opponents. But other factors also played a role, such as the ability to benefit from divisions among opponents, a tactic which greatly helped the Spaniards against the Aztecs and Incas. It is also clear that not all battles were decided by firepower. In India, for example, Babur's use of mounted archers at First Panipat was important, and the Mughals also employed war elephants, as well as troops armed with firearms and heavy cavalry with swords and lances.

The limited role of firearms was not restricted to India – where, indeed, there was no major change until the spread of the flintlock musket in the 18th century – but could also be seen in Africa, China and Persia. This was also the case at sea. Ottoman defeat at Lepanto did not indicate any marked deficiencies in their naval technology. Their opponents battered their way to

victory thanks to superior (or at least more numerous) gunnery, the fighting qualities and firepower of the Spanish infantry, and the exhaustion of Ottoman gunpowder. The normal caution of the Christian galley commanders was overridden by the charismatic leadership of Don Juan de Austria. The Ottomans, however, rapidly rebuilt their fleet, and the Christian powers soon accepted a *de facto* establishment of Spanish and Ottoman spheres of influence in their respective halves of the Mediterranean.

It is also appropriate to draw attention to the deficiencies of firearms in this period. The accuracy of smoothbore guns was limited while spherical bullets were less aerodynamically effective than their 19th-century replacements. Recharging and reloading from the muzzle (end) of the gun (rather than, as later, the breech) increased the time taken to fire, and the long reloading cycle led to acute vulnerability for the musketeers, especially from cavalry. Troops were deployed near their opponents because the ability of spherical shot to inflict lethal wounds at other than short range was limited, and was further decreased by the impact on muzzle velocity of the large windage (gap between projectile and inside of barrel) made necessary by the difficulty of casting accurate shot. This limited ability helped account for the continued popularity of body armour, as it could provide protection against most gunshot wounds.

Flodden

Date: 9 September 1513   Location: Northumberland, England

It is not to be douted, but the Scotts faught manly, and wer determyned outhir to wynne the ffielde or to dye, they wer also as well appointed as was possible at all points with armes and harness, soe that few of thaim wer slaine with arrows, how be it the billes did beat and hew thaim downe with some paine and daunger to Englisshmen.

ANONYMOUS, *THE TREWE ENCOUNTRE*, C. 1513

For James IV of Scotland and Henry VIII of England, war was a means of achieving status on an international stage. In 1513, Henry led an English invasion force across the channel. James, tied to France by an ancient alliance and mindful of previous successes in the border country, responded by opening a second front in the north. Henry received the Scottish declaration of war in his camp outside Thérounne on 11 August, 1513. He had not ignored the potential threat from Scotland and had left the defence of England in the hands of Thomas Howard, Earl of Surrey. This doughty old warrior had fought at Bosworth for Richard III. As a servant of the Tudor dynasty he had marched in pursuit of invading Scottish armies in 1496 and 1497. Now in his seventieth year and plagued by gout, Surrey had trouble walking. James unwisely mocked him as 'a crooked old earl in a cart'.

The manoeuvre for position

James had set off for the border from Edinburgh on 18 August 1513, picking up levies as he moved south. When he crossed the Tweed into England at Norham he may have had as many as 40,000 men with him. His first act was to destroy several local strongholds. He then took up a naturally strong defensive position on Flodden south-east of Branxton. Here he made his camp, digging entrenchments for his cannon, and awaited Surrey.

The English earl arrived with his army at nearby Bolton-in-Glendale on 5 September. His army was divided into two 'battles', or groups, each flanked by smaller units on their wings. The vanguard, commanded by his son Sir Thomas Howard, Lord Admiral of England, was about 9,000 strong. Its flanking units were commanded by Surrey's youngest son, Edmund Howard, with 3,000 men, and Marmaduke Constable, with 1,000 men. The main battle was Surrey's own command, 5,000 strong and flanked by 3,000 Borderers under Lord Thomas Dacre on the right, and 3,000 Lancashire and Cheshire levies under Sir Edward Stanley on the left. Surrey now waited for the Scots to attack but, to his dismay, James would not leave the natural fortress he had found. Making a skilful use

A 16th-century colour engraving of James IV of Scotland accoutred for war. The English chronicler Edward Hall paid this tribute to his reckless bravery: 'O What a noble and triumphant courage was thys for a kynge to fyghte in a battayl as a meane souldier.'

of terrain to conceal his movements, Surrey therefore executed a daring flank march, placing his army to the rear of James's position and cutting him off from Scotland.

Fatal field

Early in the afternoon of 9 September, James finally realized Surrey's intentions. He abandoned his camp and moved his own army onto Branxton Hill, whilst the English were still struggling into position through some difficult, boggy ground near Branxton village. Desertion had reduced James's army to about 34,000 men. These he divided into five battles. On the extreme left were a mixed contingent of Borderers and Highlanders under Lord Alexander Home and the Earl of Huntley. On their right was a column of pikemen under the command of the earls of Errol, Crawford and Montrose. In the centre was the king himself, with the main battle. To his right was a pike column commanded by the Earl of Bothwell. On the extreme right was the largest Highland contingent, led by the earls of Lennox and Argyll. Each Scottish battle numbered about 4,000 to

5,000 except for the king's, who had 9,000 men.

The English were still trooping into position led by Edmund Howard's small detachment, followed by the Admiral's vanguard. James appears to have been eager to catch them as they arrived piecemeal onto the field before him. He took his own place in the front rank of his mighty battle. A brief exchange of artillery fire followed. Few Englishmen were struck, but several of their cannon balls ploughed into the Scottish ranks, causing the pike columns to hasten their advance and thus disrupting their formations. Nevertheless, Home and Huntley's column scattered Edmund Howard's outnumbered command. Only a well-timed charge by Dacre's Borderers saved the English right flank from disaster. Next, Montrose and Crawford's pike column smashed into the Admiral's vanguard. In the close confines of the mêlée the English bill proved a handier weapon than the Scottish pike, and the Admiral's men hacked their way forward.

Volleys of arrows had failed to stop the advance of the two centre pike columns under James and Bothwell. These were now locked in

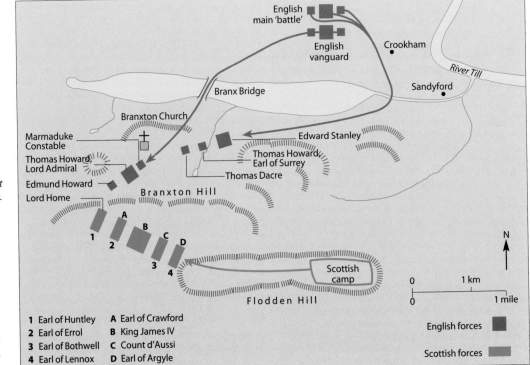

Following a risky flanking march, the English army threaded its way through some difficult, boggy ground to confront the invader's army. The Scots, having abandoned their original fortified position, were deployed on the high ground of Branxton Edge, well positioned to overrun the English as they arrived piecemeal on the field before them.

1 Earl of Huntley	A Earl of Crawford
2 Earl of Errol	B King James IV
3 Earl of Bothwell	C Count d'Aussi
4 Earl of Lennox	D Earl of Argyle

English forces

Scottish forces

Left *This contemporary woodcut shows James lying dead, while the Scottish nobility is hacked down around him.*

Below *Modern reconstruction of a common English foot soldier at Flodden, wearing a metal-plated 'jack' and a sallet helmet. The English bill, derived from a simple agricultural tool, was one of the deadliest mêlée weapons of medieval warfare.*

combat with Surrey's main battle. The Scottish king led his men to within yards of the banners that marked the earl's position, but a tenacious defence held firm. Rank after rank were hacked down by the English billmen, knight and noble, laird and commoner. On the eastern edge of the battlefield, the levies of Lancashire and Cheshire had taken the offensive, scrambling up a muddy slope to attack Lennox and Argyll's Highlanders.

Once these had been put to flight, they swept through the Scottish camp and fell on the rear of James's doomed column. Home, sensing defeat, withdrew his men from the fight as night fell. Yet for the rest of the Scottish army, there was no avenue of retreat; they fell where they stood. Only in the morning did the English realize the magnitude of their victory. They took possession of the magnificent artillery train abandoned on Branxton Hill and found the body of the Scottish king himself, wounded by arrows, killed by bill strokes.

The raids of 1513–14

Although their victory had neutralized the threat of Scottish invasion for a generation, the English were unable to dominate the border country as a whole. All Scotland feared an English incursion in the wake of the catastrophe. Yet Lord Home, although much criticized for abandoning the field, had saved enough men to defend his home-land. In a vicious series of raids and counter-raids in the year following Flodden, neither nation gained a marked ascendancy. Indeed, for nearly a century, the Anglo-Scots 'marches' (or frontier zones) remained the scene of sudden conflagration, foray and raid. Even the death of a king could not bring peace to the wild border country.

COMBATANTS

English

- 26,000 men
- Commanded by Thomas Howard, Earl of Surrey; Sir Thomas Howard, the Lord Admiral; Sir Edward Stanley; Lord Thomas Dacre; Marmaduke Constable; Edmund Howard
- 1,500 casualties

Scottish

- 34,000 men
- Commanded by James IV; Lord Alexander Home; William Graham, Earl of Montrose; Adam Hepburn, Earl of Bothwell; Matthew Stuart, Earl of Lennox; Archibald Campbell, Earl of Argyll
- 7,000–8,000 casualties

23

Tenochtitlan

Date: 13 August 1521   Location: modern Mexico City, Mexico

Cortés was beginning to feel that the siege was too long drawn out, since he had not been able to take Mexico in fifty days of it; and he wondered at the endurance of the enemy, in skirmish and combat, and at their determination not to accept peace, for he knew how many thousands of them had died at the hands of their adversaries, and how many from hunger and disease.

FROM *CORTÉS: THE LIFE OF THE CONQUEROR* BY HIS SECRETARY FRANCISCO LOPEZ DE GOMARRA, 1540

The final assault on Tenochtitlan that began in May 1521 was the pivotal event giving Spain domination over Mexico. This was not a surprise attack, but the culmination of 18 months of Aztec/Spanish contacts. The Spanish general Hernan Cortés had reached coastal Mexico in April 1519 and struck alliances with disaffected Aztec tributaries and enemies, notably the state of Tlaxcallan. Cortés's goal was conquest, yet his strategy had been to coopt Indian rulers rather than confront them with his few men. On reaching the Aztec capital on 8 November 1519 he was welcomed by King Moteuczoma Xocoyotl (popularly but incorrectly known as Montezuma), but a week later seized the unresisting king and ruled Mexico through him for over seven months before being forced to flee.

The events initiating that flight began with the arrival of Pánfilo de Narváez, a conquistador who was sent by Governor Diego Velásquez to return Cortés to Cuba for violating his orders. Cortés marched to the coast, triumphed over Narváez, and was joined by Narváez's men. Meanwhile, in Tenochtitlan and suspecting a plot, Cortés's companion Pedro de Alvarado massacred thousands of Aztecs participating in a festival, whereupon the populace rose up and besieged the Spaniards in their quarters. On learning of this, Cortés returned with Narváez's men and 2,000 Indian

Hernan Cortés was credited with conquering Mexico. Born in Castile, Spain, c. 1485, Cortés accepted the surrender of Cuauhtemoc on 13 August 1521. He died in Seville in 1547.

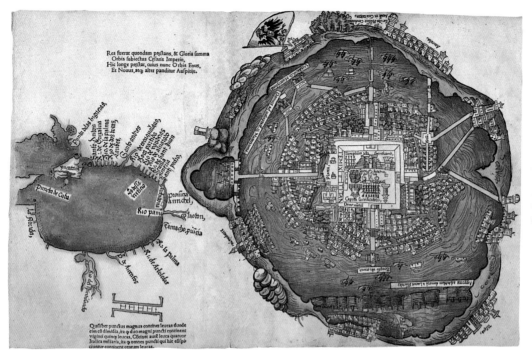

allies, and entered Tenochtitlan unopposed on 24 June. But they were immediately trapped. Spanish forays and entreaties by Moteuczoma failed and, with supplies dwindling, the Spaniards slipped out at midnight on 30 June during a heavy rainstorm. Discovered in mid-flight, Cortés and 500 Spaniards escaped, but he lost 800 Spaniards, his Indian allies and captive nobles, including Moteuczoma. After eleven days of fighting withdrawal, the Spaniards reached Tlaxcallan and recuperated for three weeks before resuming their conquests. The Aztecs reinforced their tributaries near Tlaxcallan but were unable to stop the Spaniards, whose success secured their rear and the road to the coast. This road was then used to transport enough men to double their numbers during the following year.

Moteuczoma's brother, Cuitlahua, became king, but soon died of the smallpox brought by Narváez that killed 40 per cent of the Indians in central Mexico within a year. He was succeeded by his nephew, Cuauhtemoc, in a climate of general political disruption. Many contenders to the throne drove bargains for Spanish help, notably Ixtlilxochitl, would-be king whose brother ruled Tetzcoco, the empire's second city.

Unable to consolidate immediate control over their eastern tributaries in the face of the Spanish/Tlaxcaltec forces, the Aztecs adopted a defensive strategy. Tenochtitlan was connected to the shore by three major causeways which could be severed without impeding either the canoes that supplied the city or the canoe-borne Aztec troops in their attacks on the Spaniards throughout the Valley of Mexico. So when Cortés re-entered the valley on 30 December 1520, the Aztecs did not oppose him.

Preparations for the siege

Politically, Cortés wooed disaffected cities in and around the valley to deprive the Aztecs of supporters and supplies. And on the Spaniards' arrival, Tetzcoco's king fled to Tenochtitlan, leaving Ixtlilxochitl in control of the city, its food supplies and men, and an ideal beachhead for a Spanish attack.

Militarily, Cortés's first priority was to isolate Tenochtitlan. His major assault drove straight into the centre of the valley along a peninsula to Ixtlapalapan, which would cut Tenochtitlan off from the agricultural breadbasket in the southern lakes. But marching along the lakeshore subjected Cortés to Aztec canoe assaults, the attack failed and he narrowly escaped.

Cautious but undeterred, Cortés launched two encircling campaigns, each lasting over two weeks. The first, begun on 3 February, struck anti-clockwise north through the least populous areas around to Tlacopan before Aztec reinforcements forced him to withdraw. Then, on 5 April, Cortés began his southern encirclement. Dense popula-

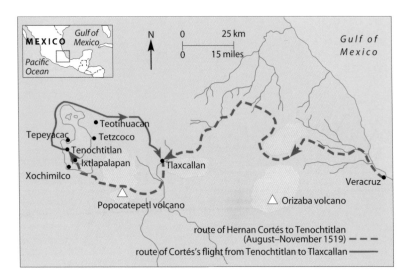

tions and proximity to the lakes prevented a repetition of the northern assault, so he marched clockwise south of the valley. He conquered cities en route, then re-entered the valley from the southwest and attacked Xochimilco before being repulsed. These two thrusts covered only three-quarters of the valley's circumference, but they blocked every major pass in or out, cutting the Aztecs off from outside support. And they lay the groundwork for the siege itself.

Cortés's advantage lay less in his own men and arms, than in what they added to his Indian allies' men and arms. Aztec and Tlaxcaltec armies were comparably armed, which often resulted in stalemates, and Cortés's men were too few to alter that balance. But unlike Indian arms, Spanish cannons, arquebuses, crossbows and mounted lancers could all penetrate the opposing lines. So Cortés's primary contribution would be in punching through and disrupting opposing lines, while his Indian allies exploited breaches they could not create alone.

After cutting off the valley from external support, tightening the noose further required control of the lakes. Throughout the campaign, the Spaniards had been subjected to canoe assaults and, regardless of the effectiveness of Spanish arms, an unsupported attack along the narrow exposed causeways was hopeless. Accordingly, Cortés ordered 13 brigantines to be built, each over 13 m (40 ft) long, with 12 oarsmen, 12 crossbowmen and arquebusiers, 1 artilleryman and 1 captain. When they were launched at Tetzcoco on 28 April, the siege began in earnest.

Above *Route of Cortés and his men from the Gulf coast to Tenochtitlan in 1519 and their flight from Tenochtitlan to Tlaxcallan in July 1520.*

Right *The forces of Pedro de Alvarado advanced from Tlacopan, Gonzalo de Sandoval from Ixtlapalapan and Pedro de Alvarado from Coyohuacan. Once the latter two armies linked up on the causeway, Sandoval and his forces withdrew to Tepeyacac and advanced onto that causeway.*

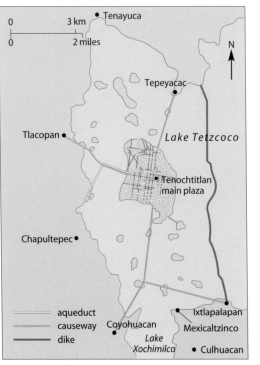

The siege

The remaining land forces were divided into three armies of around 200 Spaniards and 20,000–30,000 Indians each. Alvarado and Cristóbal de Olid left Tetzcoco on 22 May, followed by Gonzalo de Sandoval on 30 May, to coordinate their arrivals at the three major causeways. Destroying en route the aqueduct at Chapoltepec that brought freshwater to Tenochtitlan, Alvarado encamped at the Tlacopan (western) causeway, while Olid encamped at

CONQVISTA DE MEXICO POR CORTES... Nº 7

Coyohuacan and Sandoval at Ixtlapalapan, the latter two (southern) causeways joining before reaching the capital.

Cortés then launched his armada, convincingly defeated the first Aztec fleet he encountered, breached the Ixtlapalapan causeway and sailed to Coyohuacan, where he scattered the canoes opposing Olid's forces. With brigantine support, Olid and Sandoval both reached the causeways' juncture on 31 May, which freed Sandoval to block the last major (northern) causeway, to Tepeyacac.

With food and water slowed to a trickle, Tenochtitlan's great populace now became a liability and its larger forces could not be brought to bear on the causeways' limited fronts, where the effectiveness of Spanish arms was concentrated. The Aztecs adopted counter-measures that slowed the assault, but were ultimately futile. Spanish advances during the day were lost at night as the Aztecs widened breaches and rebuilt

defences. Eventually, Cortés ordered camps to be established wherever the advance stopped for the day, and the slow Spanish progress resumed.

Some canoes slipped through the brigantines' blockade, but too few, and famine soon gripped Tenochtitlan. As the fortunes of war shifted to the Spanish side, so too did towns in the valley, but their progress was precarious. On 30 June, 68 Spaniards were captured during one assault. Ten were slain immediately and their heads thrown back into Spanish lines; the rest were sacrificed that night on the Great Temple, in full view of the Spanish camp. Their faces were skinned, tanned and sent to wavering allies as a warning. Encouraged, the Aztecs attacked with renewed vigour for four days and most of Cortés's allies left. But the assault eventually waned, the Spanish camps were not overrun, Cortés began his offensive once more and his Indian allies returned.

Once the fighting entered the city, the Aztecs attacked from flanking buildings and rooftops,

A later, romanticized painting of The Taking of Tenochtitlan by Cortés, *1521, by an artist of the Spanish school.*

101

and the Spaniards razed everything in response. Burning and levelling the buildings before them, the Spaniards fought toward the centre, until Cuauhtemoc finally agreed to negotiate. The fighting slackened but, when negotiations failed to materialize, Cortés resumed his attack. And on 13 August, the Spaniards broke through the last defences. Cuauhtemoc fled with a canoe fleet but was overtaken by a brigantine and surrendered, ending the siege.

Drawing from Diego Durán's Historia de las Indias de Nueva España e Islas de la Tierra Firme *depicting Cortés besieged in Tenochtitlan before his flight. The Spaniards were besieged in the Palace of Axayacatl, and the attacking Aztec warriors are indicated by the glyph of a stone and cactus denoting Tenochtitlan.*

Aftermath

The conquest of Tenochtitlan was effectively the conquest of Mexico. Some cities resisted unsuccessfully, but most capitulated without a struggle, consolidating the Spanish victory and opening up Mexico to Spanish colonization and exploitation. That victory encouraged the conquest of Peru ten years later and also opened Asia to trade, which ran from Manila to Seville through Mexico City. And the silver and gold of the New World overwhelmed Spain, fuelling development throughout much of Europe, stimulating colonial expansion by other powers and irreversibly changing the world.

COMBATANTS

Spaniards and Indian allies

- Spaniards: *c.* 2,000 men involved throughout two years, armed with falconets, arquebuses, crossbows, swords, fewer than 20 horses and 13 brigantines; Indian allies: *c.* 100,000 men, comprising soldiers from Tlaxcallan, Huexotzinco, Tetzcoco, Chalco and Chollollan, all armed with similar weaponry to the Aztecs

- Spanish commanders: Hernan Cortés, Pedro de Alvarado, Cristóbal de Olid, Gonzalo de Sandoval; Indian allies commanders: Ixtlilxochitl (Tetzcocans), Chichimecateuctli (Tlaxcaltecs)

- *c.* 1,000 Spaniards died (100 in the final assault); casualty numbers of Indian allies unknown

Aztecs

- Likely to be *c.* 100,000 men; armed with obsidian-bladed oak broad-swords, thrusting spears, slings, bows and arrows; protected by shields and quilted cotton armour

- Commanded by Moteuczoma Xocoyotl until 30 June 1520, Cuitlahua until early December 1520, then the Aztec king Cuauhtemoc until his surrender on 13 August 1521

- Unknown casualties

Pavia

Date: 24 February 1525   Location: Lombardy region, northern Italy

*I have taken all necessary measures; my supplies are ready and my troops
are paid. I am expecting 1,400,000 francs next month and I have summoned fresh troops.
I have not crossed the Alps in person or invaded Italy with 30,000 good infantry and the
support of a fleet with 6,000 or 7,000 troops on board to stop now. I want nothing less
than the entire state of Milan and the kingdom of Naples.*
FRANCIS I, *STATE PAPERS OF HENRY VIII*, VOL. 6, 359, NOVEMBER 1524

When Francis I succeeded to the throne of France in 1515, the Great Italian Wars had already raged for over a quarter of a century. Francis himself faced a particularly acute strategic crisis: in 1516 his Habsburg rival, Charles V, became both King of Spain and Holy Roman Emperor. France could now expect invasion from Germany, the Netherlands or Spain. Charles's English ally, Henry VIII, threatened France from across the Channel. In 1523–24 a rebellion at home, led by Charles Duke of Bourbon, had to be quashed. Yet the audacious Francis resolved to carry the war to the Habsburgs, by leading French armies back into the Italian peninsula.

The capture of Milan

Francis's main objective was the wealthy Duchy of Milan, against which his fortunes ebbed and flowed. At Marignano, 1515, he was victorious; at Bicocca, 1522, he was defeated. Possession of Milan eluded him. In October 1524, Francis launched another invasion across the Alps, and with around 33,000 men, his army was twice the size of Imperialist forces defending Milan. The French army was of a high quality too: Swiss, Landsknecht (formidable German infantry) and Italian mercenary infantry supported by French heavy cavalry and an impressive artillery train. Charles de Lannoy, the Imperialist commander, withdrew his forces into Lodi and Pavia, and abandoned Milan to the French on 26 October.

Francis was urged by his older, more experi-enced commanders, such as Louis de la Tremouille and Jacques de Chabannes, Seigneur de la Palice, to strike directly at the main Imperial-ist force at Lodi. However, his young friend Guillaume Gouffier, Seigneur de Bonnivet, per-suaded him to besiege Pavia instead, which was closer to Milan. The commander of the Lodi garri-son, Fernando Francesco d'Avolos, Marquis de Pescara, exclaimed in relief, 'We were defeated; soon we will be victorious.'

Francis I of France as depicted by Jean Clouet. This portrait was probably painted in the same year that catastrophe overtook the king at Pavia. Chivalrous and brave, but a poor general, he was lucky to escape the battlefield with his life.

The siege of Pavia

Pavia was a difficult proposition for a besieger; to the south, the River Ticino (called Ticinus in Roman times, see Cannae p. 33) formed a strong natural defence, while all other approaches were defended by the city walls. The 6,000-strong German and Spanish garrison was commanded by the capable and determined Antonio de Leya. Premature assaults on the city on 21 November were repulsed, and an ingenious attempt to divert the Ticino was thwarted by heavy rainfall. The siege settled down into a wearying contest of artillery duels, sorties and skirmishes.

Francis detached 6,000 of his own troops, under John Stuart Duke of Albany, to threaten the kingdom of Naples. This expedition failed to draw significant Imperialist troops away from Lombardy, but it did persuade Pope Clement VII to enter into a secret treaty supporting Francis's cause. Even as Imperialist forces gathered under Lannoy and Charles Duke of Bourbon, the French king remained confident and insisted that Pavia would soon fall.

The Imperialist gamble

By February 1525, the Imperialists knew they were running out of time. Their troops' pay was in arrears and a mutiny threatened. Yet an attack on the strong French positions around Pavia seemed a desperate gamble. The French army still numbered around 30,000, marginally more than the Imperialists had assembled. Their gun batteries were well-entrenched and much of the army was stationed in a walled park to the north of the city, containing the fortified hunting lodge, Castello Mirabello.

Attempts to draw the French from these positions by feinting at Milan had failed. Little option was left but to try to assault the French positions around Pavia. This would combine a surprise attack on the park with a strong sortie from within the besieged town itself. During the night of 23 February, sappers breached the wall of the park in three places. The work was done quietly and slowly. It was already dawn on 24 February when Imperialist troops began to move into the park.

The fighting at Pavia ebbed and flowed through the wooded expanses of Mirabello Park and around the siege-lines surrounding the city.

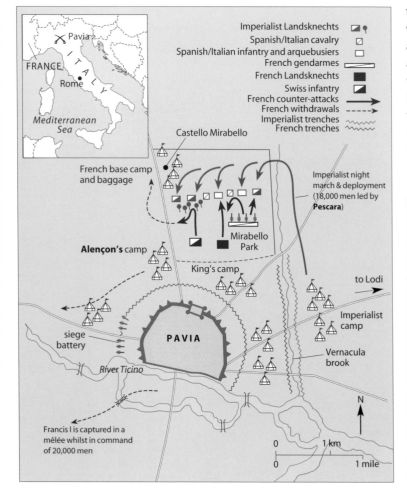

COMBATANTS

Imperialists

• 28,000 men

• Main commanders: Charles de Lannoy; Fernando Francesco d'Avolos, Marquis de Pescara; Charles Duke of Bourbon; Avolos d'Aquino, Marquis de Vasto; Georg von Frunsberg

• 1,500 casualties

French

• 30,000 men

• Main commanders: King Francis I; Louis de la Tremouille; Jacques de Chabannes, Seigneur de la Palice; Guillaume Gouffier, Seigneur de Bonnivet; Charles de Valois, Duc d'Alençon

• 10,000 casualties

The battle in the park

The first objective of the attack was Castello Mirabello, which was seized by 3,000 arquebusiers led by Avolos d'Aquino, Marquis de Vasto. Yet Imperialist troops now came under a heavy fire from French cannon that seemed to have been expecting the attack. Gaps were torn through the ranks of some Imperialist units as they attempted to form up. The Imperialist Landsknechts, under their famous captain Georg von Frunsberg, fared better, pushing deeper into the park where they soon encountered a large body of Swiss pikemen. The French defence seemed uncoordinated, with bodies of troops arriving piecemeal into the battle. But the Swiss were well known for their courage and discipline and held the Landsknechts for over an hour before finally withdrawing from the field in some disorder.

Fresh Imperialist troops continued to march through the breaches into the park, marshalled by Bourbon. They were screened by a force of about 1,600 Spanish cavalry under Lannoy. To his dismay, he could now see over 3,000 French men-at-arms forming up before him. Francis was at the head of his heavy cavalry and was determined to drive the Imperialists from the field personally. The Spanish horse wheeled to meet the threat but the thundering French charge easily smashed through them, scattering the survivors. A stream of enemy horsemen fled the field, carrying Lannoy with them. The French king exclaimed in triumph, 'Now is the time to call me Duke of Milan!' Yet it swiftly became apparent that he had ridden to catastrophe, not victory.

The mass of French horsemen had masked the cannon that had been doing so much damage to

Rupert Heller, The Battle of Pavia, *1525 (c. 1529). The importance of gunpowder weapons, both cannon and hand-held arquebuses, at Pavia is well-illustrated in this spirited depiction of the fighting.*

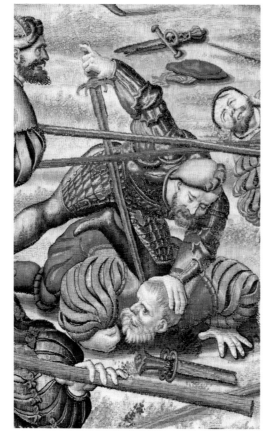

German Landsknecht mercenaries are locked in combat in this detail from a contemporary tapestry. At Pavia, Imperialist Landsknechts clashed with the Landsknechts of the 'Black Band', who fought for France, in a bitter mêlée with no quarter given.

The French king himself was caught in one of these desperate mêlées. Unhorsed, he fought valiantly in his own defence as the nobility of France was cut down around him. Lannoy would claim to have saved Francis's life, intervening to protect him from an inglorious death at the hands of an arquebusier. More likely, an ugly scuffle took place around Francis, as a number of men competed to make him a prisoner and claim a king's ransom. To be captured was a miserable fate for a king, but Francis was more fortunate than most of his friends and counsellors. The dead included both Bonnivet and Tremouille. Richard de la Pole, Duke of Suffolk, the exiled Yorkist claimant to the English throne, fought and died amongst the men of the Black Band.

The sortie by the garrison of Pavia proved as successful as the Imperialist advance through the park. Swiss troops had been driven from their positions around the Five Abbeys district and the earthworks at Torre del Gallo. The last-formed body of French troops on the field was the 5,000-strong command of Charles de Valois, Duc d'Alençon, which had been based outside the park, west of Pavia. Alerted to the disaster by the routers fleeing past his camp, Alençon accepted that the battle was lost and retreated towards Milan. By mid-morning the fighting was over.

The Treaty of Madrid

Remarkably, the victors failed to capitalize on France's misfortune. In January 1526, the captive Francis signed the Treaty of Madrid by which he renounced his claims to Italy and surrendered the French province of Burgundy to the Holy Roman Emperor. On his release from captivity, however, he declared the treaty 'contrary to all reason and equity'. Skilful diplomacy forged a new alliance with the Papacy, Venice, Florence and Francesco Sforza of Milan. Whilst, in time, this league would itself prove fragile, it allowed Francis to pursue once more his ambitions in Italy. The mighty struggle between the Valois and Habsburg dynasties would drag on until the Treaty of Cateau-Cambrésis, of 1559. And yet there was to be no peace, for Europe was by then entering the dark era of the Wars of Religion.

the Imperialist infantry, and the gunners had ceased firing. The Marquis de Pescara seized this respite to reorganize his infantry. Unsupported and isolated, the king and his men-at-arms were soon hedged in by an impenetrable wall of pikes. Unable to manoeuvre, they were an easy target for the thousands of arquebusiers lurking out of reach in the copses and broken ground of the park. As they fell, halberdiers and swordsmen moved in to finish them off. Some French infantry hurried to their king's aid but simply met their own destruction. German Landsknechts in French service, the renowned 'Black Band', clashed with their Imperialist counterparts. It was a particularly bitter encounter and Frunsberg's men gave no quarter as they hacked their compatriots down.

Fought in a thick mist, in broken, wooded terrain, the fighting at Pavia was often a bewildering series of scattered skirmishes and sudden encounters between bodies of enemy troops.

Panipat 1526

Date: 21 April 1526   Location: Haryana district, northern India

*By the grace and mercy of Almighty God this difficult affair was made easy to me,
and that mighty army, in the space of half a day, was laid in the dust.*
ZAHIR-UD-DIN MUHAMMAD BABUR, APRIL 1526

Timur the Lame (1336–1405), ruler of Samarkand, had carved out a rich Asian empire, from his base in Islamic Transoxiana (see Ankara p. 78). Yet his successors had struggled to retain his legacy. By 1494, it was left to an 11-year-old boy, Zahir-ud-din Muhammad Babur, to attempt to recover the fortunes of the dynasty. Babur's language and paternal ancestry were Turkish. His mother was a Mongol, a descendant of Chinghis (Genghis) Khan. The empire he would found would derive its name from this line of descent: Mughal. Babur was a lover of literature and an accomplished poet, but his early life was dominated by a harsh military education.

Three times Babur won, and then lost, Timur's capital of Samarkand, before being driven back to Kabul by the Usbeks in 1511. In 1514, his Persian allies were defeated at Chaldiran by the Ottoman sultan, Selim the Grim. Accepting that he could not recover the former Timurid domains, Babur turned his attention to India. His small army already displayed the best qualities of its Turkish and Mongol heritage, being predominantly a well-disciplined and mobile force of skilled horse archers. Babur also learned from the Ottoman use of gunpowder weapons. He armed much of his infantry with matchlock handguns and established an impressive artillery train.

The invasion of India

Babur began his campaign in 1519 by subduing the hill tribes who blocked his invasion route into the Punjab. Thereafter, he launched a number of incursions into northern India itself. Babur's adversaries were principally Afghans, who had migrated to the plains under the Lodi dynasty. He was able to establish a brief alliance with the unreliable Daulat Khan Lodi, viceroy of the Punjab, and his uncle Alam Khan, who together sought to overthrow the sultan of Delhi, Ibrahim Lodi. Yet Daulat Khan's intriguing, which eventually destroyed the alliance, and Usbek pressure on Babur's homeland, delayed a serious invasion attempt. Only in 1525 was Babur able to resume his march into India. An enemy army under Daulat Khan melted away before his advance. Sultan Ibrahim himself now took the field.

Panipat: triumph of horse and gun

Sultan Ibrahim's army reputedly numbered 100,000 men, ten times the size of Babur's invasion force, and was accompanied by 1,000 war

Babur's dispositions at Panipat allowed for a potent mixture of stalwart defence based on field fortifications and gunpowder weapons, and a devastating mobile offence: the tulughma *manoeuvre of the horse archers. Unable to fight its way forward and enveloped by the swarms of enemy cavalry, Ibrahim's army was soon 'laid in the dust'.*

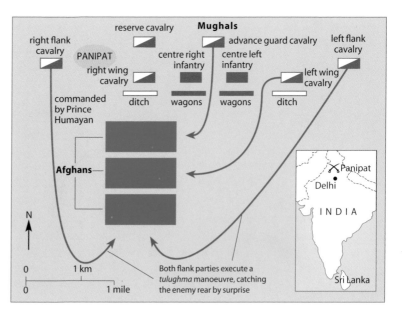

elephants. Yet Babur was undaunted; he thought the sultan a young and inexperienced commander 'who marched without order, retired or halted without plan and engaged in battle without foresight'. He intended to use a close combination of firepower (his enemy possessed no gunpowder weapons) and the mobility of his cavalry to negate Ibrahim's numerical advantage.

On 12 April 1526, Babur took up a position with his right flank anchored on Panipat, north of Delhi. In the centre of his battle line, he stationed his cannon and matchlock men. Imitating the Ottomans at Chaldiran, he fortified their position with 700 wagons chained together and a line of breastworks. Similarly, he strengthened the position of both his left and right flanks with defensive ditches, and an *abatis* (wall of felled trees). Gaps a bowshot wide were left between fortified positions, in order to allow the cavalry to advance when opportunity arose. Remarkably, Babur was able to work on his field fortifications for eight days in the presence of Ibrahim's army, which was singularly inactive after its arrival at Panipat. During this time, Babur's horsemen rode up to the enemy lines and fired arrows into his camp without provoking a response.

On 20 April, Babur attempted a night attack on Ibrahim which miscarried badly in the darkness. This little victory emboldened Ibrahim and his men and, during the course of the following day they finally deployed for battle. Babur had divided his army into six main divisions: right and left centre, right and left wings, advanced guard and a reserve. He had also, true to Mongol traditions, detached two flanking parties of light cavalry, one on the extreme left, the other, commanded by his son Prince Humayan on the extreme right. These bodies of horsemen would execute the *tulughma*, a wide enveloping manoeuvre that would attack the enemy from the rear once they were fixed in battle.

On 21 April the ponderous Afghan army finally moved to attack, with a concentrated assault on Babur's right wing. Babur's reserve moved to

Akbar the Great, Babur's grandson, besieges Ranthambhor in 1568. It was Akbar who finally consolidated Mughal rule in India, but the process began with victory at Panipat.

support the threatened portion of the line, but Ibrahim's men were quickly stalled at the field fortifications. The rear ranks pressed forward, without comprehending that they drove their comrades onto the *abatis* or into the ditches. From behind Babur's defences, bow, matchlock and cannon poured a merciless fire into the disordered masses. Cavalry moved through the gaps that had been left for them and drove off the elephants with flights of arrows. The men of Babur's left wing now advanced. For a brief time they were held, until fresh troops filtered forward from the centre in support of the counter-attack. The Afghans made a number of desperate charges, but each was repulsed in turn and the survivors driven back onto their own ranks.

Whilst the battle raged in the centre, the *tulughma* was skilfully executed. The flanking detachments were soon behind the Afghans, cutting off any avenue of retreat and firing arrow after arrow into the packed ranks of trapped men. As Babur recalled, his enemies 'could neither move forward against us nor force a way for flight'. Ibrahim himself was cut down, fighting bravely to the last alongside thousands of his men. By midday the battle was over.

Birth of an empire

In the immediate aftermath of victory, Delhi and Agra were seized. From this base, Babur consolidated his hold on northern India, defeating the Rajputs at Kanua in 1527, and storming the fortress at Chandiri in 1528. On his death in 1530, Babur ruled an empire that included Kabul, the Punjab and Delhi. It stretched eastward as far as Bihar and south to Gwalior. He bequeathed to his successors, too, an army that proved to be a formidable instrument of conquest. Thus were the foundations of the Mughal empire, that would come to dominate the Indian sub-continent, laid at Panipat.

COMBATANTS

Mughals

• 10,000 men

• Main commanders: Zahir-ud-din Muhammad Babur; Prince Humayan

• Few casualties

Afghans

• 100,000 men

• Main commanders: Sultan Ibrahim Lodi; Vikramajit Singh of Gwalior

• 15,000 casualties

Mughal armoured elephant, c. 1600. Babur's men fought with a potent mix of Mongol and Turkish tactics. As the Mughals established themselves in India they integrated indigenous forces into their armies too, including the formidable, if not wholly dependable, war elephant.

Mohács

Date: 29 August 1526   Location: southern Hungary

The division of the Janissaries attacked the contemptible infidels (gavurs)
three or four times with musket fire and tried to force them back.
FROM THE CAMPAIGN DIARY OF SULTAN SÜLEYMAN, 1526

Above left *After his accession to the throne, Süleyman the Magnificent turned against the Ottomans' Christian enemies.*

Left *Louis II, who failed to mobilize the country's forces in time, was thrown from his horse and killed while escaping.*

By the early 16th century the Ottoman empire had emerged as a significant military power that controlled the Balkans, Asia Minor, the Black Sea littoral, the eastern Mediterranean and most of the Middle East. Compared to this vast empire of Süleyman I (1520–66), Louis II of Jagiello's (1516–26) Hungary, the only regional power in central Europe that in the 15th century had been capable of halting the Ottoman advance, was now a small and weak country. Resources of the Ottoman empire and Hungary respectively in the early 1520s give a clear picture of their differences. Territory: 1,500,000 sq km (580,000 sq miles) v 300,000 sq km (116,000 sq miles); populations: 12–13 million v 3.1–3.5 million; Central Treasury revenues: 4.5–5 million gold ducats v 0.3 million gold ducats; and potential mobilizable forces: 110,000–130,000 men v 40,000–50,000.

Recognizing that his father's wars against the Safavids in eastern Anatolia could not be continued due to economic, military and religio-political reasons, Süleyman turned against the empire's Christian enemies in Europe, where his major opponents were the Habsburgs and their Hungarian neighbours. By occupying Belgrade and Zimony (1521), Orsova (1522) and Szörény (1524), the Ottomans had assumed control over the lower Danube as far as Belgrade by the mid-1520s, while the Hungarians lost the most important castles of their southern border defence system.

The causes of the 1526 Ottoman campaign are hotly debated. Some historians claim that it was a response to King Louis's 'provocations', the king's refusal of Süleyman's peace offers and the Hungarians' interference in the sultan's two Rumanian vassal principalities, especially in Wallachia, whose 'voevode' or lord repeatedly rebelled against the Ottomans with Hungarian backing. Others maintain that all these were mere pretexts – that the conquest of Hungary had been Süleyman's main objective from the beginning of his reign and that he carried it out according to his plan of 'gradual conquest'. Given Süleyman's pragmatic and often reactive policy, the empire's multiple commitments and constraints, the insufficiently understood nature of Ottoman ideology, propaganda and decision-making, it is wise not to overstate the importance of religio-political imperatives with regard to Ottoman imperial planning.

The opposing forces

In the 1526 campaign the Ottoman army may have numbered some 60,000 provincial cavalry (the Rumelian and Anatolian troops) and standing forces (janissaries [the sultan's elite infantry troops], cavalry and artillery) and perhaps another 40,000–50,000 irregulars and auxiliaries. Due to the long, four-month march, rainy weather and sieges, a good portion of this army must have been lost by the time it reached Hungary. Thus the estimate of Archbishop Pál Tomori, commander-in-chief of the Hungarian army, who, based on

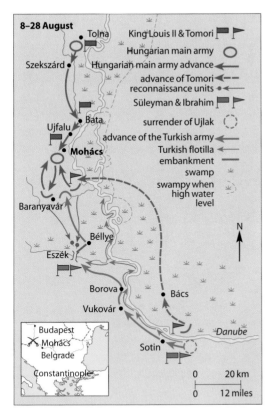

8–28 August

Tolna — King Louis II & Tomori
Szekszárd — Hungarian main army
— Hungarian main army advance
— advance of Tomori
— reconnaissance units
Újfalu — Süleyman & Ibrahim
Bata — surrender of Újlak
Mohács — advance of the Turkish army
— Turkish flotilla
— embankment
Baranyavár — swamp
— swampy when
— high water
— level
Béllye
Eszék
Borova
Vukovár — Bács
Danube
Sotin

Budapest
Mohács
Belgrade
Constantinople

0   20 km
0   12 miles

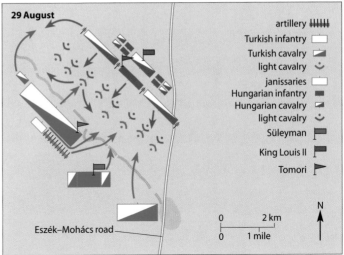

29 August

artillery
Turkish infantry
Turkish cavalry
light cavalry
janissaries
Hungarian infantry
Hungarian cavalry
light cavalry
Süleyman
King Louis II
Tomori

Eszék–Mohács road

0   2 km
0   1 mile

N

intelligence he received, put the whole fighting force of the sultan's army at about 70,000 men, seems more realistic than the exaggerated figures of 150,000 to 300,000 men suggested by later historians. However, even this more modest estimate suggests a considerable Ottoman numerical superiority. Since the Croatian and Transylvanian forces, numbering some 10,000 to 15,000 men each, could not join the king in 1526, the Hungarian army that met the Ottomans south of Mohács – near the intersection of modern Hungary, Croatia and Yugoslavia – was only about 25,000 to 30,000 strong. A similar Ottoman superiority can be seen with regard to firepower: whereas the Ottomans deployed some 200 cannons, mainly small-calibre ones, the Hungarians had only about 80 cannons.

The battle

The battlefield was bordered by the marshes of the Danube from the east and by a plateau 25 to 30 m (82–98 ft) high from the west and south. The Hungarian command planned to charge against the much larger Ottoman army in increments as it descended from the steep and, given the heavy rainfall in the weeks before the battle, slippery plateau.

Facing southwest, the army lined up in two echelons. On the right and left wings of the first echelon stood the Hungarian heavy cavalry, facing the Rumelian and the Anatolian *timariot* cavalry of the sultan respectively. The 10,000-strong Hungarian infantry stood ten ranks deep in the middle facing the janissaries. Louis II stood in the second echelon behind the Hungarian infantry, whereas Süleyman, guarded by his central cavalry, stood behind the janissaries. Ottoman cannons were placed in front of the janissaries.

However, this battle order evolved only gradually. The Hungarians initiated the combat when only the Rumelian army was on the plain. Süleyman and his cavalry were still descending from the plateau and the Anatolian troops of the right flank were further behind. The skirmishes of the light cavalry forces were already underway when the Hungarian artillery opened fire at the Rumelian army about to camp on the plain. It was followed by the cavalry charge of the Hungarian right flank that broke the resistance of the Rumelian cavalry. But instead of chasing the fleeing enemy, the Hungarians set out to loot. By then, the janissaries had arrived at the bottom of the terrace and inflicted major destruction on the

Far left *Between 8 and 28 August, the 70,000-strong Ottoman army made its way along the western side of the Danube, finally reaching a plateau, where they turned to face the Hungarian troops below.*

Above *Thanks to their position, the outnumbered Hungarians successfully routed the Rumelian cavalry, which was the first to arrive on the plain. Failing to capitalize on this early advantage, however, the Hungarians were then easy prey for the Ottomans, whose highly skilled janissaries finished off the battle.*

'Battle of Mohács' from the Süleymanname of Arifi transcribed in 1558. To the right, the sultan is backed by a phalanx of tall-hatted janissaries. This was the human barrier against which the Hungarian cavalry dashed itself to pieces. The janissaries' firepower proved decisive.

Hungarians with their volleys. Although the Hungarian infantry and the left wing fought bravely, they were unable to break the obstacles erected in front of the cannons and janissaries and were slaughtered by janissary volleys. Contrary to general belief, it was not the Ottoman cannons (which shot beyond the Hungarians) but the insurmountable wall and firepower of the janissaries that figured decisively in the Ottoman victory.

The consequences and historical significance of the battle

Such a grave defeat had not been inflicted on the Hungarian armed forces since the battle of Muhi in 1241 against the Mongols. The king, most of the magnates and prelates, about 500 noblemen, 4,000 cavalry and 10,000 infantrymen perished. Hungary also lost its century-and-a-half-old struggle to contain the Ottoman advance into central Europe. More importantly for Europe, the battle led to the direct confrontation of the Habsburg and Ottoman empires, for a group of Hungarian aristocrats elected Archduke Ferdinand of Habsburg, younger brother of Charles V, as their king (1526–64). However, Ferdinand was able to control only the northwestern parts of

Hungary, for the middle and eastern parts were under the rule of János Szapolyai, also elected king of Hungary (1526–40), whose pro-Ottoman policy temporarily postponed the clash. Szapolyai's death in 1540 and Ferdinand's unsuccessful siege of Buda in the spring and summer of 1541 triggered the sultan's campaign which led to the Ottoman occupation of central Hungary, and turned the country into the major continental battleground between the Habsburgs and Ottomans.

COMBATANTS

Ottomans

- 60,000–70,000 men
- Commander-in-Chief Sultan Süleyman the Magnificent (1520–66)
- Unknown casualties

Hungarians

- 25,000–30,000 men
- Commander-in-Chief Archbishop Pál Tomori; King Louis II of Jagiello (1516–26)
- 14,000–15,000 casualties

Lepanto

Date: 7 October 1571 Location: near Naupactus, Gulf of Patras, Greece

…In five months they [the Ottomans] have built 150 vessels with all the artillery and equipment needed….Already their general is prepared to set out to sea at the end of this month with two hundred galleys and one hundred galliots, of corsairs and others…I should never have believed the greatness of this monarchy, had I not seen it with my own eyes.
DE NOAILLES, FRENCH AMBASSADOR IN CONSTANTINOPLE, TO CHARLES IX ON 8 MAY 1572,
SEVEN MONTHS AFTER THE BATTLE OF LEPANTO

On 7 October 1571, the allied fleet of the Holy League destroyed the Ottoman navy. Contemporaries celebrated the victory of united Christendom over the 'infidel' Turks. Historians have claimed that the battle signalled the 'decline of the Ottoman empire' and the 'rise of the West'. But did Lepanto yield major strategic advantage for the West?

Ottoman challenge: the conquest of Cyprus 1570–71

By the second half of the 16th century the Ottoman empire had become a major power that controlled the Balkans, the Middle East, the Black Sea and the eastern Mediterranean. For Grand Vizier Sokullu Mehmed Pasha (1556–78), whose political grand designs included the unsuccessful Don–Volga and Suez Canal projects (1569) to encircle Istanbul's Safavid rivals and to counter Portuguese imperialism in the Red Sea and Indian Ocean respectively, the conquest of Cyprus seemed a long-overdue task. This Venetian-held island was a nuisance in the Ottoman-controlled eastern Mediterranean, for it offered a safe haven for Christian corsairs who endangered Ottoman lines of maritime communication between the capital and Egypt, the richest province of the empire, and preyed on Muslim merchant and pilgrim ships. Failure to eliminate Christian privateering would cause severe economic losses and weaken Istanbul's legitimacy in the Islamic world. Cyprus was a tempting target too for its known richness in land and taxes as well as for its closeness to Ottoman logistical bases, an important consideration given the war galley fleets' limited radius of operation.

During the 1570 campaign the Ottomans mobilized some 208 to 360 vessels and at least 60,000 land forces. Despite its up-to-date, 'trace italienne' fortifications, Nicosia, the capital of Cyprus, fell on 9 September after a 46-day siege. Shorter Ottoman lines of supply and reinforcement that enabled the besiegers to outnumber the defenders at a ratio of 6 to 1, Ottoman skills in siege warfare, the dismal performance of the Venetian relief fleet plagued by typhus and desertions, the incompetence of Nicosia's Venetian commander, as well as local support the Cypriots afforded the Ottomans against their detested Venetian overlords, all played a role in the conquest. The ferocity of the three-day sack of Nicosia persuaded the other Venetian forts to surrender, except for the eastern port garrison of Famagusta, which was finally captured on 1 August 1571 after withstanding seven general assaults and 74 days of heavy bombardment. Although the Ottomans agreed to generous terms of capitulation, the massacre of Muslim pilgrims, kept in the garrison, provoked Ottoman retaliation. On 5 August, the Venetian officers were beheaded and governor Bragadino, who had ordered the killing of the Muslims, was skinned alive, his hide stuffed with straw and paraded along the Anatolian coast and Istanbul.

Right Naval Battle of Lepanto *by Andrea Micheli 'Vicentino' (1539–1614). Displayed in the Doge's Palace, Venice, this picture celebrates the great Christian victory, in which Venice had a leading role.*

Below *Admiral Ali Pasha, a land commander with no experience in naval warfare, was largely responsible for the Ottoman defeat.*

Western response: the Holy League and the battle of Lepanto

On 25 May 1571 the Holy League of the Papacy, Spain, Venice, Genoa, Tuscany, Savoy, Urbino, Parma and the Knights of Malta was proclaimed in Rome. The League's purpose was to fight a perpetual war against the Ottomans and the Muslims of North Africa, and to recapture Cyprus and the Holy Land. The signatories agreed to provide 200 galleys, 100 ships, 50,000 infantry and 4,500 light cavalry along with the necessary weaponry and supply.

The fleet of 1571, led by Don Juan de Austria, 23-year-old half-brother of Philip II, assembled in Messina in early September and reached Corfu on 26 September. Here the alliance was informed that the Ottoman navy, which had raided Crete and Venice's Adriatic possessions during the summer, had returned to Lepanto (a harbour town on the north side of the Gulf of Patras). On 4 October the Christians learned of the fall of Fama-

Below *Although the 24-year-old Captain General of the Holy League fleet, Don Juan de Austria, was an inexperienced commander, he proved an able diplomat and managed to keep together the fragile alliance.*

gusta and Bragadino's torture. The news sparked desire for vengeance, giving the fragile alliance unusual unity of purpose.

Meanwhile, Ottoman scouts informed their commanders about the arrival of a Christian fleet off Cephalonia. At a war council held on 4 October, Pertev Pasha, commander-in-chief (*serdar*) of the 1571 campaign and Uluc Ali Pasha, governor (*beylerbeyi*) of Algiers, were of the opinion that the Ottomans should take a defensive position in the Gulf of Lepanto, citing the undermanned nature and exhaustion of the navy. However, it was Müezzinzade Ali Pasha, admiral (*kapudan*) of the navy, a land commander with no experience in naval warfare, who prevailed. He ordered his fleet to attack the Christians.

The opposing navies clashed on 7 October in the Gulf of Patras. The numbers of vessels given in the factfile are somewhat misleading, for they do not contain the *galiots* in the Christian fleet and exclude all *fustas*, smaller transport ships, from both navies. Estimated figures of soldiers and weaponry indicate that the Holy League slightly outnumbered the Ottomans in terms of combatants and auxiliaries – 62,100 to 57,700 – and had a substantial advantage regarding firepower – 1,334 to 741 guns. Ottoman accounts also underline that their fleet was undermanned due to losses during the 1571 campaign and to the fact that many of the soldiers aboard the coastal beys' ships had already left for the winter.

The battle started before 11 am with the engagement of the inshore squadrons. Ottoman commander Mehmed Suluk almost outflanked Agostino Barbarigo's galleys manoeuvring between the shoals and the Venetians. The Venetians lost several galleys and Barbarigo was mortally wounded. However, unengaged galleys of the Christian left wing and vessels from the rearguard sent in by another Holy League commander, Don Álvaro de Bazán, turned the defeat into victory, destroying the entire Ottoman right wing in two hours.

Meanwhile, a fierce mêlée developed between the Christian and Ottoman centre, following a head-on clash of the two flagships, Don Juan's *Real* and Ali Pasha's *Sultana*. Ali Pasha planned to counter Christian firepower superiority by using his reinforcements from the reserve until Mehmed Suluk and Uluc Ali outflanked the Christian wings.

Despite losses from the cannons of the galleasses (warships with auxiliary oars), Ottoman galleys penetrated the Christian ranks and Ali Pasha's men even boarded the *Real*. Soon, however, the Ottoman centre was overwhelmed. When Ali Pasha was killed and his *Sultana* taken by the *Real* in tow, the Ottoman centre collapsed. All the Ottoman ships here were sunk or taken,

This reconstruction of Lepanto shows the crucial phases of the battle and the deployment of galleys on either side.

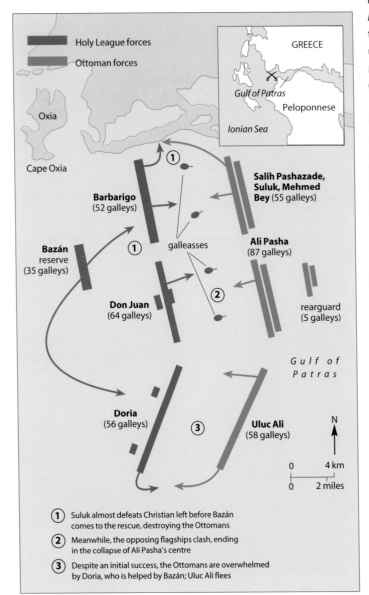

- Holy League forces
- Ottoman forces

GREECE

Gulf of Patras

Peloponnese

Ionian Sea

Oxia

Cape Oxia

Barbarigo (52 galleys)

Salih Pashazade, Suluk, Mehmed Bey (55 galleys)

galleasses

Bazán reserve (35 galleys)

Ali Pasha (87 galleys)

Don Juan (64 galleys)

rearguard (5 galleys)

Gulf of Patras

Doria (56 galleys)

Uluc Ali (58 galleys)

N

0 — 4 km
0 — 2 miles

① Suluk almost defeats Christian left before Bazán comes to the rescue, destroying the Ottomans

② Meanwhile, the opposing flagships clash, ending in the collapse of Ali Pasha's centre

③ Despite an initial success, the Ottomans are overwhelmed by Doria, who is helped by Bazán; Uluc Ali flees

COMBATANTS

The Holy League

- (Venice, Habsburg Spain, the Papacy, Malta, Genoa, Savoy): 62,100 combatants; 2,300 rowers; 202–219 galleys; 6 galleasses; 1,334 guns

- Commander-in-Chief Don Juan de Austria; Agostino Barbarigo; Gian Andrea Doria; Don Álvaro de Bazán

- 33 galleys lost/disabled; 23,000 dead/wounded

Ottomans

- 57,700 combatants; 19,000 rowers; 205 galleys; 35–68 *galiots*; 741 guns

- Commander-in-Chief Müezzinzade Ali Pasha; Salih Pashazade; Mehmed Bey; Suluk/Sirocco Mehmed; Uluc Ali Pasha

- 25,000 dead; over 3,486 captured; 84 galleys & *galiots* destroyed; 127 captured

and almost the entire population of their crews mercilessly massacred.

The clash between the seaward squadrons started later, for Uluc Ali and Gian Andrea Doria, the most skilled sea captains on either side, both tried to outmanoeuvre the other. While the bulk of his galleys engaged Doria's right and centre, Uluc Ali managed to inflict serious damage upon some 15 of Doria's galleys that had broken formation at the left flank.

Uluc Ali proceeded to attack the Christian centre's right flank in order to help the overwhelmed Ottoman centre. It was too late. Ali Pasha was already dead and Bazán sent his remaining reserve against Uluc Ali. Realizing that he could not save the day, Uluc Ali escaped into the open sea with some 30 galleys. The Christian victory was complete. The Holy League fleet destroyed almost the entire Ottoman navy with its crew and ordnance.

Significance

When in 1572 an entirely rebuilt Ottoman navy emerged from Istanbul under the new *kapudan*, Uluc Ali, it seemed as if Lepanto had altered the balance of power little. It is true that Cyprus was never regained and that the Holy League collapsed as Venice concluded a treaty with Istanbul in 1573, and as Spanish resources were redirected to meet new challenges in the Netherlands. It is also true that in 1574 the Ottomans retook Tunis, capturing also the Spanish garrison of La Goletta. But Lepanto did save Venice and its remaining Mediterranean possessions (most notably Crete) and the western Mediterranean from further Ottoman conquests. While the galleys were rebuilt by 1572, it took decades for Istanbul to replace the crews, especially the skilled Muslim marines, sailor-arquebusiers and naval archers. And Uluc Ali was too good a seaman to challenge the Christians with his green navy.

Battle of Lepanto by Hendrick Vroom the Younger (c. 1591–1661). The battle, which halted further Ottoman expansion in the Mediterranean, also marked the apogee of galley warfare.

The Armada

Date: 31 July–8 August 1588   Location: English Channel

*I don't know who had the idea that we should join forces
[with the Army of Flanders] in a place with such powerful currents, with a
shore so open and liable to cross-winds, and with so many sandbanks....*
DON FRANCISCO DE BOBADILLA, COMMANDER OF THE ARMADA'S ARMY FORCES,
TO DON JUAN DE IDIÁQUEZ, PHILIP II'S SECRETARY, 20 AUGUST 1588

King Philip II (1527–98) was the most powerful ruler in Christendom and the first who controlled territories around the globe. The Armada operation showed that there were limits even to his power.

In 1585, the successes of Philip II of Spain's Army of Flanders caused Queen Elizabeth to send English forces to help the Dutch. A Spanish victory over the Dutch rebels might endanger her regime. Indeed the aim of Philip's 1588 campaign was to overthrow England, the main threat to his power. If England were defeated, the Dutch revolt would collapse and raids against Spanish and Portuguese colonies and trade would end. Philip believed that most Englishmen and Dutchmen were still Catholics at heart and willing to accept new regimes. Success here might also lead to a rapid victory for the Catholic and pro-Spanish side in the French Civil War. Philip hoped to win these three wars with one major offensive and establish a firm Spanish hegemony over western Europe.

Preparations

During 1586 two plans to invade England evolved. The Duke of Parma, commander of Philip's army in the Netherlands, suggested that 30,000 of his men should be sent in barges across the English Channel in a surprise assault. The Marquis of Santa Cruz, commander of Philip's Atlantic fleet, planned to send 55,000 soldiers from Spain on a drastically enlarged fleet. By September 1587 Philip had merged this into one plan, to be executed with available resources: the Atlantic fleet was to sail to the Channel with part of the invasion army to protect the transportation of Parma's army to the Thames estuary.

The deployment of a large force from southern to northern Europe was a huge administrative undertaking and the departure of the fleet was repeatedly delayed. In February 1588 Santa Cruz died and Philip appointed the Duke of Medina Sidonia as his successor. The duke was an experienced administrator and his social position gave him the authority to command. When the 'Armada' (Spanish fleet) left Lisbon in late May it had 29,000 men on 24 major warships, 47 armed merchantmen, 21 transports and 35 small vessels. Contrary winds and gales made its progress slow and it spent over a month in La Coruña for repair.

The element of surprise was lost and England had plenty of time to mobilize. 34 royal warships and 192 private vessels with around 16,000 men served during 1588. However, most of the private vessels were small and many were auxiliaries. In terms of tonnage, possibly half of the English fleet were purpose-built warships, including private warships. The comparable Spanish figure was about one third of the fleet.

Combat

In mid-July the English intended to make a pre-emptive attack on the Armada in Spanish ports, but southerly winds kept them back. When the Spanish sailed into the Channel on 30 July, most of the English fleet was in Plymouth. The Armada formed its combatants and transports into a wide crescent, with additional groups of ships as tactical reserve. The intention was to fight in line abreast, and the heavy guns were probably concentrated fore and aft rather than in the broadsides. The Spanish knew that they were inferior in gunfire, while the English knew that they must avoid boarding as the Armada had a much superior infantry. Philip had no illusions that his fleet, with a high percentage of slow and unwieldy merchantmen, could bring the nimble English warships to close combat, but he was confident that it could fight off an English attack. If the Armada reached Parma's army and protected its crossing, it had achieved its purpose.

The English fleet easily gained the windward position. As westerly winds prevailed in the Channel they took a position aft of the Spanish formation, which they attacked from the rear. In the first battle, off Plymouth on 31 July, the English fleet was divided in two parts, commanded by Lord Howard of Effingham and Sir Francis Drake. The ships attacked individually or in small groups, firing their bow guns, broadsides and stern guns in succession, after which they hauled off to windward for reloading and to give place to the ship next astern. The rate of fire was slow and the effect of gunfire at long distance was limited.

Two Spanish ships were seriously damaged but only by accidents, and both were abandoned to the English – a sign that Medina Sidonia had no intention of fighting a decisive battle. He reformed the fleet into a vanguard and a larger rearguard, both sailing in line abreast and he formed groups of fast warships, which could be sent to any part of the formation. On the morning of 2 August, off Portland Bill, the wind for some hours gave the Armada the weather gauge. Medina Sidonia tried to bring about a close-range battle but the English avoided it. Long-distance gunfire continued until late afternoon but with little effect on both sides.

Next day the English fleet was divided into four squadrons, apparently for better control. On 4 August, the Armada passed the Isle of Wight and a new battle developed. The duke may have let a few ships trail as bait to lure the English into close combat. He may even have tried to use the Solent as a sheltered harbour. If these were his intentions, they both failed. Again, damage was limited, but both sides now lacked ammunition and refrained from further combat.

Queen Elizabeth (1533–1603) ruled a medium-sized power and she normally followed a cautious foreign policy. Long-term investments in a navy made her able to keep control of the English Channel even when attacked by a formidable enemy.

Sailing fleets were dependent on winds and the performance of their worst sailors. The Armada was delayed by unfavourable winds, and westerly winds made it difficult to return through the Channel. In the Atlantic it suffered from heavy gales and the slower ships ran out of food.

The Armada anchored off Calais in the evening of 7 August. The English main fleet was strengthened with the squadron which had been guarding the narrow straits. The first phase of the Spanish operation had been successful, but now geography and the complexities of a combined operation conspired to cause disaster. Since 1574, the Dutch rebels had controlled the deep-water ports on their coasts. They now blockaded the ports in Flanders, preventing Parma's vessels there from reaching open water. Furthermore, the sea outside these ports was shallow and did not allow the deep-drafted Armada ships to sail close enough to break the blockade.

With no deep-water base for the Armada, Parma's invasion would have had to be launched immediately, before the Armada's provisions ran out. But without control of the shallow waters, Parma's fleet could not even set sail – a problem which ought to have been solved at planning stage. Parma and Medina Sidonia had believed for too long that the other had the solution, while Philip had underestimated the Dutch willingness to fight.

During the night of 7 August, the English sent eight fire-ships to drift into the Armada. The Spanish ships cut their anchor cables and escaped, but the formation lost its cohesion. During 8 August, in the battle off Gravelines, the English fleet attacked aggressively at close range

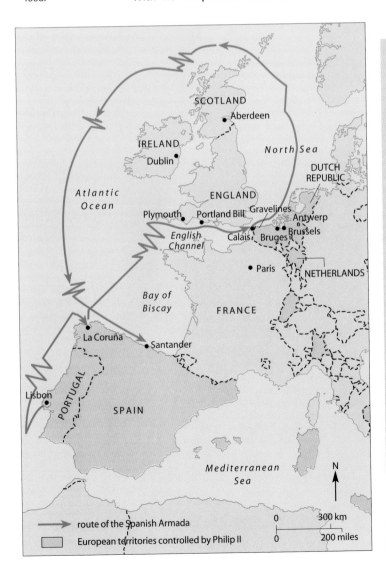

route of the Spanish Armada

European territories controlled by Philip II

0   300 km
0   200 miles

N

COMBATANTS

English & Dutch

- *English* naval forces during 1588: 23 major and 11 minor royal warships and 192 private vessels, of which around 30 may be counted as major combatants; total approximate displacement (calculated): 20,000 tonnes of royal warships and 30,000 tonnes of private ships; around 16,000 men, of whom 1,500 were soldiers; *Dutch*: over 100 coastal warships

- *English* commanded by the Admiral of England, Charles Lord Howard of Effingham; *Dutch* commanded by Justin of Nassau

- *English*: small losses in combat, but several thousand died from disease and insufficient provisions; *Dutch* losses unknown

Spanish

- Forces in late May 1588: 20 warships (galleons), 47 armed merchantmen, four galleasses (warships with auxiliary oars), four galleys, 21 transports and 31 small vessels; total approximate displacement (calculated): 50,000 tonnes; 8,000 seamen, 2,000 oarsmen and 19,000 soldiers

- Commanded by Don Alonso Pérez de Guzmán el Bueno, Duke of Medina Sidonia

- *c.* 9,000 soldiers and possibly 5,000 seamen and oarsmen killed, taken prisoner, lost in shipwrecks, missing; at least 35 ships lost, two captured by the English, two by the Dutch

and the effect of their gunnery markedly increased. Medina Sidonia could gradually re-form his fleet, but four ships were lost and several damaged. Early on 9 August it looked as if the Armada would be stranded on the sandbanks off Flanders, but it was saved by a shift in the wind. Unbeknown to the Spanish, if Parma's army had been able to pass the sandbanks, the battle-worn but unbroken Armada might have been able to protect its crossing. The English fleet had spent its ammunition and could not resume fighting for weeks. Without a port, the Armada had no alter-native but to return to Spain.

With the prevailing winds and a seemingly superior British fleet at sea it was judged best to sail around the British Isles. The fleet was gradu-ally scattered by gales and a total of 28 ships sank at sea or were wrecked on the Scottish and Irish coasts when seeking shelter to repair and get water. The first ships arrived in Spain on 21 Sep-tember, but stragglers continued to arrive for about a month. Probably around half of the men

who sailed did not return, mainly due to ship-wrecks and disease. The victors did not fare much better in fact, as epidemic disease and logistical breakdowns caused the deaths of thousands of seamen, despite minimal losses in action.

Outcome

The Armada campaign did nothing to change the political and strategic situation. Philip's attempt to win all his wars with one offensive strike failed, and the English still retained control of the Channel and the freedom to make raids on Spanish trade. The rise of England to maritime and naval pre-eminence came later and only after a long period of Dutch maritime supremacy. Philip diverted Parma's army to the civil war in France. The Dutch gained much territory and time to develop their army and navy, while the French gradually rallied round their new king, Henry IV, against Spanish intervention. Spain did, however, remain the most powerful European state until the mid-17th century.

In this painting, the artist has brought together the two main events of 8 August. In the background the English fireships are making their night attack off Calais, while the English and Spanish ships in the foreground are fighting off Gravelines, a battle that lasted from the morning to the evening.

Seventeenth Century

As before, key battles were waged between and within military systems. A leading example of the former was Shanhaiguan (1644), the battle that led both to the capture of Beijing by the Manchu, and the first conquest of the country by non-Chinese forces since the Mongol invasion in the 13th century: Beijing had been sacked by the Mongols in 1215. The Ottoman defeat outside Vienna in 1683, in contrast, marked a crucial end to the attempt to exert force on Christian Europe, and was followed by the Austrian conquest of much of Hungary.

Within systems, there were battles that played a major role in leading to the unification of states and ending civil conflict, such as Sekigahara in Japan (1600), and Naseby in England (1645). The 17th century also saw important battles between states, with Breitenfeld in 1631 and Nördlingen in 1634. Breitenfeld established Gustavus Adolphus of Sweden as the leading general of the Thirty Years War. The defeat of the Imperial army led many German Protestant princes to rally to Gustavus, whereas – had he been defeated – the Catholic Habsburg Holy Roman Emperor Ferdinand II would have established a degree of practical control in the empire that would have been unassailable. The fluidity of war was indicated three years later, when the Swedes were defeated outside Nördlingen, although, as at Breitenfeld, size played a key role. In each case the outnumbered army was defeated.

The net effect of these battles was to ensure that no single power dominated Christian Europe. The competitive military emulation that this 'multipolarity' caused resulted in an increase

The Relief of Vienna, 1683. Christian Europe celebrated the safety of its most prominent bulwark with considerable relief. The Ottoman commander was punished with strangulation.

Engraving by Matthaeus Merian the Younger showing the battle of Nördlingen. Battles in the Thirty Years War were usually won by experienced and motivated troops whose dispositions had been well arranged. Numerical superiority could also be crucial.

in the aggregate effectiveness of Christian European powers, and also kept their forces combat-worthy. Victories reflected the combination of numbers, command skills and fighting quality. For example, at Naseby, the well-disciplined cavalry on the Parliamentary right under Oliver Cromwell defeated the Royalist cavalry opposite and then turned on the veteran, but heavily outnumbered, Royalist infantry in the centre, who succumbed to an overwhelming attack.

Nothing in the European world compared to the scale and drama of the overthrow that accompanied Ming China. Shanhaiguan was a victory for Manchu cavalry over the static military system and warfare of China, but the lack of unity on the Chinese side was also important. This weakened resistance and, in some cases, directly abetted the Manchu advance. From 1582 China had suffered weak emperors, increasingly arbitrary central government, oppressive taxation and growing financial problems.

Having conquered China, the Manchu drove on to overcome rebellion and, in the 1690s, to conquer Mongolia and defeat the Dzhungars of

Xinkiang. The Manchu system had delivered a decisive verdict, despite the difficulty of the terrain, the distance from Chinese sources of supply and the long months of campaigning. The combination of effective forces and successful logistical and organizational systems made the Manchu army the best in the world.

The Mughals, the leading land power after China, encountered serious setbacks both within India and in neighbouring regions, especially in frontier zones where the terrain was not suited to their forces, such as Afghanistan. In comparison, the European military impact on India was of minor importance, and the same was also the case elsewhere in South and East Asia and in Africa. Where native peoples were fewer, however, notably in eastern North America and Siberia, Europeans made important inroads: the English and French infiltrated North America, while the Russians advanced across Siberia to the Pacific Ocean. The Europeans also competed within their expanding world, the Anglo-Dutch wars of the 1650s, 1660s and 1670s being waged in west Africa, North America and northern South America, as well as in European waters.

Sekigahara

Date: 21 October 1600   Location: Gifu Prefecture, Japan

*The arts of peace and the arts of war are like to wheels of a cart which,
lacking one, will have difficulty in standing.*

KURODA NAGAMASA (A SAMURAI WHO FOUGHT FOR IEYASU AT SEKIGAHARA), *NOTES ON REGULATIONS*, 1568–1623

U p until the end of the 16th century, the Japanese archipelago had witnessed about 250 years of rivalry and domestic conflict, of which over a century consisted of more or less intensive warfare. A warrior elite held power. Successful warriors were endowed with landed property comprising rights to rule over smaller or larger groups of dependent farmers. The granting of rights to rule over land and people in exchange for military service resulted in a social hierarchy that reminded early European visitors to Japan of the Middle Ages, and induced them to apply the terminology of feudalism in their descriptions of this warrior aristocracy.

Indeed, the hierarchy of Japanese military land-holders displayed some striking similarities with the social order of medieval Occidental knights, but differed in at least one crucial respect. Whereas in the medieval Occident, knights occupied the top echelon of rulership manifest in the offices of the emperor and the several kings, the Japanese warrior elite established and maintained its position as a social sub-system within the comprehensive political framework headed by the emperor, or Tennô. The Tennô continued to be regarded as the supreme legitimizer of secular power and was thus not himself part of the warrior elite. Consequently, the rivalries and military campaigns that the warriors fought among themselves were never contests about the 'unity' of Japan, even in the 13th century when there were two rival branches of the imperial dynasty backed by opposing warrior factions.

Tosei gusoku armour from the Momayama period (late 16th to early 17th century) and made of iron, leather, lacquer, silk, wood and silver leaf. This suit was owned by Kuroda Nagamasa (1588–1623), daimyo – or feudal lord – of a domain in Chikuzen province, and was worn by him at the battle of Sekigahara.

The rival powers

Nevertheless, there was an incremental process through which, in the course of the 16th century, a few warriors elevated themselves to more powerful positions and higher social status than their rivals and, in consequence of their superior power and authority, positioned themselves as overlords over large parts of the archipelago.

At the end of the 16th century, the most powerful of these warrior aristocrats were Oda Nobunaga, Takeda Shingen, Uesugi Kenshin, Toyotomi Hideyoshi and Tokugawa Ieyasu. From 1573, Oda was in actual control of most of the archipelago, only to be murdered in 1583 by a group of retainers wary of excessive power in the hands of one man. However, Toyotomi Hideyoshi succeeded in taking over Oda's position and became the virtual ruler of Japan (except the northern island of Hokkaido), established his headquarters in the old imperial capital of Kyoto and erected Osaka Castle as his military stronghold. When he died in 1598 he left behind an infant son under the regency of his five most powerful vassals, namely Tokugawa Ieyasu, Maeda Toshiie, Uesugi Kagekatsu, Mori Terumoto and Ukita Hideie. The regents soon resumed their rivalries and tried to knock each other out.

Within these campaigns, Ieyasu – whose stronghold was in the Nagoya area and whom Hideyoshi had dispatched to the Kanto plain around modern Tokyo – managed to attract the largest number of retainers and was lucky to survive his rivals. After Maeda Toshiie's premature death in 1599, Ieyasu attempted to become

Hideyoshi's sole successor and moved into Osaka Castle. But as soon as the following year, he relocated the core part of his forces to the Kanto area to fend off a possible rising of Uesugi's men. Ieyasu's departure from Osaka allowed his enemies to gather forces of about 128,000 men, mainly from western Japan (the 'Western Army'), in an effort to check Ieyasu's rising power. In October 1600 these forces, led by Ishida Mitsunari, gathered around the passage at Sekigahara through a mountainous area east of Kyoto that blocked the westward road from Nagoya. Mitsunari's forces were determined to launch a surprise attack against Ieyasu to prevent him from returning to Kyoto and Osaka. But Ieyasu obtained intelligence about his rivals' plans and appeared well prepared.

Prelude to battle

Ieyasu's 'Eastern Army' of about 75,000 men encountered their foes in good order and with

A gun manual produced by the Inatomi School. Firearms were introduced to Japan by Portuguese sailors in 1543.

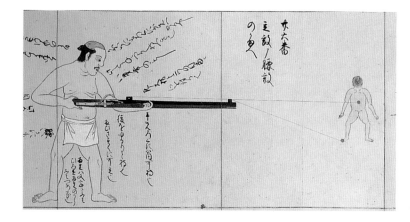

their commander's knowledge that Kobayakawa Hideaki, one of Mitsunari's men, was determined to betray his lord during the battle. Sixteenth-century Japanese armies were composed of small warrior bands with kin affiliation, local connections or dependence on a lord. Although these small bands were integrated into tactical formations under an overarching command structure, they strove to fight autonomously as much as possible. Bands were often separated from their comrades by the terrain – intervening hills, rivers or buildings that complicated the coordination of battle action. Moreover, the deployment of mounted archers allowed for rapid movement across the battlefield, not always by strict execution of given commands. Portable firearms used by infantrymen added a static element to the battle as, under the constraints of 16th-century muzzle-loading technology, firearms could only be reloaded through a lengthy process during which their bearers were essentially unarmed and

needed protection by other forces or linear defence works. Portable firearms were therefore insignificant, and tactics remained dominated by weapons like longbows, useful during rapid and autonomous battle action. As a consequence, the battle of Sekigahara evolved as a sequence of combats between small warrior bands.

The battle itself

Ieyasu's forces launched an attack in the early hours of 21 October 1600 and a mêlée began that lasted until noon with no real advantage falling to either side. Hideaki's units did not participate until Ieyasu employed rifles and, almost as if this was a signal, Hideaki gave orders to attack Mitsunari's forces. This treacherous move proved decisive and forced Mitsunari to flee from the battlefield while his remaining troops surrendered. Ieyasu lost approximately 6,000 men while about 9,000 men from the Western Army were killed in action. Ten days later, Ieyasu entered Osaka as the

A detail of The Battle of Sekigahara, *attributed to Tosa Mitsuyoshi (Edo period, no later than 1611–12). This pair of eight-fold screens was made using ink, colour and gold leaf on paper.*

dominant regent for Hideyoshi's son and actual ruler of Japan, while Mitsunari was captured and decapitated.

Aftermath

Ieyasu did not stay in Osaka but returned to the Kanto plain, where he established himself at a seaport conveniently located at the end of a Pacific Ocean bay that stretched deep into the main island of the archipelago. This place had a small fortress and was used as a fishing port under the name Edo (modern Tokyo). The Chinese characters used to write Edo can be translated as 'water gate', perhaps an appropriate name for a location where several rivers meet at the ocean. Yet it is unclear whether the name had this meaning before the Chinese characters were chosen to represent it in writing. Ieyasu chose Edo as the seat of his government once the Tennô in Kyoto had, in 1603, agreed to make Ieyasu the Shogun, the highest-ranking military ruler. As holder of this office, Ieyasu could act as the effective ruler of the country by the Tennô's authority, even if Toyotomi Hideyoshi's family continued to articulate claims that Hideyoshi's son was the rightful ruler of Japan. The conflict between Ieyasu and the Toyotomi clan continued for more than ten years until Ieyasu provoked the battle of Osaka in 1615, where he defeated the Toyotomi and their followers. Ieyasu died in the following year. He had already passed the Shogun's office to his son Hidetada in 1605, and it remained with their descendants until 1867.

Tokugawa Ieyasu had completed Hideyoshi's design for the establishment of a central military government under the Tennô's nominal suzerainty, but sought to create his own centre of government at a distance from the court in Kyoto. Ieyasu's deputies in the provinces were obliged to spend some time and more money at the centre in Edo, where they had to leave hostages behind. Through this system the Tokugawa clan retained control even in remote parts of the archipelago and maintained domestic peace for about 200 years from the mid-17th century.

Ieyasu also followed Hideyoshi's example in trying to demilitarize the warrior elite and disarm the lower-ranking warriors. While the high-ranking warriors continued to be able to carry their swords, the centrally enforced 'sword hunt' decrees promulgated by Hideyoshi were extended to include firearms, which remained in use solely for hunting purposes. The Tokugawa also exercised strict control over fortresses. The only major fortress that they allowed to be newly built was Himeji Castle, the centre of Tokugawa government for areas west of Osaka. And in a decree issued in 1615, Ieyasu requested that elite warriors should devote their skills to non-military activities while continuing to practise the martial arts with or without weapons.

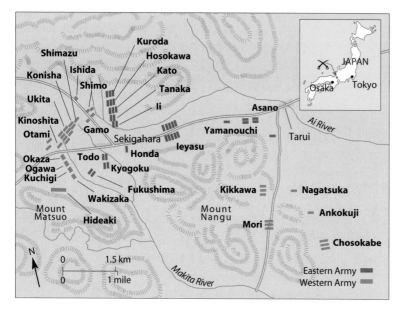

Tokugawa Ieyasu, commander of the Eastern Army, advanced westwards through the valley at Sekigahara. At around noon on the day of battle, Hideaki, Wakizaka and Kikkawa led the turncoats who betrayed Mitsunari to ensure defeat for the Western Army and victory for Ieyasu.

COMBATANTS

Eastern Army
- *c.* 75,000 men
- Commanded by Tokugawa Ieyasu, and helped by Kobayakawa Hideaki
- *c.* 6,000 dead

Western Army
- *c.* 128,000 men
- Commanded by Ishida Mitsunari
- *c.* 9,000 dead

Breitenfeld

30

Date: 17 September 1631   Location: north of Leipzig, Germany

*Breitenfeld was not what we call a 'decisive' victory, in that it did not decide the war.
But it was a major victory, a turning point.*
WILLIAM P. GUTHRIE, *BATTLES OF THE THIRTY YEARS WAR*, 2002

The Thirty Years War (1618–48) was essentially a struggle over the correct interpretation of the political and religious constitution of the Holy Roman Empire. The Austrian Habsburg dynasty ruled both the empire and a monarchy that stretched into Hungary. Infighting at the end of the 16th century encouraged parts of both the empire and the monarchy to seek greater political and religious autonomy. Faced with late 16th-century rebellions in both areas, Emperor Ferdinand II tried to reassert his authority, prompting a backlash that began in Bohemia and spread to Germany after 1618.

Background to the conflict

Ferdinand was determined to impose his interpretation of the imperial constitution that gave limited toleration for Lutherans, but not Calvinists. He had no desire to become embroiled in the prolonged struggle of his Spanish cousins against the Protestant Dutch rebels and was reluctant to accept Spanish military assistance, leaving him dependent on Lutheran Saxony and Catholic Bavaria. The latter was permitted in 1619 to reconstitute the Catholic League, an organization the Habsburgs had previously suppressed as too sectarian, but which now provided powerful assistance in crushing Ferdinand's original opponents. Danish intervention widened the war in 1625, encouraging Ferdinand to raise his own army under Albrecht Wenzel von Wallenstein (1583–1634), an enigmatic Bohemian noble.

Fearing that the emperor was becoming too powerful, the League combined with other princes to force Wallenstein's dismissal. The two

armies remained separate, but command of both was given to the League general, Jean Tzerclaes Count Tilly (1559–1632).

Tilly was an experienced and respected soldier, but also war-wounded and past his prime, while his forces were demoralized by Wallenstein's dismissal and major reductions in strength. At this point, King Gustavus Adolphus of Sweden intervened in order to sustain his own Baltic empire. He deftly evaded Tilly's superior forces while rallying the support of Protestant German princes; it was not until Elector John George of Saxony arrived that he felt strong enough to give battle just north of Leipzig.

Jean-Jacques Walter's painting of Gustav-Adolph at the Battle of Breitenfeld, c. 1632. In the background can be seen the Swedish cavalry attack.

The two armies

Controversy surrounds Tilly's decision to fight the much larger Swedish-Saxon force. Many blame the impetuous cavalry general Count Pappenheim, who considered Tilly senile. Allegedly, he led the imperial advance guard so close to the Swedish army that Tilly was forced to come and rescue him. In fact, Tilly was keen to fight, having sought battle all summer. He knew that most of the Saxons were raw levies and gambled on his veterans being able to defeat the enemy's superior numbers.

Tilly deployed north of Breitenbach village facing open fields sloping gently down to the Loderbach stream. The centre comprised 18,700 imperial and League foot soldiers grouped into four brigades of three 'tercios' or large infantry regiments with two batteries in front. The brigade on the right occupied the Galgenberg Hill, the only significant high point on the battlefield. The right wing was commanded by Count Fürstenberg who had the best cavalry regiments, totalling 3,150 troopers, supported by Count Isolano with 950 Croatian light cavalry, as well as the 1,200-strong Wangler infantry regiment.

The left, under Pappenheim, comprised 3,800 heavy cavalry, backed by the 1,500-strong Holstein infantry regiment. Five unenthusiastic cavalry regiments, totalling 2,000 dispirited troopers, were left in reserve under Colonel Erwitte. Tilly's exact intentions are unknown, but the massing of his best troops on the right suggests he intended to crush the Saxons first and then turn on the Swedes.

The Saxons deployed separately under the nominal command of their elector, but in practice led by General Arnim. Their ten battalions totalling 12,100 infantry deployed much like the imperial foot in relatively deep formations. They were flanked by two groups of six squadrons, totalling 5,200 cavalry, and had a battery of 12 guns to their front.

The Swedes were in thinner formations to maximize firepower. Their seven infantry brigades totalled 11,930 men, each subdivided into three battalions and deployed with one battalion in front and two behind in support. Four of the brigades formed the first line with another 1,010 musketeers and 500 cavalry in immediate support behind. The other three brigades were in the second line with only 700 cavalry in support.

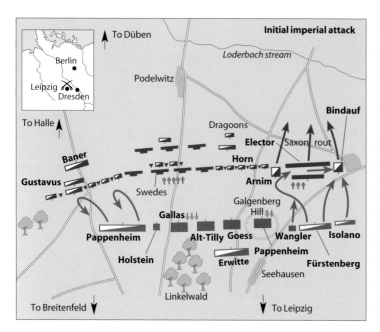

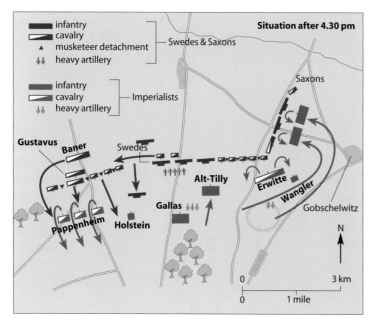

Above left *The imperial right routed the Saxons but the Swedes remained firm.*

Left *The imperial army crumbled as the Swedish counterattack started.*

Two cavalry wings stood either side of this infantry centre, each with its first line interlaced with musketeer detachments to add fire support to the cavalrymen's pistols. The entire line was supposed to fire simultaneously once the enemy cavalry came within pistol range. The Swedish horse would then charge home. Many commentators held this tactic to be superior to the caracole of the imperial cavalry, whereby a unit would ride within range of the enemy and then each rank would fire its pistols and return to the rear to reload. Though copied by other armies into the 1650s, the Swedish system was not an unqualified success, as Breitenfeld was to show.

Count Gustav Horn commanded the left with 1,250 cavalry and 940 musketeers in the first line and 1,050 more cavalry in the second. A detachment of 460 dragoons stood to the rear in support. The right was nominally under General Johann Baner, but in practice Gustavus Adolphus was in charge directly throughout much of the day. The king clearly intended to make his main attack here and massed his best men – 2,450 Swedish and Finnish horse – in the first line, backed by 860 musketeers. Another 950 cavalry made up the second line.

The battle

The Swedes and Saxons advanced from Düben early on 17 September, forcing a crossing over the Loderbach after a stiff fight with the Croat cavalry who set fire to Podelwitz village as they retreated to join Tilly. Tilly's artillery opened fire around midday as the allies came within range, but the Swedes and Saxons closed to within 600 m (1,970 ft) before returning fire; the cannonade continued for two hours with the imperialists losing twice as many men. Some claim this stung the imperial horse into action, while others suggest Tilly ordered an attack. Either way, both Fürstenberg and Pappenheim went forward shortly after 2 pm. The latter was met by a massed volley from the Swedish left wing and recoiled to join the Holstein infantry that were coming up in support. However, the Swedish 'charge' failed to break the imperial horse that launched another six attacks over the next two hours.

Fürstenberg had greater success. The Saxon cavalry put up little resistance, particularly the 1,500 levies making up most of the right-hand group who fled before contact. This exposed the flank of the infantry that were rolled up by the imperial cuirassiers who then hit the other group of Saxon horse on the left. Most of the Saxons fled, but around 1,000 cavalry under Arnim stayed to join the Swedes, while some infantry continued to resist for a while around the gun line.

Fürstenberg was unable to exploit his success. Some of his men went off in pursuit of the Saxons, while the others got lost in the great clouds of dust thrown up by every movement across the bone-dry plain. The attack had also outpaced the imperial foot that set off around 2.30 pm in an arc to the right, intending to strike Swedes in the flank. The Goess and Pappenheim brigades, along with

Cuirassier's armour, Dutch, from about 1630. Only the best-clad troopers would have worn such a fine suit as this.

A copper engraving of Breitenfeld by Matthaeus Merian from his Theatrum Europaeum *(1637). Note the fugitives scattering from the tight formations and the clouds of gunsmoke and dust.*

Erwitte's cavalry reserve, marched round to attack from the east, while the Alt-Tilly brigade approached from the south.

Horn had time to improvise a new line along the Leipzig-Düben road by bringing up the second line of infantry from the centre. The imperial units arrived at different times, making a series of uncoordinated attacks that were all beaten off with heavy loss. Meanwhile, the imperialists had become over-stretched, opening serious gaps in their centre. Both Horn and Gustavus counter-attacked shortly after 4 pm, routing both Pappenheim's cavalry and Erwitte's horse. The imperial foot struggled to leave the field, but many units were cut off and either killed or forced to surrender. Pappenheim rallied 1,400 cavalry from his wing to cover the retreat.

Aftermath

The League's army was ruined and its political organization wound up four years later. Tilly died a broken man shortly after, while Wallenstein was recalled to rebuild the imperial army. Breitenfeld established Gustavus Adolphus's military reputation; yet luck had played a considerable part in his victory. Swedish tactics proved superior, but the margin was only slight and has often been exaggerated. Gustavus went on to defeat Wallenstein at Lützen in November 1632, but at the cost of his own life, marking the high point of Swedish influence in the empire. Sweden retained territory in northern Germany until 1815.

Nördlingen

Date: 6 September 1634 Location: Bavaria, southern Germany

The greatest victory of our times.
GASPAR DE GUZMAN, COUNT-DUKE OF OLIVARES, 1634

Nördlingen stands in stark contrast to Breitenfeld (see p. 129) as a crushing imperial victory that destroyed Sweden's hope of ending the Thirty Years War on its terms. After Gustavus Adolphus's death, Chancellor Oxenstierna sought a safe way to extricate Sweden from the war whilst retaining its territorial gains on the north German coast. He reorganized Sweden's Protestant German allies into the Heilbronn League with an army under Duke Bernhard of Weimar (1604–39) to assist the Swedes under Count Gustav Horn (1592–1657). Saxony refused to cooperate, weakening the League, while Oxenstierna switched most of the Swedish veterans to hold the Baltic shore. The personal animosity between Weimar and Horn reflected the growing rift between Sweden and her allies. In contrast, Spain diverted her Dutch war reinforcements to southern Germany for that year's campaign to help the main imperial-League army under the emperor's son, Ferdinand, king of Hungary, assisted by the general Count Matteo Gallas.

Swedish plans

Heartened by news of the Spanish approach, the imperialists besieged Nördlingen in Swabia. If the town was not saved, the Heilbronn League would probably collapse. Weimar wanted to attack the besiegers, but the more cautious Horn preferred to wait for expected reinforcements. Accusing his colleague of cowardice, Weimar persuaded the other senior officers to endorse his plan.

Weimar and Horn were northwest of Nördlingen, while the imperialists were encamped southeast of the town on the other side of the River Eger. As it was too dangerous to force a crossing directly, the allies set off at sunrise on 5 September westwards along the Böpfingen road to cross further upstream. They then moved south to pick up some of their reinforcements at Neresheim around 11.30 am. Leaving their baggage guarded by 2,700 militia from Württemberg, they marched eastwards back towards Nördlingen. By seizing the Arnsberg hill behind the imperial army, they hoped King Ferdinand would be forced to abandon the siege.

Unfortunately, they had little knowledge of the terrain. They arrived on the Arnsberg plateau in mid-afternoon, but found that there was still the Rezen valley and a further line of hills between them and the imperial flank. These hills ran northwest to southeast in two groups (Himmelreich, Ländle and Lachberg divided from the Heselberg and Allbuch), then met a second line of hills running northwards to Nördlingen and the imperial camp (Schönfeld, Adlerberg, Staffelberg and the Galgenberg). The two hill lines intersected with the Eger to make a triangle enclosing a relatively open plain called the Herkheimerfeld.

Action on 5 September

The 12,000 imperialists were encamped east of Nördlingen, together with the 6,000 Bavarians under Duke Charles IV of Lorraine. They had been joined the day before by 15,000 Spaniards under Prince Fernando, the younger brother of King Philip IV of Spain. Like his cousin King Ferdinand, he had been given an experienced advisor: the Marquis of Leganes.

Weimar had raced ahead and left his artillery to clog the only road over the Arnsberg, impeding Horn's advance. Around 3 pm Weimar's men

The Victory of Nördlingen *by Cornelius Schut, 1635. This typical early Baroque painting shows the youthful Ferdinand triumphing with divine assistance.*

This contemporary painting by Pieter Meulener conveys a good impression of the often confused fighting of most 17th-century battles.

encountered Spanish dragoons and Croat light cavalry posted from the Himmelreich to the Allbuch. Having cleared the ground as far as the Lachberg, they were halted by the arrival of another 500 Spanish musketeers. Horn finally arrived around 10 pm, fought another two hours to clear the Heselberg, and decided to leave the Allbuch till the following morning

During the night, Horn deployed in four lines between the Heselberg and the Rezen, with two infantry brigades and three squadrons in the first line. Seven squadrons stood behind these, with three infantry brigades in the third line and another eight squadrons in the fourth. Horn intended to seize the Allbuch at dawn and use his cavalry to exploit his success. Weimar deployed on the hill line from the Ländle to the Heselberg to cover him. He put his three infantry brigades on the Heselberg and a battery of 20 heavy guns on the Lachberg. His 21 squadrons were divided into three groups, one behind the infantry and two behind the guns. Colonel Taupadel and 1,000 dragoons covered the left flank. The imperialists guessed their opponents' intentions and posted a strong force to hold the Allbuch, whilst placing the rest on the ridge running north to Nördlingen in case Weimar made a dash to relieve the town.

Main battle

Things went wrong for the Swedes from the start. Horn's cavalry attacked ahead of his infantry by mistake, becoming embroiled in a skirmish in the Rezen valley, leaving the foot to storm the hill alone. The first assault captured one of the entrenchments, but was disorientated by an exploding powder wagon and driven back by the crack Idiaquez regiment.

Horn sent in three more attacks, but by 7.30 am it was clear he was not going to take the hill alone. Weimar had been cannonading the main imperial position since 5 am, whilst Taupadel's dragoons skirmished with the Croats on the plain. He decided to attack, hoping to relieve the pressure on Horn by distracting the imperialists' attention. He launched 2,000 cavalry onto the plain, while General Thurn attacked the Allbuch with two of his infantry brigades.

This fatally split Weimar's army. Thurn was harassed by the Spanish cavalry, and cavalry sent by Horn to help were in turn hit by Lorraine's Bavarians and routed. Less than half of Thurn's infantry escaped back to the Heselberg and, by this time, Weimar was losing the fight on the plain. By 10 am he had no cavalry left, whereas Gallas had a reserve. Horn abandoned his fruitless

COMBATANTS

Swedes and the Heilbronn League

- 13,300 infantry, 10,150 cavalry, 68 guns

- Swedes: commanded by Count Gustav Horn;
  Heilbronn League: commanded by Duke
  Bernhard von Weimar

- 8,000 killed, 4,000 captured along with all guns
  and baggage

Imperialists

- 20,000 infantry, 13,000 cavalry, 64 guns

- Imperialist army: commanded by Count Matteo
  Gallas (under overall command of King
  Ferdinand of Hungary); Spanish: commanded by
  Diego Felipe de Avila de Guzman, Marquis of
  Leganes (under overall command of Prince
  Fernando, Cardinal-Archbishop of Toledo)

- 1,500 killed, 2,000 wounded

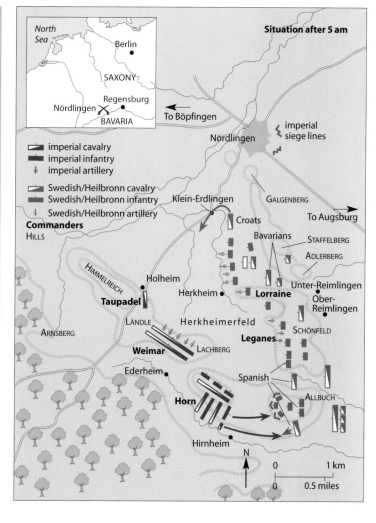

assaults and headed back up the Rezen valley intending to ford at Ederheim, covered by Weimar's remaining men on the Heselberg and Lachberg. However, Gallas's fresh troops tipped the balance, routing the Swedish horse and joining the Bavarians and Spanish in sweeping Weimar's remaining infantry off the hills. Only Horn's leading brigade managed to cross before the Bavarians seized Ederheim. His rearguard managed to escape downstream, but the centre was cut off and captured. The Croats had meanwhile turned Weimar's left and reached Neresheim, where they massacred the Württembergers guarding the baggage.

Consequences

Along with White Mountain (1620), Nördlingen was the greatest imperial victory of the war. The emperor imposed the Peace of Prague (1635) as his solution to the conflict, but French intervention and Swedish resistance ultimately frustrated this and forced his successor to accept a less favourable settlement at Westphalia in 1648.

Above right *The first Swedish attacks got underway in the early morning.*

Right *The imperial-Spanish army delivered its death blow.*

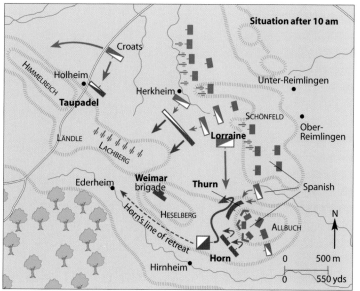

Shanhaiguan

Date: 27 May 1644   Location: Hebei province, northeast China

*My court wanted to reinforce the eastern frontier's defences and buttress
the capital and ordered me to relinquish Ningyuan and defend Shanhaiguan.
Bandits suddenly rebelled against Heaven and toppled the emperor. Unfortunately
for the late emperor, the people of the capital were not loyal, and a group of
traitors opened the gates and welcomed the bandits.*
WU SANGUI'S LETTER TO THE QING (MANCHU) EMPEROR, 20 MAY 1644

In the middle of the 17th century, the Ming dynasty was suffering internal rebellions as well as incursions by the increasingly powerful Manchu people to its northeast. Although Ming China was a vast, wealthy empire, its corrupt and ossified government was no longer able to maintain an effective army or react to crises. When rebels seized the capital Beijing, the central government collapsed and the emperor committed suicide. Caught between the rebels and the Manchus, Wu Sangui – the general commanding the Ming army defending Beijing from the northeast – allied himself with the latter and crushed the rebels at Shanhaiguan. This avenged the Ming emperor, but opened the door for the Manchu conquest of China.

Context

Frequent famines in the 1630s–1640s fomented widespread peasant rebellions, exacerbated by the government's weak response. By 1641 a rebel army led by Li Zicheng had grown large enough that he was able to capture Luoyang, an important walled city, and then Kaifeng the following year. Many of the Ming army's best generals could not, however, be reassigned from the northern steppe frontier, where they faced the growing Manchu threat. The inept Chongzhen emperor and his hopelessly factionalized court failed to

A Chinese sword (dao), possibly dating from 1572 to 1620.

decide on anything, so when Li Zicheng seized Beijing on 25 April 1644 and the abandoned emperor hung himself, generals like Wu Sangui were left militarily and politically stranded on the border. Rather than join the Manchus, Wu initially resolved to accept Li's offer of terms.

On his way to surrender to Li, however, Wu heard that the rebels had butchered his entire family. He returned to Shanhaiguan, defeating two rebel attacks on his position on 5 May and 10 May. Wu tried to open negotiations with Li over the disposition of the Ming heir apparent, but Li had already left Beijing and was heading for Shanhaiguan with his 60,000 veterans.

Wu Sangui's position was critical. He was about to face a force equal or superior to his own, with no hope of Ming aid, and without a route of retreat or escape. He had no choice but to turn to the Manchus, whom his uncle and several cousins already served. The Manchus themselves had just completed a major policy review, concluding that it was time to shift from episodic raiding of Ming territory into long-term conquest. Accordingly, they resolved to use the excuse of crushing the rebels who had overthrown the Ming emperor to launch a major invasion. The Manchu army began its march south on 14 March, almost a week before Wu Sangui's envoys arrived. Wu's request for aid, and the news that the Chongzhen emperor was dead, reinforced the Manchus' claim to a righteous purpose and shifted their route of march through Shanhaiguan.

Nurhaci, the first Manchu leader, leads the Manchus in storming a Chinese city. Illustration from the 'Manju i yargiyan kooli' (Manchu Veritable Records), by Men Yingzhao, Beijing, 1781.

Battle

Leaving a strong force to garrison Shanhaiguan, Wu Sangui deployed his main army near the Sha River, a few kilometres west of the city. Li Zicheng's troops faced him in a broad and deep line. When the battle opened early on 27 May, the Manchu army had just arrived before Shanhaiguan. Wu Sangui formally surrendered to Dorgon, the Manchu regent, while his forces made repeated charges into the rebel lines. Wu's forces sustained heavy casualties without breaking the rebel lines, and would have been badly defeated had the Manchu cavalry not then ridden around the rebel's left flank in a blinding sandstorm. As the rebels realized who their new attackers were, their army collapsed.

Aftermath

Li Zicheng fled back through Beijing, pausing long enough only to have himself enthroned as emperor and to set fire to the city and its imperial palaces. The Manchu army followed soon after, occupying Beijing without resistance on 5 June. Wu Sangui was sent in pursuit of Li, while the rest of the Manchu army used the excuse of putting down rebellion and stabilizing the situation to conquer north China.

The battle of Shanhaiguan was crucial not in allowing the Manchus through the Great Wall – something they had accomplished by force repeatedly before – but in giving them the chance to smash Li Zicheng's army and spread across China's Central Plain as a rescuing force.

COMBATANTS

Manchu & Ming

- Manchu: *c.* 100,000 men; Ming: army numbered *c.* 50,000, and Ming local militia *c.* 50,000
- Manchu: commanded by Dorgon; Ming army led by Wu Sangui
- Exact casualties unknown, but Wu Sangui's main troops suffered heavy casualties

Rebels

- *c.* 60,000 men
- Commanded by Li Zicheng
- Exact casualties unknown, but Li Zicheng's army is recorded as having lost many 'tens of thousands of corpses on the field'

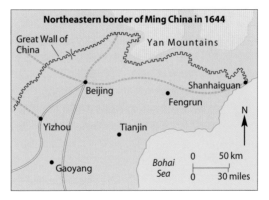

Northeastern border of Ming China in 1644

Great Wall of China

Yan Mountains

Beijing

Shanhaiguan

Fengrun

Yizhou

Tianjin

N

Gaoyang

Bohai Sea

0   50 km
0   30 miles

A map showing the Great Wall defence line and the route between Shanhaiguan and Beijing.

33 Naseby

Date: 14 June 1645   Location: near Northampton, central England

King and kingdom were lost.
EARL OF CLARENDON, CHARLES I'S ADVISER AND THE ROYALIST HISTORIAN OF THE WAR,
HISTORY OF THE REBELLION, 1702–04

Charles I on Horseback with Monsieur de St Antoine *by Anthony Van Dyck, 1633. His Royal Majesty, an image of power prior to defeat.*

N aseby ensured the defeat of the Royalist cause in the English Civil War of 1642–46, a defeat that was to help determine the direction of British history, and the character of the state and society of what became the key imperial power in the world.

War broke out as a result of widespread suspicion of the autocratic and Catholicizing policies of Charles I (reigned 1625–49). This suspicion was focused by the Long Parliament that met from late 1640. Charles's inability to retain political control of the situation led him to attempt a coup, forcibly entering Parliament on 4 January 1642 to seize his most virulent opponents, only to find that they had already fled. As both sides prepared for war, Charles left London to rally support, a foolish move as the history of civil conflict in England demonstrated the importance of seizing the capital's resources and institutions.

As determined minorities polarized the nation, fighting began at Manchester in July 1642. Charles, whose support was strongest in the north, Wales and Cornwall, advanced on London, narrowly winning the battle of Edgehill (23 October 1642), but was checked at Turnham Green to the west of London (13 November 1642). He retreated to establish his headquarters at Oxford, his best chance of winning the war lost.

In 1643 the Royalists made major gains, especially in western England, where Bristol was stormed, but their sieges of Gloucester and Hull both failed. In 1644 a Scottish army intervened on the Parliamentary side, and a joint force heavily defeated the major Royalist army in the north at Marston Moor (2 July 1644). Like many battles, although not Naseby, Marston Moor arose from an attempt to relieve a siege, in this case besieged York, by Parliamentary and Scottish forces.

This clash prefigured the battle at Naseby the following year. After the 27,000-strong Parliamentarian/Scots army launched a surprise attack on the 18,000-strong Royalists at about 7 pm, the Royalist cavalry was successful on the allied right, but on the allied left their cavalry, under Oliver Cromwell and Alexander Leslie, drove the opposing Royalist cavalry from the field. The infantry struggle in the centre ended when Cromwell's cavalry joined the assault on the Royalist infantry.

The allies lost about 1,500 men, the Royalists 3,000 and their cannon, but, more seriously, their cohesion was broken and the Royalist cause in the north fatally defeated. York surrendered on 16 July and this was followed by the overrunning of most of northern England. Nevertheless, further south, Charles's forces continued to hold most of Wales, western England and the southern Midlands. Charles felt able to reject advice that he negotiate with Parliament, advice that he again rejected in January 1645.

The 1645 campaign

In response to the continued resilience of the Royalists and the defeat of the Earl of Essex, the leading Parliamentary commander, at Lostwithiel (2 September 1644), and the incompetence of their commanders at the inconclusive Second Battle of Newbury (27 October 1644), the Parliamentary forces were reorganized as the New Model Army, led by Sir Thomas Fairfax, with Oliver Cromwell as commander of the cavalry. An opportunity to destroy the main Royalist field army was provided by the developing contest for control of the Midlands in the late spring of 1645. Prince Rupert of the Rhine, Charles I's nephew, stormed Leicester on 30 May with 10,000 Royalists. This threatened Parliamentary control of nearby Northampton and the two armies clashed outside the village of Naseby, 17 km (11 miles) northwest of Northampton, on 14 June.

Left *Military success took Oliver Cromwell from the Huntingdonshire gentry to become Lord Protector in 1653, the most dramatic example of upward social mobility in British history. His portrait here was painted by Robert Walker, c. 1650–53.*

Below *Like other battles of the period, Naseby was one that flowed more on the cavalry flanks than in the infantry centre.*

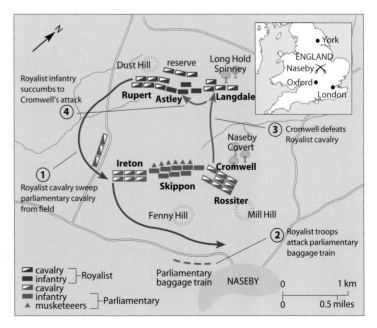

The battle

The Royalists, deployed like the Parliamentarians with infantry in the centre and cavalry on the wings, were heavily outnumbered, but the battle, which began at about 10 am, was decided by the superior discipline of the Parliamentary cavalry. The cavalry on the Royalist right, under Rupert, swept the cavalry of Henry Ireton's Parliamentary left from the field, but then dispersed to attack the Parliamentary baggage train, which offered easy looting.

In contrast, on the Parliamentary right, the cavalry under Cromwell defeated the Royalist cavalry opposite under Sir Marmaduke Langdale, but then retained sufficient control to turn on the veteran, but heavily outnumbered, Royalist infantry in the centre. These were already heavily engaged, with the inaccuracy of individual muskets countered by the proximity of the opposing lines and their close-packed nature. The Royalist infantry had advanced and driven back the front line of the New Model's infantry, but Fairfax had deployed the most experienced troops in the second line. They had held fast,

Musketeer of the English Civil War. Muskets were heavy weapons, slow to fire and of limited accuracy and reliability. As a result, fire was delivered in volleys and at close range.

advancing and stopping the Royalist infantry. It was this struggle that Cromwell swayed by attacking the flank and rear of the Royalist infantry. Attacked by both infantry and cavalry, the Royalist centre succumbed, with about 5,000 men taken prisoner. The Royalists also lost all of their artillery. Charles I had proved a poor commander, not least for failing to use his reserve effectively. He fled the battlefield.

Reasons for victory

The New Model Army's equipment and tactics were essentially similar to those of their opponents; the major difference was that they were better disciplined and supported by a more effective infrastructure and supply system. Promotion was by merit and Cromwell, in particular, favoured officers and men imbued with equal religious fervour to his own. This contributed to their disciplined response to the uncertainty of battle, and interacted positively with Cromwell's command skills. The contrast between Prince Rupert and Oliver Cromwell was one of different attitudes towards responsibility, position, quality and merit. The New Model Army prefigured the Continental Army of the American War of Independence, the republican army of the French Revolution, and the Red Army in the Russian Civil War. In each case, the army served as the expression of the political thrust of the revolution, as well as providing its force.

The Parliamentary victory took three hours and, like Marston Moor, was very much an attack

The Kings Army

The ReBells Army

victory. Also like Marston Moor, and the French victory over the Spaniards at Rocroi in 1643, Naseby indicated the continued decisive battlefield role of cavalry. Command skills were also crucial. The ability to grasp and exploit the initiative and to make good use of the terrain were both important. Cromwell's victories over the Scots at Preston (1648) and Dunbar (1650) were to be particularly good examples of the former. Command skills were also seen in the degree of success when retaining control over cavalry, the decisive factor at Naseby, and one that was far from easy.

Consequences

Naseby was a decisive victory with decisive results. It led most Royalists to appreciate that the war was over. Carlisle had successfully resisted a Scottish siege once the previous October, but it asked for terms when news of Naseby arrived. With the main field army heavily defeated, the Royalist situation was one of inexorable collapse,

although, hopeful of success in Scotland and naturally stubborn, Charles still refused to negotiate. Thanks to superior Parliamentary firepower, the principal Royalist army in the west was defeated at Langport on 10 July, while Bristol was successfully stormed on 10–11 September. The Parliamentarians were also victorious at Rowton Heath near Chester on 24 September. By the end of 1645, the Royalists had been pushed back into Wales, southwest England and isolated strongholds in the Midlands. The pace of Parliamentary attack continued in early 1646 with the capture of Chester on 3 February and the overrunning of much of Devon. On 5 May 1646, Charles gave himself up to the Scottish army in England. The remaining Royalist strongholds then surrendered or were captured: Worcester on 23 June, Oxford next day, and Harlech Castle in February 1647. The social and ideological politics of the New Model, however, made it impossible to demobilize, and it was to serve as the basis for the dictatorship that Cromwell imposed.

The nature of Naseby as a combined arms engagement emerges clearly from this picture. Pikemen and musketeers were interdependent.

34

Vienna

Date: 15 July–12 September 1683 Location: eastern Austria

I cannot believe that the Vezir proposes to go to Vienna, and that so ambitious a design can be based on such mediocre forces. It is possible that brutal resolution of this kind may be inspired by sheer pride; but the judgment of God will fall upon them.

EMPEROR LEOPOLD'S AMBASSADOR, ALBERT CAPRARA, AFTER HE LEFT THE OTTOMAN ARMY AT ESZÉK ON 12 JUNE 1683

In 1683, about a century and a half after the first unsuccessful siege of Vienna in 1529, the Ottomans were again in front of the walls of the Habsburg capital. This was a major change in recent Ottoman-Habsburg relations, which were relatively peaceful in the first half of the 17th century due largely to Habsburg commitments in the Thirty Years War (1618–48) and the protracted Ottoman-Venetian war over Crete (1645–69). The hostilities broke out in the 1660s, in a decade that saw a series of Ottoman conquests in Hungary (1660 and 1663), Crete (1669) and Poland-Lithuania (1672) under the able leadership of Grand Viziers Köprülü Mehmed Pasha (1656–61) and his son, Köprülüzade Fazil Ahmed Pasha (1661–76).

Increased Ottoman military activity and capability were linked to the reforms introduced by the Köprülü Grand Viziers, which strengthened Istanbul's authority and improved its administrative-financial capabilities. Recent revival of Ottoman military fortunes and Vienna's conciliatory policy towards the Ottomans, exemplified by the Treaty of Vasvár (10 August 1664), which acknowledged the latest Ottoman conquests in Hungary (Várad and Érsekújvár/Neuhäsel) despite a decisive Habsburg victory at Szentgotthárd (1 August 1664), were interpreted in Istanbul as signs of Habsburg weakness.

Above left *The Grand Vizier's failure at Vienna forged an anti-Ottoman coalition that eventually recaptured Hungary.*

Left *Jan III Sobieski's triumph at Kahlenberg is celebrated as one of the major victories in Polish history.*

Emperor Leopold's ineptness against the Hungarian insurgents in the 1670s and, especially, Imre Thököly's successful insurrection (1681–83) that resulted in the establishment of yet another pro-Ottoman client state, Thököly's 'Middle Hungarian Principality' in Upper Hungary (between the Habsburg-controlled Royal Hungary and the Ottoman-vassal Principality of Transylvania), all reinforced the Ottomans' perceptions of Habsburg vulnerability. Louis XIV's policy of 'reunions' – capturing territories in his northeast frontier merely because they were granted to him in past treaties – and perceived Habsburg military weakness persuaded Grand Vizier Kara Mustafa Pasha that the time had come to challenge Vienna. As it turned out, his assessment of international politics and of Ottoman and Habsburg capabilities proved to be wrong.

The road to Vienna

Rumours of a possible Ottoman attack against the Habsburgs circulated from the 1670s onwards, but Kara Mustafa managed to secure the sultan's support for his planned campaign only in August 1682. Sultan Mehmed IV (1648–87) and his army left Edirne, the old capital, on 1 April 1683. They reached Belgrade in early May, where the janissaries, cannoneers and the bulk of the provincial cavalry from Asia Minor and the Arab provinces joined the army. Sultan Mehmed decided to stay in Belgrade and appointed the Grand Vizier commander-in-chief. The decision to lay siege to the Habsburg capital, instead of Komárom (Komorn) and Győr (Raab) that had been the official targets of the campaign, was taken either in Székesfehérvár on 25 June or in the military camp nearby Győr, sometime between 1 and 7 July.

On 7 July the Grand Vizier left the camp at Győr for Vienna with the main army, leaving Ibrahim Pasha – the *beylerbeyi* or governor of Buda – with 25,000 Ottoman and 10,000 Tartar soldiers to besiege Győr. The Grand Vizier reached Vienna on 14 July with an army of about 90,000 men. Of the Ottoman vassals only the Tartars took part in the actual fighting.

The siege

Emperor Leopold and his court left Vienna on 7 July for Linz and Passau. The defenders of Vienna under Count Ernst Rüdiger von Starhemberg numbered some 16,000 men: 10,000 infantry and 6,000 cuirassiers. They were strengthened by 8,000 citizens and 700 university students fit for military service. The city's fortifications had been modernized in the 1670s and reinforced before the siege. Due to the indefatigable diplomacy of Pope Innocent XI (1676–89), effective military assistance was also on its way.

After a failed preventive siege against Érsekújvár, the Habsburg forces – commanded by the talented Duke Charles of Lorraine (1643–90) – tried to secure the left bank of the Danube while waiting for the Polish allied troops. The latter were to join the relief army according to an 'everlasting offensive and defensive alliance', signed in Kraków by the representatives of the emperor and Jan III Sobieski, king of Poland (1674–96), on 31 March, a day before the sultan had left Edirne. The Habsburg and papal diplomacy also secured the participation of some 10,000 Bavarian troops and a like number of Saxon soldiers, led by the electors of Bavaria and Saxony, Maximilian II Emanuel and Johann Georg III respectively.

By 15 July Vienna had been encircled and cut off. The very same day the siege began in earnest with heavy bombardment that lasted for the next two months. Throughout the siege, the Ottomans con-

centrated their attacks against the walls between the Burg Bastion and the Löbl Bastion. However, as in 1529, the Ottomans lacked heavy siege artillery, and moreover, their 130 field guns and 19 medium-calibre cannons were inferior in number to the defenders' 260 cannons and mortars. The defenders did lack sufficient ammunition, however, which explains why only one to two shots per weapon were fired daily during the

Ottoman cavalry forces were the backbone of the Ottoman army, with a mobilizable force of more than 100,000 men. The sipahi (Turkish cavalryman) usually wore mail shirt and helmet, and his weapons included sabre, recurved bow and a small round shield.

siege. Ottoman trench and mine attacks, of which the sultan's soldiers were experts, proved more effective than Ottoman bombardment. But the defenders stood firm, made frequent sorties, repaired the walls and stopped the besiegers by hastily erected fortifications behind the breaches. It was not until 2 September that the Ottomans could take the Burg Ravelin. On 6 September another mine exploded under the Burg Bastion and the defenders, who had by this time lost about half of their strength and were weakened by dysentery and food shortage, expected a decisive final assault. Instead, Kara Mustafa paraded his army in front of the walls to force the city to surrender. Had the Grand Vizier launched this final assault instead, he might have been able to take it before the arrival of the relief army.

The crucial battle at Kahlenberg

The decisive battle took place on 12 September near Kahlenberg, at the edge of the Vienna Woods. The relief army of 75,000–80,000 men and 160 cannons was gathering northwest of Vienna. The troops from Bavaria, Saxony, Franconia and Swabia numbered about 35,000–40,000 men and

joined the imperial forces of 20,000 men under Lorraine. Arriving last, King Jan Sobieski's Polish troops could have numbered some 20,000 men.

Underestimating the strength of the relief army, Kara Mustafa left most of his janissaries in the trenches and planned to destroy the allied

COMBATANTS

Christians

- (Austrian Habsburgs, Germans and Poles) Defenders of Vienna: 16,000 soldiers and 9,000 citizens; relief army at the battle of Kahlenberg: 75,000–80,000

- Commander-in-Chief of the defence forces of Vienna: Count Ernst Rüdiger von Starhemberg; commander-in-chief of the relief army: Jan III Sobieski, king of Poland

- 2,000 casualties

Ottomans

- 90,000 men during the siege; c. 50,000 at the battle of Kahlenberg

- Commanded by Grand Vizier Kara Mustafa Pasha

- 10,000 casualties

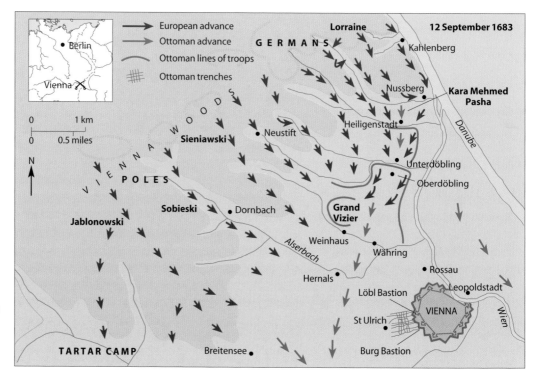

The battle at Kahlenberg, 12 September 1683. This reconstruction shows the distribution of forces and their movements.

Christian troops with a decisive cavalry charge. Although Ottoman chroniclers put the number of the Ottoman forces at Kahlenberg at 28,400 men, with Tartar and other auxiliary troops it must have reached some 50,000 men, despite carrying only 60 field guns. Due to bad intelligence, Kara Mustafa expected the Christian attack on 11 September and ordered his soldiers to stay awake throughout that night.

The battle actually started at dawn on 12 September, between the Ottoman advance forces under Kara Mehmed Pasha and the Christian left wing under Lorraine near Nussberg. Lorraine's forces, strengthened by the Saxons, soon reached the Ottoman right wing, commanded by Ibrahim Pasha. The Bavarians and Franconians also descended from the slopes further inland and joined the fight against the Ottoman right wing and the middle. Sobieski's Poles on the Christian right wing advanced slowly because of difficult terrain, but by 1 pm the Polish vanguard had reached Dornbach. Although the Ottomans fought bravely, an overall Christian attack that started after 3 pm, in the fiercest heat, decided the fate of the battle. The Ottoman left wing and the Tartars were unable to withstand the charge of the Polish cavalry and dragoons, who were the first to reach the Ottoman encampment from the west. By 6 pm the Ottomans were defeated. Those who had not been slaughtered fled the battlefield, leaving ample booty, the whole Ottoman camp, for the Christians.

Significance

Vienna was saved by a coalition of central European countries, whose army proved tactically superior and, for the first time in the history of Ottoman-European land confrontations, matched the Ottomans in terms of deployed manpower and weaponry, as well as in logistical support.

The Grand Vizier's defeat led to his downfall and execution, soon followed by the dethronement of his master, Sultan Mehmed IV. More importantly, Kara Mustafa's 1683 campaign provoked the creation of an anti-Ottoman coalition, also called the Holy League. In the ensuing Long War of 1684–99 the Ottomans lost Hungary, Sultan Süleyman's most prestigious conquest (see Mohács p. 110). Although the Ottomans were far from defeated: the early 18th century saw Ottoman military resurgence and success as well as the limits of Habsburg military capabilities. The peace treaty of Karlowitz that ended the Long War signalled a new era in the history of Ottoman-Habsburg, and more generally in Ottoman-European, relations.

This picture by Franz Geffels captures both the siege and the battle, with King Sobieski – the hero of the battle – in the foreground (right). Notice the elaborate Ottoman siege works (trenches, mines) in the background.

Eighteenth Century

In the 18th century there were two important developments. First, European forces were increasingly successful against non-Western opponents – Belgrade in 1717 was a key victory: the Austrians under Prince Eugene defeated the Ottoman army seeking to relieve the besieged city. In a difficult position, Eugene resolved on a surprise attack and won. It was a confused engagement that was not a matter of clear-cut formations exchanging fire, and was followed by the surrender of Belgrade. There was also a major victory outside Europe, at Plassey in northern India in 1757. Until this point, despite the European impact in the Americas and Siberia, there had been little success on land to report from the rest of Asia or indeed Africa. But the British victories in India were the first to change this situation.

Secondly, the major battles fought by European forces within the Western world outside Europe continued to be against other European forces, as with the battle between British and French troops outside Quebec in 1759. But from 1775, rebellion by colonists became an added factor: British rule was challenged in the Thirteen Colonies that were to become the core of the independent United States of America, and led to key American victories at Saratoga in 1777 and Yorktown in 1781. These battles showed that American success involved not only avoiding defeat but also forcing British armies to surrender, although at Yorktown they had the vital assistance of the French navy, which prevented the relief of the besieged British position. The American achievement was particularly marked given British experience in power projection and,

The battle of Poltava in 1709, saw the emergence of Russia as a great power. In this conflict Peter the Great defeated the Swedish king, Charles XII (see p. 153).

A more distant view of the battle of Poltava, painted c. 1750 by an artist of the Russian School.

specifically, in operations in North America against the French and the Native Americans. Rebellion against European rule was subsequently to spread, first against the French in the 1790s and 1800s, leading to the creation of Haiti, and then against Spanish and Portuguese rule in Latin America.

Within Europe, the key battles did not arise as a consequence of civil wars, but instead reflected the struggle for dominance between states. The 1700s saw the failure of the French effort to seize hegemony in western Europe, especially with defeat at Blenheim in 1704. Again, command skills proved crucial. The Anglo-Dutch-Austrian victory over the Franco-Bavarian army was largely due to the tactical flexibility of John Churchill, 1st Duke of Marlborough – in particular his ability to retain control and manoeuvrability. The decisive factors were mastery of the terrain, the retention and management of reserves, and timing of the heavy strike in the centre where the opposing line was broken. Victory was followed by the conquest of Bavaria. Russia's victory at Poltava (1709) led to the fall of the Swedish empire in northern Europe, while Rossbach (1757) confirmed the

new-found reputation of Prussia under Frederick the Great. Frederick's ability to grasp and retain the initiative, and the disciplined nature of his outnumbered army, were decisive. The rise of Prussian power owed everything to success in battle. Rossbach was also a very serious blow to French military prestige, and led to pressure in France for widespread military reform.

A very different force was victorious at Jemappes in 1792, the columns of Revolutionary French soldiers bringing to an end Habsburg rule of the Austrian Netherlands (modern Belgium), and adding a strong ideological factor to conflict in Europe. The *leveé en masse*, a general conscription ordered in 1793, raised large forces, such that French armies were able to operate effectively on several fronts at once, matching the opposing forces of much of Europe.

Casualty rates in the battles of this period were formidable. At Poltava the Swedes suffered terrible casualties, as their attack on well-defended Russian positions exposed them to superior forces and artillery. Only 14 of the 700-strong Uppland regiment, and 40 of the 500 in the Skaraborg battalion, survived.

Blenheim

35

Date: 13 August 1704   Location: near Donauwörth, Bavaria, modern Germany

*From a church tower you would have seen the enemy repulsed on one flank
and we on the other, the battle rippling to and fro like the waves of the sea,
with the entire line engaged in hand-to-hand combat.*
FROM THE MEMOIRS OF THE COMTE DE MÉRODE-WESTERLOO, 1702–12

Western Europe in the late 17th century had been dominated by the power of Louis XIV of France (r. 1643–1715), and it was this power that was decisively checked at the battle of Blenheim. In 1701, France and Austria had taken up arms in the War of the Spanish Succession. In 1702, concerned about the consequences of the inheritance of the Spanish dominions by Louis's grandson, Philip, Britain and the Dutch entered the war on the Austrian side.

Britain committed the bulk of her military power in the traditional nearby region of military activity, the Low Countries, but in 1704 the British had to strike further afield. In alliance with Elector Max Emanuel of Bavaria, French forces had invaded southern Germany. In 1703–4, a combination of the two with Hungarian rebels seemed about to extinguish Habsburg power, and thus to destroy the basis of Britain's alliance strategy: the use of Austrian strength to resist French expansion.

The British response was organized by one of the greatest of British generals, John Churchill (1650–1722), then 1st Earl of Marlborough. He thwarted Louis XIV's plans by a bold advance, at the head of an Anglo-German army, from the Rhineland to the Danube Valley. This was the most decisive British military move on the continent until the 20th century and, unlike the Waterloo campaign in 1815 (see p. 193), was a combination of the strategic and the tactical

John Churchill, 1st Duke of Marlborough, a master of coalition warfare and of tactical surprise. Portrait attributed to Michael Dahl, c. 1702.

offensive. The advance was a formidable logistical challenge: depots of supplies were established along the route, providing the troops with fresh boots as well as food. Such depots enabled the army to maintain cohesion and discipline, instead of having to disperse for supplies.

The campaign was a great triumph for mobility and planning, both in strategy and on the battlefield. The French had been kept unsure of Marlborough's destination by feints. Having arrived in Bavaria, Marlborough stormed the Schellenberg Heights north of Donauwörth, but Max Emanuel had been joined by the French under Marshal Camille de Tallard. Although the Franco-Bavarian army was larger, Marlborough, joined on 12 August by the Austrians under Prince Eugene, forced a battle at Blenheim on the north bank of the Danube.

The battle of Blenheim was more of a successfully planned encounter than many battles of the period, but fighting quality was necessary alongside adroit planning.

The battle

Blenheim was hard fought, with about 31,000 dead or wounded in just one day. The Franco-Bavarian army had a strong defensive position,

with Tallard covered by the Nebel stream, but it was soundly beaten. Allied victory was largely due to Marlborough's flexibility: in particular to his ability to retain control and manoeuvrability, an ability that contrasted with the failure of the opposing generals both to coordinate operations, and to respond to particular crises. The decisive factors were mastery of the terrain, the retention and management of reserves, and the timing of the heavy strike. Having pinned down much of the French infantry in defensive engagements in and around the villages of Blenheim and Oberglau, into which the French fed their reserves, Marlborough launched the substantial force he had kept unengaged at the centre of Tallard's army. He was able to achieve a local superiority in what he made a crucial part of the battlefield. The initial British cavalry attack there was checked by the French, who had assumed that they would be able to drive back any British advance in the centre, but British infantry and artillery support blocked the advance of the French cavalry, and it was then unable to resist the second British cavalry attack.

This led to the rout of the French cavalry, followed by the retreat of the Franco-Bavarian left under Max Emanuel and the surrender of 10,000 French infantry on the right in the village of Blenheim, their retreat cut off by British infantry who had exploited the victory in the centre.

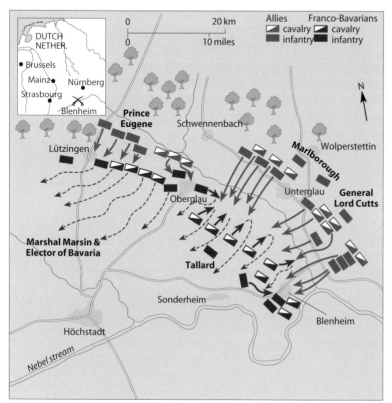

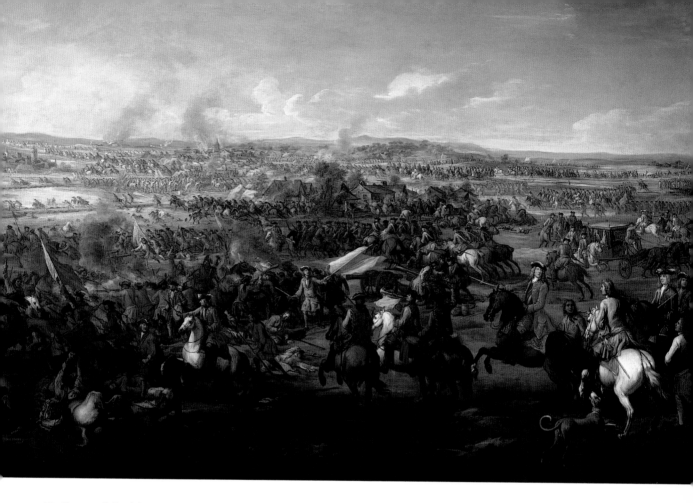

Marlborough had been more successful than his opponents in integrating cavalry and infantry, his cavalry were better trained for charging and the artillery, under Colonel Holcroft Blood, manoeuvred rapidly on the battlefield, brought forward to help support the breakthrough in the centre. Cool and composed under fire, Marlborough had proved a master of the shape and details of the battle. He kept control of his own forces and dictated the tempo of the conflict, moving and committing his troops decisively at the most appropriate moment.

The British army

Under Marlborough, the British army reached a peak of success that it was not to repeat in Europe for another century. The combat effectiveness of British units was superb, especially the fire discipline and bayonet skill of the infantry, and the cavalry's ability to mount successful charges relying on cold steel. Extensive experience of campaigning and battle in the 1690s had been an important factor in this success, and also played a

vital role in training the officers and in accustoming the troops to immediate manoeuvre and execution. This was the most battle-experienced British army since those of the civil wars of the 1640s, and the latter did not take place in battles that were as extensive – or sieges of positions that were as well fortified – as those that faced Marlborough's forces.

The cavalry composed about a quarter of the army. Like Gustavus Adolphus of Sweden in the Thirty Years War, Marlborough made his cavalry act like a shock force, charging fast, rather than as mounted infantry relying on pistol firepower. He used a massed cavalry charge at the climax of Blenheim, Ramillies (1706) and Malplaquet (1709). The infantry, drawn up in three ranks, were organized into three firings, ensuring that continuous fire was maintained. British infantry fire was more effective than French fire, so that the pressure of battlefield conflict with the British was high. The artillery was handled in a capable fashion: the cannon were both well positioned on the field, and re-sited and moved forward to

The Battle of Blenheim *by John Wootton, c. 1743, a major painter of battles. In 1743, the memory of Blenheim was a painful one, as its brilliant success was not to be repeated in the War of the Austrian Succession. George II's victory over the French at Dettingen did not have the same consequences as Blenheim.*

The Blenheim Tapestry, *1715. The memory of Blenheim was kept alive at the new palace built for the Spencer-Churchill Dukes of Marlborough in the Oxfordshire countryside.*

affect the tempo of the battle. As Marlborough was Master-General of the Ordnance as well as Captain-General of the Army, he was able to overcome institutional constraints on cooperation.

Marlborough's battles were fought on a more extended front than those of the 1690s, let alone the 1650s, and thus placed a premium on mobility, planning and the ability of commanders to respond rapidly to developments over a wide front and to integrate and influence what might otherwise have been a number of separate conflicts. Marlborough anticipated Napoleon's skilful and determined generalship in this respect, and was also successful in coordinating the deployment and use of infantry, cavalry and cannon on the battlefield.

Casualty rates, however, were very high. The exchange of fire between nearby lines of closely-packed troops, the battlefield use of artillery against such formations, and cavalry engagements relying on cold steel all produced high casualties. Some 1,500 of the 4,000 British troops who stormed the Schellenberg Heights in 1704 were killed or wounded.

Consequences

Blenheim was followed by the conquest of southern Germany as Bavaria was 'taken out' of the war. After both the battle and the subsequent retreat to the Rhine, most of the Franco-Bavarian army was no longer effective. The Allies were able to take the major fortresses of Ulm, Ingolstadt and Landau before the close of the year. French forces were not to campaign so far east again until 1741. Marlborough won other battles, but none had the dramatic impact of Blenheim, in part because that victory had ended the danger of the anti-French alliance collapsing.

Marlborough also found that victory did not end the difficulty of obtaining co-operation among the Allied forces, and this, combined with differences in military and diplomatic strategy among the political leaders, especially Dutch caution, made his task very difficult. Nevertheless, he benefited personally, becoming a duke, while Parliament provided the funds with which in Oxfordshire he built a major palace named after his great victory, an unprecedented reward for a British general.

Poltava

Date: 8 July 1709   Location: eastern Ukraine

God today in his great mercy has granted us a matchless victory over the enemy.
In short, their entire force has been defeated.
PETER THE GREAT, 1709

The battle of Poltava marked the turning point in the epic struggle of the Great Northern War (1700–21) that decided the balance of power in northern Europe and marked the emergence of Russia as a great power. The war began with a combined attack by Russia, Denmark and Saxony-Poland. The Allies hoped to partition Sweden's Baltic empire between them, but seriously underestimated the young king Charles XII. Having knocked out Denmark within a few months, Charles defeated Tsar Peter the Great at Narva in November 1700. Russia remained at war, but could do little to prevent Charles overrunning both Poland and Saxony by 1706. The Swedes rested in Saxony, creating considerable apprehension as to their next move. Aware that Russia was rebuilding its forces, Charles turned eastwards through Poland and into the Ukraine in 1707.

The main army of 38,000 crossed the Berezina and defeated a Russian force at Holowczyn in July 1708. But it was clear that Peter's forces were much improved. The Russian army was already being transformed before he became Tsar in 1696. Peter stepped up the programme of integrating western European ideas and technology with native experience and numbers. Though unsuccessful at Narva, the Russians were gaining confidence and already displaced most of the hired foreigners in the senior ranks by 1708. Military doctrine was revised after Holowczyn to give greater emphasis on firepower to counter the Swedish shock (*gå på*) tactics. However, Peter was

Victory symbolically crowns Peter the Great on the field of battle in this painting attributed to Gottfried Danhauer.

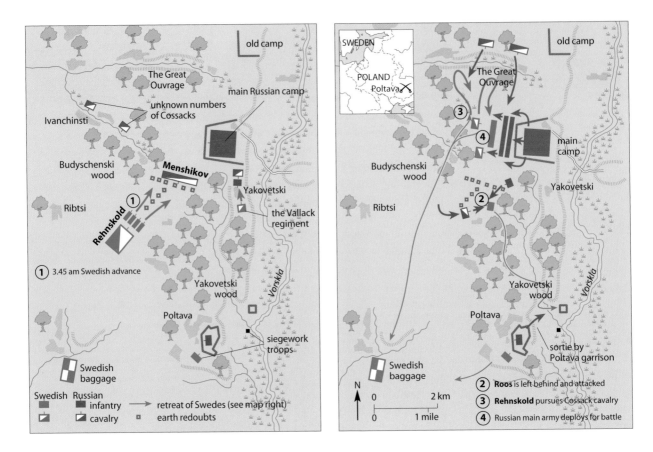

Above left *The Swedish infantry assault overran the first redoubts.*

Above right *The Russian counter-attack trapped and destroyed most of the Swedish army.*

not yet ready for a major battle and continued to retreat, destroying the countryside as he went.

The Swedes suffered grievously in the harsh winter of 1708 after their supply convoy was captured at Lesnaia in October. Intending to open the route northeast to Moscow, Charles besieged the small town of Poltava on the Vorskla, a tributary of the Dnieper. The place was poorly fortified, but the Swedes lacked proper equipment and the siege dragged on. Charles needed a decisive victory to win fresh ground and convince the Turks and Tartars to join him. Peter also sought battle and moved across the Vorskla to an entrenched camp north of Poltava. Charles was wounded in the foot during a small skirmish and had to be carried about in a litter. Nonetheless, he resolved to attack, entrusting tactical command to Field Marshal Rehnskold (1651–1722).

The Russian position

The Swedes had a formidable task. The main Russian army was entrenched in a rough rectangle backing onto the bluffs above the Vorskla. There were only three exits and the approach was strewn with obstacles. There were 51 infantry battalions totalling 25,000 men inside with 73 guns, many of which were on platforms to fire over the parapet. Any approach from the west was blocked by the Ivanchinsti stream and Budyschenski wood, both watched by Cossack cavalry. The Yakovetski wood extended from the southern side as far as Poltava and was guarded by another 1,000 infantry and a similar number of Cossacks. Poltava was held by a further 4,000 foot and 28 guns. This left only a narrow route between the two woods. A line of earth redoubts was built to block this with another line extending at right angles towards the Swedish camp so as to enfilade any attacking force. Eight battalions totalling 4,000 men held these redoubts together with 16 guns, while 9,000 cavalry in 85 squadrons drew up behind under Prince Menshikov (1673–1729). The latter had another 13 light cannon attached.

COMBATANTS

Russians

- 30,000 infantry; 9,000 cavalry; about 3,000 Cossacks; 102 guns, plus the Poltava garrison
- Commanded by Prince Alexander Danilovitch Menshikov (under the overall command of Tsar Peter the Great)
- 1,345 killed and 3,200 wounded

Swedes

- 9,500 infantry; 12,800 cavalry; 32 guns and up to 5,000 Cossacks
- Commanded by Field Marshal Count Carl Gunther Rehnskold (under the overall command of King Charles XII)
- 6,900 killed and wounded, plus 2,800 (mostly wounded) prisoners. Another 13,558 soldiers and 5,000 civilians were captured at Perevolochna

Aware that other Russian forces were in the vicinity, Charles was forced to detach 1,800 cavalry (off the map) south of Poltava. Another 1,100 infantry, 200 cavalry and 2 guns held the siege lines around the town, with 1,000 Polish light cavalry in the Yakovetski wood. Most of the artillery was left behind with the baggage that was guarded by 2,000 horse and Charles's Cossack allies. This left only 18 battalions (8,200 men), 109 squadrons (7,800 men) and a mere 4 guns for the assault. Charles intended to rush past the redoubts before dawn and attack the entrenched camp. By concentrating his entire force at one point, he hoped to break in and roll up the Russians who would be crowded together inside. This had worked at Narva, but now Charles was facing a very different Russian army.

The Swedish attack

The Swedes were delayed by the late arrival of their cavalry and did not advance until 3.45 am on 8 July, by which time it was already light. Worse still, the battalion commanders were not told whether they should move past or storm the redoubts. As a result, six battalions got left behind under Major General Roos. Menshikov counter-

attacked, but was beaten off by the Swedish cavalry that also cleared the Cossacks from the Budyschenski wood. Most of the Russian cavalry fled northwards to a gully called the Great Ouvrage, pursued by the Swedish horse, but some rallied under Menshikov south of the camp.

Rehnskold regrouped the Swedish infantry in a depression about 1 km (0.6 miles) west of the enemy camp, but was unable to make the main attack because Roos' group was still on the wrong side of the redoubts. Roos had lost over 1,000 men trying to take the redoubts. He now had no idea where the main army was and retreated into the Yakovetski wood with 1,600 survivors. Realizing his predicament, Menshikov sent a strong force of infantry and dragoons to catch him. Roos was finally forced to surrender near Poltava at 9.30 am after heroic resistance.

Peter had learnt his lesson at Narva, and now advanced smartly out of his camp to attack the main Swedish force. Leaving a small force to hold the camp, he massed 22,000 infantry in two lines, flanked by his dragoons who had now rallied. The Swedes could muster barely more than a single line of foot, while most of their cavalry were still reforming after their earlier efforts. Nonetheless, they stuck to their offensive tactics and charged the Russians. Some battalions managed to close, despite heavy musket and artillery fire, but the Swedes were overwhelmed by superior numbers and dissolved in rout.

Swedish surrender

Charles and the survivors fled south to Perevolochna where their path was blocked by the Dnieper River. The king and his escort managed to get across, but the rest were too demoralized to resist once the Russians arrived and surrendered on 13 July. Having been stripped, the Swedes were forced to watch the execution of the Cossacks who had joined them and were then marched off into captivity. Charles escaped to exile in Turkey, before returning to Sweden and dying in action in 1718. Sweden relinquished most of its Baltic empire in the 1721 peace settlement, that confirmed Russia's new status as a great power.

King Charles XII of Sweden wearing the same austere blue and yellow uniform as the rest of his army.

Belgrade

Date: 15 June–22 August 1717   Location: modern Yugoslavia

There is no doubt that the blood which is going to flow on both sides will fall like a curse upon you, your children and your children's children until the last judgment.
GRAND VIZIER SILAHDAR ALI PASHA TO EUGENE OF SAVOY, APRIL 1716

Habsburg-Ottoman relations remained relatively calm following the peace treaty of Karlowitz (1699). Both empires waged wars on other fronts. The War of the Spanish Succession and the Hungarian insurrection of Ferenc Rákóczi II tied up Vienna's resources. The Ottomans were fighting successful wars against the Russians and the Venetians. Prince Eugene of Savoy, Imperial Field Marshal and President of the Viennese Aulic War Council, watched Sultan Ahmed III's recent conquests in the Morea (Peloponnese) and Crete with great suspicion. On Eugene's suggestion, the Habsburgs formed a defensive alliance with Venice in 1716, leading to Istanbul's declaration of war against Vienna.

The war of 1716–17

The 1716 campaign resulted in major Habsburg victories. The Imperial army, 70,000 strong and commanded by Eugene, met the Ottoman army under Grand Vizier Damad Ali Pasha, the victor of the Morea campaign, at Pétervárad (Peterwardein), northwest of Belgrade on the right bank of the Danube. Without Tartar and Wallachian auxiliaries, even the paper strength of the regular Ottoman forces was hardly more than 70,000: 41,000 janissaries and 30,000 *sipahis* (Turkish cavalry). The battle of Pétervárad (5 August 1716) ended with the defeat of the Ottoman troops with some 6,000 dead, including the Grand Vizier. Despite severe Imperial losses of 4,500 dead and wounded, Eugene decided to besiege Temesvár, the centre of an Ottoman province since 1552 and a strong Ottoman fortress guarded by 12,000 men. Temesvár's

defenders resisted the siege for 43 days, but eventually gave up the fortress on 16 October. During the winter, Eugene made preparations for next year's campaign, the main objective being to recapture Belgrade, the strongest Ottoman military base that controlled the main invasion route against Habsburg Hungary.

The battle of Belgrade

On 15 June 1717, using pontoon bridges, the Imperial army under Prince Eugene crossed the Danube at Pancsova (Pančeva), east of Belgrade. By 18 June Belgrade was surrounded and the Imperialists were busy building their protective entrenchments against the fortress (counter-valation) and the approaching relief army (circumvallation). Eugene's army had a paper strength of 100,000 men, over 100 field guns and a strong siege artillery train. Defended by the Danube from the north and the Sava from the west, Belgrade was guarded by 30,000 men and 600 cannons under Sarı Mustafa Pasha. When the

Rejected by Louis XIV, Prince Eugene of Savoy entered the service of the Austrian Habsburgs, scoring many victories for them in the War of the Spanish Succession and against the Ottomans.

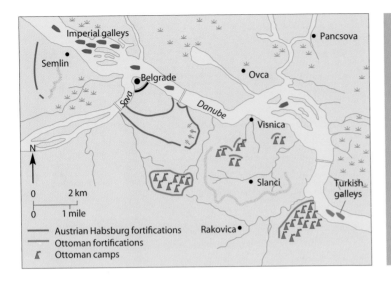

Imperial galleys

Semlin

Belgrade

Sava

Danube

Pancsova

Ovca

Visnica

Slanci

Rakovica

Turkish galleys

N

0   2 km

0   1 mile

—— Austrian Habsburg fortifications
—— Ottoman fortifications
Ⴑ Ottoman camps

COMBATANTS

Austrian Habsburgs

- 100,000 men (paper strength)
- Commanded by Prince Eugene of Savoy, Imperial Field Marshal (1663–1736)
- 5,000 casualties

Ottomans

- Ottoman defenders of Belgrade: 30,000; Ottoman relief army: over 100,000 (paper strength)
- Commanded by Grand Vizier Hacı Halil Pasha
- 10,000 casualties

Above *This reconstruction shows the deployment of forces and the countervallation and circumvallation built by Eugene.*

Below *Eugene crowned his career with the battle of Belgrade, after which he retired as the most successful general of the Austrian Habsburgs.*

Ottoman relief army under Grand Vizier Hacı Halil Pasha arrived on 27 July, Belgrade had been seriously destroyed by the Habsburg bombardment.

The paper strength of the Ottoman forces was well above 100,000 men. However, contemporaries noticed that regular troops composed only 'a small proportion of their whole body. The rest…are a mob…ignorant of all discipline, and are neither armed nor trained sufficiently well to make a stand against a regular force.' Knowing the weakness of his forces, the Grand Vizier chose not to engage Eugene's army in an open battle. Instead, he kept up a deadly artillery fire on the Imperialists from his elevated position to the east of the city, against which the circumvallation gave little protection. The Imperialists were caught between the defenders' and the Ottoman

field army's artillery fire. Eugene had to act quickly if he was to save his army, which was suffering not only from enemy fire but also from dysentery.

Hoping that the besieged would not be able to fight for some days after the large explosion on 14 August, Eugene decided to attack the Ottoman army on 16 August. While he left 10,000 men in the trenches facing the fortress, Eugene unleashed his remaining forces in the early morning when the thick fog cleared that had concealed the Imperialists' movements. Thanks to the courageous Bavarians and at the expense of over 5,000 dead, the Imperialists destroyed the Ottoman army, capturing all 150 pieces of the Ottoman artillery and the Grand Vizier's camp. The Ottomans, who lost perhaps as many as 10,000 men, retreated towards Niş. A day after the battle the defenders of Belgrade, who – blinded by windy weather conditions – had remained passive during the battle, surrendered. On 22 August, Eugene and his men moved into the city.

Significance

The Habsburg-Ottoman war of 1716–17 was the briefest of the military conflicts between the two empires. With the conquest of Belgrade and the Temesvár region, Prince Eugene of Savoy crowned his career as the most successful military leader of his time. The following peace treaty of Passarowitz (1718) restored the 'natural' Danube borderline between the two empires.

Rossbach

Date: 5 November 1757 Location: west of Leipzig, Germany

*When our great Frederick arrives
and just claps his knee
then the entire imperial army
pandours and French flee*
CONTEMPORARY SONG

Rossbach was the most complete victory won by Frederick the Great of Prussia. Frederick began his reign in 1740 with a surprise attack on Austria, grabbing the valuable province of Silesia. Austria was forced to acknowledge this loss five years later, but planned revenge. A radical shift in European alliances brought France, Russia and Sweden on Austria's side by 1757. They resolved to dismember Prussia and destroy its formidable military potential.

Preparations for conflict

Fearing attack, Frederick struck first in August 1756 by invading Saxony (now northwest Germany), hoping to seize this as a forward base in the coming war. This move played into Austrian hands, enabling it to legitimize its own war of revenge as defence of the Holy Roman Empire. In keeping with its defensive character, the empire relied on its constituent territories to second their own troops to form the Reichsarmee, or imperial army. Limited coordination was provided by the ten 'circles', or regional organizations, of the German territories. However, the more ambitious princes ruling larger territories frequently refused to subordinate their forces to the circle organization and made their own arrangements, while their smaller neighbours often had to raise their contingents from scratch.

Frederick the Great shortly after the battle of Rossbach. The action is celebrated for the Prussian tactics of disciplined movement, cavalry shock and infantry firepower.

These shortcomings were to have a major impact on the outcome of Rossbach, but the wider political circumstances were probably more significant. Most German territories were reluctant to follow Austria's lead. The members of the three northern circles were largely allied to Prussia and Britain and formed their own army to oppose the French. Austria was supposed to provide 36,200 men from the Austrian and Burgundian circles. Yet it needed its own army to invade Silesia and sent only 8,200 men, mostly hussars and 'pandours', or light infantry from the Habsburg Balkan provinces. The other five circles fielded 33,000 men, only 10,000 below their official quotas. Militarily it would have made sense to use these forces as garrison troops, but politically the imperial army had to be at the forefront of the campaign to liberate Saxony. Command was entrusted to the Prince of Sachsen-Hildburghausen, an experienced admin-

istrator, but a singularly unsuccessful general. He had to collaborate with a French army under the Prince de Soubise, a man who owed his command largely to his connections at court. It was agreed that the joint force would invade Saxony from Thuringia, while the main Austrian army captured Silesia. Frederick would have to divide his forces to meet these two threats.

However, they had not reckoned on the speed of the Prussian response. Frederick left his main army to hold Silesia while he dashed with 27 battalions and 45 squadrons to confront the Franco-Imperial army. He gambled on defeating this first and then hurrying back before the Austrian operations were fully underway. The Prussians crossed the Saale River in western Saxony to camp between the villages of Bedra and Rossbach, opposite the enemy position 4 km (2.5 miles) away. The French mustered 30,200 men in 49 battalions and 40 squadrons with 32

This rather stylized contemporary picture shows the Franco-Imperial army on the point of collapse.

heavy guns. Most of the imperial army was detached covering the flank and rear, leaving just 10,900 in the camp. These were divided into 12 battalions and 39 squadrons, 13 heavy guns, and included 3,860 Austrian cavalry and light troops.

The Franco-Imperial advance

Hildburghausen persuaded a reluctant Soubise to agree to attack Frederick on 5 November 1757. Five French brigades under the Comte de St Germain were to pin down the Prussians by advancing onto the Schortauer Heights, while the main army swung south and then east to turn the enemy flank. The Austrian light troops under Loudon would occupy the Gallows Hill and act as a link between St Germain and the main force. Soubise merely hoped that Frederick would go home, but Hildburghausen wanted to fall on him and destroy his army.

The plan was basically sound, but let down by poor coordination and the demoralized state of the allied army that had run out of food. Soubise set off at 9 am without having recalled foraging parties or the horses set out to graze, leaving the gunners to manhandle their pieces. Communication between brigade commanders was almost non-existent and the cavalry were soon 2 km (1.25 miles) ahead of the infantry, while the imperial foot were squeezed out by their French colleagues and dropped even further behind.

Shortly after 1.30 pm the allies observed the Prussian tents suddenly collapse and within minutes the Prussian army disappeared behind the long ridge of Janus Hill. Both generals were convinced Frederick was retreating and Soubise wrote jubilantly to Paris reporting victory.

Frederick appeared to be unconcerned all morning, but General Friedrich Wilhelm von Seydlitz had ordered the cavalry to saddle up and so was ready to move when his king finally decided to act. A few troops were left at the campsite to watch St Germain, while the infantry formed up behind the Janus Hill and the cavalry assembled further to the east. A battery of 18 heavy guns was placed on the summit and opened up at 3.15 pm at the Franco-Imperial cavalry who had now arrived north of Reichardtswerben.

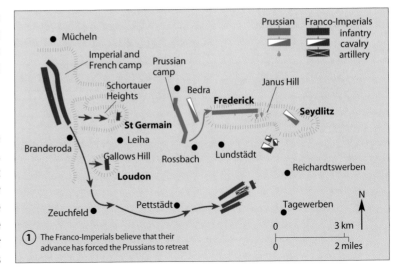

① The Franco-Imperials believe that their advance has forced the Prussians to retreat

② The Franco-Imperial cavalry retreats after a surprise Prussian attack from behind Janus Hill

③ Prussian infantry and cavalry combine forces to surround and overwhelm the Franco-Imperials

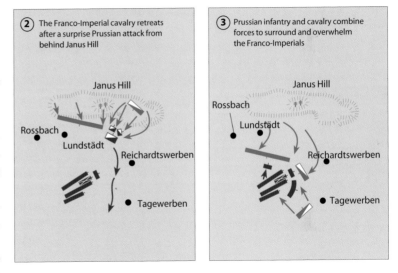

Thinking that Frederick was merely covering his retreat, the allies continued their advance, bringing their infantry to within 750 m (820 yds) of their now-stationary cavalry and moving eight guns forward to reply. Seydlitz's cavalry suddenly swept over the hill and bore down on the Franco-Imperial horse that had yet to deploy from column of march. Only two regiments were out in front, but these managed to delay the Prussians long enough for some others to form into line. The Prussian first line recoiled, but the second swept forward and broke the leading Austrian and French regiments. Most of the imperial cavalry, unused to manoeuvring, was swept away, but one south German contingent fought

Top *Allied forces try to turn the Prussian flank.*

Above left *The initial Prussian attack.*

Above right *The final Prussian attack prompts the rival army to flee.*

161

The Széchényi Hussar regiment of the Austrian contingent with the imperial army, from a contemporary illustration.

on until attacked in the confusion by the Austrian hussars. Soon, the entire allied cavalry was in retreat to Reichardtswerben where they panicked and fled. Seydlitz halted southwest of here to regroup. The mêlée had lasted just half an hour.

The leading allied infantry brigades halted once the cavalry engagement started, but their commanders neglected to tell those leading the rearward units, who continued to press forward, increasing the confusion. The Prussian infantry now raced over the hill and swung into a single line to maximize firepower. The French regiments at the head of the allied columns had deployed in columns for a bayonet attack, but wilted under the hail of shot that was increased by the fire of the Prussian battalion guns. They gave way, disordering the units behind them just as Seydlitz launched a second cavalry attack. The French infantry collapsed, and fled through the imperial regiments behind them. Most of the latter now ran off, though the Hessen-Darmstadt regiment stayed to help cover the retreat along with St Germain and Loudon's men.

In a mere two hours, the Prussians had killed or captured a quarter of the enemy for scarcely any loss themselves. The French suffered further during their hasty retreat over the next two weeks, while the imperial army virtually disintegrated.

Rossbach and German history

This ten-to-one ratio of losses is extremely rare in 18th-century battles, magnifying the scale of the Prussian triumph. Frederick's military reputation was restored after defeats earlier that year, and he went on to win another striking victory over the Austrians at Leuthen in Silesia that December. The two successes convinced Britain to continue its backing for Prussia, greatly contributing to Frederick's survival during the subsequent five years of war. Austria abandoned its plans to recover Silesia and made peace on the basis of the pre-war status quo in February 1763.

The immediate military consequences were far less dramatic. Hildburghausen resigned, but the imperial army reassembled and fought on with some success until the end of 1762. Later writers largely ignored the divisive impact of the Seven Years War on German politics, using Rossbach as a symbol of Prussia's allegedly superior political and military organization. In fact, over-confidence and inept leadership turned simple defeat into disaster. While Rossbach is celebrated for the Prussians' disciplined movement, cavalry shock attacks and infantry firepower, it was the French who pointed to the future with their mixture of linear and column formations. All these elements were to be refined by Napoleon and contribute to Prussia's own disaster at Jena in 1806.

Plassey

Date: 23 June 1757   Location: Bengal, northeast India

Gentlemen, this morning at one o' clock we arrived at Plassey grove and early in the morning the Nabob's whole army appeared in sight and cannonaded us for several hours and about noon returned to a very strong camp…upon which we advanced and stormed the Nabob's camp….Our loss is trifling, not above 20 Europeans killed and wounded.
ROBERT CLIVE TO THE SELECT COMMITTEE OF THE EAST INDIA COMPANY, 1757

Plassey was a relatively minor engagement, but one with important consequences. Britain was the dominant European military power in India in 1756, but the local states were becoming stronger as the Mughal empire declined. The French and the British East India Companies were part of a more general process of state-building in India, but also linked to international power systems in the shape of French and British interests. European influence in India saw the spread of flintlock rifles, bayonets, prepared cartridges and cast-iron cannon. Not until the 18th century in India did cavalry progress to infantry bearing firearms, while superior firearms and effective tactics greatly improved artillery.

The initial crisis in Bengal arose as a result of the British needing to defend their position. In June 1756 the newly acceded Nawab of Bengal, Siraj-ud-dowla, stormed the poorly defended British position in Calcutta, Fort William, confining his captives in the 'Black Hole'. Robert Clive, Lieutenant Governor of Fort St David, the major British position in southeast India, was instructed to retake Calcutta. In command of 850 British soldiers and 2,100 Indian sepoys (trained to fight like British regulars), Clive regained Fort William in late December, largely thanks to the guns of Rear-Admiral Charles Watson's supporting naval squadron. The Nawab's advance on Calcutta was then checked by Clive, Siraj-ud-dowla made

As with many battles, the small scale of this conflict bore no relation to the vast consequences that were to stem from it.

COMBATANTS

Anglo-Indian force

• 850 British troops; 50 naval gunners; 2,100 Indian sepoys

• Commanded by Robert Clive

• *c.* 60 casualties

Indians

• *c.* 50,000 men

• Commanded by Siraj-ud-dowla, Nawab of Bengal

• *c.* 500 casualties

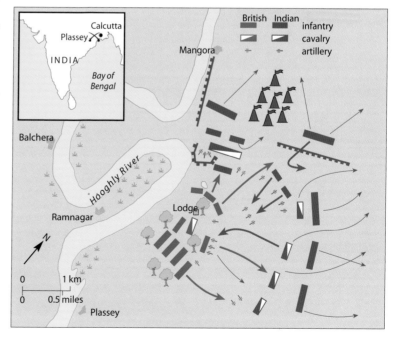

the flanks and his ten field guns and howitzers. An artillery duel began and Clive withdrew his men into the grove. The Indians made no real effort to attack, with the exception of a cavalry advance that was driven back by grapeshot, and Mir Jaffir's men were deliberately inactive. Rain then sabotaged most of the Nawab's guns, but the British gunners kept their powder dry. As the Indian artillery (manned by Frenchmen) retreated, Clive advanced to man the embankment surrounding a large pond to the front of his position. An Indian infantry attack was repelled by Clive's artillery and infantry fire and, as the Indians retreated, Clive's men advanced rapidly, storming the Indian encampment. The Nawab had already fled.

Consequences

Casualties were slight, but the political consequences were important. The subsequent defection of Mir Jaffir, whose son had the Nawab killed, was a dramatic example of how the British benefited from their ability to win local allies. Mir Jaffir was installed as the Nawab's successor, enabling Clive to establish himself as a politician with a gift of over £250,000. The British victory at Buxar in October 1764 led to the Treaty of Allahabad (1765) which recognized the British position in Bengal and Bihar: the Mughal emperor conferred the right to collect revenue and conduct civil justice, the *diwan*, on the East India Company. Bengal and Bihar were to provide a solid source of revenue and manpower, and to be the basis of British imperial power in Asia.

The number of troops at Plassey was far fewer than those who fought at the Third Battle of Panipat on 14 January 1761, when Afghan invaders of India defeated the Marathas in probably the largest land battle of the century; but, in terms of the long-term history of South Asia and consolidation of an Indian state, the British victory at Plassey was more important.

Above *Francis Hayman, one of the leading painters of the age, depicts* Robert Clive and Mir Jaffir *after the Battle of Plassey, c. 1760.*

Below *A matchlock musket or torador from Lahore, India (late 18th century). British-trained troops using more efficient flintlocks benefited from their fire quality.*

peace and, on 9 February 1757, recognized Calcutta as British.

Concerned about the French presence in Bengal, Clive next attacked their fort at Chandernagore, an advance made possible by excellent navigation in the waters of the Hooghly River. Close-range fire from Watson's warships was instrumental in its fall on 23 March. Suspicious, however, of intrigues between the Nawab and the French, Clive determined to replace the Nawab and reached an agreement with one of his generals, Mir Jaffir. Clive then marched towards the Nawab's capital at Murshidabad, taking the fort at Cutwa en route.

Battle

The Nawab stationed his army to block Clive's advance near the village of Plassey, where the two forces met on 23 June 1757. Clive deployed his men in front of a mango grove with an acute angle of the river behind him, the sepoys on

Quebec

Date: 13 September 1759   Location: eastern Canada

We stood to receive them; they began their fire at a distance, we reserved ours, and as they came nearer fired on them by divisions, this did execution and seemed to check them a little, however they still advanced pretty quick, we increased our fire without altering our position, and, when they were within less than an hundred yards, gave them a full fire, fixed our bayonets, and under cover of the smoke the whole line charged.
ANONYMOUS BRITISH PARTICIPANT, 1759

The clash that ensured that North America would draw on British rather than French culture, the battle outside Quebec, was the result of the British determination to capture the French bases in Canada. Conflict between the two powers had broken out anew in North America in 1754, but the French largely held their own until the 1758 campaign. On 9 July 1755, they and their Native American allies ambushed and routed a force of British regulars advancing on Fort Duquesne (modern Pittsburgh, Pennsylvania). In 1756, the French drove the British from the southern shores of Lake Ontario, capturing Forts Ontario, George and Oswego, and in 1757 they bombarded Fort William Henry at the head of Lake George into surrender.

In 1758, however, the balance of advantage shifted. William Pitt the Elder, the most dynamic British minister, had written of the need for 'an offensive war....The King is of opinion, that the taking of Louisbourg and Quebec can alone prove decisive'. In 1758, Pitt planned a three-pronged offensive on Canada. A British frontal attack on Fort Carillon at the southern end of Lake Champlain on 8 July was repulsed with heavy losses – nearly 2,000 killed or wounded; but the French lost their major North American naval base, Louisbourg on Cape Breton Island on 26 July. This opened the way to a British amphibious advance up the St Lawrence River. The third prong captured Fort Duquesne.

Naval power played a key role in British success. The British were able to move forces within their imperial system, and to stop the French from doing the same. The blockade of Brest (the leading French naval base) made it difficult for France to send substantial reinforcements to, or to maintain important trade links with, their colonies. French insurance premiums for ships to Quebec rose from about 5 per cent in 1755 to over 50 per cent in 1758, and were seldom obtainable in 1759, a year in which many of the merchantmen sent to Canada were captured.

In 1759, benefiting from reliable pilots and nearby harbour facilities at Halifax, both of which had been lacking during previous attempts in 1690 and 1711, the British navy convoyed a force of 8,640 men, including 6,560 British regulars and 1,190 American militia, under James Wolfe to just outside Quebec. Although young, Wolfe was experienced and had a well-deserved reputation for energy and determination. The relatively small forces involved in trans-oceanic operations, and the close similarity of their weapons and methods of fighting, put a great premium on leadership (especially the ability to understand and exploit terrain), as well as on morale, and unit cohesion and firepower.

Wolfe arrived near Quebec on 26 June, but the natural strength of the position, French fortifications, and the skilful character of the Marquis de Montcalm's dispositions thwarted him for over two months. Wolfe's initial operations along the Beauport Shore were unsuccessful: on 31 July

A skilled commander, Louis-Joseph, Marquis de Montcalm had been particularly effective in the early stages of the war.

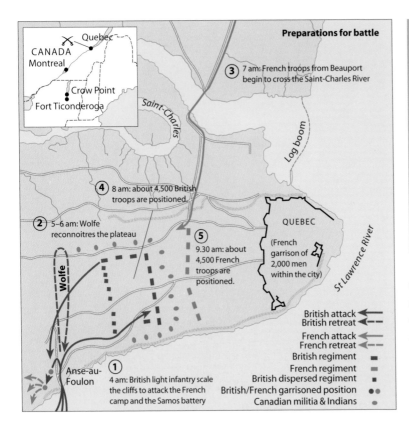

Preparations for battle

CANADA
Montreal
Quebec
Crow Point
Fort Ticonderoga

Saint-Charles

Log boom

③ 7 am: French troops from Beauport begin to cross the Saint-Charles River

④ 8 am: about 4,500 British troops are positioned

② 5–6 am: Wolfe reconnoitres the plateau

⑤ 9.30 am: about 4,500 French troops are positioned

QUEBEC
(French garrison of 2,000 men within the city)

St Lawrence River

Wolfe

Anse-au-Foulon ① 4 am: British light infantry scale the cliffs to attack the French camp and the Samos battery

British attack ◀━
British retreat ◀╌╌
French attack ◀━
French retreat ◀╌╌
British regiment ▬▬
French regiment ▬▬
British dispersed regiment ■ ■
British/French garrisoned position ●●
Canadian militia & Indians ●

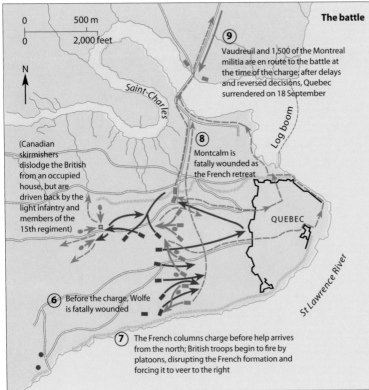

The battle

0 — 500 m
0 — 2,000 feet

N

Saint-Charles

Log boom

⑨ Vaudreuil and 1,500 of the Montreal militia are en route to the battle at the time of the charge; after delays and reversed decisions, Quebec surrendered on 18 September

(Canadian skirmishers dislodge the British from an occupied house, but are driven back by the light infantry and members of the 15th regiment)

⑧ Montcalm is fatally wounded as the French retreat

QUEBEC

St Lawrence River

⑥ Before the charge, Wolfe is fatally wounded

⑦ The French columns charge before help arrives from the north; British troops begin to fire by platoons, disrupting the French formation and forcing it to veer to the right

COMBATANTS

British
- *c.* 4,500 men
- Commanded by Major-General James Wolfe
- *c.* 658 killed or wounded

French
- *c.* 4,500 men
- Commanded by Major-General Marquis Louis-Joseph de Montcalm
- 644 killed or wounded

an attack on French positions was repelled by Montcalm's large army, with the British suffering 440 casualties to the French 60. As winter approached, it seemed increasingly likely that the British would fail, although, at least, they avoided the heavy losses to disease suffered by British expeditions in the West Indies.

Wolfe risked a bold move. James Cook, later famous as the explorer of the Pacific, had thoroughly surveyed the St Lawrence, while British warships had passed beyond Quebec from 18 July onwards and made upriver raids on 8 August. The army was to follow. On 1–3 September, British troops left the Montmorency camp and moved along the southern bank of the river opposite Quebec. On 10 September Wolfe, having reconnoitred the river, decided to land at Anse-au-Foulon to the west of the city, a move requiring a secret redeployment that was skilfully handled.

After delays due to the weather, the British landed in the early hours of 13 September. Some 200 light infantry scaled the cliffs and successfully attacked a French camp of 100 men from the rear. Another 385 men landed and overran the Samos battery. The remainder of the British force, about

Above left *Early on 13 September 1759, British regiments started to land southwest of Quebec. Preparation was crucial to the correct positioning of troops.*

Below left *The battle was speedily over, the French columns proving unable to prevail over the firepower of the British lines.*

5,140 men, then landed and advanced to the Plains of Abraham to the southwest of the city.

The battle

Montcalm was in a strong position, with a total of 13,000 men in the area and fresh troops approaching Wolfe's rear, but, instead of waiting on the defensive and uniting his forces, he chose to attack with the men immediately available. The French advanced in columns, but their centre veered to the right, and their formations became disorganized. The British waited until the French were about 30 m (100 ft) away, then opened regular volley fire. This close-range onslaught caused the French columns to disintegrate and retreat before the British began their bayonet charge. Wolfe had already been fatally wounded before the French advance, and Montcalm was mortally wounded as his troops retreated.

French and British casualties were comparable, but French morale was shattered. Quebec had not been captured, in part because the presence of 1,500 Canadian militia on the right flank of the French force persuaded the British not to pursue the French into the city. The French were still in control of the major fortified position and 2,000 more French troops arrived immediately after the battle in the British rear, leading the British to send the 48th and 35th regiments and two field pieces to meet them. At a council of war, the French officers decided not to risk battle again, but to retreat upriver. The decision to retreat was reversed on 17 September but, even as a French relief force approached Quebec, it surrendered on 18 September, far earlier than was necessary. The relief force was less than 5 km (3 miles) from Quebec when Commandant de Ramezay surrendered the city.

Consequences

The capture of Quebec was the key blow to French rule in Canada, but its impact was enhanced by successful advances on other fronts, with the British capturing Fort Niagara on 26 July and Carillon (renamed Ticonderoga) on 27 July. In early 1760, the French army still in Canada

A View of the Taking of Quebec. *This painting underestimated the difficulty and hazard of scaling the cliffs.*

Edward Penny, The Death of General James Wolfe, 1763. A totemic scene of sacrifice for the cause of empire that prefigured that of Nelson at Trafalgar. The audience at a theatre in Birmingham, England, on 17 August 1791 was promised a 'grand serious pantomime' culminating in Wolfe's death.

advanced to try to recapture Quebec: the British position there was weakened by the closure of the St Lawrence by ice, which deprived the troops of naval support and supplies. On the very same battleground, the British were defeated in the battle of Sainte-Foy (28 April 1760), which was in many respects a replay of the 1759 battle: the French had 4,200 men, the British 3,870. The French carried the day with a bayonet charge that benefited from a lack of order in the British force, and the British retreated with heavier casualties into Quebec: 1,088 dead and wounded, compared to 833 French casualties.

The melting ice, however, enabled a British fleet to arrive with reinforcements on 16 May. Yet again, naval power proved decisive. The French

fell back on Montreal. That summer, British troops advanced from Quebec, Ticonderoga and Lake Ontario, and the greatly outnumbered French – 3,520 to 17,000 men – under the Marquis de Vaudreuil (Governor-General of New France), surrendered at Montreal on 8 September. Three days later the fort at Trois-Rivières, between Quebec and Montreal, surrendered.

The 1760 campaign was an impressive triumph of resources and planning, but it is appropriate that the fall of Quebec should receive most attention. At that stage, the fate of the war was more in the balance. Moreover, Wolfe in his death provided a powerful icon of self-sacrifice and success, an image of imperial warfare that was to possess great potency.

Saratoga

41

Date: 19 September–17 October 1777   Location: New York state, eastern USA

…rash projects, visionary enterprises, and disastrous events.
BRITISH PAMPHLET DESCRIBING THE SARATOGA EXPEDITION

The defeat of an entire British army in 1777 was a key event in the winning of independence by the Americans. It was also the total failure of a bold strategy comprising cutting the rebellious Thirteen Colonies in half along the Hudson corridor. The British army in Canada advanced south, easily capturing Fort Ticonderoga on Lake Champlain on 6 July and then advancing to the Hudson through difficult wooded terrain, made harder by the Americans felling trees in order to block the creeks. All war involves risk and not to have pressed on, having taken Ticonderoga so easily, would have been to make no contribution to what appeared likely to be the decisive campaign. If the British were tired, their opponents were also in a poor state, affected by low morale and desertion, and uncertain how best to respond to the British commander John Burgoyne's advance. Major-General Philip Schuyler had written about Ticonderoga on 5 July:

'Should an accident befall us in that quarter and the troops be lost we shall be in a disagreeable situation, with little else besides militia; with not a single piece of heavy or light artillery, and not one artillery man…we have no cartridge paper.'

Instead of resisting, they fell back.

A detached part of the British force, however, was defeated near Bennington on 16 August, while, having crossed the Hudson on a bridge of rafts on 13 and 14 September, Burgoyne foolishly pressed on towards an American army that was growing in numbers and moving north from Albany. He underrated the risks, not least because he was well aware of his lack of accurate information.

The battle

On 19 September, Burgoyne approached the American commander Horatio Gates's position, which was fortified by breastworks and redoubts, on Bemis Heights, a heavily wooded area north of Stillwater on the western side of the Hudson. The advance was a disaster. Americans under Benedict Arnold and Daniel Morgan advanced to meet the British centre at Freeman's Farm, about 2 km (1 mile) north of Bemis Heights, and Morgan's riflemen inflicted serious casualties. Every time the British advanced, the Americans withdrew, sniping from 180 m (200 yds) and killing officers in particular. The British fought bravely but they did not reach Gates's entrenchments.

Burgoyne was at fault for failing to coordinate his three advancing units, and for exposing his troops in an engagement in which they lost the initiative without possessing a strong defensive position to fall back on. Fortunately for Burgoyne, Gates, an overrated general, refused to leave his entrenchments in order to support Morgan and Arnold, while the British were assisted by an advance of German auxiliaries under General Frederick Riedesel, which eventually turned the American right flank. Burgoyne was left in command of the battlefield, but he had lost about 600 men, compared to 300 Americans, while Gates still blocked the route south. The British advance had failed to fulfil its operational goals and had revealed serious weaknesses in British tactics.

Charles Willson Peale's portrait of Horatio Gates, 1782. Successful at Saratoga and an effective administrator, Gates was to be heavily defeated by the British at Camden in 1780 and was soon after replaced by Nathanael Greene.

Burgoyne decided to try again, but he then postponed his attack in order to see what impact a British advance up the Hudson from New York under General Sir Henry Clinton would have. On 28 September Burgoyne wrote to Clinton informing him that he was outnumbered and cut off from Canada and had provisions only until 20 October. Clinton had only a small force, but on 6–7 October he advanced, seizing Forts Montgomery, Clinton and Constitution. These, however, were still far from Burgoyne's position.

Since the engagement of 19 September, Burgoyne's increasingly exposed army had been affected by falling morale, decreasing supplies and desertions. At a Council of War on 5 October, his officers pressed Burgoyne to retreat while there remained a chance, but he obdurately responded by calling for a full-scale attack on

Gates, whose army had increased to 11,469 effectives, compared to 6,617 in Burgoyne's force. When it was pointed out that the thick woods made it impossible to obtain accurate information, Burgoyne proposed a reconnaissance in force that could be broadened into a full attack to turn the American flanks. Attempted on 7 October, this was repelled by the Americans, although Gates's refusal to commit all his troops limited the extent of the disaster. The British lost 600 troops, including several important officers, while there were about 130 American casualties.

The battle destroyed the morale of Burgoyne's army, and on 8 October the British began to retreat, leaving their wounded, a measure that further hit morale. The Americans, however, had already fortified the opposite bank of the Hudson to prevent a crossing. Burgoyne was persuaded to abandon the guns and baggage, and retreat by forced marches in order to cross the Hudson above Fort Edward, but, when he discovered that the route was also blocked, he countermanded the march. Encamped at Saratoga, Burgoyne's army was reduced to waiting for Clinton, while exposed to constant fire.

Benedict Arnold, the hero of Saratoga, is unhorsed as the Americans encounter a group of Riedesel's Hessians. Arnold was seriously wounded at Bemis Heights. In 1780 he entered into treasonous correspondence with the British, but was then discovered and forced to flee.

COMBATANTS

Americans
- Eventually 21,000 men
- Commander-in-Chief General Horatio Gates; General Benedict Arnold, General Daniel Morgan
- *c.* 430 casualties

British
- 7,000 men
- Commander-in-Chief General John Burgoyne; General Simon Fraser; German auxiliaries led by General Frederick Riedesel
- Entire British force taken as prisoners of war

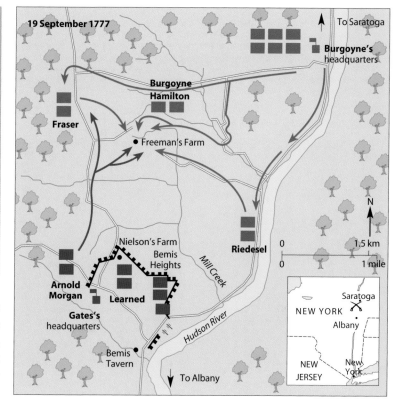

Clinton's men were pushing forward, but on 14 October Burgoyne began negotiating with Gates, and on 17 October the army surrendered. Keen to settle because he was concerned about Clinton's advance, Gates agreed to terms under which Burgoyne's troops were to return to Britain on condition that they did not serve again in America. This type of parole was natural to European combatants and Gates, an ex-major in the British army, believed that he was acting according to normal conventions. Worried that those who surrendered and were returned to Britain would simply replace other soldiers who could be sent to fight, however, Congress disavowed the convention and kept the soldiers as prisoners of war. The British troops ended up in Virginia, marching all around the back country till late in the war.

Burgoyne's approach to forest operations had been insufficiently flexible. The British general, Simon Fraser, was shot down by Morgan's marksmen on 19 September, or his German counterpart Riedesel might have succeeded in defeating the Americans. But with Burgoyne in command, the

Above right *The first attack. The British force was checked, but Riedesel led a counter-attack on the American right, enabling Burgoyne to achieve a drawn battle by nightfall.*

Below right *Burgoyne's final attack. After being checked, Burgoyne and his army left the British wounded on the battlefield and retreated to Saratoga where terms were agreed.*

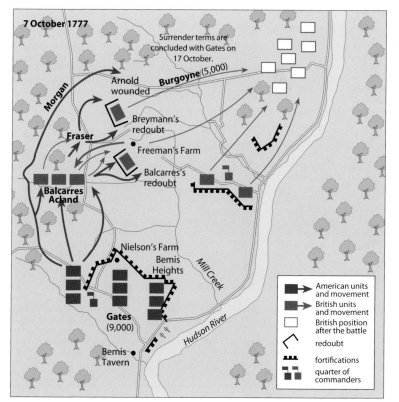

British suffered seriously from poor leadership. To be 'Burgoyned' – surrounded and captured – became a common term.

Consequences

The loss of the troops was serious, but so also were the strategic consequences. Thereafter the British did not attack south from Canada. As a result, they adopted a maritime strategy that centred on control of ports and coastal areas without the additional dimension of overland capability provided by an offensive force based in Canada. This reduced the strategic options open to the British. Saratoga marked the end of any serious prospect of cutting off New England from the rest of America. Had Burgoyne retreated, he would have been in a position to advance and threaten the upper Hudson again. The campaign also served as a warning to those thinking that the Americans had really only one important field army and, consequently, that its defeat would signal the end of the war. When Burgoyne's advance had first been considered, it had been assumed that the sole significant risk would be if Washington moved against him. Instead, Burgoyne had been defeated while Washington campaigned near Philadelphia.

The notion that the militia or Morgan's sharp-shooting riflemen won Saratoga is a hoary old tradition no longer accepted by modern scholars; but one that again reflects the emphasis on volunteerism and the strength of sturdy amateurism in the American military myth. Saratoga powerfully contributed to this myth over the following century. It was seen as a victory for a distinctly American way of fighting. It was indeed the case that, in August 1776, militia forces defeated a British detachment at Bennington, which was a major blow to the campaign. Furthermore, Gates's force of Continentals at Saratoga was only enabled to stand and fight because of the large numbers of militia who had rallied to their support. Most of the fighting on the American side, however, was done by Continentals detached from Washington's army under Arnold.

Saratoga had a major impact in America and Europe, raising the morale and prestige of the Revolution. By helping to demonstrate American resilience, the campaign led France closer to intervention.

The surrender of General Burgoyne was the reward for rashness, a failure to understand the geographical and strategic situation, and a lack of support from other British generals. Paroled, Burgoyne was appointed commander-in-chief in Ireland in 1782.

Yorktown

Date: 29 September–19 October 1781   Location: Virginia, eastern USA

There was nothing to be seen but bombs and cannonballs raining down on our entire line.
FROM THE DIARY OF JOHANN DÖHLA, WHO FOUGHT FOR CORNWALLIS AT YORKTOWN, 1781

The surrender of the British force at Yorktown led to the end of the American War of Independence, as it caused a crisis of confidence in the continuation of the war and resulted in the fall of the British government. It was a decisive battle, won with few casualties. The defeat more particularly marked the failure of both British land-sea coordination and of the strategy for 1781 which had led Cornwallis to march north across North Carolina and into Virginia. A lack of Loyalist support made hopes of conquering Virginia idle, and Cornwallis's operations there lacked a clear strategic purpose. If pacification was the British objective, wandering into Virginia, however destructive, was not going to secure it. Moreover, Cornwallis was reduced to establishing a position on Chesapeake Bay in response to orders to cover an anchorage for British warships. This represented a dangerous loss of flexibility and the initiative, because the Americans and their French allies were preparing to act.

Nevertheless, at this stage, the war had not been lost. It was apparent that neither the British southern strategy nor the advance into Virginia had brought the anticipated gains, but – as earlier around New York City – the British had shown in the south that they could gain and hold important points and defeat American forces.

A watercolour of American soldiers at Yorktown, painted by a French officer, Jean-Baptiste-Antoine de Verger, includes a black infantryman of the First Rhode Island Regiment. This is the only known contemporary rendering of a black soldier in the Continental Army.

Furthermore, the economic burden of the struggle was becoming more punishing for the Americans. Hyperinflation had wrecked the American economy, and units mutinied in early 1781. Nathanael Greene, the commander of the American forces in the south, complained on 13 August 1782, 'The supply is so trifling compared to our wants that it has served little other purpose than to mock our distress....Murmuring and discontent prevailed among the soldiers to a great degree.'

Furthermore, had the British successfully preserved their positions in America and pursued their maritime war against France and Spain, they could have hoped to divide their rivals. This was not to be, however, as the British provided their opponents with an opportunity that they appreciated and grasped. Cornwallis settled on Yorktown, a defensive position that had little to commend it, being unfortified, low-lying and commanding no ground, although it did have an anchorage suitable for ships of the line. George Washington had hoped to attack the British base of New York City, but rapidly took advantage of the possibilities created by Cornwallis's moves. American and French troops, including the crucial French siege train, were moved south into Virginia.

Top *A small and short siege by European standards, but a crucial one. This view is painted by Louis Nicolas van Blarenberghe.*

Above George Washington *by James Peale (after Charles Willson Peale c. 1787–90). Yorktown was the pinnacle of Washington's military career.*

The British naval response was inadequate, in large part because Admiral Rodney refused to send sufficient ships from the West Indies, and the French were able to build up a crucial local superiority in naval strength. As a result, on 5 September at the battle of the Virginia Capes, the British Admiral Thomas Graves found himself outnumbered 24 to 19 in ships of the line. In the battle, neither side had any ships sunk, but the clash was decisive in that it prevented Graves from relieving Cornwallis's army.

Meanwhile the net closed. French troops had landed near the entrance to the James River on 1 September, while on 14 September Washington reached the Williamsburg peninsula. Two days later, reassured by a promise of naval support, Cornwallis wrote, 'If I had no hopes of relief I would rather risk an action, than defend my half-finished works, but as you say [Admiral] Digby is hourly expected, and promise every exertion to assist me, I do not think myself justified in putting the fate of the war on so desperate an attempt.' He soon had no option. The Franco-American force took up positions round Yorktown on the night of 28 September and the next day.

The battle

Encouraged by the promise of relief, Cornwallis

abandoned his outer works on the night of 29 September in order to tighten his position and increase the density of his defence in the face of the more numerous besiegers. Washington's men occupied the outer works on 30 September, although they had to cope with heavy fire from Cornwallis's cannon until, on 6 October, their own artillery arrived. The besiegers were then able to begin conventional siege-works against what was, by the standards of the age, a vulnerable and weakly fortified position.

On the night of 6 October, the besiegers began to dig the first 'parallel', a trench parallel to the fortifications and a crucial part of normal siege-works. They completed it on 9 October and, that afternoon, began the bombardment with a larger and heavier artillery force than that of Cornwallis, causing many casualties and damage, and badly affecting the morale of the defenders.

On 11 October, Cornwallis wrote,

'…nothing but a direct move to York River, which includes a successful naval action, can save me. The enemy made their first parallel on the night of the 6th at the distance of [550 m] 600 yards, and have perfected it, and constructed places of arms and batteries with great regularity and caution. On the evening of the 9th their batteries opened and have since continued firing, without intermission with about 40 pieces of cannon, mostly heavy, and 16 mortars…many of our works are considerably damaged; with such works on disadvantageous ground, against so powerful an attack we cannot hope to make a very long resistance.'

On 12 October a postscript reads:

'Last night the enemy made their second parallel at the distance of [270 m] 300 yards. We continue to lose men very fast.'

Many of Cornwallis's cannon had been silenced by the bombardment, while a lot of his troops were wounded or ill. On the night of 14 October, the besiegers bravely stormed the two redoubts that obstructed the path of the second parallel to the river, and thus further curtailed the British perimeter. Cornwallis wrote the next day, 'Experience has shown that our fresh earthen works do not resist their powerful artillery….The safety of the place is therefore so precarious that I cannot recommend that the fleet and army should run great risk in endeavouring to save us.'

The end

On 16 October, a sortie designed to spike the besiegers' guns had only a limited and temporary effect. Cornwallis therefore decided to try to cross the York River to the British outpost at Gloucester by night and then to attack the French force

Above Charles Cornwallis, 1st Marquess Cornwallis, *by Thomas Gainsborough, 1783. Defeated at Yorktown, Cornwallis rescued his reputation with success in India (1791–92) and Ireland (1798).*

Fighting with backs to the river was never recommended, and weak fortifications did not greatly improve the situation for the British.

blockading that position. The first detachment crossed the river successfully late that day, but a violent storm prevented the boats from crossing a second time, and, by the time the weather improved, it was too late to mount an attack and Cornwallis had to recall the first wave. Under a ferocious bombardment that could not be countered, Cornwallis decided to abandon the position.

On 17 October Johann Conrad Döhla, a member of the Ansbach-Bayreuth forces in Cornwallis's army, recorded, 'At daybreak the enemy bombardment resumed, more terribly strong than ever before. They fired from all positions without let-up. Our command, which was in the Hornwork, could hardly tolerate the enemy bombs, howitzers and cannonballs any longer.' That day, the fourth anniversary of Burgoyne's surrender at Saratoga, Cornwallis proposed an armistice in order to settle terms for his surrender. After negotiations on 18 October, the British troops marched out of their ruined positions the following day to surrender to the tune of 'The World Turned Upside Down'.

Although the British still held Charleston, New York City and Savannah, Yorktown was effectively the end of British efforts in North America. It led to the fall of Lord North's cabinet in March 1782, and its replacement by a government under the Marquis of Rockingham pledged to negotiations with the Americans. On the world scale, however, Britain did less badly. The temporary and localized superiority the French fleet had enjoyed off the Chesapeake was not the consequence, nor cause, of a climatic battle in which one fleet destroyed the other and there was no decisive shift in naval advantage against Britain. Instead, on 12 April 1782, Rodney inflicted a serious defeat on the French fleet off the Iles des Saintes. Had it come earlier there might have been a very different result at Yorktown.

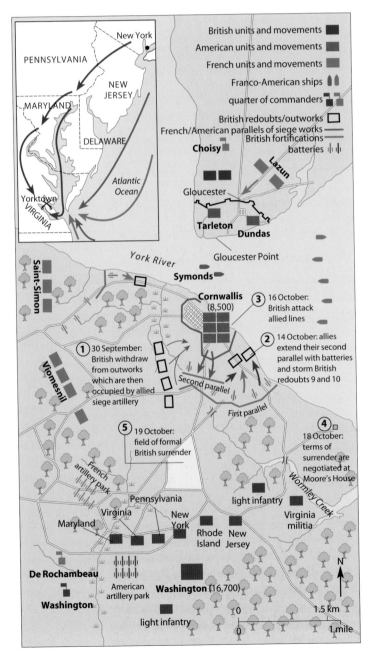

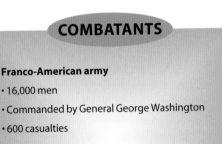

COMBATANTS

Franco-American army
- 16,000 men
- Commanded by General George Washington
- 600 casualties

British
- 6,000 men
- Commanded by General Lord Cornwallis
- Entire force taken prisoner

Jemappes

Date: 6 November 1792   Location: near Mons, southwest Belgium

There was not a unit in the French army that was not [at first] beaten,
and that did not [then] close with the enemy with cold steel.
FROM THE MEMOIRS OF GENERAL CHARLES FRANÇOIS DUMOURIEZ

Jemappes was the first major defeat of a professional army in Europe by a force imbued with the revolutionary principle of motivated 'citizens-in-arms'. This form of organization stemmed from the French Revolution of 1789 and was expected to sweep the supposedly uninterested mercenaries from the field.

However, the Revolutionary Wars (1792–1802) were far more than a simple clash of opposing ideologies and their respective military institutions. Few outside France believed that war was inevitable and thought the Bourbon king only had himself to blame for failing to implement the reforms of more enlightened monarchies elsewhere. Prussia, Russia and Austria were far more interested in the problems of eastern Europe. France remained a monarchy, but the new liberal government of the National Convention failed to resolve its underlying problems. As radical, moderate and conservative factions jostled for power, war increasingly seemed a welcome way out of the domestic impasse. The region of the Austrian Netherlands – modern Belgium and Luxembourg – had been in upheaval since 1787 and it was widely predicted in Paris that the inhabitants would welcome the French as liberators. The

A contemporary etching of the battle of Jemappes showing the French heroically storming the Austrian positions.

Convention declared war on the Habsburg emperor and directed the 34,000-strong Armée du Nord to invade Belgium on 29 April 1792.

The campaign of 1792

Though the French greatly outnumbered the Austrians on the frontier, they fled south at the first encounter. France appeared on the point of complete collapse, creating an opportunity for Austria and Prussia to settle their own differences at its expense. In return for acknowledgment of its greatly enhanced position in eastern Europe, Prussia backed Austria's bid to seize Alsace and Lorraine from France under cover of an invasion intended to restore Louis XVI's authority.

The overconfident allies made poorly coordinated attacks on northeastern France late that summer. The main Prussian army met a hastily assembled French force at Valmy, 160 km (100 miles) east of Paris on 20 September 1792. After a cannonade, the Prussians withdrew having lost only 184 men. This otherwise insignificant engagement had major political repercussions. The next day the National Convention abolished the monarchy and proclaimed a republic. Short of supplies, the allies retreated in disarray, allowing the French to invade the Rhineland and send more troops to the Belgian frontier.

Command of the northern sector was entrusted to General Charles François Dumouriez (1759–1823), a minor aristocrat with 34 years experience in the royal army. Dumouriez's reinforced Armée du Nord now numbered 90,000 men, giving him a clear advantage over the 50,000 Austrians, most of whom were dispersed on internal security and garrison duty. Sending smaller columns to distract the Austrians along the frontier, Dumouriez pushed his main force towards Mons, aiming for Brussels. His troops were a mix of the old royal army and new volunteer forces. There were 32 line battalions and 38 more battalions of volunteers, giving 35,000 infantry, plus 3,000 cavalry in 10 line regiments and four free companies. The 100 guns were served by experienced professional artillerymen.

The Austrians were commanded by Field Marshal Albert Duke of Sachsen-Teschen (1738–1802) who could muster only 13,200 men in 14 battalions, 16 squadrons and 54 heavy guns to confront the invaders. He deployed on a ridge south of the small town of Jemappes, with his front protected by a stream, entrenchments and the village of Quaregnon.

Battle is joined

After three days of skirmishing, Dumouriez finally approached early on 6 November. He deployed in three groups, each in two lines. The left under General Ferrand was directed to seize Quaregnon, while the right under Dampierre swung past Frameries to outflank the Austrians and cut them off from Mons. The centre would then make the main attack. Things did not go quite to plan.

After three hours of preliminary bombardment the Austrians were clearly outnumbered

'Departure of the volunteers.' The wine bottle may be a reference to the French practice of living off the land.

French

- Armée du Nord (38,000 men; 100 guns)
- Commanded by General Charles François Dumouriez
- 4,000 killed and wounded

Austrians

- 13,200 men; 54 guns
- Commanded by Field Marshal Albert Duke of Sachsen-Teschen
- 305 killed, 513 wounded and 423 taken prisoner

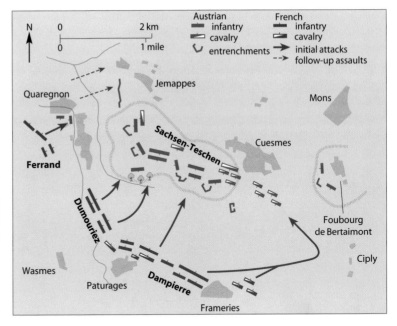

and outgunned. Dumouriez ordered Ferrand to start his assault at 10 am. The French infantry formed battalion columns and advanced rapidly towards Quaregnon, redeploying into line to fire at the defenders. Supported by their main battery, the Austrians threw them back. The first line of the French centre then advanced in battalion columns to make the main attack around noon. Twice beaten back by heavy fire, the French made some progress once Ferrand finally took Quaregnon. However, the right wing had made little headway in the face of fierce resistance and was unable to prevent the Austrians breaking off at 2 pm and escaping past Mons.

The Austrians lost 1,241 men, and though the French claimed a huge victory, their frontal assaults had proved costly and they suffered 4,000 casualties.

A revolutionary victory?

Later generations proclaimed Jemappes as 'a true revolutionary victory', typified by the verdict of Georges Lefebvre, the great historian of the French Revolution, who wrote that 'it had been won in an open attack without astute manoeuvres and by the sans-culottes who rushed the enemy to the martial strains of the *Marseillaise* and the *Carmagnole*, swamping the adversary with sheer force of numbers'. While numerical superiority clearly played a major part, it was not a clear-cut victory of a modern, revolutionary army over an outmoded opponent. Regulars from the

royal army formed over half of Dumouriez's troops, still resplendent in their white Bourbon uniforms. When the attack wavered, the men were rallied by the 19-year-old Duc de Chartres, the future King Louis Philippe who ruled France 1830–48. The Austrians retreated on Cologne, abandoning the Netherlands to the French. However, they were back within a year and retook most of the province before a more convincing defeat at Fleurus in June 1794.

The political significance of Jemappes far outweighed its military importance. Emboldened by the success, the National Convention declared its determination two weeks later 'to give fraternal support to all people who wish to regain their liberty', effectively committing France to a protracted offensive war that would eventually lead to the Napoleonic empire. Domestic politics took a radical turn, first with the execution of Louis XVI on 21 January 1793 and then the Jacobin Terror of April 1793 to July the following year. The regulars were merged with the volunteers to create a single revolutionary army, backed by universal conscription decreed in August 1793. Accompanied by accelerating anti-clericalism, such measures proved deeply divisive and Dumouriez was one of the many officers who subsequently defected to the Austrians.

This map shows the disparity between the opposing forces, with the outnumbered Austrians stretched to defend their position against three times the number of French.

Nineteenth Century

The Western conquest of much of the world, especially in Africa, Oceania and Southeast and Central Asia, was a major theme of warfare during this century, leading to a series of battles such as Omdurman (1898), in which larger non-Western forces were defeated. In the West, there were also battles arising from conflict within states, as with Antietam (1862) and Gettysburg (1863) in the American Civil War (1861–65), or between states, as with Trafalgar (1805), Leipzig (1813), Waterloo (1815), Mexico City (1847), Inkerman (1854) and Sadowa (1866). This internal struggle for control sometimes arose from separatist conflicts, and there is not much to choose between those in which the separatism failed, such as the American Civil War, and those where they were successful, such as Ayacucho in 1824, a crucial battle in the Latin American Wars of Independence against Spanish rule.

During the century, there were important technical developments in battlefield capability and operations. Land warfare was transformed by the continual incremental developments in firearms, such as the introduction of the percussion rifle and the Minié bullet, both in the 1840s, and, subsequently, of breech-loading cartridge rifles. The net effect, for both handheld firearms and artillery, was substantial changes in precision, mobility and speed of use. Commanders, however, faced the problem of how best to respond to developments. Due to defensive firepower, massed frontal attacks on prepared positions became more costly. The firepower shown by the British in Napoleon's final defeat at

Prussian efficiency, technological superiority and tactical sophistication were established at the battle of Sadowa (see p. 215) in 1866, when Moltke's forces defeated the Austrians under Benedek.

Waterloo was surpassed by the time of the American Civil War, in which both sides learned the necessity of throwing up entrenchments as a consequence of fighting each other to a costly draw at the battle of Antietam (1862). Already at Inkerman, attacking Russian columns, seeking to close to bayonet point, took heavy casualties from the Enfield rifles of the British and were defeated.

Bayonets and rifled muskets were increasingly supplemented by, or even downplayed in favour of, field fortifications and artillery: looking towards the situation in the two World Wars, infantry tactics responded. In the Sadowa campaign, the Prussian tactic of concentrating strength on the skirmishing line, and adopting more extended formations that were less dense than columns or lines, and thus less exposed to fire, commanded attention. However, Prussian skill at the operational and tactical levels and poor Austrian leadership, had not prevented many difficulties from arising, not least at the hands of Austrian artillery.

More generally, in the century after Waterloo in 1815, greater and more predictable production of munitions flowed from a more streamlined and systematized manufacturing process. The overall result was a degree of change far greater in pace and scope than that over the previous century.

This was even more the case with logistics, command and control, and naval warfare, as the railway, the telegraph and steam power affected both nearby campaigns and those waged at a distance. The combination of all three made it possible to apply and direct greater resources, and in a more sustained fashion, than hitherto. This supported imperial expansion, although, as before, it was valuable to be able to elicit support within those subject to pressure. Indeed, much of the fighting for imperialism in South Asia and West Africa was done by local troops recruited and trained by the British and French respectively. In East Asia, Japan successfully modernized its military under Western pressure, but China was less able to do so. Japan joined in the naval revolution stemming from major advances in naval armour, gunnery and propulsion.

Command of the sea through battle was emphasized by late-19th-century theorists, particularly the influential American, Alfred Thayer Mahan, and from the 1890s the leading powers all developed battleship navies. The potency of naval gunnery increased as breech-loaders replaced muzzle-loaders, as quicker-firing guns and high-explosive armour-piercing shells were introduced, and as ships were redesigned to allow for guns mounted in centreline turrets.

Charge of the 21st Lancers at Omdurman, 2 September 1898, painted the following year. British infantry and artillery were more effective than those of their enemy, devastating the Mahdists.

Trafalgar

Date: 21 October 1805   Location: off southern Spain

This battle must be considered as an exception to the actions hitherto engaged on account of the manner in which the enemy attacked; it was a concourse of individual engagements over a small area.
VILLENEUVE'S CHIEF OF STAFF, COMMANDER J-B PRIGNY, 1805

This famous naval battle was fought off the southwest corner of Spain between a British fleet of 27 ships of the line commanded by Vice Admiral Horatio, Viscount Nelson, and a combined fleet of 18 French and 15 Spanish ships of the line under the command of the French Vice Admiral Pierre, Comte de Villeneuve.

Trafalgar was a consequence of the collapse of the Emperor Napoleon's impracticable dreams of invading Britain in 1805. These failed at the first serious hurdle when Villeneuve's combined Toulon and Cadiz fleet was repulsed from its intended junction with the Brest fleet by a waiting British squadron – under Admiral Calder off Ferrol on 22 July 1805 – and put back to Vigo and then to Cadiz. Napoleon decided instead to march eastward against the more accessible target of the Austrian and Russian armies.

The combined fleet at Cadiz was now to be used in the Mediterranean to protect the emperor's exposed Italian flank against British and Russian amphibious attack. Deciding that Villeneuve's indecisiveness would prevent him forcing his way past the blockading British fleet, Napoleon sent a new commander, Admiral Rosily, to take the fleet to Italy.

News of Rosily's impending arrival, and of the withdrawal of part of the watching British fleet for resupply at Gibraltar, encouraged Villeneuve to

Below left *Vice Admiral Horatio, Viscount Nelson.*

Below right *The newly discovered (2000) sketch by Nelson of his battle plan: after considering (in top half) a manoeuvre to 'double' the enemy line, he develops (bottom half) his idea of breaking their line in two places, shown by his vigorous scratches.*

Nicholas Pocock's painting of the closing stages of the action at the battle of Trafalgar (see second map on the opposite page). In the distance the French van escapes south-southwest and to the left the French Achille catches fire and explodes.

set aside his misgivings. He took his fleet to sea on 19–20 October, hoping to rescue his reputation by implementing the emperor's orders himself. As the combined fleet left harbour, a chain of frigates and battleships reported its movements back to Nelson, whose fleet was hovering beyond the horizon. Anticipating that it would be bound for the Mediterranean, he moved his fleet south-east to intercept it.

Preparations for battle

Nelson, the foremost admiral of the age, had taken command only three weeks before, but he had a clear idea of how he would fight. This was communicated to his captains over dinners at which he raised morale amongst his newly formed blockading fleet. He and Napoleon were unique in their time in always seeking battles of annihilation. A result of this sort would be impossible to achieve by traditional line-ahead manoeuvres in the short daylight hours of late October. Nelson's victorious encounters with the Spanish at Cape St Vincent in 1797, and with the French at the Nile in 1798, had revealed their poor gunnery. He decided to risk a head-on attack by two columns.

His own (12 of the line on the day) would cut the enemy centre, capture their admiral and hold back the enemy van from interfering in the decisive action, which would be achieved by focusing superior numbers (15 of the line under Collingwood) on overwhelming the enemy rear. To restrict the damage from a head-on attack against the enemy broadsides he looked to get in

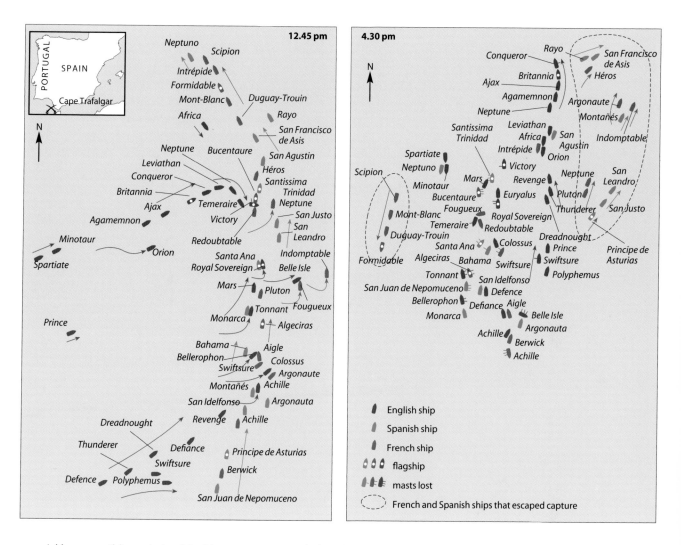

12.45 pm

4.30 pm

PORTUGAL
SPAIN
Cape Trafalgar

N

● English ship
● Spanish ship
● French ship
●●● flagship
●●● masts lost
⌒⌒ French and Spanish ships that escaped capture

as quickly as possible, ordering his ships to carry full sail and extra studding sails until they reached the enemy line, instead of the normal fighting rig of topsails only (which avoided the mainsails being set alight by gun flashes). His largest first- and second-rate battleships headed his columns since they were best able to absorb damage, had the weight to break up the enemy line, and carried most guns to take on the concentrated fire power until the ships behind arrived to help.

Villeneuve, who had been at the Nile, correctly foresaw that Nelson would not fight an orthodox line-against-line battle, but instead concentrate against part of his fleet. To counter this he formed a fast squadron of observation under the Spanish Admiral Gravina (*Principe de Asturias*) to act separately from the line of battle wherever it was

needed, and instructed all his captains to join the action as soon as possible. He also urged boarding tactics to vitiate the superior British gunnery.

In the event, however, he was let down by his subordinates. Gravina tamely attached his ships to the rear of the line (where he saw that Colling-wood was aiming), rather than using his freedom of action to manoeuvre against Collingwood's flank and disrupt his attack. Admiral Dumanoir (*Formidable*), commanding the allied van, allowed himself to be mesmerized by Nelson's initial feint towards the van before attacking the centre, and was consequently late in ordering his ships to turn back and support the centre, a movement further delayed by the very light wind which necessitated launching his ships' boats to tow them around.

Above left *12.45 pm: Collingwood's column had already engaged and Nelson broke the line in* Victory *at the head of his column.*

Above right *4.30 pm: part of the allied van escaped south-southwest after failing to rescue* Bucentaure *and* Santissima Trinidad; *the rest of the van and survivors from the rear escaped to Cadiz.*

185

Admiral Pierre Charles Jean-Baptiste Silvestre, Comte de Villeneuve, commander-in-chief of the combined French and Spanish fleet.

Action

Collingwood – in his newly refitted, first-rate *Royal Sovereign* – was first to break through the allied line at about midday. Nelson headed his column through the centre in *Victory* at 12.45 pm and the battle then continued until about 4.30 pm. The first British ships into action took the bulk of casualties as they found themselves surrounded by enemy ships. Nelson himself was killed by a French sharpshooter, as were two captains in Collingwood's division.

However, as more British ships entered the newly opened gaps in the enemy line, so their superior gun drill and mutual fire support in a mêlée action proved their worth. French attempts to use boarding tactics were blasted to pieces by the British upper-deck heavy-calibre carronades (short guns). Two admirals were killed, as well as a commodore and six captains. Nine Spanish and eight French ships were captured (including Villeneuve and his flagship *Bucentaure*) and another French ship caught fire and exploded. Eleven limped back to Cadiz with the mortally wounded Gravina, and Dumanoir escaped northward with four of the van.

A savage storm followed the battle, lasting several days, while the British struggled to keep their own damaged ships and their captures afloat. In the end Collingwood saved all his own ships and four of his captures. During the storm, on 23 October, five of the allied survivors made a daring sortie from Cadiz and managed to rescue two captured vessels, but one of these was subsequently wrecked, as were three of the rescuers. All the remaining captures foundered or were wrecked on the adjacent coast, or destroyed by the British to avoid their recapture.

Total casualties on the British side were 449 killed and 1,214 wounded, and in the Franco-Spanish combined fleet 4,408 were killed or drowned and 2,545 wounded, many of these included among 7,000 prisoners. On 3 November Dumanoir's four fugitives were intercepted in the Bay of Biscay by Sir Richard Strachan as they tried to reach Rochefort, and all were captured, bringing the total loss of the combined fleet to 24 out of the 33 battleships engaged.

COMBATANTS

British

- Total crews 21,456 men: 18,134 seamen, 3,322 marines; 3-decker 'first rates': 3 x 100 guns; 3-decker 'second rates': 4 x 98 guns; 2-decker 'third rates': 1 x 80 guns, 16 x 74 guns, 3 x 64 guns; 4 frigates, 1 schooner, 1 cutter
- Commander-in-Chief Vice Admiral Horatio, Viscount Nelson; second in command Rear Admiral Sir Cuthbert Collingwood
- 449 killed, 1,214 wounded

Franco-Spanish combined fleet (Allies)

- French: total crews c. 15,000; 2-decker 'third rates': 4 x 80 guns, 14 x 74 guns; 5 frigates, 2 corvettes. Spanish: total crews 11,817; 4-decker 'first rate': 1 x 130 guns; 3-decker 'first rates': 2 x 112 guns, 1 x 100 guns; 2-decker 'third rates': 2 x 80 guns, 8 x 74 guns, 1 x 64 guns
- Commander-in-Chief: French fleet and combined fleet: Vice Admiral Pierre, Comte de Villeneuve; Spanish fleet: Admiral Don Federico Gravina
- French: c. 3,370 killed or drowned, 1,160 wounded, 5,000 taken prisoner, 2,500 taken prisoner but escaped in the storm after the battle; Spanish: 1,038 killed or drowned and 1,385 wounded, 3,000–4,000 prisoners, some of whom escaped in the storm after the battle, and all the wounded were returned by Collingwood

Significance of the battle

The annihilation battle that Nelson had sought was largely achieved – more ships of the line were taken than in any previous battle of the sailing era. But the immediate effects of Trafalgar were small. It prevented the combined fleet from interfering in Mediterranean operations, but those operations – the Russo-British invasion of Naples – were themselves invalidated by French victories at Ulm and Austerlitz. Trafalgar did not stop Napoleon's path into Europe, but it greatly set back any attempt to resume his westward ambitions. It gave the British breathing space to rebuild their deteriorating fleet and encouragement to continue the fight despite the defeat of their allies.

Napoleon sought to hide the British victory from the French people (his coldness to Villeneuve drove the latter to suicide when he returned on parole in 1806) and he was to rebuild his fleets, but he never rebuilt the confidence among their commanders and crews to take on the British navy successfully. Spain was the greatest loser. She never replaced her fleet, and the loss of her sea power contributed to the loss of her vulnerable American empire. Yet even Spain drew consolation from the valiant and prolonged resistance of their scratch, untrained crews to the murderous British onslaught. The stigma of subservience to the French was cast off and later generations saw this as the heroic, bloody birth of a new Spain – the start of the restoration of national honour that would lead to the Peninsular War and the ultimate rejection of French rule.

Trafalgar was the last great naval battle of the age of sail, and the benchmark by which all future naval battles were to be compared. The dead victor and his victory became immortalized in central London by Nelson's column in Trafalgar Square. Nelson left the British nation with a naval triumph that was a cornerstone to the prestige of the British navy and symbol of British naval mastery for another century, up to the battle of Jutland (see p. 232).

The Fall of Nelson. Mortally wounded early in the action by a sharpshooter in the tops of the French Redoubtable, Horatio Nelson lived long enough to hear of the extent of his victory.

45

Leipzig

Date: 14–19 October 1813   Location: eastern Germany

Never had any field of battle, in modern history, been so inundated with human gore.
But thus, and only thus, could the inordinate vainglory of Napoleon be for ever eclipsed,
offering a memento appalling to nature, but truly beneficial to mankind.
General Count Gneisenau, *The Life and Campaigns of Field Marshal Prince Blücher*, 1815

Imperial Guard, Foot Grenadier. Napoleonic infantryman in summer full dress (indicated by white gaiters).

Fought over six days in October 1813, Leipzig was the largest battle of the Napoleonic Wars, both in terms of its battle-field and the numbers engaged. Napoleon's heterogeneous *Grande Armée* faced forces from the entire European coalition, giving rise to its other name: the 'Battle of the Nations'. Thanks to the presence of Francis of Austria and Tsar Alexander, along with Napoleon and the kings of Prussia, Saxony, Sweden and Naples, it is also known as the 'Battle of the Three Emperors'.

Background

Napoleon's empire had begun to unravel following his disastrous invasion of Russia from which only a tenth of his army returned at the beginning of 1813. Prussia defected at the end of December 1812, joining Russia in declaring a 'War of Liberation' on 16 March that was backed by Britain and soon by Jean-Baptiste Bernadotte, one of Napoleon's marshals, who was now Crown Prince of Sweden. Napoleon improvised a new army to meet this threat to the east but, despite a series of minor victories, he was unable to defeat the allies in eastern Germany and agreed an armistice on 4 June. Austria took the opportunity to declare its hand for the allies.

Political rivalries simmered under the surface, but the allies at least agreed to operate in three separate armies. The Army of Bohemia was the largest and was led by Prince Schwarzenberg, the nominal allied commander-in-chief. Though unimaginative, Schwarzenberg had the tact nec-

essary to preserve allied harmony and was later toasted by the Prussian Marshal Blücher as 'the commander-in-chief who had three monarchs at his headquarters and still managed to beat the enemy'. Blücher commanded the Army of Silesia, composed of Prussians and Russians, while a similarly mixed force, backed by a Swedish corps and a tiny British contingent, made up the Army of the North under Bernadotte.

Napoleon hoped to defeat his three enemies in detail, but they deftly avoided contact. When he finally caught Schwarzenberg at Dresden he was unable to achieve the decisive victory he sought and he had to retreat into northwestern Saxony. After the defection of Bavaria on 8 October, it became imperative to save Saxony, his chief remaining central European ally. Two corps were left in Dresden while the main army concentrated at Leipzig, Saxony's second city.

14 October

Victory remained within Napoleon's grasp if he could defeat Schwarzenberg before the others arrived, and his chances were improved by the nature of the terrain. Leipzig lay at the confluence of the Elster and Pleisse rivers. The ground between the rivers south of the city was marshy and wooded, as was much of the area generally to the west.

Since Tsar Alexander refused to deploy any Russians west of the Pleisse, Schwarzenberg only posted 32,000 Austrians in these sectors, keeping the rest of his army east of the river. Blücher and the Army of Silesia were advancing across the sector northwest of the city, with Bernadotte trailing some way behind. Napoleon deployed the bulk of his troops on the main battlefield southeast of the city with his outer line of 41,000 men under King Joachim Murat of Naples.

Schwarzenberg's advance guard clashed with Murat's post at the village of Liebertwolkwitz early on 14 October. Murat launched a series of counter-attacks with his cavalry throughout the morning, his claims of success persuading Napoleon to stand and fight, rather than escape to the west while the road was still open. In fact, both sides had lost around 2,000 men, but the allied casualties were quickly made good by the arrival of the rest of Schwarzenberg's army.

Napoleon completed his deployment on 15 October, increasing his forces southeast of Leipzig to around 120,000 men, giving him a decided advantage over Schwarzenberg's 100,000. However, the latter could expect the Russian and Prussian reserves to join him, whilst Blücher was fast approaching the city from the northwest. Napoleon had only 40,000 men north of Leipzig, with another small force at Lindenau protecting the vital escape route to the west.

16 October

The main battle on 16 October fell into two distinct parts as Schwarzenberg assaulted Napoleon's forces southeast of the city, while Blücher attacked around the village of Möckern to the north. Schwarzenberg's first wave went in at 8 am against the French-held line of villages from Markleeberg through Wachau to Kolmberg. The French replied with a furious artillery barrage that intensified once the fog lifted at 10 am and expended over 80,000 shots. Schwarzenberg realized he was too weak to carry the entire position and fell back to his start line around 11 am. The Austrians west of the Pleisse also retired after some initial successes, having failed to hold onto Lindenau or force a crossing at Connewitz.

Above right *The French successfully defended their position as the allies slowly converged on Leipzig.*

Right *Superior numbers told as the allies crushed the surrounded French.*

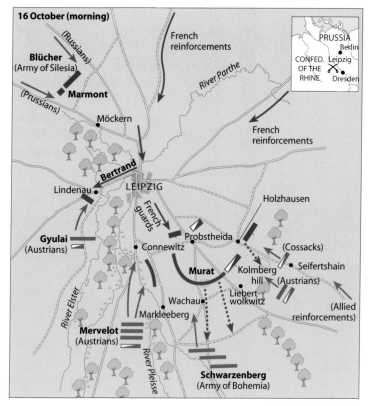

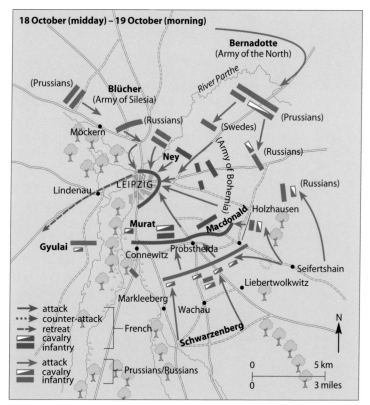

French School, The Battle of Leipzig, This 19th-century picture gives a good impression of the scale of the battle.

Sensing weakness, Napoleon counter-attacked, hoping to turn the allied right around Seifertshain. Initially, local successes encouraged him to feed in ever more troops until the attack became general by 2 pm. Murat led a massed charge of 10,000 cavalry to punch through the thinning allied ranks, but was repulsed by the allied reserves. Reinforced, Schwarzenberg held out against three further infantry assaults. Napoleon refused to commit his reserves for a final blow, and instead left this sector around 2.30 pm to concentrate north of Leipzig.

Marshals Marmont and Ney had only two corps to hold the Möckern position against Blücher's entire Army of Silesia. They ignored Napoleon's orders to join him south of the city, but the Aus-trian attack on Lindenau compelled them to detach troops later in the morning. Fortunately, Blücher's army was strung out along its approach road and only 20,000 Prussians were in place to attack at 3 pm. The French retook Möckern three times before finally being driven out with 10,000 casualties. The Prussians lost 8,000 and were unable to advance further because of nightfall.

Overall, Napoleon had held his ground, but he had been unable to capitalize on his local superi-ority south of the city. He had lost 25,000 irreplaceable troops to the allies' 30,000. It rained throughout 17 October and both sides spent the day repositioning their forces for the final battle. Schwarzenberg's army now numbered around 170,000, while Bernadotte at last arrived with his

60,000 to reinforce Blücher's remaining 40,000. The allies were convinced Napoleon would try and escape northeast and so directed Bernadotte to march in a wide arc across the Parthe to attack Leipzig from this direction. Blücher would have to continue his assault alone until Bernadotte's men could reach their new position. In fact, Napoleon was considering escaping westward and reinforced his outpost at Lindenau, whilst pulling his remaining 150,000 troops closer to the city.

18 October

It took until 2 pm before Schwarzenberg was fully in place to attack the new French position from Connewitz through Probstheida to Holzhausen. The allies took most of the villages after bitter fighting. Around 5,000 Saxons and Württembergers defected to the allies around 4.30 pm. Afterwards, Napoleon blamed them for his defeat, but the final arrival of Bernadotte south of the Parthe proved far more significant. Blücher also made progress and the French were forced back towards the city.

The French were now nearly out of ammunition. The baggage had already left at 11 am and the withdrawal continued throughout the day and night through Leipzig and along the 2-km (1.24-mile) causeway across the swamps to Lindenau. The allies started shelling this route the next morning while they renewed their attack on the city itself. The situation was critical, but not yet desperate until the French engineer in charge of

Francis I of Austria, Frederick-Wilhelm III and Tsar Alexander of Russia meet on the battlefield after Napoleon's great defeat at Leipzig (19th-century painting).

the vital bridge over the Elster panicked and blew it up, cutting off the rearguard of 20,000 French and Poles still in Leipzig.

Aftermath

Napoleon escaped with only 80,000 men, but defeated another Austro-Bavarian army that tried to block his route at Hanau. He held out in France until overwhelming allied forces compelled him to abdicate on 11 April 1814. Leipzig encapsulates the characteristics of a major Napoleonic battle. It was a hard-fought action extending over several days as fresh units converged on the field. Cavalry still played a major tactical role, along with massed artillery and infantry assaults. The experience was open to very different interpretations by Jomini and Clausewitz (the two leading military theorists of the 19th century), both of whom were present as staff officers in the allied armies.

COMBATANTS

Allies

- Armies of Silesia, Bohemia and the North, totalling 342,000 men with 1,500 guns
- Commanded by Prince Karl Philipp von Schwarzenberg
- 22,600 Russians, 16,000 Prussians, 14,900 Austrians, 200 Swedes killed and wounded

French

- *Grande Armée* totalled 195,000 men with 900 guns (by 14 October only *c.* 177,000 men/ 700 guns)
- Commanded by Emperor Napoleon
- 13,000 dead; 23,000 wounded (mostly also captured); 15,000 captured; 5,000 deserted; 325 guns and 900 wagons lost

Waterloo

46

Date: 18 June 1815   Location: south of Brussels, Belgium

I never saw such a battle…and never before did I gain such a victory.
I trust it is all over with Napoleon Bonaparte.
DUKE OF WELLINGTON

Far left *Francisco Goya's* Portrait of the Duke of Wellington, *1812.*

Centre Napoleon in his Study, *painted by Jacques-Louis David in 1812.*

Left *An 1828 portrait of Field Marshal Gebhard Blücher.*

Fought on 18 June 1815, the battle of Waterloo constituted the climactic moment in the 23-year conflict known as the Revolutionary and Napoleonic Wars. In brief, three years after the French Revolution of 1789, war had broken out between France and Austria and Prussia (see Jemappes p. 177), who were quickly joined by most of the rest of Europe. Fighting continued on and off until 1802, but in that year France's last remaining opponent – Britain – was forced to make peace. Though France had experienced some failures, she can on the whole be said to have got the better of the struggle. However, the triumph of 1802 was squandered. Under the leadership of Napoleon Bonaparte, the successful general who had seized power in 1799, France continued to disturb the peace, and in May 1803 Britain was provoked into renewing the conflict. After a long, complicated struggle, Napoleon, who had become emperor of France in 1804, overreached himself. Thus, after defeat at Leipzig in 1813 (see p. 188), in 1814 he was overthrown by overwhelming odds and forced to abdicate.

With France in the hands of Louis XVIII, Napoleon was sent to the minuscule Mediterranean island of Elba, where he was expected to live out his days as a minor princeling dependent on a subsidy paid by the French government. This subsidy, however, was only paid sporadically, and the erstwhile emperor may also have feared that Louis intended to have him murdered. With news coming in that France was in a state of growing unrest, Napoleon sailed from Elba at the head of his tiny army. Landing on the French coast on 1 March 1815, he marched on Paris. Finding that his army would not fight Napoleon, Louis fled into exile. By 20 March, then, Napoleon was back in the capital. Views on his return were mixed –

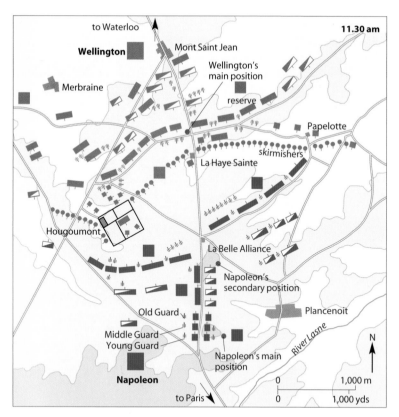

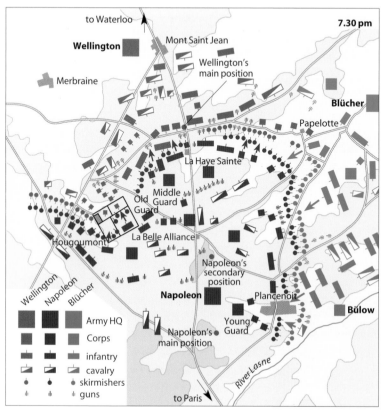

there was, in fact, considerable disaffection – but the soldiers of the old imperial army were willing enough to fight for him, and he soon had a force of some 280,000 men at his disposal. This, meanwhile, was just as well: currently assembled to discuss a definitive peace settlement at Vienna, the powers of Europe unanimously declared war on Napoleon and declared him an outlaw who was to be overthrown at all costs.

The campaign

If he was to win the coming conflict, Napoleon knew that he had to strike hard and fast so as to inflict such a blow on the allies that some or all of his opponents would decide that they would do better to make peace. The allied forces garrisoning Belgium being the most accessible target, by early June 120,000 men were heading for Brus-

Above left *By 11.30 am, Wellington's main line was on the ridge near Mont Saint Jean, Napoleon down the slope below.*

Left *A final assault by the French Imperial Guard had been repulsed, and Blücher was closing in for the kill from the east.*

sels. Opposing them were two armies: 93,000 British, Dutch, Belgians, Hanoverians, Nassauers and Brunswickers under the Duke of Wellington, and 117,000 Prussians under Field Marshal Blücher. To deal with these opponents Napoleon had, again, but one hope, except this time the trick was to get his army between the two opposing forces and defeat first one and then the other.

Rather than marching on Brussels by the direct road (a plan that would only have driven Wellington straight into the arms of the Prussians), he led his army to a position due south of the Belgian capital and crossed the frontier at Charleroi, the road that led from that town to Brussels marking the exact spot where the responsibilities of one army ended and the other began. It was a good plan – Wellington, in particular, was taken completely by surprise and caught with his army spread out far to the west watching the main Paris-Brussels highway – and the allied armies were not in good shape: of Wellington's 30,000 British soldiers, many were little more than raw recruits, and the Dutch, Belgians and Germans

(Prussians and non-Prussians alike) were mainly unwilling conscripts with little enthusiasm for the struggle. Yet the French were also less well placed than they might have been: few of Napoleon's best commanders were available, whilst the army was badly equipped and much affected by rumours of treason and disaffection. And it was not long before the plan broke down very badly.

Having crossed the frontier on 15 June, the following day the French came up against Blücher at Ligny, whilst they at the same time contacted the leading elements of Wellington's forces at Quatre Bras. Vigorous offensives at both places might have won the day for Napoleon, but although the emperor carried the day at Ligny, he failed to rout the Prussian army, which was able to draw off in reasonable order.

Still worse, meanwhile, at Quatre Bras the French forces commanded by Marshal Ney failed to inflict any significant damage at all. Nor were Wellington and Blücher even driven apart: whilst the former retreated north towards Brussels, the latter headed not east for the German frontier but

An artist's impression of Waterloo. Wellington, at far left and holding a telescope, gives orders to an officer during the height of the battle.

rather north towards Wavre. The German commander thereby kept open the possibility that he might join up with Wellington, despite feeling rightly let down by his British counterpart ('humbugged', as he put it, by Napoleon, Wellington had got Blücher to fight at Ligny by promising that he would come to his aid when he knew full well that this was a physical impossibility). And, last but not least, the French forces were no longer even united. While Napoleon followed Wellington with 73,000 men, 33,000 men went after Blücher under Grouchy.

The battle

With rain falling in torrents, on the evening of 17 June Wellington's troops reached a ridge called Mont Saint Jean, 3 km (2 miles) south of Waterloo. It was here the next day they turned to fight. The ridge provided excellent 'reverse slope' positions for the allied army whilst several roads led from the battlefield to the Prussian position at Wavre. Forward of the main line, meanwhile, three isolated farms – Hougoumont, La Haye Sainte and Papelotte – offered excellent defensive bastions.

Even now, however, Napoleon might have won, but the ground was deep in mud and so the emperor delayed a while to allow the sun to dry out the battlefield a little. And when the French did attack, their efforts were clumsy and uncoordinated. First, large numbers of infantry became bogged down in fighting round Hougoumont on Napoleon's left flank; second, a clumsy attack on Wellington's left-centre was mauled by British cavalry; and third, the bulk of Napoleon's own cavalry was thrown away in a series of unsupported charges on the allied right-centre.

Only late in the day did more careful planning pay off by delivering La Haye Sainte to the French and opening up Wellington's over-stretched and exhausted forces to destruction. But the Prussians saved the day. Having heard the sound of the guns, Blücher had immediately got all the

COMBATANTS

Army of the Lower Rhine

- 75,000 men (effectively engaged: 28,000); 264 guns
- Commanded by Gebhard Blücher von Wahlstadt
- Casualties: 7,000

Army of the Netherlands

- 68,000 men (30,000 British; 20,000 German; 18,000 Dutch-Belgian); 155 guns
- Commanded by the Duke of Wellington
- Casualties: 8,600 British; 4,000 Dutch-Belgian; 3,000 German

Army of the North

- 73,000 men; 252 guns
- Commanded by Napoleon Bonaparte
- Casualties: 25,000 killed and wounded; 17,000 captured or lost to desertion

men he could on the road (a development that Grouchy singularly failed to prevent). Since early afternoon, then, large numbers of Prussians had been arriving on Napoleon's right flank. By dint of great courage, the French were holding their own against them, but there were now too few reserves to make the capture of La Haye Sainte count for anything. Thus, with evening drawing on, Napoleon made one last effort to break Wellington's line, sending forward what little was left of the infantry of the Imperial Guard. But the men involved were hopelessly outnumbered, and they had no sooner reached the ridge than they were overwhelmed. Seeing the Guard break, the rest of the army was affected by panic in its turn, and within a few minutes most of Napoleon's army was in flight.

Impact and consequences

At the simplest level, Waterloo ended the career of Napoleon Bonaparte, the erstwhile emperor soon finding himself on board a ship bound for St Helena, where he died in 1821. By the same token, of course, it also enshrined Wellington as British hero of heroes. Beyond that it effectively put an end to 150 years of French dreams of dominance in western Europe. Yet even had Napoleon won at Waterloo, he would sooner or later have met his end somewhere else, the consequence being that the real significance of the battle is not political or diplomatic but rather military. Waterloo provided Europe's generals with the concept of the titanic clash of arms that could settle entire wars at a single stroke. As such, it was to become a fatal mirage – the fount, indeed, of the tragedy of 1914.

At the conclusion of the battle French soldiers flee, pursued by the Prussians under Blücher.

197

47

Ayacucho

Date: 9 December 1824 Location: southern Peru

Opinion in Peru, General, is that of the entire world, in that everyone wants to be king of his own home; as to the decision to take up arms, certainly you have more troops and a better position than we have, but your soldiers are not the equal of ours, as you will see in the hour of combat.

GENERAL JOSÉ MARÍA CÓRDOBA TO GENERAL ANTONIO MONET, 9 DECEMBER 1824

In June 1824 Revolutionaries responded to the Royalist recapture of Lima by voting new powers for the charismatic Peruvian leader Simon Bolívar and General Antonio José de Sucre. Bolívar and Sucre inflicted a minor military reverse on Royalist forces at Junín in July. Bolívar then took a force towards Lima, leaving Sucre to handle an expected Royalist counter-offensive.

That offensive was led by Viceroy José de La Serna, who believed that the Royalist cause in Peru was doomed. He hoped to establish a provisional government and invite a Bourbon prince to come to Peru and assume the throne. Despite his pessimism about Spain's future political control of Peru, he was confident that he could defeat Sucre's army. La Serna moved his 9,300 soldiers north of Sucre's forces near the town of Ayacucho (the name means the 'Corner of the Dead' in Quechua), located approximately 300 km (186 miles) southeast of Lima. By doing so he hoped to cut the Revolutionaries off from the sea and any possible reinforcement by the new army Bolívar was trying to raise near Lima. The altitude of the Ayacucho region, as high as 2,800 m (9,000 ft), promised to further limit Sucre's ability to manoeuvre.

La Serna's forces outnumbered those of Sucre, who had just 5,780 men, most of them from Gran Colombia and Peru. La Serna tried to use his superior numbers to encircle Sucre, who responded by adroitly moving his men out of harm's way and establishing a defensive position on the plain of

Fought on a plain in the Andes Mountains, Ayacucho's open spaces allowed a smaller Peruvian force to outmanoeuvre a larger Spanish force.

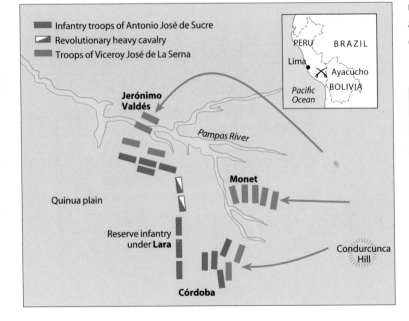

Infantry troops of Antonio José de Sucre
Revolutionary heavy cavalry
Troops of Viceroy José de La Serna

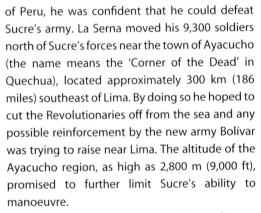

COMBATANTS

Peruvians (Revolutionaries)
• 5,780 soldiers
• Commanded by Antonio José de Sucre
• 309 dead, 607 wounded

Royalists
• 9,300 soldiers
• Commanded by Viceroy José de La Serna
• 1,400 dead, 700 wounded, 2,500 captured

Quinua that was well protected by ravines. During the night, Sucre and his officers worked out a plan to allow La Serna to attack first, then respond with reserves. They divided their forces into four divisions, with two regiments of heavy cavalry in the centre and four battalions of infantry on either flank. Three battalions of infantry under General Lara formed a reserve capable of responding to La Serna's attack.

The 'Battle of the Generals'

At dawn on 9 December the Royalists attacked Sucre's right, which was commanded by General José María Córdoba. This attack failed, as did an attack on the centre by forces led by the Royalist general Antonio Monet. The Colombians under Córdoba responded with a bayonet attack that drove back the left of the Royalist line, breaking their ranks and allowing the Revolutionaries to introduce their cavalry and infantry reserves. Royalist reserves unwisely advanced, leaving themselves in a position to be encircled by Revolutionary forces.

Despite having been outnumbered, Sucre won a fast and relatively bloodless battle. The entire action had taken less than 80 minutes. Total Revolutionary casualties were just over 300 dead and 600 wounded.

Royalist casualties, on the other hand, were astonishingly high. They suffered 1,400 dead, 700 wounded and 2,500 captured. Among the captured were the majority of the Royalists' most important officers. Viceroy La Serna himself became a prisoner of war, as did 15 generals, 16 colonels and 68 lieutenant colonels. The high number of senior officers lost gave this battle the nickname 'Battle of the Generals'. The Royalists could not afford the loss of so much of their senior military and administrative leadership.

Aftermath

Sucre gave the Royalists honourable terms of surrender. La Serna agreed to withdraw all Royalist forces from Peru, making it independent of Spain. Sucre then moved into Upper Peru, and at Chuquisaca he proclaimed the independence of that province in August 1825. He renamed Upper

Peru 'Bolivia' in honour of Simon Bolívar.

The victory at Ayacucho effectively ended Spanish control in South America. The impacts of the Napoleonic Wars meant that Royalist forces could not expect reinforcements from Europe. The last sizeable Spanish force surrendered at Callao in January 1826. Sucre became Bolivia's first constitutional leader, but soon resigned in the face of an insurrection. Chuquisaca was later renamed Sucre in his honour.

Antonio José de Sucre (1793–1830) on horseback at Ayacucho, 1824, during the War of Independence against Spain.

Mexico City

Date: April–September 1847 Location: central Mexico

…one of the most unjust [battles] ever waged by a stronger against a weaker nation.
THE VERDICT OF THE PERSONAL MEMOIRS OF ULYSSES S. GRANT, 1885–86

The military operations conducted by the United States in the early stages of its war with Mexico (1846–48), south of the Rio Grande, had failed to bring decisive results. In October 1846 President James K. Polk decided to strike directly at Mexico City, the capital; but, as a Democrat, he nursed severe reservations about the officer best equipped to undertake this hazardous mission, Major General Winfield Scott. Polk suspected that Scott would use a successful campaign as a springboard for a Whig presidential candidacy in 1848.

Nevertheless, on 23 November 1846 Scott received orders to begin

Above *Portrait of General Antonio Lopez de Santa Anna, President of Mexico.*

Right *Major General Winfield Scott, c. 1849. Although querulous, vain and pompous, Scott was the central figure in the US army's adoption of professional methods during the Mexican War.*

planning the operation. On 9 March 1847 he landed with 10,000 men near the port of Vera Cruz, and took it 20 days later after a short siege. Scott's strategy for the Mexico City campaign reflected methods previously used further north. American forces would advance rapidly into the hinterland, utilizing the full available space, and seize their objectives rapidly before the Mexicans could concentrate overwhelming force. The civil population would be treated relatively gently to prevent any guerrilla uprising that could jeopardize vulnerable supply lines.

Scott faced enormous logistical problems because his army had to surmount the sierras that stretched before him. The further he advanced, the longer his lines of communication back to Vera Cruz became. Scott, for all his self-absorbed pomposity that earned him the nickname 'Old Fuss and Feathers', had an astute military brain and was a keen student of military history. To offer detailed advice on the planning process, Scott created his 'little cabinet', the first properly functioning general's field staff in American military history. Its members included some of the most talented young officers in the US Army, including Robert E. Lee, P. G. T. Beauregard and George B. McClellan (see Antietam p. 206).

March across Mexico
On 10 April 1847 Scott began his march on Mexico City. The long American columns toiled up the narrow mountain paths, conscious that they were about to take part in an epic military adventure. The Mexican *caudillo* (military strongman-turned-leader) General Antonio Lopez de Santa Anna, who combined the presidency with

command of the army, rushed down from northern Mexico to block Scott's path.

In a brilliant series of out-flanking manoeuvres, Scott successively turned Santa Anna out of strong defensive positions at Cerro Gordo (18 April) and Contreras (18–20 August). Scott had been forced to wait for nearly three months at Puebla as the enlistments of 7,000 volunteers had expired, and he could not advance further without reinforcements.

By August 1847 Scott could field 10,738 men in four divisions. This was hardly a huge force and Mexico City could boast strong fortifications. The city had to be approached along causeways through extensive marshes in the beds of dried-up lakes (see Tenochtitlan, ancient Mexico City, p. 98). The points of entry were covered by defensive lines and forts, the strongest being El Peñon. Santa Anna had 25,000 men to hold the city, divided into three field armies.

Scott's success at Contreras had allowed him to advance on the city from the south and avoid El Peñon. As Scott approached Mexico City he received a request from Santa Anna for an armistice to which he acceded. But Scott was convinced of Santa Anna's knavery and suspected that the Mexicans were defying its terms by melting down church bells to make new cannon at an improvised foundry at Molino del Rey. Scott determined to attack it the following day. He succeeded in taking it, but at heavy cost; he lost 700 lives, while the Mexicans sustained 2,000 casualties and 700 prisoners. Nor could Scott's officers find any evidence of cheating.

Storming the city

Although an error, the seizure of Molino del Rey brought American forces right up to the walls of the fortress at Chapultepec. Scott decided to storm it without delay. On 12 September he announced impulsively that he would attack that day; but he was persuaded by brevet Lieutenant Colonel Robert E. Lee to wait until the following morning, thus allowing the artillery bombardment to have more effect. So at 8 am on 13 September three of Scott's divisions moved forward to the assault: John A. Quitman from the south, Gideon J. Pillow from the southwest, and William J. Worth from the west. The infantry brandished scaling ladders, clambered up the walls, surged over them, and by 9.30 am Chapultepec had fallen into American hands. Thereafter the divisions of Quitman and Worth pushed on to the Belem and San Cosme gates respectively. Both

The seizure of Chapultepec was the key moment in the storming of Mexico City. Superior artillery and gunpowder prepared the way for the American assault.

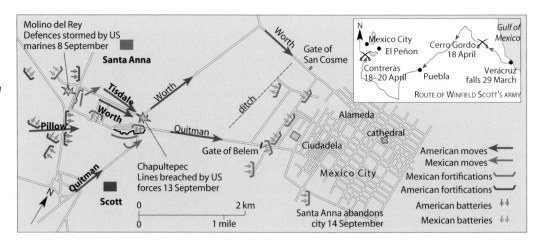

The defence of Mexico City depended on its outer ramparts. Once these surrendered, Santa Anna decided to abandon the city rather than fight for every street.

gates had been taken by nightfall. But Scott entertained real doubts as to whether he could seize the city and hold it – he had suffered 900 casualties and was running low on ammunition.

The Mexicans, however, solved Scott's dilemma for him. Santa Anna commanded a demoralized army that had fought bravely but ultimately failed to hold Mexico City's strong-points. He decided to abandon the capital and withdraw north to Guadalupe Hidalgo. On 14 September Mexico City surrendered and Quitman's troops marched into the Grand Plaza and raised the American flag. Within the hour Scott and his staff arrived to take the salute.

Hostilities still rumbled on for several weeks with Santa Anna refusing to give up. He tried to retake Puebla and force Scott's withdrawal by harrying US supply lines. But he failed in these small operations as he had in the greater and, resigning the Mexican presidency, on 11 October he was relieved of military command.

Scott's campaign against Mexico City repre-sents a masterly achievement that displays high qualities of planning and generalship. Given the length of his supply lines, a single error might have led to catastrophe; but he did not take counsel of his fears. Scott's timing and logistical judgment could not have been bettered.

The Treaty of Guadalupe Hidalgo

The Mexican War did not formally end until the signing on 2 February 1848 of the Treaty of

COMBATANTS

United States forces

• 10,738 men

• Commanded by Major General Winfield Scott

• 900 casualties

Mexican forces

• 25,000 men

• Commanded by General Antonio Lopez de Santa Anna

• 4,000 casualties

Guadalupe Hidalgo. Mexico ceded more than half its national territory, California, plus the New Mexico territories, and the US gained the frontier of the Rio Grande (over 1 million sq. km [half a million sq. miles]). In return Mexico received $15 million, plus a further $3,250,000 to pay outstand-ing claims against it by US citizens.

The Mexican War served notice of the US determination to be the paramount power in North America. It facilitated the establishment of a continental republic stretching from the Atlantic to the Pacific Oceans. Alas, by acquiring so much new territory from Mexico, Scott's victory revived sectional debate as to its future character. Slave or free? Such questions affected the North-South balance; ultimately, the political crisis of the 1850s would end in the catastrophe of secession and civil war.

Inkerman

49

Date: 5 November 1854   Location: southwest Crimea, Ukraine

Quel abbatoir!

GENERAL P. F. J. BOSQUET, ON SEEING THE PILES OF BODIES AROUND THE SANDBAG BATTERY, 5 NOVEMBER 1854

The Crimean War of 1854–56 arose from Russia's attempts to expand southwards at the expense of the Ottoman empire and from the determination of Britain and France to prevent that. Russia occupied Turkey's Danubian provinces in July 1853; Turkey declared war in October and Britain and France the following March. When the Russians, threatened by Austrian intervention, withdrew from the Danubian theatre, the allied armies focused on the Crimean peninsula and the destruction of the naval base at Sevastopol from which Russia controlled the Black Sea and threatened Constantinople.

The campaign

The Anglo-French forces landed on 14 September and, moving south towards Sevastopol, fought a major battle at the Alma River. Though Sevastopol was soon under siege, most of the Russian army remained at large in the peninsula's interior and could communicate with the incompletely invested town and threaten the besiegers. The Russians sought to break through to the British supply harbour at Balaklava on 25 October, and the next day a Russian sortie probed the right extension of the British-held part of the siege line.

Though recognizing the vulnerability of this flank, the allied commanders, Canrobert and Raglan, chose to concentrate their limited resources on a decisive assault on the town before winter closed in. Menshikov, the Russian commander-in-chief, was under pressure from the Tsar to strike early to break the siege and expel the invaders from the Crimea; the arrival of reinforcements from the Danube theatre now gave him marked superiority in manpower and artillery. He designed a decisive blow of his own through a pincer movement aimed at the weak British right. Two converging forces would scale and seize the thinly defended Inkerman Ridge and occupy the Chersonese plateau behind the besieging forces, while diversionary attacks occupied the French. Menshikov entrusted field command to General Dannenberg who had arrived with the Danubian troops.

The battle

The Russian attack began in the dark early hours

The Crimea was the first campaign to be recorded by photography, though actual battle remained beyond the limited technology. Here Roger Fenton's exposure of the Light Division's encampment shows the open and vulnerable nature of British dispositions above Balaklava.

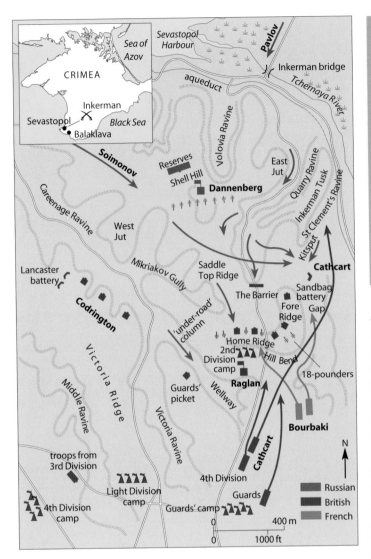

2nd Division commander, Brigadier General Pennefather, decided to throw men forward as they became available to reinforce his pickets rather than withdraw to the plateau to await larger reinforcement. This tactic prevented the superiority of Russian numbers and guns (artillery had been installed on Shell Hill, supplemented by two gunboats in the bay below) from having full effect.

Neither side was fully aware of the other's numbers and dispositions, even when the mist partially cleared and a series of fierce and disconnected encounters developed along the ridges and scrub-lined ravines of the plateau's edge. Though the Minié rifle used by some of the British was markedly superior to the Russian muskets, the detrimental effect of overnight rain on these rifles, ammunition shortages and the close engagement meant that there was unusually heavy reliance on the bayonet in hand-to-hand fighting. The Coldstream Guards made eleven bayonet charges. The frenzied and improvised resistance of Pennefather's division of 3,000 men broke Soimonov's advance, killing the Russian general himself, so that the British line on Home Ridge was still intact when Pavlov's division arrived. Raglan, present on the field, left local responses to sector commanders, but made two crucial decisions: to request French assistance (earlier declined) and to order up two 18-pounder siege guns to counter the enemy's artillery.

The above map illustrates the narrow front of the engagement along the ridges, interspersed by ravines, above Sevastopol. This concentration served the British defenders well and reduced the effect of superior Russian numbers.

of Sunday 5 November. Infantry 19,000-strong with supporting artillery, commanded by Lieutenant General Soimonov, advanced from Sevastopol towards the right end of the British lines on Inkerman Ridge. A second force of 16,000 men under Lieutenant General Pavlov, accompanied by Dannenberg, was to make a simultaneous advance across the Tchernaya River to join Soimonov's troops in breaching the British lines. But repairs to Inkerman bridge and Dannenberg's changes to Menshikov's timetable prevented the conjunction of the two forces which attacked consecutively instead of simultaneously. Aided by darkness, drizzle, mist and the terrain, Soimonov achieved total surprise, but the British

The much larger French forces had faced two diversionary attacks, the first a fierce sally from the town on the left of the siege line, the second a feint attack south of the plateau from a force of 22,000 commanded by General Gorchakov. The weakness of the pressure from Gorchakov left the French General Bosquet confident enough to dispatch several of his regiments northwards to assist the British. In this second phase, as arriving detachments were thrown in desperately, the battered British line developed a gap, with confusion and indiscipline among commanders contributing to the problem. Only the impact of the 18-pounders in clearing the enemy artillery and the arrival of Bosquet's regiments (mainly Zouaves) turned the day and, after taking heavy casualties, Dannenberg ordered withdrawal.

The clear superiority of Russian resources, aided by the advantage of surprise, had not achieved victory. Failures of co-ordination among Russian commanders and the forward engagement by British troops – restricting the enemy to a narrow front and difficult terrain where his full resources could not be deployed – had permitted the line to be held until the French arrived. Inkerman, a wholly defensive and reactive battle as fought by the allies, would stand as 'a soldier's battle', as well as a notably bloody one. One junior officer concluded, 'We owe our existence as an army to the pluck of the private soldiers.'

The impact

The initial outcome of the battle was negative for both sides. The British were shaken, only the heroism of the infantry having prevented a disaster, and casualties were high (50 per cent in some units). One general suffered a nervous breakdown and another advised the abandonment of the whole campaign. The planned assault on Sevastopol was now impossible and the siege had to continue over the winter. A great storm which destroyed the British supply ships and depot at Balaklava on 14 November increased the privations and losses through the winter of 1854–55. Major reinforcements were poured into the Crimea to give the allies military superiority.

The impact on the Russian side was even greater. A third major battle had failed to dislodge the invaders and, as the allied build-up proceeded, it was clear Sevastopol was doomed. After a last break-out attempt, the town fell in September 1855 and the war ended as an Anglo-French victory. The Treaty of Paris (1856) demilitarized the Black Sea and stalled Russia's expansion at Turkey's expense for 20 years. Russia's loss of the aura of military invincibility retained since 1815 would have profound domestic and international consequences. But the international standing of Palmerston's Britain was confirmed and that of the Emperor Louis Napoleon's France enhanced.

Even this romanticized depiction of the death of Lieutenant General Sir George Cathcart, who had rashly led his men into a ravine exposed to Russian fire, conveys something of the battleground confusion at Inkerman.

50 Antietam

Date: 17 September 1862   Location: Sharpsburg, northwest Maryland, USA

The present posture of affairs, in my opinion, places it in the power of the Government of the Confederate States to propose with propriety to that of the United States the recognition of our independence.
ROBERT E. LEE TO JEFFERSON DAVIS, 8 SEPTEMBER 1862

President Abraham Lincoln visited McClellan's troops at Antietam on 1 October 1862. Frustrated with his commander, he sarcastically described the Army of the Potomac as 'McClellan's bodyguard'.

The Maryland Campaign of September 1862 in the American Civil War, culminating at Antietam, resulted from the strategic reverses inflicted on Union arms by Confederate General Robert E. Lee. The Seven Days' Battles (25 June–1 July) had saved the Confederate capital, Richmond, and the second battle of Manassas had re-established the Confederate frontier along the Potomac River. On 5 September Lee's Army of Northern Virginia entered Maryland.

Preparations for battle

President Abraham Lincoln reacted to this crisis decisively. He called for another 300,000 volunteers, recalled Union forces from the South Atlantic and Kanawha Valley and, most controversially, appointed Major General George B. McClellan as commander of all Union forces in the Washington area. As a Democrat, McClellan was regarded by some of Lincoln's cabinet as a political enemy and, despite demonstrating astute organizational qualities, the Seven Days' Battles had shown him to be more concerned with avoiding defeat than defeating the enemy. He now redeemed himself by instituting an intensive training programme and bringing new recruits into the Army of the Potomac. By 7 September McClellan had got his troops into the field, but almost one quarter of them (some 20,000 men) had not seen action before.

Lee's self-confidence led him to underrate Union resilience, and the speed of McClellan's reaction took him by surprise. He had counted on at least three weeks to allow his troops to rest, refit, and move through the western (Unionist) counties of Maryland towards Pennsylvania. Lee intended to stay on northern soil until November, eroding support for the continuation of the war and forcing Lincoln to acknowledge Confederate independence. He told Colonel William Allan in 1866, 'I went into Maryland to give battle', hoping to out-manoeuvre Union forces and strike a lethal blow that would win the war for the South.

The Army of Northern Virginia had to spread out to forage off the country. On 9/10 September

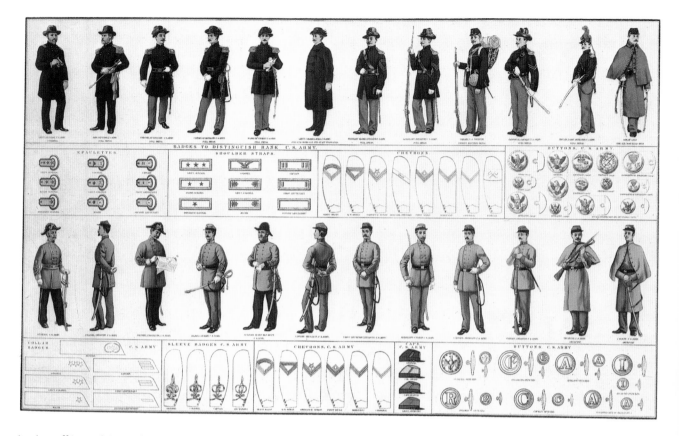

Lee's staff issued Special Order No. 191 detailing his dispersal. Most significantly, Major General Thomas 'Stonewall' Jackson and 38,000 men had been sent back to 'intercept' the Federal garrison at Harper's Ferry. A copy of this order – the famous Lost Order – was found by Union troops and handed to McClellan. He waved it exuberantly in the air, an act noticed by a Confederate spy. It would appear doubtful that Lee knew the precise cause of McClellan's elation for some time, although he did recognize that his plans had been compromised.

Lee had, in any case, already lost the initiative. On 12 September Union troops entered Frederick, Maryland, and Lee had only one division available to protect his rear, that of D. H. Hill. On 14 September McClellan attacked Hill at the battle of South Mountain, but unfortunately did not exploit his success. In an effort to shield Jackson's force Lee ordered a retreat via Keedysville, from where on 15 September he spotted the Sharpsburg Heights and discerned their strength as a defensive position for his army.

Shortly afterwards he received a despatch from Jackson predicting the fall of Harper's Ferry (an unanticipated siege). Lee thus ordered a concentration of the army at Sharpsburg.

At this point Lee had yet to make up his mind whether to offer McClellan battle on this ground or withdraw. But a return to Maryland at a later date would have ruined the strategic momentum of the campaign. The Sharpsburg Heights offered a confusing series of interlocking hills that might deceive McClellan as to Lee's numerical weakness, giving Lee valuable time. With the meander of the Potomac behind him, the Confederate flanks could safely rest there, but he had no avenue of escape should McClellan break his front. By midday on 15 September, Lee had only 15,000 men and 100 guns with him, accepting an enormous risk by making a stand at Sharpsburg.

Jackson arrived on the morning of 16 September (minus A. P. Hill's division), considerably adding to Lee's strength. That afternoon the cavalry commander, Major General J. E. B. Stuart, reported the arrival of Union troops, first Major

Union and Confederate uniforms in 1861, the 'War of the Blue and the Gray'. The choice of gray was chosen by the Confederate president, Jefferson Davis, who had been a cadet at West Point and always admired the gray of the cadets' uniforms.

General Joseph Hooker's I Corps, followed shortly afterwards by XII Corps under Major General Joseph Mansfield. At 4 pm both corps started to cross the Antietam Creek and approach the Confederate left, but McClellan took no further action that day. He forfeited surprise by advertising his strength and then granted Lee another day to make his preparations.

McClellan's onslaught degenerated into a series of piecemeal attacks. Lee could thus concentrate his reserves at key points to repulse them.

McClellan commanded 75,000 men and 275 guns. The Union artillery was superior in both range and weight of ordnance, and McClellan concentrated his guns on his right at Poffenberger Hill behind the North Woods. McClellan foolishly believed that the Confederates outnumbered him, when Lee barely had 50,000 men ready for battle. His plan to weaken both Confederate flanks with attacks then smash Lee's centre demanded tight tactical control and neat timing. Alas, McClellan made his headquarters far in the rear and did not appear on the field once. Consequently, his plan broke down into a series of piecemeal frontal attacks, none of which was strong enough to defeat Lee's army on its own.

Action

On 17 September the Union assault opened on the right at 5 am. Hooker intended to seize the high ground around the Dunker Church. Once taken, Lee's army could be driven into the Potomac. Confederate artillery placed on Nicodemus Hill enfiladed the Union infantry as they marched forward. Jackson commanded this sector and resisted Hooker's onslaught stubbornly. XII Corps received the order to advance at 7.30 am, but Mansfield fell mortally wounded and his divisions attacked piecemeal. Lee sent Jackson one division from the centre and another from the right. Jackson's strengthened line held.

The second phase of the operation began at about 9 am, when Major General Edwin V. Sumner's II Corps thrust towards the Confederate

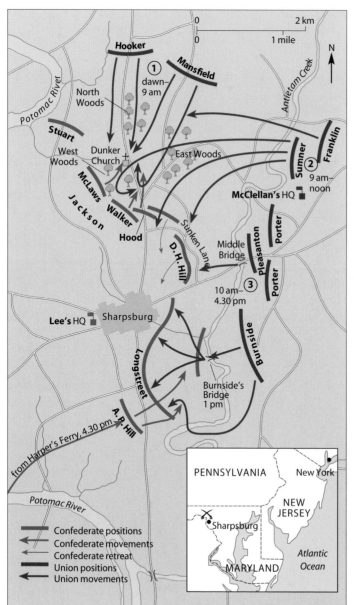

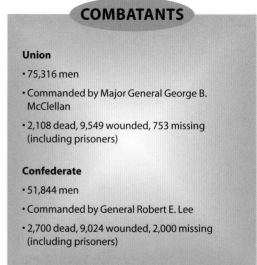

COMBATANTS

Union

• 75,316 men

• Commanded by Major General George B. McClellan

• 2,108 dead, 9,549 wounded, 753 missing (including prisoners)

Confederate

• 51,844 men

• Commanded by General Robert E. Lee

• 2,700 dead, 9,024 wounded, 2,000 missing (including prisoners)

Very high casualties resulted from the close proximity of the two armies, the power of their artillery and the desperate nature of the fighting.

centre. This was the weakest part of Lee's position because a dale ran through it to the Potomac. D. H. Hill's division covered the vital hinge, a sunken lane, linking it to the Confederate left flank.

McClellan let this attack go forward as an unsupported frontal assault – contributing to the wearing-out process that it should have been held back to exploit. Sumner's three divisions became confused by the ground, diverged, and then made three separate assaults. Lee struggled to resist them and committed R. H. Anderson's division to support D. H. Hill, but at 1.30 pm the Confederates were driven out of the sunken lane.

The battle seemed to be going against Lee. One of Sumner's divisions renewed the assault on the Dunker Church and for a couple of hours this fell into Federal hands. Lee worked feverishly to patch up his line, but by 2.30 pm he had no more reserves to commit. One weak division of 2,400 men covered his entire right flank. Then another disaster occurred. At long last Burnside's IX Corps drove back Confederate skirmishers and crossed the Rohrbach (now Burnside's) Bridge, climbed the bluffs over Antietam Creek, and belatedly advanced on Sharpsburg to cut off Lee's retreat. Lee failed to rally the fleeing Confederates and, in a dramatic flourish, A. P. Hill's division from Harper's Ferry arrived. 'General Hill', said a delighted Lee, 'I was never so glad to see you. You are badly needed.' In the nick of time, Hill's Light Division charged Burnside's exposed left flank and drove it back over the creek.

On 18 September Lee stood his ground, claiming the field and thus the victory, which McClellan made no effort to challenge. The following day Lee withdrew back to Virginia, his troops exhausted. The Army of the Potomac had also been drained by the experience and remained largely in the locality for another six weeks. Although technically a draw, Antietam remains one of the most decisive and bloody battles of the American Civil War, each side sustaining losses of about 12,000 men.

Consequences

Antietam frustrated Lee's efforts to gain a decision in the Confederacy's favour that year. It also dashed the very slight chance that Great Britain and France might intervene on the South's side. The withdrawal of Confederate troops offered Lincoln enough of a strategic victory to justify the issue on 22 September of the preliminary Emancipation Proclamation. It freed no slaves, except those on Confederate territory, but signalled Lincoln's harsher approach to the South. He sought nothing less than a Confederate surrender or the destruction of the Southern social system based on slavery. Although a persuasive case has been made that Antietam made foreign intervention more likely because of humanitarian fears of a servile war, Britain only had 'mediation' in mind, not military intervention. Lincoln could have brushed this aside.

In sum, Antietam provided the all-important foundation for the eventual Union victory. It could also lay claim to be one of the most decisive battles of the Americas. Without it the United States could not have established an *imperium* in the western hemisphere by the 1880s as a prelude to world power.

Gettysburg

Date: 1–3 July 1863   Location: southern Pennsylvania, USA

The dead dying and the wounded begers all decription. They lay in Piles about the Brest Works and for miles they lay lyke Wheat Bundells in a good hearvest field – Men, horsis, Mules, Broken Canan, Canan Caridges, Bugles, Drummes, Swords, and Muskettes law stewd all over the fields – grain feelds all Stompt in the Earth. The most horabel Sight man ever saw.
LETTER FROM A WISCONSIN SOLDIER AFTER THE BATTLE

Gettysburg was probably the most important battle of the 1861–65 American Civil War. Following his brilliant victory at Chancellorsville in May 1863, General Robert E. Lee, commander of the Confederate Army of Northern Virginia, convinced Confederate President Jefferson Davis to allow him to carry out an invasion of Pennsylvania. Lee intended this as a spoiling attack to delay an anticipated invasion by Major General Joseph Hooker's Federal Army of the Potomac (see Antietam p. 206). It would allow Virginia a chance to recover from the ravages of war and the Confederacy could draw resources from the rich Pennsylvania countryside. Bringing the war home to the North might also aid the peace movement there, and if the South could win a great military victory, it would certainly aid Southern chances of securing diplomatic recognition abroad. Although the Union had a slight edge in manpower (about 85,000–90,000 to some 70,000 Confederates) the numbers were closer than they had been recently or would be in the future.

On 3 June Lee's army began moving west. Hooker took a parallel route north of the Rappahannock, keeping his own forces between Lee and the Federal capital. Lee slipped across the Blue Ridge, moved north through the Shenandoah Valley and crossed the Potomac north through Maryland and into Pennsylvania. Securing Harrisonburg would allow Lee to cut Union communications to the west. He would also be in

210

position to threaten a number of eastern cities, including Baltimore and Washington, and hoped thereby to force Hooker to attack him.

By the end of June Lee's three corps, under Lieutenant Generals Richard Ewell, A. P. Hill and James Longstreet, were all in Pennsylvania but widely scattered. Because there had been no word from his cavalry commander, Major General J. E. B. ('Jeb') Stuart who was to secure the Confederate right flank in the march north, Lee assumed that the Federal Army was not a threat. But Stuart had become separated from the main Confederate Army and forced to circle behind the northward moving Union troops. On the evening of 28 June, with his own forces dangerously dispersed, Lee learned that Hooker's army was massed near Frederick, Maryland, closer to portions of Lee's army than these were to each other. Lee had to concentrate at once. If he did not do so, his army would be destroyed piecemeal.

The Confederates assembled at Gettysburg, a little town of 2,400 people and major road hub. The Army of Northern Virginia came in from the northwest, the Army of the Potomac from the south. Union forces also had a new commander, Major General George Gordon Meade. Hooker had been quarrelling with his superiors in Washington, and on the 28 June President Abraham

Artistic rendering of fighting between Union troops (left) and Confederate soldiers (right) during the second day of the battle, 2 July 1863. Hand-coloured lithograph published by Currier & Ives.

Lincoln replaced him. Hooker had been a capable corps commander, but he had dithered and allowed Lee (with half his numbers) to win a brilliant victory at Chancellorsville in May. Lincoln and his advisors doubted Hooker could stand up to Lee; while it often took Meade some time to make decisions, he was nevertheless a reliable and unflappable commander.

Preliminary contact between the two forces occurred near Gettysburg on 30 June. Union cavalry under Brigadier General John Buford entered Gettysburg and sighted A. P. Hill's Confederate infantry scavangers west of the town. Buford sent back word to Major General Joseph Reynolds, commander of the Union I Corps and of Meade's left wing. Buford decided to try to hold Gettysburg as both sides rushed resources forward.

Union and Confederate positions at Gettysburg, 3 July 1863.

The battle

The battle of Gettysburg lasted three days. The first day, 1 July, was a Confederate victory. Reynolds reached the town in mid-morning and moved his infantry forward to replace Buford's cavalry. Reynolds was killed while directing the placement of units. In early afternoon, Major General Oliver Howard's Union XI Corps reached the field, taking up positions north of Gettysburg.

In fierce fighting that followed, the Confederates drove the Union troops back through Gettysburg into strong positions on Cemetery Hill and Culp's Hill. Reynolds and Buford had purchased just sufficient time, for the resultant Union defensive line – which came to be known for its shape as the Fishhook – was Meade's greatest single advantage. The Fishhook was anchored on the right by Culp's Hill. It ran westward to Cemetery Hill, then south along Cemetery Ridge to the two Round Tops. Union cavalry screened the flanks. The Confederates, meanwhile, occupied Seminary Ridge, a long, partially wooded rise running north and south parallel to Cemetery Ridge. The first day's battle had been costly for the Union; two-thirds of the 18,000 Federals who fought on 1 July were casualties.

The second day revealed the advantage of the Fishhook, as Meade, operating from interior lines, could more easily shift about troops and supplies than could Lee. Longstreet urged an effort to

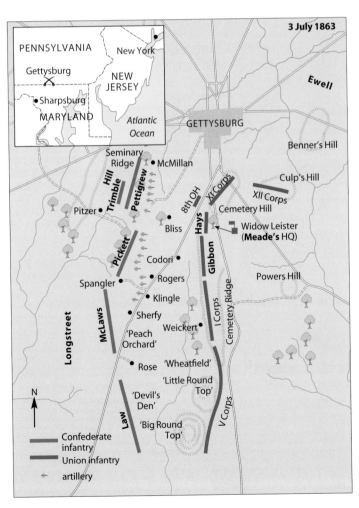

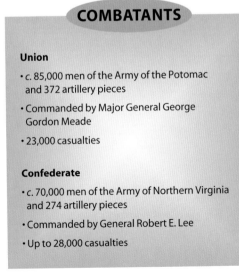

COMBATANTS

Union

• *c.* 85,000 men of the Army of the Potomac and 372 artillery pieces

• Commanded by Major General George Gordon Meade

• 23,000 casualties

Confederate

• *c.* 70,000 men of the Army of Northern Virginia and 274 artillery pieces

• Commanded by General Robert E. Lee

• Up to 28,000 casualties

Far left *Major General George Gordon Meade, commander of the Union Army of the Potomac.*

Left *General Robert E. Lee, commander of the Confederate Army of Northern Virginia.*

secure the Round Tops at the south of the Union defensive line and then swing around behind the Union forces threatening Baltimore and Washington, to draw Meade from his defensive positions. Lee, however, planned a two-pronged attack on the Union flanks.

These attacks occurred one after the other, enabling Meade to contain both. Longstreet's march beyond the Union left and its observation posts took much of the afternoon. Nonetheless, the Confederate attack by two divisions against the Union left under Major General Daniel Sickles, commander of III Corps, was successful. Sickles had foolishly left Cemetery Ridge and moved in advance of the rest of the Union line, forming a salient that was completely unsupported.

Fighting here raged through locations that became famous: the Peach Orchard, the Wheatfield, Devil's Den and Little Round Top. Meade now shifted forces south and, although Sickles's men were driven back to Cemetery Ridge, they held that position. The Confederates also failed to take Little Round Top, thanks to Colonel Joshua Chamberlain's badly outnumbered 20th Maine Regiment, rushed there just in time. Had the Confederates been successful here, it would have enabled Longstreet to enfilade the entire Union line.

The fighting then shifted to the Union centre. Although Hill attacked with insufficient numbers, one Confederate brigade briefly secured a lodgement on Cemetery Ridge. To the north, at twilight two Confederate brigades were driven back from Cemetery Hill, and Ewell's attack on Culp's Hill was also rebuffed. The second day ended a draw.

On the third day Lee planned a massive Confederate attack from Seminary Ridge against the center of the Union line, held by Major General Winfield Scott Hancock's II Corps. The Confederate cavalry under Stuart, which had arrived only

Below *Participants in a modern reconstruction of the battle of Gettysburg.*

the day before, was to sweep around the Union line from the north, but was defeated 8 km (5 miles) east of the battlefield by Union cavalry.

At about 1 pm, the Confederates began a massive artillery barrage with some 160 guns from Seminary Ridge. More than 100 Union guns on Cemetery Ridge replied in a two-hour cannonade. Then the guns all fell silent and the Confederates began their assault over 1.5 km (1 mile) of open ground in ranks the same distance wide, battle flags flying as if on parade. There were three divisions in the charge, with Major General George Pickett's in the centre. The two others faded away and streamed back towards the Confederate lines, leaving Pickett's division alone and exposed to enfilading Union fire. Only a few hundred Confederates reached the Union line, where they were halted. Out of about 12,000–13,500 men, Pickett lost between 8,000 and 10,000 that day.

Lee then shortened his line. He remained in place along Seminary Ridge the next day, hoping that Meade would attack him, but the Union commander refused to take the bait. Finally, on the night of 4 July Lee decamped, taking advantage of darkness and heavy rain to withdraw down the Cumberland Valley and into Virginia, with captured booty and even 6,000 prisoners.

Aftermath

In the battle itself, Meade lost some 23,000 men. Lee's losses were as great as those of the Union and possibly as high as 28,000 men. Although the South trumpeted a victory, cooler heads could see that this was a Confederate defeat. The Army of the Potomac had at last lived up to its promise. The Union victory at Gettysburg, coupled with the simultaneous success at Vicksburg, Mississippi, decisively tipped the military/diplomatic balance in favour of the North. From this point, the Confederacy was on an unrelenting slide to defeat.

A dead Confederate soldier in the Devil's Den, Gettysburg.

Sadowa

Date: 3 July 1866   Location: modern Sadová, Czech Republic

The path was crammed with men fleeing from the right wing. Cavalry, infantry, artillery, trains, everything; we couldn't clear them out or restore any kind of order. Our columns were broken up. The enemy directed his fire into this overfilled ravine and every ball hit home. We retreated, leaving thousands dead.
AN AUSTRIAN OFFICER AT SADOWA, 1866

Prussia's victory over Denmark in 1864 led to the Prussian acquisition of the provinces of Schleswig and Holstein. Austria soon led a coalition that included Bavaria, Saxony and Hanover to resist further Prussian gains and to balance an Italian-Prussian alliance. With war looming, Prussian forces, under the command of General Helmuth von Moltke, mobilized and prepared for deployment in June 1866. The superiority of Prussian staff work soon yielded important advantages. Moltke used six different railway lines to concentrate three armies across a 500-km (312-mile) arc in Bohemia, catching the much slower Austrians off guard.

Not expecting so rapid a movement and concentration of his opponent's forces, Austrian General Ludwig von Benedek had suffered a series of local defeats before placing his forces between the towns of Sadowa and Königgrätz. His deployment was better suited to the 18th than the 19th century. The Austrians deployed with their backs to the Elbe River, their right flank sitting on low ground, their left flank virtually unprotected. This position was ill-suited to their lines of retreat and their reserves were too close to the main forces. The Austrians thus placed themselves in a position to be encircled if the Prussians could locate them and strike quickly.

Far left *One of the designers of the modern general staff system and an early convert to railways, General Helmuth von Moltke grasped the importance of planning and preparation.*

Left *General Ludwig von Benedek's heroic status at Solferino (1859) was destroyed after Sadowa, when Austria made him a national scapegoat for the loss.*

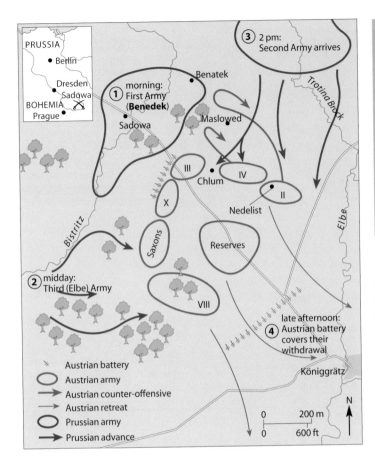

PRUSSIA
- Berlin
- Dresden
- Sadowa
BOHEMIA
- Prague

① morning:
First Army
(**Benedek**)

Benatek

③ 2 pm:
Second Army arrives

Trotina Brook

Maslowed

Sadowa

III
Chlum

IV

II

X

Nedelist

Saxons

Reserves

② midday:
Third (Elbe) Army

VIII

Bistritz

Elbe

late afternoon:
④ Austrian battery
covers their
withdrawal

Königgrätz

Austrian battery
Austrian army
Austrian counter-offensive
Austrian retreat
Prussian army
Prussian advance

N

0 ——— 200 m
0 ——— 600 ft

The Austrian position left exposed flanks that the better-armed Prussians were able to exploit.

COMBATANTS

Prussians
- 225,000 men
- Commanded by General Helmuth von Moltke
- 9,000 dead and wounded

Austrians and Saxons
- 230,000 men
- Commanded by General Ludwig von Benedek
- 20,000 dead and wounded; 20,000 prisoners

Benedek had gained fame by saving the Austrian army in the wake of the defeat at Solferino in 1859. Now he commanded a demoralized and polyglot force that was almost 60 per cent Slav. These soldiers cared little for a war to decide who would become master of Germany. Austrian staff work was clearly inferior to that of the Prussians, leading Benedek to become pessimistic about Austria's ultimate chances of winning the war. He had already asked his emperor to sue for peace and been refused. Now he was poorly positioned, poorly informed and poorly armed.

Moltke needed to win a quick war to keep France neutral and avoid long supply lines from Prussia. His scouts located the Austrians on 2 July amid a driving rain storm. Moltke planned to advance the next morning with all three of his armies and cut the Austrians off from retreat with his cavalry. If all went to plan he could destroy Benedek's army, despite both forces being roughly equivalent sizes, *c.* 250,000 men each.

Nevertheless, as Moltke himself once observed, no plan survives first contact with the enemy. Due to a failure of his telegraphic communications, the Second Army did not receive its orders and thus did not attack. By mid-morning Austrian artillery had held the other two Prussian armies at bay, leaving them few gains except in a wooded area in the centre known as the Swiepwald. The Austrians unwisely decided to counter-attack to reclaim the woods, advancing directly into the path of solid Prussian infantry using breech-loading rifles known as needle guns. These weapons allowed the Prussians to disperse, fire lying down, and remain concealed.

The Second Army arrival

By midday the Austrians had been bloodied, but showed few signs of breaking. They did not, however, know of the approach of the Second Army. Upon hearing the sounds of the battle in the morning the Second Army began advancing, reaching the right flank of the Austrian army at around 2 pm. The Prussians advanced in dispersed formations, hitting the same exhausted units that had been attacked in the Swiepwald. The subsequent advance of the Prussian First Army in the centre held the Austrian centre in place, leaving the right flank to face the withering fire of the Second Army by itself. It soon collapsed, taking with it any hope of Austrian victory. Poor weather slowed the Prussians enough to allow Benedek to order counter-attacks to cover a retreat. He was thus able to extricate his army as

he had done at Solferino seven years earlier.

The Austrian army survived, but it had been badly hit. More than 40,000 Austrians were killed or wounded and a further 20,000 had become prisoners of war. Prussia lost just 9,000 men in all. Militarily, Sadowa helped to establish the reputation of the Prussian army, particularly that of its General Staff. Prussian efficiency, technological superiority and tactical sophistication clearly outclassed those of their opponents. Prussia used the same system, with a few refinements, to defeat France in the 1870–71 Franco-Prussian War .

The Treaty of Prague

The political ramifications of the battle were just as impressive. In the Treaty of Prague, signed on 23 August, Austria agreed to exclude itself from German affairs and recognize Prussian dominance of the North German Confederation. Having lost their influence in Germany, Austria decided to move its power east and south. Conse-

quently, it negotiated with Hungary to form the Dual Monarchy in 1867. Thereafter, Austrian influence would be directed into central Europe and the Balkans. The defeat at Sadowa also forced Austria to abandon its campaign in the Veneto, allowing Italian forces to retake Venice and embark on the final stages of unification.

The terms that German Chancellor Otto von Bismarck presented to the Austrians at Prague were in fact more generous than they need have been. With Austria thoroughly beaten on the battlefield and its leaders fearful of revolution, Bismarck could have demanded much harsher terms. Although the Prussians did demand an indemnity, Austria lost none of its territory. The two German powers remained on relatively good terms in the years immediately following the war. By 1879 relations between the two states were cordial enough to lead to the conclusion of the Dual Alliance, the first step in the interlocking alliance system that led Europe to war in 1914.

This painting captures some of the confusion in the midst of battle. More organized Prussian staff work made the Prussians better suited to deal with this uncertainty, providing an important advantage on the battlefield.

Omdurman

Date: 2 September 1898   Location: near Khartoum, central Sudan

It was not a battle, but an execution.
G. W. STEEVENS, *WITH KITCHENER TO KHARTUM*, 1898

C. M. Horsfall's post-Omdurman portrait of Kitchener, now ennobled and a celebrity, conveys the image of forbidding sternness and ruthlessness its subject cultivated.

Omdurman was the highpoint of the success of British military imperialism against native resistance and ended the Mahdiyya, the dervish state in the nominally Egyptian Sudan. Though Britain had occupied Egypt in 1882, control of the Sudan was lost to the Mahdi's militantly revivalist Islamic movement. Defeats for British-led forces had culminated in the death of General Charles Gordon at Khartoum in 1885.

Britain and Egypt, the latter effectively ruled by the British Consul-General Lord Cromer, left the Sudan to the Khalifa, the Mahdi's successor, for a decade. Avenging Gordon's death was a popular cause in Britain, but it was not the motive for the reconquest of 1896–98. Lord Salisbury, Conservative Prime Minister, ordered a diversion to aid the Italians, defeated by Abyssinia at Adowa early in 1896, and to head off any alliance between Abyssinia, the Khalifa and France. But the successful Egyptian advance south along the Nile towards Dongola showed the willingness of native troops to fight fellow-Muslims, and London learned of a French military expedition heading for the Upper Nile Valley.

Salisbury and Cromer decided that the forces commanded by Major-General Herbert Kitchener, the Sirdar (commander) of the Egyptian Army, should take Omdurman, the dervish capital, and secure control of the whole Nile Valley. British resources and reinforcements were committed to the expedition, though it remained nominally Egyptian and around two-thirds of both manpower and money were provided by Egypt.

The expedition

The essence of Kitchener's campaign lay in transport and supply. He overcame the problems of distance and desert by constructing the Sudan Military Railway across the great bend of the Nile, 616 km (383 miles) in all, inspiring Winston Churchill to declare 'The Khalifa was conquered on the railway'. The line ensured the rapid flow of supplies, reinforcements and prefabricated sections of the armed river steamers which gave Kitchener effective control of the Nile and its banks, as the rising waters of the river's seasonal flood made the cataracts crossable. At the Atbara in April 1898 a Mahdist force 12,000–16,000 strong was defeated, but thereafter the dervishes offered no significant resistance as the Anglo-Egyptian army advanced along the river. The Khalifa staked all on a great battle before his capital.

The battle

The invaders reached the plains before Omdurman on the west bank of the Nile on 1 September. Native 'friendlies' secured the east bank, and artillery and the gunboats shelled the city and its defences. A great dervish army was already taking the field and Kitchener decided to protect his forces overnight within a large, semi-circular encampment backing onto the river, where the gunboats lay, with a *zariba* (thorn-wall) erected on the desert side. A night attack would have reduced the advantage of allied firepower and given the dervishes their best chance of breaching the *zariba*, but instead battle commenced in the light of early morning.

There were two phases to the battle. In the first phase, Kitchener's main forces fought an essentially defensive engagement from within the *zariba*; in the second, they moved out to advance on Omdurman and cut off the dervish retreat (Kitchener was nervous of street-fighting in a hostile city).

The first phase was dominated by the weight of Anglo-Egyptian firepower as the enemy infantry charged the perimeter en masse across the plain. The numerically superior dervishes had little artillery, no machine-guns and only muskets and obsolescent rifles with poor quality ammunition, in contrast to their opponents' modern weaponry. Kitchener's artillery, 80 pieces including those on the gunboats, opened up with shrapnel at 2,750 m (3,000 yds), the 44 Maxim guns at 1,650 m (1,800 yds) and the infantry's rifles at 1,370 m (1,500 yds).

The Egyptian battalions had the Martini-Henry rifle, the British the new Lee-Metford smokeless magazine rifle. Few dervishes survived to within 270 m (300 yds) of the perimeter and none reached it. Churchill, an eye-witness, thought the slaughter 'a mere matter of machinery'. The only allied setback was that cavalry and Camel Corps squadrons, stationed outside the *zariba* towards the Kerreri Hills, were driven further northwards by dervish cavalry; only the intervention of gunboats saved them from a mauling.

The annihilation of the dervish charges persuaded Kitchener to leave the perimeter and

Below *The campaign left valuable photographic records. Here Kitchener is shown directing operations. His refusal to employ a chief-of-staff handicapped him as a field commander, but his preparations before the battle were still decisive.*

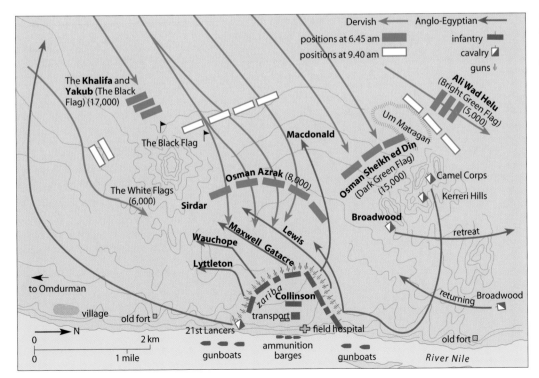

Left *The development of the battle in its two phases, before and after the main allied forces left the zariba. Both, though, were contests between dervish numbers and Anglo-Egyptian firepower.*

advance on Omdurman to cut off the remaining enemy. The decision was premature. In this second phase his forces suffered heavier losses and came close to serious reverses, and were now beyond the support of the gunboats. Kitchener had underestimated the Khalifa's reserves, held back behind hills. A cavalry charge by the 21st Lancers (in which Churchill participated) won three VCs but was both unnecessary and expensive, severe casualties among men and horses leaving the squadron unfit for pursuit duties.

The abandonment of standard echelon formation in the rush for the city left the Egyptian infantry division, commanded by Lieutenant Colonel Hector Macdonald, exposed on the advance's northwest flank and it was attacked by the Khalifa's forces from the west and then by dervishes returning from the north. 'Fighting Mac' re-aligned his division to face west and then north while under attack and fought off the assaults until relieved.

Again the weight of western firepower had told against mass charges of natives, mostly spearmen, despite their courage. Now the Khalifa's remaining forces retreated from the field and the allied march on Omdurman resumed. The city was occupied with little resistance and the harrying of the escaping dervishes continued, though the Khalifa was not finally hunted down until the following year.

The impact

This overwhelming victory emphasized the gulf between Western and native weaponry, and their respective tactics. The dervish mass charges only intensified the effect of superior allied firepower. Churchill dignified it as 'the most signal triumph ever gained by the arms of science over barbarians'. The impact of Adowa effaced, European

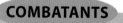

COMBATANTS

Anglo-Egyptian forces

- 8,200 British and 17,600 Egyptian and Sudanese soldiers
- Commanded by Major-General Sir Herbert Kitchener
- 48 killed; 434 wounded

Dervish forces

- c. 52,000 warriors
- Commanded by the Khalifa Abdullahi
- 9,700 killed; 10,000–16,000 wounded; 5,000 captured

might now appeared as irresistible in Africa. Strategically the outcome was decisive for British control of the whole Nile Valley, the Sudan being declared an Anglo-Egyptian condominium. Marchand's French expeditionary force which had earlier reached Fashoda was soon confronted by Kitchener's forces. After some days of international tension, Paris agreed to withdraw and concede the Nile Valley to British control. The dream of a British-dominated East Africa was closer to reality. The victory was received rapturously in Britain and Kitchener became a popular hero, despite some press criticism of the killing of dervish wounded. Any illusions about the invincibility of British forces in colonial fields would soon, however, be punctured by the Boer War.

Robert Kelly's depiction of the Khalifa's flight was wholly imaginative, but still suggests the impact which the exotic image of dervish power had on British opinion.

Modern Times

The 20th century brought a dramatic change in the range and nature of battle. Aerial combat was added, as in the defensive British victory over the Germans in the Battle of Britain (1940) and the successful American air attack on Japan (1945), and its combination of land and sea combat greatly changed both. At sea, the major exchanges between capital ships – a crushing Japanese victory over the Russians at Tsushima in 1905 and the Anglo-German battle-fleet draw at Jutland in 1916 – were replaced by conflicts dominated by air power. America's victory at Midway in 1942, for example, turned the tide in the war in the Pacific. The sinking of four heavy Japanese aircraft carriers and the loss of many aircraft and pilots shifted the naval balance, as the initiative and arithmetic of carrier power moved rapidly against the Japanese.

Air power was also brought in to influence the struggle with a new force in naval conflict: submarines, as with the Anglo-American victory over the German submarines in the battle of the Atlantic in 1943. Other factors also played a role, not least the effectiveness of convoy escorts, the Allied ability to intercept and decipher German naval codes, and the building of far more merchant shipping from 1942, particularly by the Americans. Air power had only played an ancillary role in the land battles of World War I, such as Tannenberg (1914), Verdun (1916) and the Allied offensive on the Western Front (1918), and they continued to be largely artillery and infantry affairs, although tanks played a supporting role in 1918.

During World War II, in contrast, air power was more important, as seen in the battle for

Massed American tanks in training for the Gulf War (1991), a conflict that led to 2003's Iraq War. The introduction of armoured vehicles was a key development in modern war.

dominance in the western half of Eurasia. This took the Germans as far east as Stalingrad on the Volga, but they were fought to a standstill there despite a massive commitment of resources. When, in turn, the Soviets counter-attacked, Hitler failed to respond with the necessary flexibility and forbade a retreat from Stalingrad before it was encircled. Thereafter, the Soviets advanced, driving the Germans back to the Elbe by 1945, a distance greater than that achieved by any European force for over a century. A key campaign was Operation Bagration in 1944, which overran Belarus (White Russia or Belorussia) and took the Soviets close to Warsaw, in the process destroying much of the German Army Group Centre and causing over half a million casualties as the Germans were outgeneralled and outfought.

There was also a web of wars for hegemony in the eastern half of Eurasia. Most significant were the Russo-Japanese War, in which Tsushima was the decisive battle at sea; the war in the Pacific between the USA and Japan from 1941 to 1945, in which Midway stopped the Japanese, and the American air attack on Japan ended the war; the Chinese Civil War, one of its key battles being Huai-Hai (1948–49), which led to Communist dominance; and the attempts to define the Communist position in East Asia, which led to the Korean and Vietnam Wars. The French defeat at Dien Bien Phu in 1954 led them to withdraw from Vietnam, and although the Americans – who eventually replaced them – thwarted the Communist assault in 1968 (the Tet Offensive), their inability to secure victory led to withdrawal in 1973, which was followed by the Communist overrunning of South Vietnam in 1975.

There were bloody conflicts elsewhere in the world, most particularly in Africa, but they did not focus on large-scale battles. The Iraq War of 2003 indicated clearly that victory in battle was not the same as success in war. American technological superiority, resources and training were important in leading to the rapid overthrow of Iraqi forces, but the effectiveness of guerrilla warfare and terrorist attacks challenged the sense of political control. This contrast is unlikely to diminish over the next century.

A German propaganda picture, falsely building up confidence during Stalingrad. The difficult urban terrain greatly hindered the Germans, who were then surrounded by an effective counter-attack.

Normandy, when British and American forces defeated the Germans in the key struggle for control of France in 1944. Subsequent attempts to use air power as a war-winning tool were not always successful, for example in the Vietnam War, but could be very important, as with the American-led attacks on Iraq in 1991 and 2003.

Many of the key battles of the first half of the century – Tannenberg (1914), Moscow (1941), Stalingrad (1942) and Bagration (1944) – focused on the struggle between Germany and Russia for

Tsushima

Date: 27 May 1905   Location: Island in the Korea Strait

The fate of the empire rests upon this one battle; let every man do his utmost.
(SIGNAL FLOWN FROM FLAGSHIP *MIKASA*) ADMIRAL HEIHACHIRO TOGO, 1.55 PM, 27 MAY 1905

Tensions between Russia and Japan over spheres of influence in Korea and Manchuria led to a rupture of diplomatic relations on 6 February 1904; two days later, without declaring war, the Japanese launched a surprise attack against the Russian Pacific squadron, sending ten destroyers into Port Arthur where they torpedoed two battleships and a cruiser, all of which were subsequently repaired. In the first high-seas action of the Russo-Japanese War, the Battle of the Yellow Sea (10 August 1904), Admiral Heihachiro Togo's Combined Fleet turned back an attempt by the Russian Pacific squadron to break out of Port Arthur and run for Vladivostok. Neither side lost a ship in the engagement, but the unprecedented range at which the battle was fought (between 8,000 and 9,000 m / 8,700–9,800 yds) drew worldwide attention.

Over the following months, Japanese siege guns sank four battleships and two cruisers at Port Arthur; the Russians ultimately scuttled a fifth battleship there to keep it out of enemy hands when the base surrendered (2 January 1905). Meanwhile, after the loss of an armoured cruiser in the Battle of the Sea of Japan on 14 August 1904, a Russian cruiser squadron based at Vladivostok did not venture out for the rest of the war. Japanese losses in 1904 were limited to two battleships, a small armoured cruiser and two protected cruisers (all of which struck mines) and a third protected cruiser, sunk accidentally in a collision with another Japanese warship.

After the defeats of August 1904 the Russians resolved to relieve Port Arthur with reinforcements sent from the Baltic. Admiral Zinovy Rozhestvensky's Second Pacific squadron, including most of the Russian Baltic Fleet, departed for the Far East on 15 October. Mishaps along the way included the Dogger Bank Incident (21–22 October 1904), in which jittery Russian gunners mistook a group of British North Sea fishing trawlers for 'Japanese torpedo boats', sinking one and damaging six. Afterwards only the most strenuous diplomatic efforts by France (which considered Britain and Russia natural future allies against Germany) kept Britain from declaring war.

Rozhestvensky divided his fleet off the coast of Spain, sending the smaller units to the Indian Ocean via the Mediterranean and the Suez Canal, while the battleships proceeded around the Cape of Good Hope. In January 1905 he reunited his forces off Madagascar, where he received news of the surrender of Port Arthur. In an attempt to make up for the ships lost there, Rozhestvensky received as reinforcement the Third Pacific squadron under Rear Admiral N. I. Nebogatov, a

Above left
Portrait of Admiral Rozhestvensky (1848–1909), who commanded the Russian Second and Third squadrons at Tsushima.

Above right *His enemy counterpart Heihachiro Togo (1848–1934) commanded the Japanese Combined Fleet at Tsushima.*

force consisting of older or smaller battleships and cruisers not included in Rozhestvensky's squadron owing to their lack of speed and firepower. Cruising via the Suez Canal, the Third squadron joined the Second in April 1905, at Camranh Bay in French Indo-China. The combined force then steamed northward to meet the surviving units of the Russian cruiser squadron at Vladivostok.

The battle

As Rozhestvensky's long column neared the war zone, Admiral Togo planned to intercept it in the Korea Strait as it passed the island of Tsushima. The Japanese had 12 armoured warships (4 battleships and 8 armoured cruisers), the Russians 14 (11 battleships and 3 armoured cruisers), but Togo enjoyed a clear qualitative superiority. None

of his armoured ships was more than eight years old and three of his battleships were larger than any ship in the Russian fleet. In contrast, Rozhestvensky's fleet included the three 4,970-tonne *Admiral Ushakov*-class coast defenders, and his three armoured cruisers were actually armoured frigates more than two decades old. Aside from four 13,520-tonne battleships of the *Borodino* class and the 12,680-tonne battleship *Osliabia*, his larger warships were obsolete.

Togo opened the battle at 1.40 pm on 27 May 1905, when he initiated a crossing of the Russian 'T' from east to west at a point roughly 40 km (25 miles) east of Tsushima. When he repeated the manoeuvre from west to east, Rozhestvensky responded by attempting to steam past the Japanese to the northeast, forcing Togo to give chase. At 2.08 pm Russian guns registered the first

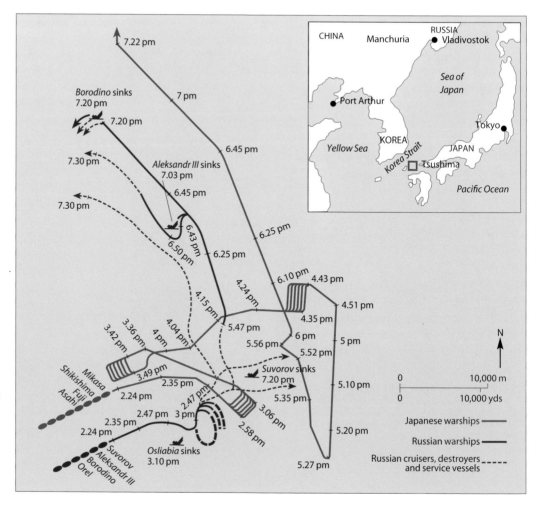

A plan of the battle of Tsushima. Action from 2.30 pm to 7.30 pm, following the first crossing of the Russian 'T' by the Japanese.

我驅逐艦速鳥朝霧冒大風雪
於順擊沈敵艦之圖

hits of the battle, against Togo's flagship, the 15,140-tonne *Mikasa*, at a range of 7,000 m (7,600 yds). Though the two fleets fought at shorter ranges than in the Battle of the Yellow Sea (at Tsushima the Japanese held their fire until closing to 6,400 m/7,000 yds), medium-calibre artillery again played little part. Once again, the Japanese advantage in speed doomed the Russian quest to reach Vladivostok but, unlike the encounter of the previous August, which had ended in a Russian retreat to Port Arthur, Rozhestvensky's fleet had nowhere else to go.

The *Osliabia* was the first casualty, sinking at 3.10 pm. As the Japanese line pulled ahead of the Russian line, Rozhestvensky doubled back and attempted to steam due north across the wake of Togo's column, but the Japanese admiral quickly doubled back to the west to cut him off. Rozhestvensky then turned away to the south, and his column began to disperse. The large stocks of coal the Russian warships carried only hastened their destruction, as widespread fires left many of them unable to defend themselves further as the Japanese closed to sink them. At the climax of the action Rozhestvensky lost three of the *Borodinos* within 30 minutes, including the flagship *Suvorov* (7.20 pm). The last fighting Russian units exchanged fire with their attackers at just 2,500 m (8,200 ft) and at such close range, medium-calibre artillery finally came into play. During the night of 27/28 May the Japanese sank or captured most of the remaining Russian warships. Rozhestvensky, severely wounded, was rescued from the *Suvorov* before it sank, only to be captured aboard a Russian destroyer. On the morning of the 28th, some 240 km (150 miles) north-northeast of Tsushima, his second-in-command Nebogatov surrendered the last of the *Borodinos* (the 13,520-tonne *Orel*) along with three smaller battleships.

Consequences

The decisive clash of battle fleets at Tsushima vindicated the 'one big battle' approach to naval warfare that Alfred Thayer Mahan had promoted in his influential work *The Influence of Sea Power upon History* (1890). The Japanese sank six

Japanese print depicting the night action of 27/28 May, during which Togo's torpedo flotilla sank several of the surviving Russian warships.

Admiral Togo's 15,140-tonne flagship, The Mikasa.

Russian battleships, one armoured cruiser and one protected cruiser, and captured another four battleships. The Russians scuttled one battleship, two armoured cruisers and one protected cruiser to prevent their capture; the three remaining Russian protected cruisers eventually made their way to Manila, to be interned by the United States. The armed yacht *Almaz* and two destroyers made it through to Vladivostok; the other sixteen smaller units were either sunk, scuttled or captured.

The Japanese lost three torpedo boats, and three of their armoured warships suffered moderate damages. The prizes they took, along with other warships raised at Port Arthur and later repaired, more than made good the losses suffered by Togo's fleet during 1904. The disastrous outcome of the largest naval engagement since Trafalgar forced Russia to the peace table. Negotiations mediated by the United States concluded in the Treaty of Portsmouth, September 1905. Russia's loss in territory (the southern half of Sakhalin Island) was minimal compared to its loss of influence in northeast Asia. Russia had to agree to transfer its lease of the Liaotung Peninsula to Japan, surrendering the naval base at Port Arthur and informal title to the former Russian sphere of influence in Manchuria. Japan also gained a free hand in Korea, which it annexed in 1910.

Contemporary naval observers had difficulty drawing lessons from Tsushima and from the Russo-Japanese War as a whole. A torpedo attack had opened the war, but neither side ever deployed a submarine. Mines sank two Japanese battleships and one Russian battleship, and concern for mines influenced the behaviour of both navies. Both made effective use of destroyers, deployed extensively in combat for the first time. At Tsushima, as at the Battle of the Yellow Sea, the big guns of the largest warships had registered hits at extraordinary ranges, thanks to new range-finders and better gun-sighting. This development ultimately overshadowed the others, providing justification for the construction of Britain's *Dreadnought* and battle cruiser designs as well as other 'all big gun' warships already on the drawing board at the time.

COMBATANTS

Japanese

- Combined Fleet: 4 battleships; 8 armoured cruisers; 7 protected cruisers; 65 destroyers or smaller vessels

- Commanded by Admiral Heihachiro Togo

- 116 dead; 538 wounded; 3 torpedo boats sunk

Russians

- Second and Third Pacific squadrons: 11 battleships; 3 armoured cruisers; 5 protected cruisers; 19 destroyers or smaller vessels

- Commanded by Admiral Zinovy Rozhestvensky

- 4,830 dead; unknown number wounded; 5,917 captured; all but 3 small vessels sunk, scuttled, captured or interned

Tannenberg

55

Date: 25–30 August 1914   Location: modern Stębark, Poland

*There is no information about the situation of the Corps of the Second Army
on the evening of the 31st.... There is no news of the XIII Corps. Isolated men
of the XV Corps are arriving in batches at Ostrolenka. A portion of the
XXIII Corps is fighting with the I Corps, a portion was with the XV Corps.*
RUSSIAN NORTHWEST HEADQUARTERS REPORT, 31 AUGUST 1914

The report above indicates the extreme state of confusion and totality of the defeat inflicted by Germany on the Russian armies at the battle of Tannenberg. It was one of the most complete victories in military history, destroying four Russian Corps despite a Russian superiority in manpower (based on their First *and* Second Armies) of nearly two to one.

The Germans had long planned to fight on the defensive in East Prussia, where the railway network facilitated rapid troop movement. German General Paul von Hindenburg had spent his retirement planning every detail of defeating a Russian invasion of East Prussia. Nevertheless, German war planning for 1914 was based on a deployment of seven armies to France, leaving just one army to face a much larger Russian force.

The defence of East Prussia became an even more critical issue in the face of a Russian mobilization that was faster than the Germans had anticipated. Russia inflicted a defeat on Germany at the battle of Gumbinnen on 20 August. The German commander, Max von Prittwitz, feared that the larger Russian forces might encircle him. When he proposed a retreat to the Vistula River, the German high command replaced him with Hindenburg, recently recalled from retirement. They also named Erich Ludendorff, one of the heroes of Germany's campaign in Belgium, as Hindenburg's chief of staff.

'The emperor trusted me'
Despite their advance, the Russians were actually

in a poor position. The commanders of the two Russian armies, Pavel Rennenkampf and Alexander Samsonov, had little information about the other's exact dispositions. The Northwest Front commander, Yakov Zhilinski, did little to resolve either the commanders' confusion or their well-known enmity for one another. As a result, the Russians moved cautiously and in a manner that did not incline them to support one another in the event of a German attack. Their communications, moreover, depended upon radio links and uncoded messages, yielding important clues to German eavesdroppers.

Upon their arrival in the east, Hindenburg and Ludendorff reviewed a staff officer's aggressive

Erich Ludendorff and Paul von Hindenburg assumed leadership of the German Eighth Army shortly before Tannenberg. Their success in directing the battle set them on a course that eventually made them the two most powerful men in Germany.

plan to insert the German Eighth Army between the Russian First and Second Armies. The plan was risky, but it fitted in with General Staff teachings about interior lines of communications and with ideas that Hindenburg and Ludendorff had discussed during their train ride east.

The German plan involved screening Rennenkampf with one cavalry division and redirecting the remainder of the German forces against Samsonov. While Samsonov moved westwards unaware of the danger mounting around him, a German corps under the aggressive

Herman von François moved east, surrounding the Russians. The main German attack then came from the southwest, thus trapping Samsonov's army. The arrival of additional forces from the north completed the encirclement.

Russian units soon found themselves attacked from several sides and suffering heavy casualties. By 28 August, Samsonov's XIII and XV Corps were engaged in fierce combat with German forces. Trapped among swamps and lakes, Samsonov could not redeploy his forces, increasing the confusion. His decision to move forward and direct operations from XV Corps headquarters left him unable to direct the battle as a whole. The next day, the XV Corps failed to break out of the encirclement and soon found its constituent units jumbled with those of the XIII. After telling his chief of staff, 'The emperor trusted me. How can I face him again after such a disaster?', Samsonov disappeared, committing suicide later that day.

Although Rennenkampf's cavalry was within striking distance of the main German attack, he remained largely ignorant of the crisis in front of Samsonov. German forces attacking Samsonov's

Above *German infantry, with their classic spike helmets, advance. Their initial mission was to defend East Prussia, but Hindenburg and Ludendorff soon developed plans to use them in a major offensive aimed at destroying two Russian armies.*

Right *The Masurian Lakes limited Russian ability to concentrate their superior numbers, providing the Germans with an enticing opportunity.*

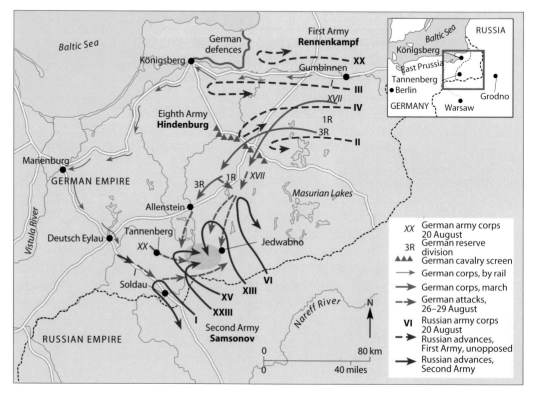

Russian soldiers fight from an improvised trench. Poor leadership and poor training doomed thousands of Russians to death or imprisonment.

right also blocked approaches to the town of Allenstein, further impeding any possible move by Rennenkampf. As it became evident that the Germans were moving large numbers of forces around him, Rennenkampf reacted by retreating his forces east. That decision undoubtedly gave him a temporary respite from German movements, but it left Samsonov with no support.

The Russians lost 30,000 dead, more than 130,000 prisoners, and 500 heavy guns. The Germans had to devote 60 trains to transporting the horses and equipment taken from the Russians. Hoffman suggested calling the great victory Tannenberg after the nearby sight of a battle in 1410 in which Polish and Lithuanian warriors slaughtered the Teutonic Knights.

COMBATANTS

German forces
- Eighth Army: 200,000 men
- Commanded by Paul von Hindenburg, Erich Ludendorff
- 10,000 dead and wounded

Russian forces
- Second Army: 150,000 men
- Commanded by Alexander Samsonov
- 30,000 dead; 130,000 prisoners

The aftermath

Tannenberg helped the Central Powers to survive the early months of the war. This victory counterbalanced the German setback at the Marne River near Paris less than two weeks later. It also helped to relieve the pressure from Austria-Hungary, whose chaotic mobilization and war planning had led to early defeats. Perhaps most importantly, Tannenberg greatly reduced any threat of a Russian invasion of the German heartland.

For Russia, this crushing defeat led its main allies, Britain and France, to have grave doubts about the fighting ability of their colossal but clumsy partner. Tannenberg left the Russians off balance, allowing the Germans to strike again at the battle of the Masurian Lakes. Between 7 and 14 September, the same German forces that had destroyed Samsonov's First Army routed Rennenkampf's Second Army. The Russians lost 140,000 more men. Only German exhaustion prevented an even greater disaster.

Combined with the end of the Schlieffen Plan in the west, Tannenberg caused a fundamental shift in German grand strategy. Hindenburg and Ludendorff became confirmed 'easterners', believing that victory was more likely against Russia than in France. In 1915 they had their chance, inflicting huge damage on Russia in the Gorlice-Tarnów campaign. Even this defeat failed to destroy the Russian giant, leaving Germany with the two-front war it knew it could not win.

56

Jutland

**Date: 31 May–1 June 1916 Location: Skaggerak Strait,
off Denmark's North Sea coast**

There seems to be something wrong with our bloody ships today.
VICE ADMIRAL DAVID BEATTY, AFTER THE EXPLOSION OF THE *QUEEN MARY*,
THE SECOND BRITISH BATTLE CRUISER SUNK AT JUTLAND, 4.26 PM, 31 MAY 1916

*Admiral Sir
John Jellicoe
(1859–1935),
commander of
Britain's Grand
Fleet at Jutland.*

After the outbreak of World War I, German strategy called for Rear Admiral Franz Hipper's battle cruiser squadron to be used as bait to draw a portion of the British Grand Fleet into battle in the North Sea with the rest of their High Seas Fleet, reasoning that if the entire German fleet could be brought to bear to destroy a part of the British fleet, Germany's numerical inferiority in capital ships could be erased in a single stroke. In the first such sortie to result in contact with the British, the battle of Dogger Bank (24 January 1915), Hipper's squadron of three battle cruisers and the armoured cruiser *Blücher* lured Vice Admiral Sir David Beatty's five battle cruisers out of Rosyth, then steamed back towards Wilhelmshaven. But in the ensuing action, the British sank the *Blücher* while not losing a ship of their own.

Kaiser Wilhelm II responded to the defeat by relieving Admiral Friedrich von Ingenohl, commander of the High Seas Fleet and Hipper's superior, for keeping the main body of German dreadnoughts too far from the battle cruisers to come to their aid or to trap the British battle cruiser squadron. The emperor subsequently kept Ingenohl's successor, Admiral Hugo von Pohl, on such a short leash that the High Seas Fleet practically rusted at anchor.

Early in 1916 Vice Admiral Reinhard Scheer succeeded Pohl and persuaded the emperor to allow the High Seas Fleet to resume sorties, with Hipper's battle cruisers again used to lure out the British. Unlike Ingenohl on the day of Dogger Bank, however, Scheer intended to keep his dreadnoughts close enough to rescue Hipper and

destroy the British forces that came out to chase him. Sorties in February, March and April of 1916 brought no contact with British capital ships, but Scheer's fourth sortie resulted in the battle of Jutland, the largest naval engagement of the war. In the predawn hours of 31 May, five battle cruisers under Hipper's command steamed northward from Wilhelmshaven, parallel with the coast of Danish Jutland in the direction of the Skaggerak Strait, with Scheer's sixteen dreadnoughts, six predreadnoughts and a host of smaller warships following some 80 km (50 miles) behind.

As at Dogger Bank, Beatty's battle cruisers came out of Rosyth to intercept Hipper, this time followed by the rest of the Grand Fleet under Admiral Sir John Jellicoe, from Scapa Flow. On the British side, as on the German, the main body of the fleet followed roughly 80 km (50 miles) behind the battle cruiser force. Owing to a recent exchange of ships between Beatty and Jellicoe, Beatty had 6 battle cruisers and 4 dreadnoughts, and Jellicoe had 24 dreadnoughts and 3 battle cruisers.

Light cruisers screening for Beatty and Hipper first engaged at 2.28 pm, just over 160 km (100 miles) west of the Jutland coast. The two battle cruiser forces began their exchange at 3.48 pm. After sighting the British battle cruisers, Hipper turned away to the south-southeast, running back towards Scheer so as to draw Beatty into battle with the entire High Seas Fleet.

The first phase of the battle, later called the 'run to the south', lasted 50 minutes. Steaming south-southeast on parallel courses, the two columns of battle cruisers duelled at a range of 11,000–14,500 m (12,000–16,000 yds). Gunfire

from the *Von der Tann* sank the *Indefatigable* at 4.02 pm, and shells from the *Derfflinger* sank the *Queen Mary* at 4.26. Twelve minutes later, when Beatty sighted the main body of the High Seas Fleet steaming up from the south, he reversed course to the north, hoping to draw the entire German fleet onto Jellicoe's advancing force.

During the second phase of the battle, or 'run to the north', neither side lost a capital ship. But the 38-cm (15-inch) guns of the four *Queen Elizabeth*-class dreadnoughts now bringing up Beatty's rear overmatched the 27- and 30-cm (11- and 12-inch) guns of Hipper's battle cruisers, now at the head of the German column, inflicting considerable damage. The Germans first encountered the main British force at 5.36 pm, when a light cruiser Jellicoe had sent on ahead met light cruisers of Hipper's group.

By 6.15 pm, Beatty's ships had joined Jellicoe's line, and the entire British force crossed the German 'T', steaming eastward in an east-west line. The old armoured cruisers *Defence* and *Warrior*, deployed with Beatty's battle cruisers at the head of the column, came under heavy fire from the German capital ships at a range of barely 7,300 m (8,000 yds). While the *Warrior* survived to be towed from the scene at the end of the day (to founder and sink the next morning), the *Defence* sank at 6.20 pm, followed by a third British battle cruiser, the *Invincible*, at 6.32 pm. Hipper's battle cruisers, still heading the German column, suffered in the exchange but remained afloat, although his flagship *Lützow* sustained enough damage to force the admiral to transfer to another ship.

By 6.45 pm, the entire German column had turned away to the southwest, only to double back to the northeast just before 7 pm. When battle resumed minutes later, Jellicoe achieved a second crossing of the 'T' by slowing his line,

German dreadnought König in dock after Jutland, where it sustained ten hits from British heavy guns. In the decade between the launching of HMS Dreadnought (1906) and the battle of Jutland, Britain had completed 42 'all big gun' capital ships (dreadnoughts and battle cruisers) to 22 for Germany. Of these, 37 British and 21 German capital ships saw action at Jutland.

leaving the lead ships of Scheer's column bearing directly into his starboard flank. By 7.15 pm the entire British line was concentrating fire on the German column from a range of 10,000 to 12,800 m (11,000–14,000 yds), scoring hits as far back as the eleventh ship. Scheer again turned away to the southwest, this time in disarray. Around 7.35 pm, with about 30 minutes of daylight remaining, Jellicoe opted not to pursue the Germans. Fear that enemy torpedoes would claim still more of his capital ships swayed him from trying for the decisive victory then within his grasp.

As darkness fell, Jellicoe reconsidered and ordered the Grand Fleet to pursue the fleeing Germans. The fifth and final phase of the battle began with the High Seas Fleet already enjoying a 16-km (10-mile) lead over its pursuer, but the British closed fast. By 8.30 pm the two fleets were steaming almost due south, the British between the Germans and the Jutland coast. Around midnight the British lost the armoured cruiser *Black Prince* after it blundered into Scheer's dreadnoughts. But the warship losses of 1 June were all German, including the battle cruiser *Lützow*, torpedoed by a German destroyer after finally being abandoned around 3 am, and the pre-dreadnought *Pommern*, torpedoed by a British destroyer at 3.13 am. Remarkably, the High Seas Fleet made it home despite the fact that, for several hours during the night of 31 May/1 June, the British fleet was actually closer to Wilhelmshaven. The Germans survived because Scheer steered a course much closer to the Jutland and Schleswig coasts than Jellicoe anticipated; steaming south-southeast, the main body of his fleet ultimately crossed the wake of the British force heading south-southwest.

Outcome

At Jutland, the Germans clearly inflicted more damage than they suffered, sinking 3 battle cruisers, 3 armoured cruisers, 1 flotilla leader and 7 destroyers, while losing 1 battle cruiser, 1 pre-dreadnought battleship, 4 light cruisers and 5 destroyers of their own. Aside from Scheer's good luck and Jellicoe's moments of caution, Jutland

The escape of the High Seas Fleet. A German artist's rendition of the action on the morning of 1 June 1916.

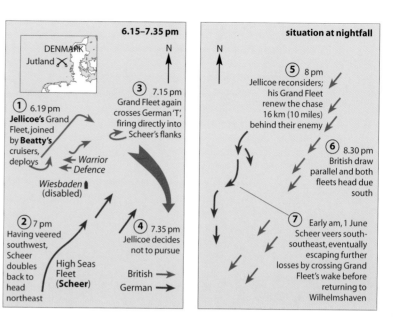

DENMARK
Jutland ✕

6.15–7.35 pm

N

① 6.19 pm
Jellicoe's Grand
Fleet, joined
by **Beatty's**
cruisers,
deploys

③ 7.15 pm
Grand Fleet again
crosses German 'T',
firing directly into
Scheer's flanks

← *Warrior*
← *Defence*

Wiesbaden
(disabled)

② 7 pm
Having veered
southwest,
Scheer
doubles
back to
head
northeast

High Seas
Fleet
(Scheer)

④ 7.35 pm
Jellicoe decides
not to pursue

British ⟶
German ⟶

situation at nightfall

N

⑤ 8 pm
Jellicoe reconsiders;
his Grand Fleet
renew the chase
16 km (10 miles)
behind their enemy

⑥ 8.30 pm
British draw
parallel and both
fleets head due
south

⑦ Early am, 1 June
Scheer veers south-
southeast, eventually
escaping further
losses by crossing Grand
Fleet's wake before
returning to
Wilhelmshaven

turned out this way largely because of the sturdier construction of the German capital ships, the unsafe handling of unstable powder supplies aboard the larger British warships, and poor fire control especially on the British side. The Germans claimed 'Skaggerak' (their designation for the battle) as a great victory, even though afterwards, the British remained in command of the North Sea. Realizing that the battle had done nothing to alter the strategic situation, on 4 July 1916 Scheer advised Wilhelm II that the only hope for victory at sea lay in a U-boat war against British commerce. The High Seas Fleet sortied into the North Sea again in August, October and November of 1916, then only once more (April 1918) before steaming to Scapa Flow to be interned under the Armistice.

Aftermath

While the war in the North Sea went their way after Jutland, the British were deeply disappointed by the battle, having expected that the much-anticipated encounter with the High Seas Fleet would result in a second Trafalgar. Jellicoe and Beatty (or, more accurately, their supporters within the officer corps) each blamed the other for opportunities missed. At the end of 1916 Beatty became commander of the Grand Fleet, when Jellicoe was appointed First Sea Lord. Meanwhile, in Germany, Wilhelm II promoted Scheer to full admiral and awarded him the Iron Cross *Pour le Mérite*, the country's highest military decoration. An officer corps historically fragmented by infighting rallied around Scheer, excusing his tactical errors at Jutland. He finally turned over command of the High Seas Fleet to Hipper in August 1918, then spent the last months of the war as Chief of the Supreme Navy Command.

Above left *The tradition of Victorian genre-painting used for moral example and fund-raising. The 16-year-old John Cornwell, V.C., Boy First Class aboard the light cruiser* Chester *at Jutland, earned a posthumous Victoria Cross for manning a gun throughout the battle, despite being mortally wounded early in the action.*

Above middle and right *Jutland evening and night action respectively. After the initial runs to the south and north, at 5.30 pm Beatty's run to the northwest drew Scheer towards the Grand Fleet.*

COMBATANTS

Germans

- High Seas Fleet: 16 dreadnoughts; 5 battle cruisers; 6 pre-dreadnought battleships; 11 light cruisers; 61 destroyers
- Commanded by Vice Admiral Reinhard Scheer
- 2,551 dead; 1 battle cruiser, 1 pre-dreadnought battleship, 4 light cruisers and 5 destroyers sunk

British

- Grand Fleet: 28 dreadnoughts; 9 battle cruisers; 8 armoured cruisers; 26 light cruisers or flotilla leaders; 78 destroyers; 1 minelayer
- Commanded by Admiral Sir John Jellicoe
- 6,097 dead; 3 battle cruisers, 3 armoured cruisers, 1 flotilla leader and 7 destroyers sunk

57

Verdun

Date: 21 February–mid-December 1916 Location: Lorraine, northeast France

Whole regiments melted in a few minutes, but others took their places, only to perish in the same way. 'It is a battle of madmen in the midst of a volcanic eruption' was the description given by a staff captain....West of the Meuse men died in the open air, but at Douaumont in the horror of darkness, they fought in tunnels, screaming with the lust of butchery, deafened by shells and grenades, stifled by smoke.

GEORGE LA HIR, *NEW YORK TIMES*, 1916

On 16 January 1916, French Commander-in-Chief General Joseph Joffre told a visitor to his headquarters at the sumptuous Château de Chantilly: 'I ask only one thing, that the Germans should attack and should do so at Verdun. Tell the government so.' Joffre was responding to criticisms that he had left Verdun relatively unguarded by removing men and heavy guns from the garrison. Lieutenant Colonel Emile Driant, a member of France's Chamber of Deputies and a battalion commander in the Bois des Caures on Verdun's outer defensive line, had written to his colleagues in Paris warning them of immense German preparations opposite his position. Joffre and his staff, Driant believed, had left Verdun unable to withstand a determined German attack. Minister of War General Joseph Galliéni had told Joffre of Driant's letter in mid-

December 1915. Joffre's confident comments one month later were meant to put the issue of Verdun to rest.

Verdun's ring of fortresses guarded the strategically important Meuse River and the eastern approaches to Paris. But Verdun held an importance out of proportion to its military worth. It was a national symbol of resistance, having withstood Prussian and German attacks for centuries. The modern French and German nations (as well as the middle ground that includes Alsace and Lorraine) owed their births to the Treaty of Verdun in 843. The city's fall would be a spectacular blow to French morale.

Accordingly, France reinvested in Verdun's fortresses in the years before World War I. By 1912 Verdun was defended by 60 individual forts and outposts. It was one of the strongest and best protected places in the world. It had held out against German attacks in 1914, leading Joffre to remove 4,000 of its heavy artillery pieces for use on other fronts. These removals, with an accompanying reduction in personnel, had prompted Driant's letters.

German plans

Germany's Chief of the General Staff, General Erich von Falkenhayn, believed that he had found a way to win the war in the west in 1916. His observations of the war's first two years in the west had led him to conclude that the defenders almost everywhere held an immense tactical

German infantrymen preparing to advance into the Verdun sector. Their commander, Erich von Falkenhayn, hoped that his methods would kill French soldiers at an acceptable ratio to German losses.

This famous photograph from Verdun shows the desperation of infantry assaults. These men are advancing in the face of German machine gun and rifle fire.

advantage and that the acquisition of territory mattered for little. Consequently, he created a battle plan that, he hoped, would force his enemies to send waves of soldiers to attack a place of tremendous significance to them, but of less significance to Germany. He could therefore methodically use the tactical advantage of the defensive to destroy enemy counter-attacks.

Verdun was custom-made for Falkenhayn's purpose. German lines of communication to the Verdun sector were sufficient to support a major offensive, while France could only supply the city through one road. If the Germans could assemble a large force without detection and capture Verdun quickly, its strategic and symbolic importance to France would compel the French to dedicate enormous military resources to its recapture. Once the battle had begun, Falken-

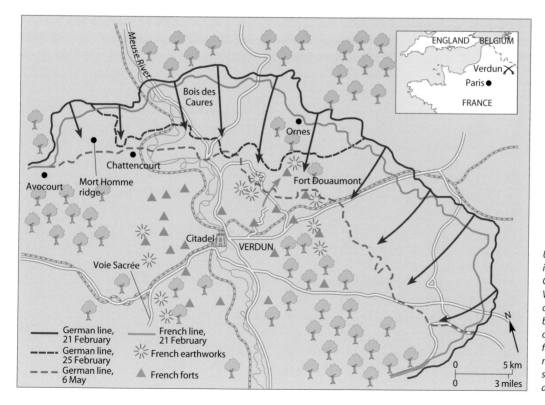

German line, 21 February

German line, 25 February

German line, 6 May

French line, 21 February

French earthworks

French forts

0 — 5 km

0 — 3 miles

Unlike most battles in this volume, the German goal at Verdun was not the capture of territory, but the elimination of the enemy's forces in a nightmarish struggle of attrition.

hayn believed, he could manage the killing in such a way that would 'bleed France white,' and attrite French forces faster and more completely than his own forces. With the French army beaten, England would seek favourable peace terms, leaving Germany free to focus on the Eastern Front in 1917.

German preparations for the attack yielded enormous advantages in both heavy artillery – 1,400 pieces in all – and manpower. Four days after Joffre's defiant statement, mounting Parliamentary pressure led him to ask General Eduoard de Castelnau to go to Verdun and assess the seriousness of the situation for himself. Castelnau agreed with Driant that an attack was imminent and that Verdun was too weak to defend itself, but his dispatch of a battalion of engineers to improve the forts was utterly insufficient to defend the city.

Germany attacks

The weakness of French defences became apparent when Falkenhayn's artillery began its assault on 21 February. German guns fired almost 2,000,000 shells. Fort Douaumont, Verdun's strongest, was the target for 120,000 shells. German infantry then advanced along the east bank of the Meuse River, marching directly at Driant's position in the Bois des Caures. The French commander and his battalion were woefully outnumbered, but held on long enough to allow those behind them to gain strong defensive positions. Driant's death on 22 February made him a great national hero, but could not prevent the Germans from capturing the position.

The slow German advance frustrated its army and corps commanders who, misled by Falkenhayn, believed that their goal was to capture Verdun. Falkenhayn, however, was pleased with the campaign's early stages. He had the 'killing cauldron' he had sought. On 25 February a small

Henri Philippe Pétain had been one of the lone advocates of defensive warfare in the years before World War I. His careful and methodical approach to defensive warfare made him the obvious choice to command the Verdun sector.

group of German advance troops found an unguarded opening into Fort Douaumont and captured it without firing a shot. Its loss was a great shock to the French people. Both sides rushed reinforcements into the Verdun sector to continue a battle that had already attained mythic status.

Falkenhayn had hoped to limit his offensive to the east bank of the Meuse in order to control the battle more carefully. Heavy French artillery fire from the west bank, however, inflicted enormous casualties. Much of that fire came from the appropriately named Mort Homme ('Dead Man') ridge. The Germans thus decided to extend their offensive to both banks of the river on 6 March. Falkenhayn's carefully managed battle quickly began to grow beyond his control.

France counter-attacks

In April, under new commander Henri Philippe Pétain, the French began counter-attacks. The back-and-forth fighting became as savage as any in the course of the war. One village changed hands fifteen times in three weeks. In a bid to recapture Fort Douaumont, the French fired 1,000 tons of artillery shells per day for four days on a plot of land measuring just 60 hectares (150 acres). In mid-July, in the wake of a Russian attack

COMBATANTS

French

- 500,000 men; 270 artillery pieces (Army Group Centre)
- Commanded by Henri Philippe Pétain (under overall command of General Joseph Joffre)
- 61,000 dead; 101,000 missing; 216,000 wounded

Germans

- 1,000,000 men; 1,200 artillery pieces (Fifth Army)
- Commanded by Crown Prince Wilhelm (under overall command of General Erich von Falkenhayn, replaced in late August by generals Paul von Hindenburg and Erich von Ludendorff)
- 142,000 dead and missing; 187,000 wounded

in the east and a joint Anglo-French offensive on the Somme River, the Germans decided to cease attacks in order to conserve manpower. By that time the two sides had fired more than 23,000,000 artillery and gas shells.

French counter-attacks continued throughout the summer and autumn. French artillery officers began using a technique called a 'creeping barrage', wherein a curtain of artillery shells preceded by 90 m (100 yds) an infantry advance. This system suppressed enemy machine-gun fire, but further stressed Verdun's already tenuous supply system. Thousands of labourers repaired Verdun's only open and passable road, which soon became known as the Voie Sacrée ('Sacred Road').

French offensives in October and November almost returned the front line to its original location in February. On 24 October the French retook Douaumont and captured thousands of German prisoners of war. The onset of winter and mutual exhaustion forced an end to the battle in mid-December. French losses are estimated at 61,000 dead, 101,000 missing, and 216,000 wounded; German losses are thought to have been 142,000 dead and missing, and 187,000 wounded. The high numbers of missing reflect the immense power of the artillery. Today, an ossuary at Verdun contains the remains of 130,000 men that could not be identified.

Verdun led to the replacement of both Joffre and Falkenhayn at the heads of their respective armies. It also forced Britain to assume the main burden for the battle of the Somme in the summer of 1916. Perhaps most importantly, Verdun created a national myth of the heroism of the French soldier. Belief in the superiority of that heroism led many Frenchmen in the inter-war years to overestimate their ability to withstand another German offensive.

Reconciliations at Verdun

Verdun remains a sacred place in French and German history. In 1963 Charles de Gaulle (himself a Verdun veteran) and Conrad Adenauer symbolically shook hands in front of the Verdun ossuary. François Mitterand and Helmuth Kohl repeated the gesture in 1984, underscoring the meaning of Verdun and the importance of learning its haunting lessons.

The destruction at Verdun shows the power of modern artillery. Many of the villages outside Verdun were damaged so badly that the French government decided to abandon them rather than rebuild them.

58

The Western Front

Date: March–November 1918   Location: near Amiens, northeast France

We are engaged in a 'wearing-out battle', and are outlasting and beating the enemy.
FIELD MARSHAL SIR DOUGLAS HAIG, 21 AUGUST 1918

Four years of destructive warfare had produced no conclusion to World War I by the early summer of 1918. On the Western Front the stalemate of late 1914 and 1915 was confirmed by the terrible attrition battles of Verdun (see p. 236) and the Somme in 1916. The next year, 1917, saw some Allied success but also another costly attrition battle at Passchendaele, while the failure of a major French offensive earlier in 1917 led to the French mutinies of that year. Only the late 1917 battle of Cambrai, using tanks and accurate artillery against German artillery, which were carefully located on maps, showed promise.

Then in March 1918, heartened by the Russian Revolution of 1917, which eliminated Russia from the Allied side, the German army launched its own large-scale offensive on the Western Front. This attack, using new infantry and artillery tactics, captured 64 sq. km (40 sq. miles) of territory, nearly split the French and British armies apart, and came close to ending the war by itself. However, the German attack lost momentum and direction, while a series of further German offensives in the spring and early summer of 1918 also failed to bring victory. These German 'peace offensives' were the final throw of the dice for the German army, since the French-led counter-offensive at the Marne in July 1918 caved in the German front, and clearly shifted the balance of the war against Germany. In retrospect this two-

British Mark V tanks supporting the 29 September 1918 Fourth Army offensive aimed at breaking the German Hindenburg Line in the Bellicourt area. The tanks carry fascines to help in crossing trenches and the St Quentin canal.

Soldiers of the Second American Division defend their position against the final stages of the German Michael offensive. The action takes place in a heavily bombarded wood on 3 April 1918 as a 37-mm gun crew fire their weapon.

week French counter-attack was the turning point on the Western Front, and led to the Allies moving onto the offensive for the rest of the war.

Overture: the battle of Amiens, 8–11 August

In early August the British Fourth Army prepared to launch a surprise attack against the German army in the Amiens area. The spearhead of the attack was composed of Australian and Canadian divisions, supported by British and French divisions on the flanks. One reason for the eventual success of this offensive was the overwhelming Allied advantage in men and material. There were 75,000 Allied troops versus 37,000 German troops, 2,000 Allied artillery pieces, 1,900 French and British planes, and numerous Allied tanks: 342 heavy Mark V tanks, 72 lighter Medium A tanks, 50 infantry-carrying tanks and 120 supply tanks. All of this overwhelmed the German defenders on 8 August, who suffered 27,000 casualties, while the Allied line advanced 12.8 km (8 miles). One scene symbolizes the fighting:

'In the valley lay a crippled tank with a couple of shell holes in her side, within were the crew, terribly mangled, a gruesome sight. On a slope less than [180 m] 200 yards away lay the other actors of the scene, two German gun crews done to death beside their guns….'

The Amiens battle continued for a further three days but the troops were exhausted, there were few tanks still running, German reserves had arrived and the old Somme trenches were holding up progress. Nevertheless, General Erich Ludendorff described the Amiens attack as the 'black day of the German army'.

The late August Allied offensives

Now the Allies began their own series of attacks along the German lines, aimed at crumbling these defences rather than trying for decisive breakthroughs. For example, the French Tenth and Third Armies fought a series of engagements from 18 August following, and two days later launched the battle of Noyon which resulted in 8,000 prisoners taken. Then on 21 August the British Third Army, supported by Fourth Army, launched a number of attacks over the next eight days called the battle of Albert, while the British

First Army followed up with offensives between 26 and 31 August in the battle of the Scarpe.

In fact the major attacks were taking place in the centre of the British line, where the strongest forces were available. Thus the Australians in Fourth Army conducted a lightning dawn attack on Mont St Quentin on 31 August , preceded by a half-hour mortar and howitzer barrage, with troops using rifle grenades and Lewis guns, and rapidly captured this important high ground. Similarly, the Canadians in First Army captured the Drocourt-Queant line on 2 September with a combined artillery, infantry and tank attack. Meanwhile, the French armies continued attacking through late August, and suffered 100,000 casualties that month, noteworthy because French forces have sometimes been criticized for not contributing strongly enough in 1918.

Reasons for Allied success

So successful were the Allied advances in late August and early September, that on 2 September General Ludendorff ordered the retreat of the German army to the Hindenburg Line. But what accounted for these Allied successes? First, it is clear the Allies possessed overwhelming advantages in men and material. For example, German losses from 21 March to the end of the war amounted to 1.76 million casualties, which could not be replaced, while in contrast the American

Ground captured by Allied offensives from August 1918 to the Armistice line of 11 November 1918. Rather than a single massive breakthrough attempt, the Allies advanced through a series of 'crumbling' attacks and offensives along the whole line. It is of interest that at the Armistice, German troops were still everywhere on foreign soil, except for a small area of Alsace.

army was landing 250,000 men per month. And while the number of German divisions on the Western Front shrank from 200 in March to only 47 'fit' divisions in September, the Allies maintained 211 divisions in the field. Then, even before the March German offensive, the German army on the Western Front could only deploy 14,000 artillery pieces against 18,500 Allied guns, 3,760 planes against 4,500 Allied planes, and by the end of the war a mere 45 tanks against 3,500 Allied tanks.

In particular, the key weapon of the Western Front, the artillery, dominated the German forces, as one official historian noted of 1918: 'For every shell the enemy sent over, he received ten or twenty back. In the bombardments…of the summer and autumn of 1918, the British artillery dominated to such an extent that the enemy retaliation was largely blind.' In addition, Allied counter-battery (the destruction of enemy artillery) worked very well by 1918, enabling Allied infantry attacks to succeed with many fewer losses. Second, the Allied armies had learnt by 1918 how to properly combine infantry (armed with Lewis guns, rifle grenades, trench mortars, bombs and rifles) with artillery, tanks and air superiority, to create an almost unstoppable attack system. Third, German morale was in such continuous decline through the second half of 1918 that desertions increased rapidly – in August, 110,000 German soldiers left the ranks.

The final Allied offensives: September and October

It is not surprising then that a series of Allied attacks in September drove the German army back in retreat from the Hindenburg Line and other defensive systems. Starting with the first major American offensive at St Mihiel from 12 to 18 September, Marshal Ferdinand Foch then launched a number of widely separated offensives designed to crumble the German line, keep the German army off balance, and prevent German reserves from reinforcing any one area.

Hence, on 26 September there was a Franco-American attack in the Meuse-Argonne area; on 27 September an attack by the British First and

Below left A British 9.2-inch gun fires as it supports troops defending against the German Georgette April 1918 offensive.

Below right An American soldier uses a field telephone in 1918. Communication by telephone was important as the war became more mobile in 1918.

Demoralized and exhausted German troops retreat in mid-September 1918 at Vauxaillon, in the Chemin des Dames area of the French Army sector. This area had seen severe fighting in 1917, which by 1918 had turned the earth into a featureless plain.

COMBATANTS

Allies

• Estimated combat strengths of forces in November 1918:
British Expeditionary Force (BEF) 1,202,000; French Army 1,540,912; Belgian Army 115,000; American Expeditionary Force (AEF): 1,078,222

• Overall Commander-in-Chief, Marshal Ferdinand Foch

BEF: Field Marshal Sir Douglas Haig (Commander-in-Chief)

French: Marshal Henri Philippe Pétain (Commander-in-Chief)

Belgian: King Albert I (Commander-in-Chief of Belgian Army Group)

AEF: General John Pershing (Commander-in-Chief); Major General Hunter Liggett; Major General Robert Bullard, Major General Joseph Dickson

• Dead, missing, wounded & captured: BEF 852,861 (throughout 1918); French 306,000 (March–Nov); Belgian 30,068 (28 Sep–11 Nov); AEF 281,627 (throughout 1918)

Germans

• Estimated combat strength in November 1918: 2,911,700

• Kaiser Wilhelm II (Commander-in-Chief); Field Marshal Paul von Hindenburg (Chief of the General Staff); General Erich Ludendorff, then General Wilhelm Groener (First Quartermaster General); Archduke Albrecht of Wurttemberg; General Hans von Boehn; General Max von Gallwitz; Crown Prince Rupprecht of Bavaria; Crown Prince Wilhelm

• Dead, missing, wounded, captured & deserted: 1.76 million (21 March–11 November 1918)

Third Armies towards Cambrai; on 28 September an attack in the north by the Belgian Army and British Second Army; and lastly an attack on 29 September by the British Fourth Army and French First Army in the centre of the Allied line. There was hard fighting in all these areas, especially against German machine gunners, and Allied casualties were often heavy (the Canadian Corps suffered its heaviest casualties of the war, 49,152, in 1918), but the Hindenburg Line and other systems were broken and the German army was in overall retreat. In certain places defences stiffened, but normally there was a German retreat, covered by their artillery and machine guns, with Allied forces following up.

The Armistice, 11 November 1918

By early October both General Ludendorff and Field Marshal Paul von Hindenburg realized that an end to the war was necessary. After protracted arguments among German generals, politicians and the German monarchy, the armistice was signed in Foch's railway carriage in the forest of Compiègne during the early hours of 11 November 1918. Hostilities ceased at 11 am on 11 November, the fifth year of the war. In summary, during 1918, the British army captured 188,700 prisoners and 2,840 guns, the French 139,000 prisoners and 1,880 guns, the Americans 43,300 prisoners and 1,421 guns, and the Belgians 14,500 prisoners and 474 guns. These statistics reveal accurately enough the relative contribution of each Allied army to the defeat of Germany on the Western Front in 1918.

Battle of Britain

Date: July–September 1940   Location: Britain and northern coastal France

*The Battle of France is over….The Battle of Britain is about to begin…Hitler knows he will
have to break us in this island, or lose the war.…Let us therefore brace ourselves to our
duties, and so bear ourselves that, if the British Empire and its Commonwealth last
for a thousand years, men will still say, 'This was their finest hour.'*
WINSTON CHURCHILL, 18 JUNE 1940

The Battle of Britain remains one of the most famous campaigns in military history and is viewed by many as the pivotal moment of World War II, when Germany's opportunity to win the war quickly and decisively was denied them. There is little doubt that the failure to knock Britain out of the war in the summer and autumn of 1940 had enormous repercussions for Hitler's regime.

In essence the Battle of Britain was an air superiority campaign fought predominantly over southern England in the late summer of 1940 between RAF Fighter Command and the Luftwaffe. It was considered crucial for the launching of *Operation Seelöwe* (Operation Sealion), the German plan to invade Britain, that the RAF be swept from the skies over the English Channel. German planners assumed that if the RAF was still

Messerschmitt 109s in 'finger four' formation over St Margaret's Bay.

London and the Thames lie vulnerable below a German Heinkel He 111 bomber, seen from an escort plane during a bombing raid on 9 July, 1940.

viable, any attempted invasion would be vulnerable to attack by the Royal Navy, protected from the Luftwaffe by British fighter cover.

The Luftwaffe

In order to achieve their goal, German commanders recognized that they would have to draw the RAF's Fighter Command into intense and sustained air battle over England in order to destroy them, and to do this they would have to threaten Britain with a major bombing campaign. Precisely how this would be prosecuted and which targets would be crucial enough to the British to force them to commit their fighters was a matter of some debate in the Luftwaffe's high command. They knew that they heavily outnumbered the RAF (2,600 aircraft to the RAF's 640 fighters), but also noted that they would be battling over England in British skies, and that many tactical advantages would reside with the RAF. German

planning staff added to their difficulties by overestimating the Luftwaffe's operational and tactical superiority, whilst underestimating the strength and capabilities of the RAF.

In equipment, the Germans fielded a variety of twin-engine bombers, such as the Heinkel He 111 and the Dornier Do 17, along with the Junkers Ju 87 Stuka dive-bomber for precision attacks. To protect them, the Luftwaffe had the Messerschmitt Bf 109 single-engine fighter, and the Messerschmitt Bf 110 twin-engine long-range heavy fighter. The twin-engine bombers were adequate, but nonetheless vulnerable to high-performance enemy fighters, especially when operating with few or no escorts. The Bf 109 was a top-class fighter but suffered from limited endurance, whilst the Bf 110 had the ability to operate over the UK for longer, but lacked the aerial combat capability to lock horns with the British fighters. The Luftwaffe, nevertheless, was

able to deploy three Luftflotten (air fleets) along the coast of northwest Europe from Norway to Brittany to spearhead the attack. Complicating matters, however, was the influence of Hermann Göring, head of the Luftwaffe, who retained control of some air units and whose executive leadership was to handicap the Luftwaffe throughout World War II.

RAF Fighter Command

British air defence was centred upon RAF Fighter Command and its supporting network of RDF ('radio direction finding' or radar) and observer corps stations, along with anti-aircraft gun batteries, balloon barrages and an array of civil defence measures. Command fell to Air Chief Marshal Sir Hugh Dowding, who had been a pivotal figure in the development of RAF Fighter Command in the late 1930s. In addition, he had stood firm against pressure to despatch more of his precious fighter

strength to France during the desperate battles of May and June, earning some criticism. In hindsight Dowding was proved correct in his assessment that Fighter Command's pilots and aircraft would be essential to save Britain, and that frittering them away on the continent in a hopeless battle was not an effective use of scant resources. Britain was also divided into four Fighter Command Groups, with 11 Group – based in southeast England under Air Vice Marshal Sir Keith Park – likely to bear the brunt.

The British had invested heavily in air defence measures in the late 1930s and the aircraft of Fighter Command were generally high-quality types. The Hawker Hurricane was the most numerous fighter, a rugged and dependable design, capable of matching anything the Luftwaffe had, save perhaps the Bf 109. In addition, the British deployed the Supermarine Spitfire, a cutting-edge, high-performance fighter to match

Paul Nash's Battle of Britain *(1941). Nash was an Official War Artist during both World War I and II.*

the Bf 109. The RAF also had the great advantage of fighting over its own territory, thus being able to recover precious numbers of downed pilots much more easily.

The campaign

The importance of the battle in the skies over southeast England is apparent from the map below. 11 Group endured the heaviest losses, but the battle was won and lost here.

The Luftwaffe's campaign began on 10 July with a series of probing raids against shipping, coastal convoys and ports. In addition, the Luftwaffe attacked the RAF's RDF stations, but was largely unsuccessful in its effort to eliminate this important element in British air defences.

The Luftwaffe then switched to attacks upon the RAF direct, 11 Group in particular. Air raids were now conducted against RAF aerodromes and stations in an effort to break Fighter Command, and thus gain air superiority over

southern England. The Luftwaffe's tactics included mixed high- and low-level attacks to confuse and surprise RDF and observer stations, trying to catch aerodrome defences unprepared. Eagle Day (or Adlertag) on 13 August saw the beginning of this determined effort by the Luftwaffe and, by early September, Fighter Command was on the brink of defeat with heavy losses and acutely stretched infrastructural support. Plans to withdraw Fighter Command's assets north to await the invasion were discussed, but Dowding and Park decided to continue contesting air superiority over the south.

In reality the Luftwaffe was enduring a chastening experience too, with heavy losses of aircraft, pilots and aircrew. The Ju 87 Stuka had already been withdrawn due to grievous casualties and questions were being raised about tactics. Göring was well aware his force was far weaker than Hitler had been led to believe, and conscious that continued losses would quickly break the Luftwaffe as a major fighting force.

The battle decided

The campaign was soon to swing Britain's way, however. The Germans had begun conducting night-time bombing raids on RAF stations, but one such attack hit a civilian area, causing the

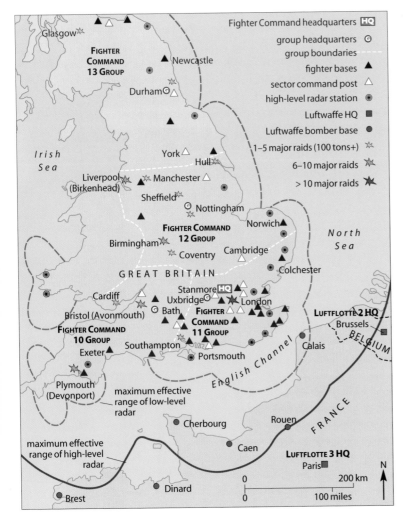

COMBATANTS

Allies

• RAF Fighter Command: 900 aircraft, of which 600 could be airborne at one time

• Commander-in-Chief Air Chief Marshal Sir Hugh Dowding

• 507 dead, 2,945 wounded, 788 aircraft lost

Germans

• The Luftwaffe: 1,800 out of 2,600 aircraft played a key role, including twin-engine bombers, dive bombers, single-engine fighters & long-range heavy fighters

• Commanded by Reichsmarschall Hermann Göring

• 1,294 aircraft lost

Left *Supermarine Spitfire Mark Is of 610 Fighter Squadron on patrol during the Battle of Britain. The Spitfire's speed and manoeuvrability made it Britain's premier fighter aircraft of World War II.*

Left *'Never was so much owed by so many to so few.' The famous quotation from Churchill's tribute to the victors of the Battle of Britain is given visual form in this photo-montage, c. 1940.*

British to retaliate by bombing Berlin. As Luftwaffe losses remained heavy and the direct attack on the RAF did not seem to be working, Hitler threw his weight behind a change of tack: direct attacks upon the British civilian population in order to break their morale and draw the RAF fighters into direct aerial confrontation.

In fact, the Luftwaffe had been very close to success and the change in tactics actually allowed Fighter Command to recover. Moreover, London was at the edge of the Bf 109's operational range, often causing German bombers to fly unescorted for part of their missions, increasing casualties still further. By mid-September there was now no chance of the Luftwaffe seizing air superiority to allow for *Operation Seelöwe* before the winter, so the battle was effectively over. The 'blitz' of British towns and cities continued throughout the winter of 1940–41, but the Germans were forced to switch to night-time attacks to reduce bomber losses, and overall effectiveness was limited. Hitler's attention had in any case by then turned towards the invasion of the Soviet Union planned for 1941 (see Battle for Moscow p. 250).

The battle in retrospect

The degree to which the result of the battle was a product of German failure or British success is a debate that will continue, but it is clear that no one factor decided the outcome. Continually shifting German priorities was a major hindrance, but this was also governed by heavy and near-unsustainable loss rates, with the Luftwaffe ill equipped for a sustained air superiority campaign. For the British, the switch to urban bombing in September came as a great relief as

their force was close to collapse, but their defence had been stout and resilient and the toll they had exacted from the Luftwaffe was a crucial factor in prompting the Germans to change tactics.

Finally, although Germany's surrender in World War II was brought about by many later campaigns, Britain's determination to continue the war after the fall of France, underpinned by their success in the skies over England in the Battle of Britain, was to lay the foundations for the combined bomber offensive, success in the Mediterranean, the liberation of western Europe and Germany's total defeat in 1945.

60 Battle for Moscow

Date: November–December 1941   Location: western Russia

We only needed another twelve kilometres to get the capital within gun range – but we just could not make it.

GERMAN LIEUTENANT IN FRONT OF MOSCOW, EARLY DECEMBER 1941

The German invasion of the Soviet Union in June 1941 caught the Red Army ill prepared and unable to cope with the tidal wave which engulfed it. Within 24 hours the Panzer spearheads (German armoured units) had penetrated up to 80 km (50 miles). By early July the Germans had overrun Latvia and Lithuania, reduced a large pocket of Soviet troops in the Bialystok area, which yielded nearly 300,000 prisoners, and were penetrating Ukraine in the south. Stalin, who had remained strangely silent for the first two weeks of the fighting, exhorted the Soviet people to fight to the last, but few outside observers believed that it would be long before the Germans were hammering at the gates of Moscow.

The Soviet capital was initially the prime German objective and the intention was to seize it before winter fell. To this end, Fedor von Bock's Army Group Centre, tasked with advancing to Moscow, had been allocated the bulk of the armour with two Panzer groups, while Army Group North, whose objective was Leningrad (present-day St Petersburg), and Army Group South, tasked with overrunning Ukraine, had just one each. On 19 July Hitler, who had been increasingly meddling in the conduct of operations, issued a new directive. Moscow, he declared, was no longer the main target. Instead, Army Group Centre was to hand over much of its armour to the other two army groups so that Leningrad could be quickly captured and the

German reconnaissance elements advancing into Ukraine, summer 1941. The Panzer spearheads were often days ahead of the main body of foot marching infantry.

prime Soviet agricultural area in Ukraine secured. This was to take place after von Bock had dealt with another large pocket around Smolensk.

The Smolensk pocket was duly reduced, with a further 310,000 Soviet troops falling into German hands. Gerd von Rundstedt's Army Group South advanced to Kiev, the ancient capital of Ukraine, which Stalin ordered to be held to the last man. Once it crossed from the Baltic states into Russia proper, Army Group North's advance became slowed by growing exhaustion and the heavily wooded terrain. Not until the beginning of September was Leningrad put under siege. Immediately, Hitler changed his mind once more. Moscow was restored as the primary objective and Army Groups North and South were ordered to return the armour that they had obtained from Army Group Centre. For Army Group North, now settling down for a long siege (it would last until January 1944), the transfer was reasonably straightforward. In contrast, Army Group South was embroiled in the capture of Kiev. This did not fall until 19 September, yielding 600,000 prisoners, and only then could von Rundstedt hand back Heinz Guderian's Second Panzer Army to von Bock. The result of this was that the 320-km (200-mile) advance on Moscow, codenamed Operation Typhoon, could not begin until 30 September. With the autumn rains due in mid-October, followed by the beginning of the grim

Russian winter, time was in short supply. Indeed, the rain began three days before Typhoon was launched.

On the Soviet side, Stalin and his high command had always been convinced that Moscow was the major German target. This was reinforced by Luftwaffe air attacks on the capital which had begun towards the end of July. This prompted a redeployment of the Soviet munitions industry east of the Ural Mountains to place

Hitler planned for Fourth and Second Panzer armies to surround Moscow, but in the face of worsening weather and Russian reinforcements it proved overly ambitious.

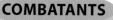

COMBATANTS

Russians

- Soviet Western, Reserve & Bryansk Fronts: 1,250,000 men (as at 30 Sep)
- Commanded by Georgi Zhukov
- 515,000 killed and captured, 144,000 wounded and sick (to 5 Dec)

Germans

- German Army Group Centre: 910,000 men (as at 30 Sep)
- Commanded by Field Marshal Fedor von Bock
- c. 200,000 casualties (to 5 Dec)

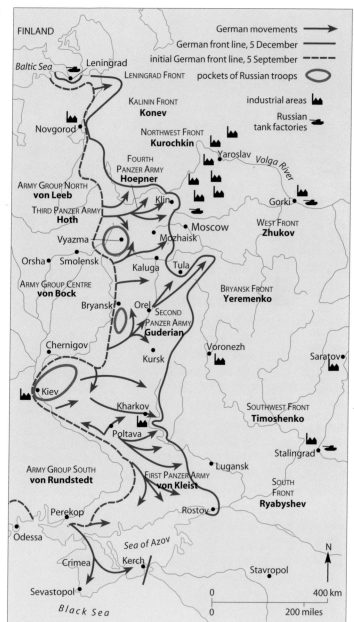

A Russian village burns as German troops tighten their grip on one of the pockets of Russian troops that they surrounded in October 1941. The task of the German infantry was to reduce the pockets which the Panzers had formed.

it out of range of the bombers. Three lines of defences were also constructed west of Moscow, largely by local labour. Facing Army Group Centre were two Soviet fronts: Semyon Timoshenko's Southwest Front of 55 divisions and Andrei Yeremenko's Bryansk Front with 26 divisions. Stalin had, however, ordered the transfer of divisions from Siberia, who were well inured to the cold, to the Moscow area.

Operation Typhoon

The renewed German offensive was spearheaded by Erich Hoepner's Fourth Panzer Army, Hermann Hoth's Third Panzer Army and Guderian's Second Panzer Army. Guderian quickly enveloped the Bryansk Front, totally trapping it by 6 October, and the following day Hoth and Hoepner similarly encircled Timoshenko. Although it took time to reduce the pockets, both Soviet fronts were completely destroyed and it seemed that the road to Moscow now lay open. But the weather

intervened. On 7 October, the very day that the Germans entrapped the Western Front at Vyazma, the autumn rains proper began. The earth quickly became a morass, drastically slowing movement. To compound the German problems, Hitler now insisted that the Panzer armies surround Moscow rather than thrust directly at the city. But the advance continued.

By mid-October the Germans were within 160 km (100 miles) of their goal. Panic now gripped Moscow. Many of the organs of government and the foreign embassies left the city. Even Stalin himself prepared to leave, but changed his mind as his train stood ready to depart. By 18 October the Germans had penetrated to within 130 km (80 miles) of Moscow and it seemed as though it were merely a matter of days before they reached their goal. But all was not going the German way. First, Stalin had appointed a tough new commander, Georgi Zhukov, whose newly formed West Front was charged with halting the German offensive.

Second, the rains, now becoming mixed with snow as October drew into November, were increasingly reducing mobility. This was aggravated by overstretched German supply lines. Many German troops were still in their summer uniforms and beginning to suffer from the cold and, because the reinforcement system could no longer cope, units were down to half strength.

Matters came to a head on 30 October, when Guderian attempted to seize Orel, 110 km (70 miles) east of Bryansk. Among the defenders was the first of the Siberian divisions to arrive and Guderian, with his fuel tanks almost dry, was surprised by the ferocity of the resistance. This and the now virtually impassable ground forced a halt.

The Germans are foiled

With the coming of November, so the frost arrived and the ground began to harden once more. The Germans hastily brought up more supplies so that the advance could recommence. Simultaneously, troop trains were rumbling westwards from Siberia, bringing a total of 40 fresh divisions to reinforce the Moscow defences. Some of these troops took part in the annual Rev-

olution Day Parade held in Red Square on 7 November in the presence of Stalin and then deployed immediately to the front. The German advance on Moscow resumed on 15 November. While the frozen ground had restored mobility, the increasing cold had a debilitating effect on the troops. Combined with the ever stiffer Soviet resistance, progress was slowing considerably.

By the end of 4 December the northern thrust had reached the Volga canal, just 32 km (20 miles) northwest of Moscow, and some reconnaissance units claimed that they could see the spires of the Kremlin. In the south, Guderian was approaching the River Oka, southeast of the city. It seemed that, with one final heave, Moscow would be in German hands. That night, however, the temperature plummeted to −35 degrees Celsius. Tank engines would not start, weapons became inoperable and frostbite was rampant among the ill-clothed German soldiers.

On 5 December Zhukov counter-attacked, his troops and vehicles better equipped to combat the cold. Hitler was forced to give permission for some local withdrawals to take place, but within 48 hours had changed his mind. In the north, the

A German battle group prepares for the final advance on Moscow, November 1941. Apart from improvised white camouflage, the troops lacked the proper clothing to cope with the Russian winter.

ЗАЩИТИМ РОДНУЮ МОСКВУ

Right *This Soviet poster reads 'We will defend our Moscow'. It was the appeal to patriotism rather than ideology which galvanized the Russian people to resist and turn back the invader.*

Below *A T-34 supports Russian infantry in a counter-attack, January 1942.*

German withdrawal was orderly, although much equipment had to be abandoned. Guderian, however, had considerably more difficulty extricating his troops from the narrow salient which they had occupied. They found themselves repeatedly cut off and fighting their way out of encirclement. The Soviet pressure was such that by late December the Germans had been driven back up to 150 km (95 miles). The Red Army continued its attacks until the end of February 1942, by which time it was exhausted.

The repulse of Army Group Centre in front of Moscow marked the end of German hopes of speedily crushing the Soviet Union. The Germans failed because they began their invasion of the Soviet Union too late in the year, and Hitler's failure to adhere to the originally agreed plan of Moscow as the primary objective imposed an additional time penalty. Consequently, the Germans found themselves facing not only a rapidly recovering Red Army, but also the harshness of the Russian winter, for which they were singularly ill equipped.

Stalingrad

Date: September 1942–2 February 1943   Location: modern Volgagrad, southwest Russia

As far as the eye can see lie soldiers crushed by tanks, helplessly moaning wounded, frozen corpses, vehicles abandoned through lack of fuel, blown-up guns and miscellaneous equipment.

HANS SCHMEIDER, NINTH FLAK DIVISION, STALINGRAD, JANUARY 1943

The origins of the long-drawn-out agony of Stalingrad during the winter of 1942–43 lay in Hitler's decision to renew his Russian offensive after the rebuff in front of Moscow in 1941 (see previous entry p. 250). Rather than make another attempt on the capital, he decided to seize the oilfields in the Caucasus, a plan that he dreamed would coincide with victory in North Africa to force the entire Middle East under his sway.

Codenamed Blue, this attack was to be conducted by Fedor von Bock's Army Group South, which was subdivided into two Army Groups: A and B. The main assault was to be carried out by the former, while Army Group B advanced to the line of the River Don, then turning southeast to Stalingrad to secure Army Group A's eastern flank on the Volga as it plunged into the Caucasus. An elaborate deception operation was mounted to make Moscow seem the principal objective and, even when plans for the Caucasus offensive fell into their hands, the Russians remained convinced it was merely a subsidiary attack.

Operation Blue is launched

On 30 June 1942 Army Group B began its advance to the Don and hoped to trap the forces initially opposing it in a pocket. Now wise to this previously successful tactic, the Russians withdrew before the pocket could be formed, but this enabled the Germans to reach the Don within a week. On 7 July Army Group A launched its assault into the Donets Basin. Again the Red Army withdrew, but the German progress was slowed by heavy rain and fuel shortages. Hitler quickly became impatient and ordered the transfer of Panzer formations and air assets from Army Group B to General Siegmund List (commander of Army Group A), leaving just Friedrich Paulus's Sixth Army, supported by some Panzer elements,

Soviet soldiers fighting a rearguard action during the German advance to the River Don, July 1942.

to continue the advance towards Stalingrad. Frustrated by what he saw as his slow progress, Hitler then sacked von Bock and dissolved his headquarters. At the same time, the two army groups were now on divergent paths – Army Group B eastwards towards Stalingrad and Army Group A southwards into the Caucasus. By mid-August the latter had overrun Maykop oilfields (despite Russia having destroyed most of the machinery) and reached the foothills of the Caucasus, while Paulus was fighting on the outskirts of Stalingrad and subjecting the city to heavy bombing. Significantly, Hermann Hoth's Fourth Panzer Army was on its way to join him, having been switched from Army Group A, which had also handed over one of its air fleets. It meant that the drive into the Caucasus began to run out of momentum as the attention of both sides became fixed on Stalingrad.

On the Russian side, Vasily Gordov's Stalingrad Front was responsible for the area. Stalin told him on 24 August that the city must be held at all costs and sent his chief troubleshooter, Georgi Zhukov, to oversee operations. While Vasily Chuikov's

Russian soldiers armed with 7.62-mm PPSh submachine guns during the costly Stalingrad street fighting.

Sixty-Second Army was made responsible for the city itself, Zhukov was aware that Paulus's flanks were vulnerable and began to organize counter-attack forces. Meanwhile, the Germans managed to press Chuikov into a narrow salient on the west bank of the Volga, but casualties were mounting. Chuikov's men, too, were becoming exhausted and running low on reinforcements. The only way that they could reach him was across the Volga, but the river was being subjected to constant artillery fire and many were lost. By the end of September a virtual stalemate had been reached.

Zhukov plans a counter-offensive

Zhukov had already organized limited counter-attacks into the flanks of the German Sixth Army, which had forced Paulus to divert forces to deal with them. As early as 12 September he conceived an ambitious plan for a double envelopment of the German forces in the Stalingrad area by launching attacks on the shoulders of the salient in which they found themselves. It took time to prepare, largely because Stalin was slow to agree that the necessary reinforcements should be

switched from Moscow to the Stalingrad area, and it was also decided to await the winter snows, when the ground would have hardened once more. One advantage which the Russians enjoyed, however, was that the Germans had been forced to deploy two low-grade Romanian armies to guard their flanks.

Security for the Russian plan, entitled Operation Uranus, was very tight. Only the Front commanders concerned – Nikolai Vatutin of the Southwest Front, Konstantin Rokossovsky of the Don Front (which had taken over from Gordov's Stalingrad Front) and Andrei Yeremenko of a newly created Stalingrad Front – were told of the outline plan. While Vatutin attacked the Romanian Third Army west of Stalingrad and Rokossovsky kept Paulus tied down through attacks into the flank of the German forces, elements of the Stalingrad Front would assault the Romanian Fourth Army to the south of the city. Uranus would be mounted on 9 November, with detailed orders issued only on the previous day. The attack had

to be postponed by ten days, however, because of delays in deploying troops, and during this time Chuikov's situation within the city became increasingly desperate.

On 19 November 1942, Vatutin and Rokossovsky launched their attacks, with Yeremenko joining the offensive the following day. The stunned Romanians soon broke and both prongs of the offensive swept southeast and northwest, on 23 November linking up at Kalach, some (80 km) 50 miles west of Stalingrad. It meant that the German Sixth Army, together with elements of Fourth Panzer Army, were now cut off. Paulus's logical action would have been to break out of the encirclement before it had time to congeal, but Hermann Göring declared that his Luftwaffe could keep the surrounded Germans resupplied. Consequently, Hitler ordered Paulus to stay put. He also tasked Erich von Manstein, one of the ablest of the German commanders, at the head of the newly formed Army Group Don, to mount a relief operation.

A German platoon pauses for breath outside the Stalingrad tractor factory, one of the most bitterly contested landmarks in the city.

At the beginning of December the Russians launched further attacks designed to split the Stalingrad pocket in two. They made little progress and were called off after a few days. On 12 December, von Manstein mounted his relief operation. Initially it made good progress, but Russian resistance stiffened and they also launched an attack further north, designed to threaten von Manstein's lines of communication. Even so, his men pressed forward, reaching the River Myshkova, just 50 km (30 miles) from the pocket, on 19 December. But the Russians had prepared defences along it, preventing the Germans from breaking through. Von Manstein suggested to Paulus that he now break out, but

Hitler's growing fixation with Stalingrad resulted in Army Group A's advance into the Caucasus running out of momentum. Thereafter the city drew in German forces like a magnet, making their flanks increasingly vulnerable to Russian attack.

the latter was under strict orders from Hitler to maintain his hold on Stalingrad and was unwilling to make sufficient forces available.

The German fate is sealed

The Russian offensive in the north had continued and was joined by one launched by the Stalingrad Front on 24 December. The twin attacks threatened to cut off a significant portion of von Manstein's forces and on 28 December Hitler gave permission for him and Maximilian von Weichs's Army Group A to his north to withdraw. This was to put them over 200 km (125 miles) away from the pocket. Not only did this make further attempts to relieve Paulus nigh on impossible, but it also aggravated his supply situation. The Germans at Stalingrad required 750 tonnes of supplies each day and the most that the Luftwaffe had achieved this far was 250 tonnes. The increased distance that the aircraft now had to fly meant that the daily supply rate would drop to 90 tonnes per day at best.

With the threat from von Manstein removed, the Russians could now move in for the kill. On 10 January 1943, Rokossovsky assaulted the pocket from the west. Within a week all the airfields bar one had been overrun by the Russians, and the Luftwaffe was reduced largely to dropping, rather than landing, supplies, most thus falling into Russian hands. Rokossovky now paused to

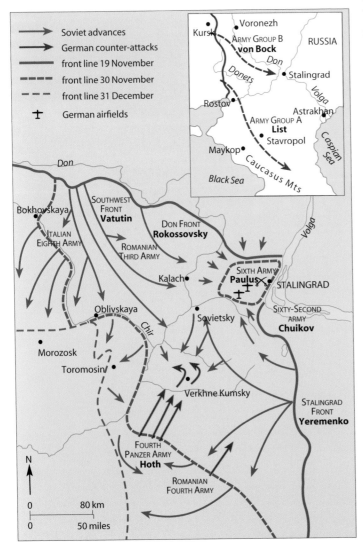

Key:
→ Soviet advances
→ German counter-attacks
— front line 19 November
--- front line 30 November
-- front line 31 December
✝ German airfields

COMBATANTS

Russians

- Russian Southwest, Don, and Stalingrad Fronts: 1,143,500 men (as at 19 Nov)
- Overall commander Georgi Zhukov
- 486,000 killed and captured, 614,000 wounded and sick

Germans

- German Sixth Army: 290,000 men (as at 22 Nov)
- Overall commander Friedrich Paulus
- 265,000 killed and captured, 23,000 wounded and evacuated

regroup and resumed his attacks on 22 January. The following day saw the last German aircraft fly out of the pocket.

Paulus was now so desperately short of food and ammunition that his 30,000 sick and wounded were denied rations. Rokossovsky's men had linked up with Chuikov in Stalingrad itself and the Germans had been reduced to two small areas. Hitler refused to countenance any form of break-out and ordered Paulus to defend to the last. On 30 January, Göring made a radio broadcast on the anniversary of Hitler's accession to power, declaring that 'a thousand years hence Germans will speak of this battle with reverence and awe.' Hitler himself promoted Paulus to Field Marshal.

On the evening of the following day Paulus, who was in the southern of the two pockets, surrendered. The northern pocket continued to resist for another 48 hours but, subjected to a final devastating bombardment, also gave in on 2 February. Of the 90,000 men made prisoner during the fighting, only some 5,000 would survive to be eventually returned to Germany. While the Russians rejoiced, Hitler declared four days of mourning. He recognized, as did Stalin, that Stalingrad was a major turning point of the war in the East. From now on it was the Russians who held the initiative as they began an advance that would eventually take them all the way to Berlin.

The haggard newly promoted Field Marshal Paulus marches into captivity. He never forgave Hitler for abandoning the Sixth Army and broadcast anti-Nazi propaganda for the Soviets.

Midway

Date: 4–6 June 1942   Location: North Pacific Ocean

This memorable American victory was of cardinal importance, not only to the United States, but to the whole Allied cause. The moral effect was tremendous and instantaneous. At one stroke the dominant position of Japan in the Pacific was reversed.
WINSTON CHURCHILL, *THE HINGE OF FATE*, 1950

Admiral Isoroku Yamamoto's plan for the Midway campaign called for Japanese forces to secure the island of Midway, at the western end of the Hawaiian chain 1,930 km (1,200 miles) from Pearl Harbor, in order to draw out the US Pacific Fleet for a decisive battle. The Americans had still not recovered from the Japanese surprise attack that had started the war; of the eight battleships in Pearl Harbor on 7 December 1941, four had been sunk and the other four damaged badly enough to remain unavailable for service six months later. None of the Pacific Fleet's carriers had been in Pearl Harbor during the

Fleet Admiral Isoroku Yamamoto (1884–1943) of the Imperial Navy and commander of the Japanese Combined Fleet at Midway.

attack, but in the battle of the Coral Sea (7–8 May 1942), the *Lexington* had been sunk and the *Yorktown* damaged so badly that Japan believed it was also destroyed. Coral Sea was the first Japanese setback of the war, forcing them to cancel an amphibious invasion of the southern coast of New Guinea. Earlier, in the wake of Pearl Harbor, the Japanese had taken Guam and most of the Philippines from the Americans, Singapore and Malaya from the British and the East Indies from the Dutch, then employed carriers to great effect in raids on Darwin, Australia (19 February 1942), and deep into the Indian Ocean on Colombo and Trincomalee, Ceylon (5–9 April 1942).

After its sortie into the Indian Ocean the main Japanese carrier force, under direct command of Vice Admiral Chuichi Nagumo, returned home for a refit before the Midway campaign. The fleet carriers *Shokaku* and *Zuikaku*, which had seen action at Pearl Harbor and Ceylon, were detached with the light carrier *Shoho* to spearhead the force intercepted in the Coral Sea. While the battle there cost the Americans the much larger *Lexington*, the Japanese lost the *Shoho*, their first significant material casualty of the war. The *Shokaku* was damaged beyond repair for the next campaign; the *Zuikaku* emerged from the battle unscathed, but lost enough aircraft and pilots to be held back too. Meanwhile, thanks to a Herculean effort in the dockyard at Pearl Harbor, the Americans would have the *Yorktown* repaired and back with the fleet in time for Midway.

In contrast to the strike against Pearl Harbor, conducted by Nagumo's First Air Fleet while

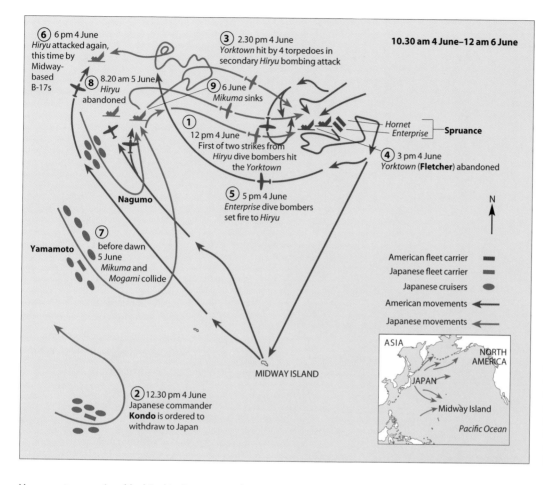

10.30 am 4 June–12 am 6 June

(6) 6 pm 4 June
Hiryu attacked again, this time by Midway-based B-17s

(3) 2.30 pm 4 June
Yorktown hit by 4 torpedoes in secondary *Hiryu* bombing attack

(8) 8.20 am 5 June
Hiryu abandoned

(9) 6 June
Mikuma sinks

Nagumo

(1) 12 pm 4 June
First of two strikes from *Hiryu* dive bombers hit the *Yorktown*

Hornet
Enterprise — **Spruance**

(4) 3 pm 4 June
Yorktown (**Fletcher**) abandoned

(5) 5 pm 4 June
Enterprise dive bombers set fire to *Hiryu*

Yamamoto

(7) before dawn 5 June
Mikuma and *Mogami* collide

N

American fleet carrier
Japanese fleet carrier
Japanese cruisers
American movements
Japanese movements

MIDWAY ISLAND

(2) 12.30 pm 4 June
Japanese commander **Kondo** is ordered to withdraw to Japan

ASIA
NORTH AMERICA
JAPAN
Midway Island
Pacific Ocean

Left *By 10.30 am on 4 June the US* Enterprise *had already bombed* Akagi *and* Kaga, *and the* Yorktown *had hit* Soryu, *rendering all three Japanese carriers out of action for the rest of the battle. This plan shows how the conflict evolved over the next couple of days.*

Below *Admiral Chester Nimitz of the United States Navy. Nimitz (1885–1966) commanded the American forces at Midway.*

Yamamoto remained behind in Japan coordinating the navy's multiple offensives of December 1941, on this occasion the entire Combined Fleet sortied, including Yamamoto in the flagship *Yamato* in overall personal command. Nagumo led the way with a force including the fleet carriers *Kaga*, *Akagi*, *Hiryu* and *Soryu*, 2 battleships, 2 heavy cruisers, and 1 light cruiser, supplemented by the light carriers *Hosho* and *Zuiho*, 4 battleships, 8 heavy cruisers, and 3 light cruisers. At the same time, Vice Admiral Boshiro Hosogawa led a diversionary strike against the Aleutian Islands with the Fifth Fleet – the light carriers *Ryujo* and *Junyo*, 3 heavy cruisers and 4 light cruisers.

The battle
Nagumo opened the battle at 4.30 am on 4 June 1942 by launching 108 of his 234 aircraft against Midway. When this first wave made its bombing-run two hours later, the island's anti-aircraft guns

shot down or damaged all but 41 planes, seriously reducing the striking power of Nagumo's four fleet carriers and giving Yamamoto second thoughts about the deployment of the four light carriers, none of which would participate in the ensuing battle. The American force, under the overall command of Admiral Chester Nimitz, steamed towards Midway from Pearl Harbor. His ships were subdivided into Task Force 16 (Rear Admiral Raymond Spruance), including the carriers *Hornet* and *Enterprise*, 5 heavy cruisers, 1 light cruiser and 11 destroyers; and Task Force 17 (Rear Admiral Frank Fletcher), including the newly repaired *Yorktown*, 2 heavy cruisers and 6 destroyers. Together the three American flattops carried 233 aircraft.

Nimitz's carriers launched their first planes between 7 and 8 am. They made their first contact with the Japanese fleet after 9 am, just as Nagumo was hesitating over whether to arm his planes for a second attack on Midway or for battle with the approaching American force. Some of the *Hornet*'s torpedo planes spotted the *Kaga* after 9 am, but failed to damage it in their attack. Then, between 10.20 and 10.30 am, dive bombers from the *Enterprise* scored hits on the *Akagi* and *Kaga*, while dive bombers from the *Yorktown* set the *Soryu* ablaze. Intense fires rendered these three Japanese carriers useless for the rest of the battle; the *Kaga* and *Soryu* each remained afloat for another nine hours before sinking, while Yamamoto ordered destroyers to torpedo the burning hulk of the *Akagi* at 5 am the following morning.

The *Hiryu*, which had taken a course to the north of the other Japanese carriers, remained

Air Attack on Japanese Carriers *by Griffith Baily Coale, c. 1942.*

COMBATANTS

Americans

- Pacific Fleet, Task Force 16 and Task Force 17: 3 fleet carriers; 7 heavy cruisers; 1 light cruiser; several smaller and supporting units including 17 destroyers and 19 submarines)

- Overall commander Admiral Chester Nimitz; Rear Admiral Raymond Spruance (Task Force 16); Rear Admiral Frank Fletcher (Task Force 17)

- 307 dead; 1 carrier and 1 destroyer sunk

Japanese

- Combined Fleet: 4 fleet carriers; 2 light carriers; 6 battleships; 10 heavy cruisers; 4 light cruisers; several smaller and supporting units including 34 destroyers and 15 submarines (NB: totals do not include units of Fifth Fleet deployed against Aleutian Islands)

- Overall commander Admiral Isoroku Yamamoto; Vice Admiral Chuichi Nagumo

- *c.* 4,800 dead; 4 carriers and 1 heavy cruiser sunk

unscathed and launched a strike against the *Yorktown* around 11 am, and a second strike at 1.20 pm. The first wave took an hour to reach its target, the second around 90 minutes, but each scored hits, and the *Yorktown* had to be abandoned just before 3 pm. The *Hiryu*'s pilots, convinced they had sunk an American carrier on the first strike, believed they had sunk a second carrier on the second strike. In any event, shortly after the *Yorktown*'s crew abandoned ship, American planes spotted the *Hiryu*, and at 3.50 pm the *Hornet* and *Enterprise* launched all of their remaining aircraft for a strike against it. They found their prey just after 5 pm, catching the crew taking its evening meal in no great sense of urgency. Four bombs tore through the *Hiryu*'s flight deck, putting it out of action and igniting fires below; the ship finally sank at 8.20 am on 5 June.

Earlier on the 5th, shortly after Yamamoto ordered the remaining ships to withdraw, the heavy cruisers *Mikuma* and *Mogami* collided in the predawn darkness, leaving both damaged and capable only of a reduced speed. On 6 June aircraft from the *Hornet* and *Enterprise* attacked the two ships as they straggled behind the rest of the retreating Japanese fleet; the *Mikuma* sank after dark that evening, while the *Mogami* escaped with heavy casualties. The *Yorktown*, abandoned two and a half days earlier, remained afloat until the morning of 7 June, when a Japanese submarine torpedoed and sank it. Meanwhile, Hosogawa's Fifth Fleet landed troops which occupied the islands of Attu (5 June) and Kiska (7 June) in the Aleutians, but this costly diversion failed to draw significant American forces away from the main body of the fleet at Midway.

Intelligence the key

Superior intelligence was key to the American victory at Midway. Thanks to the remarkable efforts in the weeks prior to the battle of a team of codebreakers led by Commander Joseph Rochefort, Nimitz knew exactly where and when the Japanese would attack. In contrast, Yamamoto sent his forces into battle thinking the *Yorktown* had been sunk at Coral Sea, and confusion over the number of American carriers he was

facing plagued Nagumo throughout the battle. Ultimately, faced with the dual objectives of attacking Midway and destroying the American fleet, Nagumo lost valuable time deliberating over whether and when to arm his planes with bombs or torpedoes; the fatal strikes against the *Akagi*, *Kaga* and *Soryu* occurred when the trio were especially vulnerable because of such hesitation. Yamamoto's chief of staff, Vice Admiral Matome Ugaki, blamed the defeat on arrogance, saying, 'we had become conceited because of past success'.

Consequences

The battle of Midway, coming just six months after Pearl Harbor, was the turning point of the Pacific theatre of World War II. Yamamoto failed to deliver the knockout blow against the US Pacific Fleet, denying Japan the short war it so desperately needed. The industrial might of the United States soon turned the tide: during the years 1942–45 Japanese shipyards completed 1 battleship, 10 carriers, 5 cruisers, 61 destroyers and 121 submarines, while American shipyards completed 8 battleships, 20 fleet and 82 escort carriers, 48 cruisers, 354 destroyers and 203 submarines. Against mounting odds, the Japanese navy went down fighting, leaving few larger units to surrender to the Allies. By the end of the war Japanese naval deaths alone numbered 300,386, just a few thousand less than the total figure for all branches of the United States armed forces on all fronts. In lives lost as well as in tonnage of material destroyed, no other defeated navy ever suffered destruction on such a scale.

US Navy SBD Dauntless dive bombers fly over a burning Japanese ship during the attack on the Japanese fleet off Midway, 4–6 June 1942.

263

63 Battle of the Atlantic

Date: 1940–43 Location: Atlantic Ocean

The only thing that ever really frightened me during the war was the U-boat peril.
WINSTON CHURCHILL, *THE SECOND WORLD WAR*, 1950

During World War II Britain perhaps came closest to defeat not in the skies over southern England in 1940 (see Battle of Britain p. 245), but in the oceanic wastes of the Atlantic during 1940–41. That winter, German U-boats attempted to enforce a blockade of Britain by exacting a crippling toll of Allied merchant shipping, with the ultimate aim of forcing the British out of the war without direct invasion.

Trade defence war

The Battle of the Atlantic was in essence a campaign centred around the Allies' efforts to move resources predominantly into and out of the British Isles via the Atlantic shipping lanes, relying in particular on the 3,000 ocean-going vessels of the British merchant navy. The Germans attempted to prevent this movement by employing surface naval units, such as the *Bismarck*, the German air force and, most importantly of all, their U-boat (or submarine) fleet. To combat this, the Allies deployed a host of defensive forces to maintain Britain's maritime links with the outside world, ranging from the Royal Navy, Royal Canadian Navy and US Navy, to air assets like RAF Coastal Command.

The campaign was also shaped significantly by a sophisticated intelligence war, on the Allied side famously based at Bletchley Park in England. In this area of the battle the British held a considerable advantage, for they were able to compromise the security of the *Enigma* encoding machines, used extensively by the German military communications and an essential part of U-boat operations. Intelligence derived from such sources was known as *Ultra*, though the process by which it was gleaned remained a closely guarded secret throughout the war and for many years afterwards.

The U-boats of the Battle of the Atlantic were still effectively submersible torpedo boats rather than true submarines, only being capable of low underwater speeds and requiring large amounts of time on the surface to recharge diesel batteries and replenish air supplies. U-boats submerged only to prevent detection for, once forced underwater, speed fell away from around 17 knots to less than 10, and the ability to prosecute attacks even on slow merchant shipping greatly receded.

With the advent of convoying in 1917, whereby the Allies began to group their merchant ships together and protect them with naval escorts and aircraft, and the later development of underwater detection equipment such as asdic or sonar, the threat of the U-boat appeared to be at an end by the late 1930s. This was certainly the opinion of the Royal Navy, and was also a view held by some in the German Kriegsmarine (Navy).

A destroyer (the smaller ship alone in the rear, right) shepherds freighters across the Atlantic in a convoy during the Battle of the Atlantic (June 1943).

Sighting the Target. *A 1943 watercolour by Georges Schreiber.*

Indeed, despite some early successes following the outbreak of war in 1939, the U-boat menace did indeed appear to be under control by 1940.

The 1940–41 campaign: the first Happy Time

However, a number of factors plunged Britain into a severe trade defence crisis by the autumn of that year. Firstly, following the fall of France in June, U-boats began to operate from French Atlantic ports, significantly cutting down their travelling time to and from the maritime approaches to the British Isles. This allowed them to spend much more time on station, searching for merchant shipping. Secondly, Allied resources were stretched to near breaking point by the various military disasters that befell Britain in 1940, there being shortages of naval escorts, aircraft and technical equipment such as radar and asdic. Finally, the German U-boat fleet, under the direction of Karl Dönitz, fully embraced new

tactics and operational methods. In order to avoid detection by asdic, U-boats began attacking on the surface and at night, where their low silhouettes would be much harder to spot. In addition, in an effort to swamp the stretched escort defences attached to each convoy, the U-boats attacked in groups, known as 'wolfpacks'. As soon as a convoy was located by the Germans – either by aircraft, individual U-boats, or from intelligence derived from intercepts and code breaking – Dönitz, from his base in Europe, would direct wolfpacks towards the target, often resulting in drawn-out battles that could last for days.

By the autumn and winter of 1940/41, merchant shipping losses were rocketing out of control, though debate continues as to how close to the brink Britain actually came. The period, nevertheless, became known to the U-boat fleet as the Happy Time, such was their success. However, a series of counter-measures was rapidly introduced by the Allies to meet the challenge. The number of escorts was slowly increased; the level of radar support allocated to convoys improved, thus largely countering the U-boat tactics of surface night attacks; air cover around Britain and out into the Atlantic improved considerably; and intelligence provided to the Admiralty and RAF Coastal Command was boosted by the increasing efficiency of *Ultra* information. Indeed, for phases of the campaign, the Allies were able to reroute convoys around congregating wolfpacks, thanks to *Ultra*. To compound matters for the Germans, U-boats began to be redirected to the Mediterranean to aid the Italian war effort. By the late summer of 1941, though British merchant shipping losses continued to be high, they were at least manageable.

Operation Drumroll: the second Happy Time

The campaign changed yet again with the entry of the USA into the war in December 1941. Dönitz and his staff correctly identified that the Ameri-

cans would be ill-prepared for the complexities of a modern anti-submarine campaign, and committed some of his best crews to patrol just off the American eastern seaboard in search of easy prey. Their success was staggering, precipitating a second Happy Time and, until the US Navy eventually accepted that they were ready to employ convoys and other counter-measures, Allied merchantmen losses were prohibitive. Many have argued that the US Navy was far too unwilling to listen to British advice or to adapt its operating practices to the realities of the campaign unfolding before them. However, new measures, tactics and equipment were eventually introduced and the losses once again brought under control.

The 1942–43 campaign

By the summer of 1942 the Allies believed that they were beginning to win the battle, but they were thrown into further crisis and, as with Operation Drumroll, it was again in part self-inflicted. Dönitz's U-boats were predominantly operating

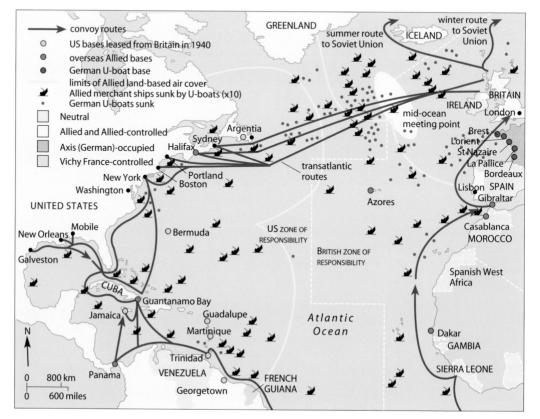

Allied merchant ships sunk between December 1941 and May 1943. The crucial area of the campaign was the central area of the North Atlantic. Losses were heaviest here, but once air cover was applied across the whole ocean in the spring of 1943, the campaign was over and the Allies had won.

in the mid-Atlantic, as far as possible from the scourge of Allied air power. Dönitz also had increasing numbers of U-boats available, and his planners argued that a period of sustained success against the British could well drive them out of the war. German efforts were further aided by the failure of *Ultra* intelligence for a substantial part of 1942, though of course Dönitz and his staff were unaware of this.

Allied losses increased dramatically, especially in the winter of 1942/43, but by the spring of 1943 the battle had finally turned decisively in their favour. They had regained the initiative in the intelligence war by breaking into *Enigma* once again and, more importantly, began deploying enough aircraft with sufficient endurance to close

the mid-Atlantic air gap, thus providing continuous air cover across the ocean. That it took a crisis as deep as that of the previous winter to prompt Allied high command to accept the need to allocate enough suitable aircraft to close the air gap is both remarkable and baffling. With this measure, however, and the increasing quality and quantity of surface escorts, U-boat losses soared, merchant ship sinkings fell away, and Dönitz was forced to withdraw his forces. The Battle of the Atlantic was over.

Consequences

With victory in the Atlantic, the Allies were free to increase the build-up of troops and equipment in Britain preparatory to the liberation of Europe in 1944–45. Without the defeat of the U-boat threat, this success would have been inconceivable. Allied shipping losses were heavy at various stages of the campaign, but in truth it was only in the winter of 1940/41 that Germany came close to victory. Even in 1942–43 when losses rose dramatically, at times even exceeding German targets, there was enough slack in the Allied shipping network to weather the storm and, once the USA was involved in the war, Allied shipping production was always likely to swamp any efforts of the German U-boat fleet. Losses on all sides were heavy during the Battle of the Atlantic, but chillingly the death rate of German U-boat crews approached 75 per cent, approximately 28,000 being killed in some 800 or so U-boats.

Above left *The American artist Georges Schreiber depicts the action below decks on a submarine before a torpedo is launched in* Stand by to Fire, *1943.*

Above right *Coast Guardsmen on the deck of the US Coast Guard Cutter* Spencer *watch the explosion of a depth charge that blasted a Nazi U-boat's hope of breaking into the centre of a large convoy. Sinking of U-175, 17 April 1943.*

COMBATANTS

Allies

- British merchant navy (3,000), Royal Navy, Royal Canadian Navy, United States Navy, RAF Coastal Command
- 11,905,000 shipping tonnes & 2,000 aircraft lost; 25,000 merchant sailors dead

Germans

- German U-boat fleet
- Commanded by Karl Dönitz
- 783 U-boats lost; 28,000 men lost/dead

64 Battle for Normandy

Date: 6 June–20 August 1944   Location: north coast of France

This day undescribe [sic] *mortar fire and wood fighting. Many casualties.*
Thank God I survived another day.
CPL G. E. HUGHES, 1ST HAMPSHIRES, DIARY ENTRY 12 JUNE 1944

O n 6 June 1944 the Allies stormed ashore on five beaches of Normandy in what is still the largest amphibious operation ever mounted. With nearly 6,500 ships and over 11,500 aircraft, 150,000 men landed at a cost of 9,000 casualties. Only Omaha beach experienced real problems, but these were largely overcome by nightfall on D-Day. It was a fitting tribute to the many months, even years, of planning and prepa-

Field Marshal Erwin Rommel inspecting coastal defences prior to the invasion of Normandy.

ration that had gone into Operation Overlord. The liberation of France had begun, but some hard fighting lay ahead.

General Bernard Montgomery, commanding the Allied ground forces in Normandy, had an overall plan. This was to draw the bulk of the German armour onto the British and Canadians in the east to enable the Americans to break out in the west. Meanwhile, the US First Army under General Omar Bradley was to seize the port of Cherbourg. The invasion had taken the Germans by surprise, and they were also well aware of the Allies' overwhelming air supremacy. Thanks to the Allied deception plans, they were not sure whether the main landing was yet to come in the Pas-de-Calais. Consequently, divisions deployed elsewhere on the English Channel coast were not immediately moved to Normandy. Those in other parts of France found their progress to the battle area impeded by the results of the pre-D-Day Allied air offensive against communications and by the activities of the French Resistance.

First steps inland

The five individual beachheads were finally linked up on 13 June, but already the Allies were pushing inland. Bayeux, a D-Day target, was liberated on 7 June, but efforts to break into Caen, the regional capital and another objective, stalled in the face of bitter German resistance. Indeed, the Germans were desperately trying to drive the British and Canadians back to the beaches with an armoured counter-attack, but the slow arrival of Panzer divisions and the disruption caused by Allied artillery and naval gunfire meant that they

268

could do little more than temporarily halt the Allied advance. Matters were made worse on 10 June when the headquarters of Panzer Group West – coordinating armoured offensive operations – was struck by Allied bombers, killing most of the staff.

The Germans continued to frustrate Montgomery's efforts to seize Caen, but a significant part of the problem lay in the nature of the Normandy terrain. Much of this *bocage* consisted of small fields enclosed by hedge-topped banks and with narrow twisting roads, a claustrophobic arena unsuitable for both tanks and attack. But such was the Allied pressure that the Germans found themselves having to commit their Panzer divisions to line holding, and were unable to mount a concerted counter-attack. So concerned were Gerd von Runstedt, the theatre commander, and Erwin Rommel, his subordinate and head of Army Group B, that they persuaded Hitler to come and see for himself. They pleaded for infantry

reinforcements and to be allowed to withdraw out of range of Allied naval gunfire. While Hitler reassured them that reinforcements were being sent, he refused to countenance any withdrawals.

The day after Hitler's conference with his commanders, 18 June, the Americans succeeded in cutting the Cotentin Peninsula. Turning north, they made for Cherbourg, which Hitler had ordered to be defended to the last. In the event, the garrison surrendered on 28 June and the Allies now had a sizeable port, although German damage to the docks would prevent their use for several weeks. In the meantime, the Allies had to continue to rely on the Mulberry artificial harbours constructed off the original landing beaches. Mulberry A supporting the American sector was seriously damaged in a storm from 19 to 21 June, which forced Montgomery to delay another attack to capture Caen. Operation Epsom was designed to seize the high ground south of the city through another thrust from the west.

Generals Eisenhower (left) and Montgomery (right) watching manoeuvres in Britain, early 1944. Despite their rigorous training, the Allied troops were ill prepared for the difficulties of fighting in the Normandy bocage.

After a promising start, it became bogged down in the *bocage* and was halted after facing resolute German counter-attacks.

Towards the break-out

Undeterred by the failure of Epsom, on 30 June Montgomery announced his strategy for the break-out. While the British and Canadians continued to tie down as much German armour as possible, the Americans would advance southwards and eastwards so as to trap the German forces as they withdrew from Normandy. In the meantime, the pressure in the Caen area was maintained. After a preliminary attack by the Canadians to seize Carpiquet airfield west of the city, the main assault was launched on 8 July, preceded by an attack by RAF Bomber Command and an intense artillery barrage, reducing much of Caen to rubble. The British troops entered and fought their way to the River Odon, but the Germans had blown the bridges and were thus able to cling onto the southern part of the city. The Americans, too, began to push southwards, their main objective the communications centre at St Lô. They found themselves advancing through some of the worst of the *bocage* and progress was slow and costly in terms of casualties. Confidence among the Allies began to flag.

But the Germans were being pressed to breaking point, with Hitler remaining adamantly opposed to any withdrawals. Von Rundstedt was sacked at the beginning of July and replaced by Günther von Kluge, whose initial confidence was soon shaken by Rommel's warning that only 10,000 men had arrived to make good the 120,000 casualties since D-Day. The prospects of the situation improving were slim in view of a major Russian offensive which was threatening to destroy the German Army Group Centre (see Operation Bagration p. 273). Indeed, the Allies

Above right
A British infantryman during the bitter battles to secure Caen in July 1944.

Right *Once the Allies were ashore in Normandy, their first task was to link up the beachheads and begin the advance inland.*

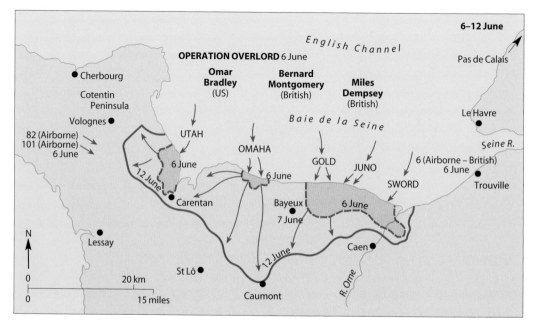

6–12 June

English Channel

OPERATION OVERLORD 6 June

Pas de Calais

Cherbourg

Cotentin Peninsula

Omar Bradley (US)

Bernard Montgomery (British)

Miles Dempsey (British)

Le Havre

Volognes

Baie de la Seine

82 (Airborne)
101 (Airborne)
6 June

UTAH

OMAHA

GOLD

JUNO

6 (Airborne – British)
6 June

Seine R.

6 June

12 June

6 June

SWORD

Trouville

Carentan

Bayeux

6 June

7 June

N

Lessay

Caen

0   20 km

St Lô

12 June

R. Orne

0   15 miles

Caumont

A British Churchill tank breasts a typical Normandy bank. This exposed its relatively thinly armoured belly to German anti-tank guns.

were comfortably winning the reinforcement race.

Montgomery, however, now came under pressure from both Prime Minister Winston Churchill and Supreme Allied Commander Dwight D. Eisenhower. Unfazed by rumours of his imminent dismissal, Montgomery approved a plan proposed by General Miles Dempsey, commanding the British Second Army, for an armoured assault in the better tank country east of Caen. Dempsey believed that this could be the Allied break-out and so did Eisenhower, who saw little prospect of an early decisive blow in the *bocage* confronting

the Americans. Montgomery, however, saw it more as a final effort to waylay the German armour in the British sector, allowing an American break-out in St Lô.

Operation Goodwood was launched on 18 July, the day after Rommel had been severely wounded, preceded by another massive RAF carpet bombing attack. Three British armoured divisions led the main attack and made good early progress against the benumbed defence. But the Germans recovered quickly and deployed tanks to the Bourguébus ridge, which dominated

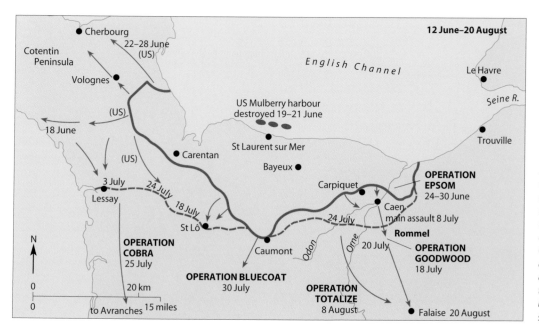

While the Americans cleared the Cotentin Peninsula, the British and Canadians in the east fought to save Caen, aiming to tie down the German armour to enable the Americans to break out southwards.

COMBATANTS

Allies

- British 21st Army Group; US 12th Army Group: *c.* 900,000 men (as at 25 July)
- Commanded by Field Marshal Bernard Montgomery
- 45,000 killed, 173,000 wounded or missing

Germans

- German Army Group B: *c.* 500,000 men (as at 25 July)
- Commanded by Field Marshal Erwin Rommel; Field Marshal Guenther von Kluge (from 17 July); Field Marshal Walter Model (from 17 August)
- 30,000 killed, 210,000 missing/captured, 80,000 wounded

US infantry on the assault during the break-out from St Lô at the end of July 1944. The man in the foreground is about to fire a rifle grenade.

the axis of advance. The British were brought to a halt, with a heavy loss in tanks, and thunderstorms then forced an end to the operation.

The break-out

Postponed for five days by bad weather, Bradley's break-out from St Lô – Operation Cobra – went ahead on 25 July, and within a few days the German resistance was beginning to crumble. Matters were not helped by von Kluge's belief that the main break-out would be in the British sector and his reluctance to switch Panzer divisions to the west. Furthermore, Operation Bluecoat, a British attack launched on 30 July close to the boundary with the Americans, was designed to act as a swinging door that would shut in the face of the German tanks.

On that same day, 30 July, the Americans entered Avranches and von Kluge was forced to admit that his left flank had collapsed. A new force, George S. Patton's US Third Army, had been landed during the previous two weeks and its role was to exploit the break-out. Patton's armour-heavy force passed through Avranches and then swung west into Brittany, south towards Nantes and Angers, and east towards Le Mans. Von Kluge realized that the game was now up and wanted to withdraw to the Seine, but Hitler insisted that he

attack the American flank and restore the situation. Four Panzer divisions therefore caught the Americans by surprise in the Mortain area on the night of 6–7 August, but swarms of Allied fighter-bombers soon stopped the attack in its tracks.

On the following night the newly created Canadian First Army launched an attack, Operation Totalize, towards Falaise, the object being to trap the German Fifth Panzer and Seventh Armies in conjunction with Patton's army. While Totalize did not actually reach Falaise itself, the German forces in Normandy were becoming progressively bottled up, but pressure from Hitler to counter-attack continued.

The Canadians resumed their advance and entered Falaise on 17 August, by which time Patton's men had reached Argentan, leaving a corridor of just 19 km (12 miles) through which the Germans could escape. On the same day Walter Model arrived to take over from the sacked von Kluge, and only now were the German forces allowed to withdraw. Those who were able streamed back across the Seine, leaving 10,000 dead and 50,000 prisoners in the pocket, which was finally sealed on 20 August. With further Allied forces having landed in the south of France on 15 August, the liberation of the remainder of the country could now begin.

Operation Bagration

65

Date: 22 June 1944   Location: Belorussia

*Ninth Army stands on the eve of another battle,
the scale and duration of which can only be surmised.*
GERMAN NINTH ARMY WAR DIARY ENTRY, 22 JUNE 1944

On 1 May 1944 Stalin informed the senior members of his staff, the Stavka, of his intentions for the summer. By this time the Russians had liberated much of their homeland which had been under German occupation. In the north they had closed up to the borders with Estonia and Latvia, while in the south they had recaptured Ukraine and were beginning to threaten Hungary and Romania. Only in the centre did a significant portion of Russian territory remain in German hands. It was Stalin's primary object to liberate Belorussia, which was held by the German Army Group Centre. The offensive was to be launched in June to coincide with the Western Allied landings in Normandy. Much emphasis was to be placed on deception

operations. In the far north the Russians were to mount an attack to force Germany's ally Finland out of the war and to prevent the German Army Group North from going to the aide of its southern neighbour once Operation Bagration, as the Belorussian offensive was codenamed, was launched. Much effort was also to be put into making the Germans believe that the main assault would be in the far south and directed at Romania and Hungary.

On the German side, Field Marshal Ernst Busch, commanding Army Group Centre, became ever more convinced that the Russians were preparing for an offensive against him. He was also well

Soviet tanks on the rampage. By 1944 the Russians had developed highly effective assault tactics based on deep penetration of the enemy's front.

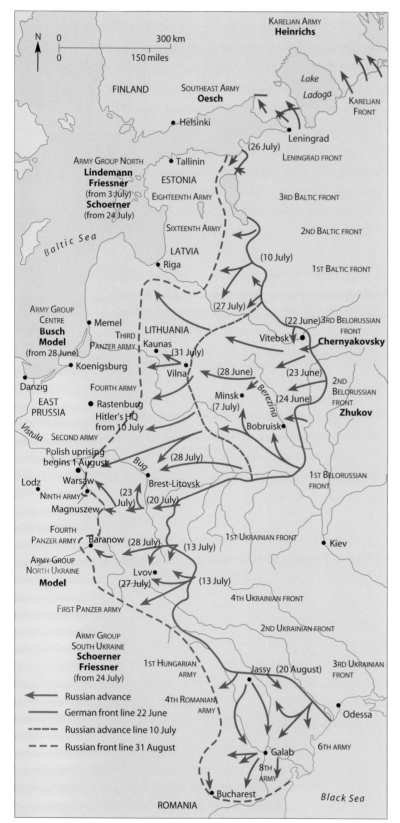

aware that his forces were holding a huge salient based on Minsk and had been forced to transfer troops to Army Group North Ukraine to the south and where Hitler and others believed that the main blow would fall. This had left his defences very stretched, but his request to shorten his line by withdrawing to the River Berezina was rejected by Hitler. Busch was further frustrated by the fact that the Russians enjoyed air superiority, which inhibited his air reconnaissance, and in the days before the assault the Russians imposed strict radio silence, denying him another intelligence source.

Bagration is launched

At dawn on 22 June 1944, the third anniversary of the German invasion of Russia, and after a short but intense bombardment, the 1st Baltic Front attacked north of Vitebsk. It took the Germans by surprise and by nightfall the Russians had penetrated to a depth of over 11 km (7 miles). The following day the 3rd Belorussian Front attacked south of Vitebsk, putting the city in danger of being cut off, and the 2nd Belorussian Front also attacked in the Orsha area, but made little progress. On 24 June the 1st Belorussian Front joined in, striking the southern part of the salient.

Faced with these multiple threats, Busch pleaded to be allowed to withdraw, but only grudgingly did Hitler relent and allow Third Panzer Army in the north to do so, although he ordered part of it to continue to hold Vitebsk, which fell within a couple of days. The withdrawal came too late, however. By 28 June Third Panzer Army had been shattered, while Fourth Army further south was desperately trying to get back to Minsk before being trapped, a fate which had already befallen Ninth Army. In short, Army Group Centre was being torn apart, not helped by partisan attacks on its communications.

Hitler, aghast at what was happening, replaced Busch with Walter Model, who was commanding Army Group North Ukraine. He also sacked Georg Lindemann, who was in charge of

The summer 1944 offensives drove the Germans out of Russia and placed Germany itself under threat.

COMBATANTS

Russians

- 2,330,000 men: Russian 1st Baltic Front and 1st, 2nd, 3rd Belorussian Fronts
- Commanded by Marshal Georgi Zhukov
- 178,000 killed and captured; 587,000 wounded and sick

Germans

- 500,000 men: German Army Group Centre
- Commanded by Field Marshal Ernst Busch (until 3 July), then Field Marshal Walter Model
- 250,000 killed, wounded and missing

Soviet infantry storm past a knocked-out PzKw V Panther during their advance towards the River Vistula.

Army Group North and wanted to carry out withdrawals because of the developing threat to the southern part of his sector. Worse was to come. The Russians succeeded in surrounding much of Fourth Army and entered Minsk on 7 July. Only the wings of Army Group Centre retained any cohesion. Six days later, the 1st Ukrainian and 1st Belorussian Fronts began to attack the northern sector of Army Group North Ukraine, intending to separate it from its desperately struggling neighbour. They created a pocket in the Brody area, which resulted in the loss of another 42,000 German troops.

On into Poland

As Army Group Centre continued to disintegrate, elements of Ivan Chernyakovsky's 3rd Belorussian Front reached Poland's 1939 eastern border on the River Bug. This occurred on 20 July, the same day that a bomb exploded during a conference Hitler was holding at his Rastenburg HQ in East Prussia. Three days later, the 1st Belorussian Front liberated Lublin and the extermination camp at Maidenek, and the northern Russian fronts increased the pressure by attacks against Army Group North. Hitler demanded that both Army Groups hold their ground, despite the liberation of more cities around them.

Yet, after an advance of 300 km (190 miles), the Russians were beginning to outstrip their supplies and their progress began to slow. This enabled Model to restore some order and even mount local counter-attacks. He could not, however, stop the 3rd Belorussian Front from swinging northwestwards towards the Latvian Baltic port of Riga and threatening to cut off the whole of Army Group North. As July came to an end, the people living on the eastern outskirts of Warsaw, the Polish capital, could hear the sounds of battle in the distance and began to believe that liberation from the Nazi yoke was finally at hand. Indeed, on 29 July a Russian-sponsored Polish radio station broadcast a call to arms. But the fighting the Poles could hear east of the Vistula was in fact the 1st Belorussian Front facing fierce counter-attacks by three Panzer divisions. It was a clear sign that the Russian offensive had run out of momentum and that the Germans were recovering. Consequently, on the night of 31 July/ 1 August the Russians went over to the defensive, but did not inform the Poles, who started a rebellion in the capital the following day.

The Warsaw uprising would continue until early October 1944, when the Germans crushed the last vestiges of resistance. All the time, the Russian forces east of the Vistula remained mere bystanders. Indeed, not until the following January would they finally liberate Warsaw. Yet Operation Bagration itself represented a major Russian victory and, with the Western Allies advancing towards Germany's western borders, the days of the Third Reich were now numbered.

66 The American Air Attack on Japan

Date: March–August 1945   Location: skies above Japan

We were going after military targets. No point in slaughtering civilians
for the mere sake of slaughter….We knew we were going to kill a lot of women
and kids when we burned that town [Tokyo]. Had to be done.
MAJOR-GENERAL CURTIS LEMAY, 1965

In the final year of World War II, US strategic air forces embarked upon a sustained bombing campaign against Japanese cities, one that ultimately reached an intensity and level of destruction unmatched in warfare before or since, and culminated in the atomic bombings of Hiroshima and Nagasaki. In the space of a few months, in particular March to August 1945, US 20th Air Force systematically destroyed dozens of Japanese towns and killed hundreds of thousands of civilians in a series of ferocious and arguably brutal firebombing raids. However, despite the best efforts of the American air forces, this campaign did not in itself force Japan's surrender and ultimately had to be supplemented by the atomic bombings and a variety of other measures.

Planning and initial raids

Long-term planning by the United States Army Air Forces (USAAF) for a bombing campaign against Japan dated back to the 1930s when specifications for a long-range four-engine strategic bomber capable of operations across oceanic areas had been drawn up, a programme that resulted in the B-29 Superfortress. American planners had also identified that Japanese urban areas, constructed with a high percentage of combustible materials, would be particularly susceptible to firebombing or incendiary raids.

However, during the early stages of the Pacific War of 1941–45, bombing Japan itself seemed a remote possibility, save the publicity stunt of Colonel Doolittle's raid on Tokyo in 1942. The earliest long-range efforts launched from China and India achieved little, and it was only with the capture of the Mariana Islands in June 1944 that a suitable base of operations, within range of Japan's major cities, fell into American hands. But the B-29, although highly advanced and clearly the most sophisticated bomber then in existence,

An American image anticipating the expected invasion of Japan in 1945. The invasion was rendered unnecessary by the surrender of Japan in August, shortly after the atomic bombings and the Soviet declaration of war.

had nevertheless been rushed into service and consequently suffered from a range of shortcomings. Difficulties centred upon the inadequately tested engines, inappropriate training, the weather and strong prevailing tail winds. Early results were disappointing and, by the end of 1944, pressure had begun to build on the USAAF to begin achieving clear results.

In January 1945, General Curtis LeMay was appointed to shake up the bombing campaign and he strove to pull the flagging elements of his command together. His tireless and single-minded approach improved morale, but results remained poor.

The torching of Japan

From March onwards, however, the campaign was transformed. LeMay, determined to demonstrate what his forces could achieve if allowed (and based largely on his own judgment), switched tactics. In essence he abandoned high-altitude, precision, daytime bombing and adopted low-level, night-time, area-bombing methods. This solved many tactical and meteorological difficulties, reduced strain on the still-temperamental engines of the B-29s and, as Japanese air defences were mainly intended for daytime operations, the already limited resistance virtually disappeared. Defensive armament on the B-29s could then be reduced, allowing even heavier payloads of bombs to be carried.

Initial results were impressive, as was the use of incendiaries (firebombs) which proved particularly effective against Japan's combustible cities. For Operation Meetinghouse, a raid conducted against Tokyo in March 1945, LeMay's command adopted the new tactics and the results were both appalling and spectacular. The heavy use of incendiaries helped to fashion a firestorm in which temperatures at the centre of the conflagration reached levels of great intensity, perhaps approaching 1,000 degrees Celsius. As many as 100,000 people died in the attack, and over one million were rendered homeless. The US air crews themselves were shocked and repulsed by the effects of the bombing, and employed oxygen masks to filter out the stench of burning flesh.

Under the tutelage of LeMay a series of similar firebombing raids followed, with cities such as Nagoya, Kobe, Osaka, Yokohama and Kawasaki receiving devastating treatment. Despite the reservations of some senior commanders, nothing was done to control LeMay's programme, reflecting the increasing desperation of the US to end the war.

The atomic bombings

However, the most controversial aspect of the air campaign was the deployment of atom bombs against Hiroshima and Nagasaki. The first nuclear weapons had been developed in the USA in the Manhattan Project, and the first was dropped by the B-29 *Enola Gay* at 8.15 am on 6 August. Perhaps 100,000 people died instantly and a new age in warfare was upon the world. It had taken dozens of bombers many hours to devastate Tokyo in March, compared to a few seconds and one bomb at Hiroshima. A second atomic bombing followed three days later on the city of Nagasaki, where another 35,000 were killed. In both cities thousands more would die subsequently because of radiation sickness and many

B-29 Super-fortresses unload their incendiaries over Japan in June 1945.

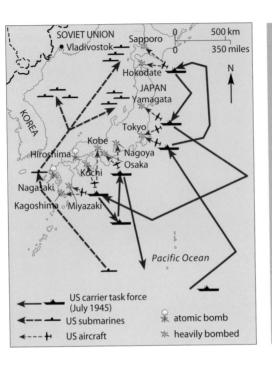

The blockade of Japan in 1944–45 was almost total and consequently devastating. The near collapse in Japanese air and naval strength from late 1944 allowed US forces free reign around the Japanese islands.

Legend	
US carrier task force (July 1945)	
US submarines	
US aircraft	
atomic bomb	
heavily bombed	

AIR CAMPAIGN

XXI Bomber Command Operations November 1944–August 1945

	Sorties	Bomb tonnage
Nov 1944	175	459
Dec 1944	492	1,759
Jan 1945	454	1,180
Feb 1945	732	1,854
Mar 1945	2,520	13,681
Apr 1945	3,246	16,383
May 1945	4,226	24,812
June 1945	5,243	32,524
Jul 1945	6,168	42,733
Aug 1945	3,145	20,936

more would suffer the after-effects for the rest of their lives. The prolonged effects of the air campaign and blockade fused with the atomic bombings, the Soviet declaration of war on Japan (8 August) and increasing realism in the Japanese military, to provoke surrender on 15 August.

Aftermath

Because of the atomic bombings, the conventional air campaign against Japan has been rather overlooked. Yet it is worth noting that more initially died in the Tokyo raid in March 1945 than in either of the August atomic bombings. However,

it is the first use of nuclear weapons that transformed our understanding of war. Some historians have argued that the atom bombs were dropped not for military reasons but predominantly to wring concession out of the increasingly recalcitrant Soviet Union, and as such should be seen as the first major act of the Cold War, as much as the last act of World War II. But whether Japan was ready to surrender on terms acceptable to the Allies prior to the atomic bombings is by no means clear and at best it was a combination of factors that forced Japan to capitulate. In reality the atomic bombings reflected the growing frustration and desperation of the USA to end the war as quickly as possible by whatever means. The level of political and diplomatic capital that flowed from this final act of the air campaign against Japan will, however, continue to be a matter of intense and bitter debate.

Ultimately, although the strategic and political effectiveness of the bombing campaign remains a matter of conjecture, there is little doubt that the raids – conventional and nuclear – threw up a whole host of political, moral and ethical concerns over excessive civilian deaths, concerns which still apply to warfare today.

Below A gruesome reminder of the aftermath of the atomic bombing of Nagasaki, 9 August 1945.

Huai-Hai

Date: 1948–49 Location: modern Xuzhou, northeastern China

You are to complete the Huai-Hai campaign in two months, November and December [1948]. Rest and consolidate your forces next January [1949]. From March to July you will be fighting in coordination with Liu Bocheng and Deng Xiaoping to drive the enemy to points along the Yangzi River, where he will dig in. By autumn your main force will probably be fighting to cross the Yangzi.

MAO ZEDONG, *THE CONCEPT OF OPERATIONS FOR THE HUAI-HAI CAMPAIGN*, 11 OCTOBER 1948

The Chinese Communist Huai-Hai campaign in 1948–49 resulted in the Nationalist retreat to Taiwan and to the founding of the People's Republic of China (PRC) on 1 October 1949. The 'loss' of China proved that Soviet-backed communism posed a serious danger, and for many Americans marked the real beginning of the Cold War. Soviet intervention, especially in denying the Nationalists access by sea to Manchuria, proved instrumental in allowing the Communists to move quickly from guerrilla tactics to conventional warfare.

Background to the Chinese Civil War

The Chinese Communist Party (CCP) was founded in July 1921. After a brief period of cooperation with the Nationalist Party, the CCP openly opposed Jiang Jieshi (Chiang Kai-shek) from April 1927 through to the end of 1936. Following the 9,000-km (6,000-mile) 'Long March' from southeast China to the northwest base area of Yan'an, Mao Zedong (Mao Tse-tung) took charge of the CCP. In the December 1936 Xi'an Incident, Jiang was kidnapped by General Zhang Xueliang and forced to form a second united front with the Communists aimed at Japan.

During the mid-1930s Mao's work *On Protracted War* divided warfare into three stages. Firstly, the Communists would be on the defensive using guerrilla tactics; secondly, they could progress to mobile war; and in a third phase that would spell victory for the CCP, the People's Liberation Army (PLA) could adopt positional warfare. At this time, Mao's strategic goal was to push Japan out of China, fighting only as far as the Yalu River (the border of Manchuria and Korea).

In November 1948, the Military Commission of the CPC Central Committee decided to establish the five-member General Front Committee to exercise unified leadership and command over the Central Plains and East China Field Armies. Left to right: Su Yu, Deng Xiaoping, Liu Bocheng, Chen Yi and Tan Zhenlin.

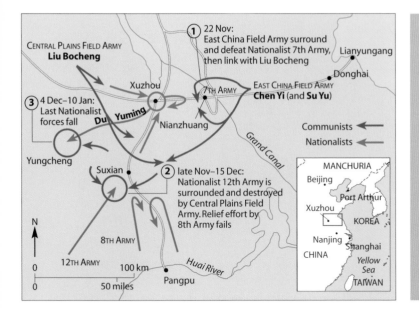

① 22 Nov:
East China Field Army surround
and defeat Nationalist 7th Army,
then link with Liu Bocheng

CENTRAL PLAINS FIELD ARMY
Liu Bocheng

Lianyungang

Xuzhou

Donghai

EAST CHINA FIELD ARMY
Chen Yi (and **Su Yu**)

7TH ARMY

③ 4 Dec–10 Jan:
Last Nationalist
forces fall **Du Yuming**

Nianzhuang

Communists ⟵
Nationalists ⟵

Yungcheng

Suxian

② late Nov–15 Dec:
Nationalist 12th Army is
surrounded and destroyed
by Central Plains Field
Army. Relief effort by
8th Army fails

Grand Canal

MANCHURIA
Beijing
Port Arthur
Xuzhou
KOREA
Nanjing
Shanghai
CHINA
Yellow
Sea
TAIWAN

N

0   100 km
0   50 miles

8TH ARMY

12TH ARMY

Huai River

Pangpu

The Communist victory at Xuzhou was the decisive battle of the Civil War. With the success of the Huai-Hai campaign, the road southwards to the Yangzi River was now open. After the Communist forces crossed the Yangzi they quickly took Nanjing and Shanghai, and pushed the Nationalist forces on to Taiwan.

As US forces advanced towards Japan, and with the end of the war in sight, the PLA opened an anti-Japanese offensive. Mao's real goal was to invade Manchuria in preparation for the final stage of the Communist-Nationalist civil war. Following the Soviet entry into the war in early August 1945, Soviet ships helped move the Communists by sea and gave them arms from Japanese stockpiles. Once in Manchuria, the PLA used the Soviet-controlled railways to move quickly into the metropolitan centres of Shenyang, Changchun and Harbin.

Renewal of the Chinese Civil War

Immediately after Japan's surrender, the civil war between Nationalists and Communists resumed. American representatives like George C. Marshall tried in vain to form a coalition government, but by 1947 both were fighting over the resource-rich, industrialized province of Manchuria.

Nationalist efforts to consolidate their power in Manchuria were foiled by Soviet control over the Manchurian ports of Port Arthur and Dalian (formerly Dairen). In particular, the Nationalist Navy, which had over 800 vessels and 40,000 men by October 1948, was denied access. According to the *China White Paper*, the Nationalists complained bitterly in November 1948 that 'the most fundamental factor in the general deterioration

of the military situation was the nonobservance by the Soviet Union of the [August 1945] Sino-Soviet Treaty of Friendship and Alliance.'

Chinese Communist authors understate Soviet help since it conflicts with Mao's claim that the CCP won unaided. However, new archival documents reveal the important role played by the USSR. In 1958, Khrushchev even reminded Mao, '…it was advantageous for you that the Soviet Army was in Port Arthur and Manchuria'.

The Huai-Hai battle

After Manchuria, the most important final campaigns of the civil war were centred around Beiping (later Beijing) and Tianjin, known as the 'Ping-Jin' campaign, and the 'Huai-Hai' campaign near Xuzhou in the northern half of Jiangsu and Anhui provinces, named after the Huai River and Haizhou. If the PLA took Xuzhou, the road to the Nationalist capital in Nanjing would open, facilitating the invasion of Shanghai and control over the vast agricultural resources of South China.

The Nationalists assembled five armies and troops from three pacification zones, totalling some 800,000 men, under the command of General Liu Zhi. On the PLA side, the Central Plains Field Army (later Second Field Army) under Liu Bocheng, and the East China Field Army (later Third Field Army) under Chen Yi, but commanded

in the field by the deputy commander Su Yu, totalled 600,000 men. Deng Xiaoping was appointed Secretary of the General Front-line Committee, which included Liu Bocheng, Chen Yi, Su Yu and Tan Zhenlin.

The final concept of the Huai-Hai campaign was to use the East China Field Army to encircle the 100,000-strong Nationalist 7th Army east of Xuzhou. Meanwhile, the Central Plains Field Army was to prevent any rescue attempt by the Nationalist forces west of Xuzhou. The pre-planned defection to the Communists of two Nationalist divisions northeast of Xuzhou on 8 November also contributed greatly to the defeat of the 7th Army at Nianzhuang, some 48 km (30 miles) east of Xuzhou. After nearly two weeks of fighting, the Nationalist army was destroyed on 22 November and its commander, Huang Baitao, killed.

While the East China Field Army was fighting east of Xuzhou, the Central Plains Field Army struck to the south and east to seize the Tianjin-Pukou Railway and cut off Xuzhou from the south. In late November, the Nationalists tried to reestablish a link with Xuzhou by having their 2nd, 13th and 16th armies attack southward while their 6th, 8th and 12th armies moved to the north. This plan failed and on 1 December the group army in Xuzhou commanded by Du Yuming abandoned the city and began moving southwest. By this time the Central Plains Field Army had already surrounded the Nationalist 12th Army between the Hui and Guo rivers southwest of Suxian. Then, on 4 December, Su Yu's East China Field Army caught up with and surrounded Du Yuming's three armies. The 12th Army was destroyed on 15 December and the last remnants of Du Yuming's force fell on 10 January 1949.

In a campaign lasting 63 days the Communists had wiped out an estimated 550,000 Nationalist troops and opened the road to the Yangzi River valley. In April 1949 the Communists crossed the Yangzi River and took Nanjing. By May, PLA forces had moved into Shanghai and were pushing into southwestern China. Soon, Jiang and his loyal followers would be forced to retreat to the island of Taiwan.

Conclusions

Without assistance from the USSR, the CCP might have faced a combined land-sea attack from the Nationalist Army and Navy. With access to Manchuria cut off by Soviet forces, the PLA moved quickly to positional warfare, which played to its strengths. The Huai-Hai victory not only helped to establish Mao Zedong's reputation as the PRC's unrivalled leader, but later Deng Xiaoping also came to power, in part due to leadership qualities demonstrated at Huai-Hai.

A modern reconstruction painting of the battle, which spelled the defeat of the Nationalist forces in mainland China. By the artist Wei Chuyu, this painting won a People's Liberation Army Art prize in 1983.

Dien Bien Phu

Date: 20 November 1953–7 May 1954   Location: northwestern Vietnam

*To occupy Dien Bien Phu and accept battle there appeared to me as the unique solution,
giving me the chance, with the forces that I had, to save Laos.*
GENERAL HENRI NAVARRE, *AGONIE DE L'INDOCHINE*, 1953–54

The battle of Dien Bien Phu was one of the most important of the entire 20th century, signalling the end of the Indo-China War and of Western colonialism in Asia. Fighting began in December 1946 between the French and the Vietnamese nationalists, the Viet Minh, led by veteran Communist Ho Chi Minh. Despite massive US aid to the French, the 1949 Communist victory in China had provided the Viet Minh with a sanctuary and supply base. The French also lost the battle for the 'hearts and minds' of the

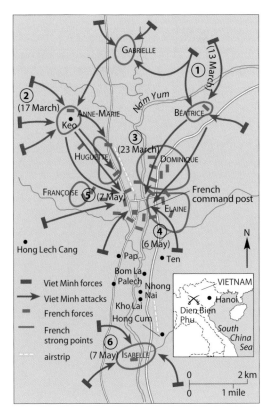

The French relied almost entirely on airborne aid and their supplies were severely reduced by the destruction of their airstrip and planes. Henri Navarre, overall French commander, had drastically underestimated the Viet Minh forces, whose persistent bombardment led to the capture of every French strong point.

people, for they failed to grant genuine authority to the State of Vietnam.

In early 1954 Viet Minh commander General Vo Nguyen Giap prepared to invade Laos. The French commander in Indo-China, General Henri Navarre, responded with Operation Castor: the establishment of a base in the village of Dien Bien Phu in far northwestern Vietnam as a blocking position astride the chief invasion route into northern Laos. He hoped to use this as bait to draw Viet Minh forces into battle, then destroy them with superior artillery and air power.

Located in an obscure valley some 321 km (200 miles) by air from Hanoi, Dien Bien Phu had a small airstrip. On 20 November 1953, 2,200 paratroops dropped into the valley, easily defeating the Viet Minh force there. Navarre assumed that, at most, Giap would commit one division, but if proved wrong he was still confident the garrison could be evacuated. But to leave the Viet Minh in control of the high ground surrounding the base would be disastrous.

Colonel (promoted to Brigadier General during the battle) Christian de Castries commanded French forces at Dien Bien Phu. These were entirely dependent on air supply by some 75 C-47 Dakotas. The French could also call on 48 B-26 and Privateer bombers, 112 Bearcat and Hellcat fighter-bombers, and a few helicopters. Around the French central command post in the village, de Castries ordered construction of a series of strong points: Béatrice, Gabrielle, Anne-Marie, Dominique, Huguette, Françoise, Elaine and Isabelle. This last post was separated from the others, 4.8 km (3 miles) to the south, and could

Viet Minh

- 49,500 troops; 20–24 105-mm howitzers, 15–20 75-mm howitzers, 20 120-mm mortars, at least 40 82-mm mortars, 80 Chinese-crewed 37-mm anti-aircraft guns, 100 anti-aircraft machine guns, 12–16 six-tube Katyusha rocket launchers
- Commanded by General Vo Nguyen Giap
- 22,900 casualties (7,900 killed, 15,000 wounded)

French

- 16,500 men; 4 155-mm howitzers, 24 105-mm howitzers, 4 120-mm mortars
- Commanded by Colonel Christian Marie Ferdinand de la Croix de Castries
- 20,000 casualties (2,242 killed, 3,711 missing, 6,463 wounded, 6,500 prisoners, plus forces lost in relief operations)

Viet Minh soldiers advance across Muong Thanh Bridge towards the French central command post. Muong Thanh was the name of the village in tribal T'ai. Dien Bien Phu is Vietnamese for the French name of 'Seat of the Border County Prefecture'.

not only be easily cut off, but it also tied down a third of the French forces. By mid-March 1954 the French had nearly 11,000 men in the valley, a third of them ethnic Vietnamese. Ultimately they committed 16,544 men there. Fortifications were inadequate, the French assuming that their artillery could quickly knock out any enemy artillery.

Giap accepted the challenge, but there was political pressure on him to do so. A diplomatic conference of the great powers was set to begin in Geneva, and a major Viet Minh military victory might bring negotiations to end the war. Giap committed four divisions to the effort, assembling some 49,500 combat troops and 31,500 support personnel.

The battle

The siege opened on 13 March with a heavy Viet Minh bombardment. Although the French added 4,000 men during the battle, Giap more than offset this with increases of his own and also steadily improved his artillery. Thousands of porters literally dragged the guns there. Ultimately the Viet Minh deployed more artillery pieces and fired more rounds than did the French.

On the very first night of the siege, 13–14 March, the Viet Minh took Béatrice. Gabrielle fell two days later. The Viet Minh also shelled the airstrip, destroying or driving its aircraft away and knocking out its radio direction beacon. C-47s still flew in supplies and took out wounded, but at great risk. The last flight in or out occurred on 27 March. During the battle, the Viet Minh shot down 48 French planes and destroyed another 16 on the ground.

Heavy casualties forced Giap to shift from costly human-wave tactics to classic siege warfare of trenches inching ever closer to the French lines. The final assault occurred on 6 May and the last French troops surrendered on the evening of 7 May. A plan to rescue the garrison or to break out came too late. The Viet Minh immediately sent their 6,500 prisoners off on foot on an 800-km (500-mile) trek to prison camps, from which fewer than half returned.

Aftermath

The outcome of the battle allowed French politicians to shift the blame to the French Army for the defeat in Indo-China and thus extricate France from the war. The Geneva Conference did subsequently hammer out a settlement for Indo-China, but it proved to be only a truce.

The Tet Offensive

Date: 30 January–24 February 1968   Location: Vietnam

With 1968, a new phase is starting. We have reached an important point when the end begins to come into view.…the enemy's hopes are bankrupt. With your support we will give you a success that will impact not only on South Viet-Nam but on every emerging nation in the world.
ADDRESS BY GENERAL WILLIAM WESTMORELAND TO THE NATIONAL PRESS CLUB,
WASHINGTON, D.C., 21 NOVEMBER 1987

Bell UH-1 'Huey' troop-carrying helicopters lifting soldiers to the combat zone during the Tet Offensive. Each Huey could transport as many as six fully-loaded soldiers.

The Communist Tet Offensive of January 1968 was a major turning point in the Vietnam War. Since Dien Bien Phu (see previous entry), fighting in Indo-China had resumed in the late 1950s, the United States defending the southern Republic of Vietnam (RVN) against a Communist insurgency directed by the northern Democratic Republic of Vietnam (DRV). When the poorly trained, ineffectively-led Army of the Republic of Vietnam (ARVN) troops were repeatedly battered by local Communist forces (Viet Cong), Washington dispatched US ground troops. An increasingly bloody stalemate developed as the regular Communist army, the People's Army of Vietnam (PAVN), infiltrated the south.

Nonetheless, in November 1967 General William Westmoreland, commander of the US Military Assistance Command Vietnam (MACV),

Wounded US Marines being transported to an aid station on an M-48 tank during the battle for the city of Hue.

returned to the United States and praised the battlefield progress, even telling a reporter, 'I hope they try something, because we are looking for a fight.' In South Vietnam, meanwhile, as US attention was riveted on a series of border engagements, PAVN and Viet Cong troops were preparing their largest military operation to date. PAVN Commander General Vo Nguyen Giap planned to draw US forces away from the populated areas, then mount a general military offensive to bring a popular uprising against the RVN government and the Americans.

The DRV leadership selected the Lunar New Year celebrations of Tet, which had traditionally been a ceasefire. ARVN units were at low strength, security was lax and even ARVN-uniformed guerrillas managed to travel undetected.

Contrary to popular myth, the offensive did not catch the Americans completely by surprise. A variety of sources indicated that PAVN/Viet Cong units were concentrating around the cities. On January 10 the commander of II Field Force, Lieutenant General Frederick C. Weyand, con-

vinced Westmoreland to pull additional US combat battalions back around the capital, making 27 battalions instead of the planned 14 in the Saigon area. It was to be one of the critical decisions of the war.

Westmoreland's chief of intelligence, Brigadier General Philip B. Davidson, did not believe that the Communists would risk alienating the people by attacking during Tet. But his chief error was in underestimating both the scale of the offensive and the tenacity of the Communists, who would risk everything in a fight for the cities.

With tension mounting, Westmoreland tried to convince RVN President Nguyen Van Thieu and ARVN Chief of the Joint General Staff General Cao Van Vien to end the ceasefire over Tet. He secured only a reduction to 36 hours and pledge of at least 50 per cent of ARVN duty troops on full alert.

The Tet Offensive

Early on 30 January 1968, PAVN/Viet Cong forces hit several locations in central South Vietnam, but the bulk of the attacks began the next night.

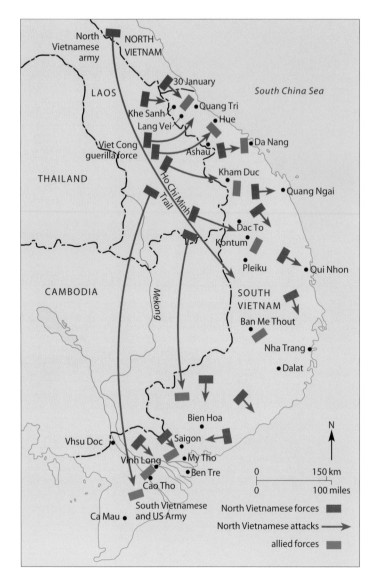

US Military Assistance Command Vietnam (MAVC) & Army of the Republic of Vietnam (ARVN)

- 85,000 men (281 manoeuvre battalions, with overwhelming advantages in tanks and other armoured vehicles, artillery, fixed wing aircraft and helicopters)

- Commanded by General William Westmoreland

- MAVC: 1,829 killed, 7,746 dead, 11 missing; ARVN: 2,788 dead, 8,299 wounded, 578 missing; Vietnamese civilians: *c.* 12,600 dead

People's Army of Vietnam (PAVN) & Viet Cong

- 197 manoeuvre battalions (99 PAVN and 98 Viet Cong; a few PT-76 tanks; some artillery and 122-mm rockets; no aircraft)

- Commanded by General Vo Nguyen Giap

- 45,000 dead, 5,800 captured

munists made a large investment of resources. Fighting was intense and house-to-house. In the 25 days it took US and South Vietnamese forces to retake Hue, half of the city was destroyed and 116,000 of 140,000 civilians were made homeless.

Aftermath

The Tet Offensive was a major Communist military defeat. Although Allied losses were the heaviest of the war to date, PAVN/Viet Cong losses amounted to half of the force committed; furthermore there had been no general rallying of the civilian population to the Communists. Support for the RVN government grew as news arrived from Hue that the Communists had executed some 5,000 'enemies of the people'. But the RVN government also faced staggering problems, particularly in caring for 627,000 newly homeless people, and pacification had suffered a serious blow.

Most importantly, the American public perceived Tet as a defeat. The offensive came as a great shock and many shapers of public opinion now forcefully objected to the war. Before the Tet Offensive, Washington was trying to win the war militarily; afterwards it sought to find a way out.

The unexpected timing and ferocity of the Communist assault shocked the United States, which barely managed to gather sufficent men in time. Despite eventually defeating the Northern Vietnamese forces, the American public perceived Tet as a defeat rather than victory.

Communist forces struck 36 of 44 provincial capitals, 5 of 6 autonomous cities, 64 of 242 district capitals and about 50 hamlets. They also hit many military installations, including 23 airfields, destroying 58 (and damaging 280) aircraft.

In the vital area around Saigon, the Communists committed the equivalent of more than two divisions. Communist sappers penetrated the US Embassy, blew up part of the large Long Binh ammunition storage dump and captured all of Bien Hoa City. Most of the fighting inside Saigon was over in a matter of days, save in the Chinese district of Cho Lon.

In the former imperial capital of Hue, the Com-

The Iraq War

Date: 19 March–14 April 2003   Location: Iraq

Decisive combat in Iraq saw a maturing of joint force operations in many ways. Some capabilities reached new performance levels....Our forces were able to achieve their operational objectives by integrating ground manoeuvre, special operations, precision lethal fires, and non-lethal effects.

GENERAL TOMMY FRANKS IN TESTIMONY TO THE US CONGRESS, 9 JULY 2003

In August 1990, dictator of Iraq President Saddam Hussein invaded and annexed Kuwait, prompting US President George H. W. Bush to gather a worldwide coalition against Iraq and launch Operation Desert Storm on 17 January 1991 – a massive air attack followed by a ground assault on 24 February that liberated Kuwait in only 100 hours. Left in power, Saddam subsequently defied the United Nations by failing to account for (and allegedly failing to destroy) all of his so-called 'weapons of mass destruction' (WMD). Frustrated UN inspectors left Iraq, UN economic sanctions continued and Britain and the United States enforced no-fly zones for Iraqi fixed-wing aircraft.

The new Bush administration

US President George W. Bush, elected in 2000, adopted an increasingly tough attitude towards Iraq, particularly following the 11 September 2001 al-Qaeda terrorist attacks against the World Trade Center in New York and the Pentagon in Washington, D.C. After Afghanistan's Taliban government refused Washington's demands that it hand over members of al-Qaeda, especially its leader Osama bin Laden, US forces invaded Afghanistan and overthrew the Taliban.

President Bush announced his intention to root out terrorism and punish those states that supported it, specifically mentioning an 'Axis of Evil' of Iraq, Iran and North Korea. The United States, supported by the British government under Prime Minister Tony Blair, secured a UN

Security Council resolution threatening force unless Iraq made full disclosure of its WMD and calling on UN inspectors regularly to report their progress to the Security Council. The Bush administration also posited a link between the Iraqi government and al-Qaeda (later not proven).

Iraq claimed it had nothing to hide, but the inspectors reported only mixed success and the Bush administration pushed for the use of force. Following a coalition of France, Germany and Russia that blocked such a resolution in the UN,

A US Airborne soldier parachutes into northern Iraq. Securing control in that area was made easier by widespread Kurdish support.

Bush and Blair decided to proceed virtually alone. Bush secured a congressional mandate and enjoyed solid US public support. Increasingly, Bush also demanded that Saddam and his family be removed from power in order to bring democracy to Iraq. Later, when no WMDs were found, Bush made this a chief justification for the war.

An Allied buildup had been underway for some time in Kuwait under US Army Central Command commander General Tommy Franks, but, in this war with Iraq, Saudi Arabia refused the use of its bases and there was no broad coalition of nations behind the United States. Some of the Gulf states, notably Kuwait and Qatar, cooperated, but Washington experienced a major setback when the Turkish government refused to allow US forces to use its territory for a northern front, a key component of the US military plan.

Operation Iraqi Freedom

The war, dubbed Operation Iraqi Freedom, began on the night of 19 March, just hours after the expiration of Bush's ultimatum to Saddam Hussein. This was to be a hi-tech war of a new kind with the bare minimum of troops and a rapier-like ground approach, rather than the sledgehammer of the previous Gulf War. Over succeeding nights, Baghdad was repeatedly struck with cruise-missile attacks and air strikes by B-1, B-2 and B-52 bombers aimed at key headquarters and command-and-control targets. Altogether the

coalition flew some 41,404 sorties during the war (93 per cent US), while no Iraqi fixed-wing aircraft took to the air. Of aerial munitions employed, some 70 per cent were 'smart' (guided weapons) and 30 per cent were 'dumb' (unguided). In 1991 only 10 per cent had been 'smart' weapons.

On the night of 22/23 March 2003, Allied aircraft landed in northern Iraq, ferrying men and supplies into the Kurdish-controlled zone and opening a northern front, not only against the Iraqi Army but also against Ansar al-Islam, a militant Islamic group with training facilities at Kalak on the Iranian border. This base was later destroyed by US Special Forces and Kurdish troops. Air strikes also occurred against the northern cities of Mosul and Kirkuk.

Meanwhile, a 100,000-man coalition ground force moved into Iraq from Kuwait on three axes to race the 482 km (300 miles) to Baghdad. In the more sparsely populated west the 3rd Infantry Division, its 3rd Squadron leading, made the most rapid progress, while in the centre the 1st Marine Expeditionary Force moved north through Nasiriya and on to Najaf and Karbala. And on the eastern part of the front the British had the difficult task of securing the port of Umm Qasr and Iraq's second largest city of Basra, with its half million, largely Shiite, population.

The British 7th Armoured Brigade covered the 112 km (70 miles) from the Iraq-Kuwait border to the outskirts of Basra in little more than a day. The

The second night of the Iraq War saw heavy coalition use of precision munitions in and around the city of Baghdad, in what was known as the 'Shock and Awe' campaign.

COMBATANTS

US and Coalition forces

- *Men*: 466,985 US personnel deployed in the area of operations (actual deployment on the ground was *c*. 130,000 in Kuwait); coalition forces included 42,987 British, 2,050 Australians and 180 Poles
  Air: 1,663 US and 115 British fixed-wing aircraft; nearly 400 US and British helicopters
  Land: 1,000 main battle tanks and 1,000 other armoured vehicles
  Sea: *c*. 150 ships, including 47 US Navy major surface combatants (5 US carrier battle groups; 2 amphibious task forces; 12 submarines; and many surface support ships); in all about one third of the US Navy; British Navy task group of 1 aircraft carrier, 1 helicopter carrier, 1 submarine and amphibious support ships; 3 Australian ships

- Commanded by US Army General Tommy Franks

- 119 US and 31 British killed

Iraqis

- *Men*: *c*. 400,000 troops of varying quality
  Air: some 255 combat aircraft, which were grounded during the conflict; perhaps 100 attack helicopters
  Land: 1,000 surface-to-air missiles (SAMs); about 2,400 major artillery weapons; some 6,000 anti-aircraft guns; about 2,200 tanks (700 T-72s); and 3,700 other armoured vehicles
  Sea: no official navy

- Commanded by President Saddam Hussein

- over 2,400 killed and 7,000 prisoners of war

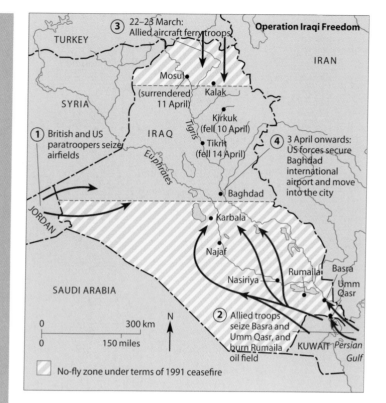

expected uprising of the Shia population there did not occur, however, thanks to memories of the abortive and costly 1991 rebellion. So long as Baath Party activists and 'fedayeen' (irregulars often in civilian clothes who attacked from civilian vehicles using machine guns and rocket-propelled grenades) remained entrenched in the city, the Shia would not rebel.

At Basra the British slowly began infiltrating their own specialized units in and out of the city, then mounting larger swift raids and, by April, the local population was helping to root out remaining Baathists. Meanwhile, the Allies had seized by *coup de main* the oil fields and key refineries north of Basra. US Special Forces secured airfields in western Iraq and, on the night of 26 March, 1,000 members of the 173rd Airborne Brigade dropped into northern Iraq to work in conjunction with lightly armed Kurdish forces against the key oil-production centre of Mosul.

A fierce sand storm on 25–26 March, logistical problems and the so-called 'Saddam Fedayeen' all delayed the move north. On 26 March the US 3rd Squadron, 7th Cavalry Regiment and other 3rd Infantry Division (ID) elements defeated an Iraqi force near Najaf in the largest battle of the war thus far, killing about 450 Iraqis.

With some units short of ammunition and food, and with an advance of 320 km (200 miles), a week into the campaign US forces went into an 'operational pause'. Saddam, meanwhile, repositioned the six elite Republican Guard divisions around Baghdad for a defence of the capital. As the Baghdad and Medina divisions moved to new positions south of the city, heavy coalition air attack destroyed much of their equipment.

On 3 April US forces reached the outskirts of Baghdad and began securing the international airport. By 5 April Baghdad was in effect under a

The Allies focused on capturing specific areas and key cities in Iraq, having mustered the support of a 100,000-strong coalition. But despite the success of their mission to depose Saddam Hussein, the conflict provoked huge controversy around the world and sparked widespread unrest among the Iraqi population.

In one of the most memorable images of the war, a US soldier watches as a large statue of President Saddam Hussein is toppled in the centre of Baghdad on 9 April 2003.

loose blockade, with the 3rd ID closing from the southwest, the Marines from the southeast, and a brigade of the 101st Airborne Division from the north. On that day a brigade of the 3rd ID pushed through downtown Baghdad, inflicting an estimated 1,000 Iraqi casualties. Operating on the assumption that war is more a test of wills than of hardware, this strike showed that US forces could move at will. On 6 and 7 April the process was repeated and, in a fierce firefight on the 6th, US forces killed an estimated 2,000–3,000 Iraqi soldiers for only one of their own lost, and moved on to occupy one of the presidential palaces.

On 7 April a coalition spokesman announced that Iraq had only 19 tanks and 40 artillery pieces left. Coalition forces held some 7,000 Iraqi POWs. The ring around the capital was now closed.

By 8 April there was at least one US brigade in Baghdad. The next day resistance collapsed in the capital as Iraqi civilians, assisted by US Marines, toppled a large statue of Saddam. There was still fighting in parts of the city as diehard Saddam loyalists sniped at US troops, but Iraqi government central command and control had collapsed. On 10 April a small number of Kurdish fighters, US Special Forces and the 173rd Airborne Brigade liberated Kirkuk. The next day, Iraq's third largest city of Mosul fell when the Iraqi V Corps commander surrendered some 30,000 men. Apart from sporadic shooting in Baghdad and massive looting there and elsewhere, the one

remaining centre of resistance was Saddam Hussein's ancestral home of Tikrit.

On 12 April the 101st Airborne relieved the Marines and 3rd ID in Baghdad, allowing them to deploy northwest to Tikrit, while the 173rd Airborne Brigade took control of the northern oil fields from the Kurds so as to prevent any possibility of Turkish intervention. The battle for Tikrit failed to materialize, and on 14 April Allied forces entered the city. That same day the Pentagon announced that major military operations in Iraq were over; all that remained was mopping up.

Aftermath

Allied air power, the rapidity of the Allied ground advance (the longest in Marine Corps history) and the ability of coalition troops to fight at night were all important in coalition success. And throughout, coalition forces endeavoured to convince the Iraqi people that they came as liberators rather than conquerors. But although the coalition had won the war, winning the peace proved more difficult than anticipated. Providing security and reestablishing public services proved major obstacles, as the Bush administration had given little thought to, and had clearly underestimated the difficulty of, post-war operations. Saddam loyalists who mounted terrorist attacks to dislodge the occupiers, animosities between Shiites and Sunni Muslims, and radical clerics all threatened to undermine the coalition military victory.

Further Reading

Ancient World

1 Marathon
Davis Hanson, V., *The Western Way of War: Infantry Battle in Classical Greece* (Berkeley, 2000)
Doenges, N., 'The campaign and the battle of Marathon', *Historia* 47 (1998),1–27
Gomme, A. W., 'Herodotus and Marathon', *Phoenix* 6 (1952), 79
Hammond, N. G. L., 'The Campaign and Battle of Marathon', *Journal of Hebrew Studies* 88 (1968), 13–57
Lloyd, A. *Marathon: The Story of Civilizations on Collision Course* (London, 1973)
Sekunda, N., *Marathon 490 BC* (Oxford, 2002)
Wees, H. V., *Greek Warfare: Myth and Realities* (London, 2002)

2 Salamis
de Souza, P., *The Greek and Persian Wars* (Oxford, 2003)
Green, P., *The Greco-Persian Wars* (Berkeley, 1996)
Herodotus, *The Histories*, trans. G. Rawlinson & intro. H. Bowden (London, 1992)
Lazenby, J., *The Defence of Greece 490–479 BC* (Warminster, 1993)

3 Gaugamela
Cohen, A., *The Alexander Mosaic: Stories of Victory and Defeat* (Cambridge, 1997)
Cummings, L. V., *Alexander the Great* (New York, 2004)
Fildes, A. & Fletcher, J., *Alexander the Great: Son of the Gods* (Los Angeles, 2002)
Fuller, J. V. C., *Generalship of Alexander the Great* (Collingdale, 1998)
Marsden, E. W., *The Campaign of Gaugamela* (Liverpool, 1964)
Rufus, Q. C., *The History of Alexander*, trans. Yardley (London, 1984)
Sekunda, N., *The Persian Army 560–330 BC* (Oxford, 1992)

4 Cannae
Daly, G., *Cannae: The Experience of Battle in the Second Punic War* (Oxford, 2001)
Goldsworthy, A., *Cannae* (London, 2001)
Livy, T. L., *The War With Hannibal,* Books XXI–XXX of *The History of Rome from its Foundation* (London, 1965)
Rosenstein, N. S., *Imperatores Victi. Military Defeat and Aristocratic Competition in the Middle and Late Republic* (Berkeley, 1990)
Shean, J. F., 'Hannibal's mules: the logistical limitations of Hannibal's army and the battle of Cannae, 216 BC', *Historia* 45 (1996), 159–87

5 Gaixia
Nienhauser, W. H. Jr. (ed.), Ssu-ma, Ch'ien [Sima Qian], *The Grand Scribe's Records, vol. 1: The Basic Annals of Pre-Han China* (Bloomington & Indianapolis, 1994)
Nienhauser, W. H. Jr. (ed.), Ssu-ma, Ch'ien [Sima Qian], *The Grand Scribe's Records, vol. 2: The Basic Annals of Han China* (Bloomington & Indianapolis, 2002)
Pan, Ku [Ban Gu], *The History of the Former Han Dynasty,* trans. H. H. Dubs (Baltimore, 1938)
Sima, Qian, *Records of the Grand Historian: Han Dynasty I,* trans. B. Watson (Hong Kong & New York, revised ed. 1993)
Twitchett, D. & Loewe, M. (eds), *The Cambridge History of China, vol. 1: The Ch'in and Han Empires, 221 BC–AD 220* (Cambridge, 1986)

6 Actium
Carter, J. M., *The Battle of Actium. The Rise and Triumph of Augustus Caesar* (London, 1970)
Dio, C., *The Roman History: The Reign of Augustus,* trans. I. Scott-Kilvert & intro. J. Carter (London, 1987)
Morrison, J.S., *Greek and Roman Oared Warships 399–30 BC* (Oxford, 1996)
Virgil, *The Eclogues, Georgics and Aeneid of Virgil,* trans. C. Day Lewis (Oxford, 1966)

7 Teutoburg Forest
'Battle of the Teutoberg Forest', *Archaeology* (Sep–Oct 1992), 26–32
Goldsworthy, A., *The Complete Roman Army* (London & New York, 2003)
Schlüter, W., 'The Battle of the Teutoburg Forest: Archaeological Research at K alkriese near Osnabrück', in *Roman Germany. Studies in Cultural Interaction*, Journal of Roman Archaeology, Supplementary Series no. 32 (Portsmouth/Rhode Island, 1999), 125–59.
Todd, M., *The Early Germans* (Oxford, 1992)
Wells, P. S., *The Battle That Stopped Rome: Emperor Augustus, Arminius, and the Slaughter of the Legions in the Teutoburg Forest* (New York, 2003)
Whittaker, C. R., *Frontiers of the Roman Empire* (Baltimore, 1994)

8 Adrianople
Ammianus Marcellinus (Loeb Classical Library), trans. J.C. Rolfe (Harvard, 1940)
Elton, H. W., *Warfare in Roman Europe: AD 350–425* (Oxford, 1996)
Hagith. S., 'On Foederati, Hospitalitas, and the settlement of the Goths in AD 418', *American Journal of Philology* 108, no. 4 (1987), 759–72
MacDowall, S., *Adrianople AD 378: The Goths Crush Rome's Legions* (Oxford, 2001)
Wolfram, H., *History of the Goths* (Berkeley, 1988)

Medieval World

9 Poitiers
Brunner, H., 'Der Reiterdienst und die Anfänge des Lehnwesens', Zeitschrift der Savigny-Stiftung für Rechtsgeschichte, Germanistische Abteilung 8 (1887), 1–38
Collins, R., *The Arab Conquest of Spain* (Oxford,1989)
Fouracre, P., *The Age of Charles Martel* (London, 2000)
France, J., 'The military history of the Carolingian period', *Revue Belge d'Histoire Militaire* 26 (1985), 81–99
France, J., 'Recent writing on medieval warfare: from the fall of Rome to *c.* 1300', *Journal of Military History* 65 (2001), 441–73
Treadgold, W., *A Concise History of Byzantium* (London, 2001)
Wallace-Hadrill, J. M. (ed.), *The Fourth Book of the Chronicle of Fredegar* (Edinburgh,1960)

10 Lechfeld
Bachrach, B. S., 'Magyar – Ottonian warfare. Apropos a new minimalist interpretation', *Francia* 27 (2000), 211–30
Bowlus, C. R., 'Der Weg vom Lechfeld. Die Kriegführung der Magyaren: Überlegungen zur Vernictung der Ungarn im August 955 anhand ihrer Kriegführung', in Worster, H. (ed.), *Tagungsband: Ausstellung Bayern und Ungarn* (Passau, 2001), 77–90
Eberl, B., *Die Ungarnschlacht auf dem Lechfeld (Gunzele) im Jahre 955* (Augsburg, 1955)
Leyser, K., 'The battle at the Lech, 955. A study in tenth-century warfare', in *Medieval Germany and Its Neighbours 900–1250* (London,

1982), 11–42
Lindner, R. P., 'Nomadism, horses and Huns', *Past and Present* 92
   (1981), 3 & 19
Sinor, D., 'Horse and pasture in inner Asian history," *Oriens Extremus*
   19 (1972), 171–84

11 Hastings
Bates, D., *William the Conqueror* (Stroud, 2001)
Bradbury, J., *The Battle of Hastings* (Stroud,1998)
Higham, N. J., *The Death of Anglo-Saxon England* (Stroud,1997)
Morillo, S., *The Battle of Hastings. Sources and Interpretations*
   (Woodbridge, 1996)
Walker, I. W., *Harold, the Last Anglo-Saxon King* (Stroud, 1997)
William of Poitiers, *The Deeds of William*, ed. R. H. C. Davis & M.
   Chibnall (Oxford, 1998)

12 Manzikert
Cahen, C., 'La campagne de Mantzikert d'après les sources
   Mussulmanes', *Byzantion* 9 (1934), 613–42
France, J., *Victory in the East. A Military History of the First Crusade*
   (Cambridge, 1994)
Friendly, A., *The Dreadful Day. The Battle of Manzikert, 1071* (London,
   1981)
Haldon, J., *Warfare, State and Society in the Byzantine World 565–1204*
   (London,1999)
Psellus, M., *Chronographia*, trans. E. R. A. Sewter (London, 1953)
Vryonis, S., *The Decline of Medieval Hellenism in Asia Minor and the
   Process of Islamization from the Eleventh through the Fifteenth
   Century* (Berkeley, 1971)

13 Hattin
Billings, M., *The Cross and the Crescent. A History of the Crusades*
   (London, 1987)
Edbury, P. W. (ed.), *The Conquest of Jerusalem and the Third Crusade.
   Sources in Translation* (Aldershot, 1996)
Hamilton, B., *The Leper King and his Heirs. Baldwin IV and the Crusader
   Kingdom of Jerusalem* (Cambridge, 2000)
Kedar, B.Z., 'The battle of Hattin revisited', in B. Z. Kedar (ed.), *The
   Horns of Hattin* (London, 1992)
Lyons, M. C. & Jackson, D. E. P., *Saladin. The Politics of Holy War*
   (Cambridge, 1982)
Riley-Smith, J., *The Atlas of the Crusades* (London,1991)
Smail, R. C., *Crusading Warfare 1097–1193* (Cambridge, 1956, 2nd ed.
   1995)

14 Liegnitz
Brent, P., *The Mongol Empire* (London, 1976)
Chambers, J., *The Devil's Horsemen. The Mongol Invasion of Europe*
   (London, 2001)
de Hartog, L., *Genghis Khan, Conqueror of the World* (London, 1989)
Marshall, R., *Storm from the East. From Genghis Khan to Khubilai Khan*
   (London, 1993)
Paris, M. *The English History,* ed. J. A. Giles (London, 1852–54)
Morgan, D., *The Mongols* (Oxford, 1986)
Saunders, J. J., *The History of the Mongol Conquests* (London,1971)
Smith, J. M., 'Mongol society and military in the Middle East:
   antecedents and adaptations', in Y. Lev (ed.), *Wear and Society in the
   Eastern Mediterranean, 7th–15th Centuries* (Leiden,1997), 249–66

15 Hakata Bay
Delgado, J. P., 'Relics of the Kamikaze', *Archaeology* 56/1 (Jan–Feb
   2003), 36–41
Friday, K. F., *Hired Swords. The Rise of Private Warrior Power in Early
   Japan* (Stanford, CA, 1992)
Farris, W. W., *Heavenly Warriors. The Evolution of Japan's Military
   500–1700* (Cambridge, MA & London, 1992)

16 Bannockburn
Barrow, G. W. S., *Robert Bruce and the Community of the Realm of
   Scotland* (London, 1965)
Barbour, J., *The Bruce*, ed. A. A. M. Duncan (Edinburgh, 1997)
Nusbacher, A., *The Battle of Bannockburn 1314* (Stroud, 2000)
DeVries, K., *Infantry Warfare in the Early Fourteenth Century*
   (Woodbridge, 1996)

17 Crécy
Ayton, A. & Preston, P. (eds), *The Battle of Crecy 1346* (Woodbridge,
   2005)
Burne, A. H., *The Crécy War* (London, 1955)
DeVries, K., *Infantry Warfare in the Early Fourteenth Century*
   (Woodbridge, 1996)
Rogers, C. J., *War Cruel and Sharp. English Strategy under Edward III*
   (Woodbridge, 2000)
Rogers, C. J. (ed.), *The Wars of Edward III* (Woodbridge, 1999)
Sumption, J., *The Hundred Years War. Trial by Battle* (London, 1990)

18 Ankara
Ahmad Ibn Muhammad (Ibn Arabshah), *Tamerlane, or Timur the Great
   Amir*, trans. J. Herne Sanders (London, 1936)
Alexandrescu-Dresca, M. M., *La Campagne de Timur en Anatolie* (1402;
   reprint London, 1977)
de Clavijo, R. G., *Embassy to Tamerlane, 1403–1406*, trans. G. Le
   Strange (London, 1928)
Hookham, H., *Tamburlaine the Conqueror* (London, 1962)
Imber, C., *The Ottoman Empire, 1300–1481* (Istanbul, 1990)
Morgan, D., *Medieval Persia, 1040–1797* (London, 1988)
Nizameddin, S., *Zafername*, trans. N. Lugal (Ankara, 1949)

19 Agincourt
Allmand, C., *Henry V* (London, 1992)
Barker, J., *Agincourt* (London, 2005)
Curry, A., *The Battle of Agincourt. Sources and Interpretations*
   (Woodbridge, 2000)
Curry, A. (ed.), *Agincourt 1415* (Stroud, 2000)
Curry, A., *Agincourt: A New History* (Stroud, 2005)
Hibbert, C., *Agincourt* (London, 1964)
Keegan, J., *The Face of Battle: A Study of Agincourt, Waterloo and the
   Somme* (London, 1976)
Nicolas, N. H., *The History of the Battle of Agincourt* (London, 1832)

20 The Fall of Constantinople
Babinger, F., *Mehmed the Conqueror and His Time*, trans. R. Manheim &
   ed. W. C. Hickman (Princeton, N.J., 1992)
Imber, C., *The Ottoman Empire, 1300–1481* (Istanbul, 1990)
Kritovoulos, *History of Mehmed the Conqueror*, trans. C. T. Riggs
   (Westport, Conn., 1954)
Melville Jones J. R. (trans.), *The Siege of Constantinople 1453: Seven
   Contemporary Accounts* (Amsterdam, 1972)
Nicol, D. M., *The Immortal Emperor. The Life and Legend of Constantine
   Palaiologos, Last Emperor of the Romans* (Cambridge, 1994)
Runciman, S., *The Fall of Constantinople, 1453* (Cambridge, 1965)
Sphrantzes, G., *The Fall of the Byzantine Empire*, trans. M. Philippides
   (Amherst, 1980)

21 Bosworth
Bennett, M., *The Battle of Bosworth* (Gloucester, 1985)
Foss, P. J., *The Field of Redemore: The Battle of Bosworth, 1485*
   (Headingley, 1990)
Goodman, A., *The Wars of the Roses* (London, 1981)
Gravett, C., *Bosworth 1485* (London, 2000)
Jones, M. K., *Bosworth 1485: Psychology of a Battle* (Gloucester, 2002)
Ross, C., *Richard III* (London, 1981)
Vergil, P., *Three Books of Polydore Vergil's English History*, ed. H. Ellis
   (London, 1844)

Sixteenth Century

22 Flodden
Barr, N., *Flodden 1513* (Stroud, 2001)
Elliot, F., *The Battle of Flodden and the Raids of 1513* (Edinburgh, 1911)
Leather, G. F. T., *New Light on Floddon* (Berwick, 1937)
Kightly, C., *Flodden: The Anglo-Scots War of 1513* (London, 1975)
MacDougall, N., *James IV* (Edinburgh, 1989)
Phillips, G., *The Anglo-Scots Wars 1513–1550* (Woodbridge, 1999)

23 Tenochtitlan
Cortés, H., *Letters from Mexico*, trans. A. Pagden (Yale, 1986)
de Sahagún, B., *Florentine Codex: General History of the Things of New Spain. Book 12 The Conquest of Mexico* (Salt Lake City, 1975)
de Sahagún, B., *The War of Conquest: How It Was Waged Here in Mexico: The Aztecs' Own Story* (Salt Lake City, 1978)
Durán, D., *The Aztecs: The History of the Indies of New Spain*, trans. D. Heyden (Norman, 1994)
Gardiner, C. H., *Naval Power in the Conquest of Mexico* (Austin, 1959)
Hassig, R., *Aztec Warfare: Political Expansion and Imperial Control* (Norman, 1988)
Hassig, R., *Mexico and the Spanish Conquest* (London, 1994)
Ixtlilxochitl, F. de A., *Ally of Cortes: Account 13: Of the Coming of the Spaniards and the Beginning of the Evangelical Law*, trans. D. K. Ballentine (El Paso, 1969)

24 Pavia
Giona, J., *The Battle of Pavia, 24 February 1525* (London, 1965)
Knecht, R. J., *Renaissance Warrior and Patron: The Reign of Francis I* (Cambridge, 1994)
Konstam, A., *Pavia 1525: The Climax of the Italian Wars* (London, 1996)
Oman, C., *A History of the Art of War in the Sixteenth Century* (London, 1937)
Taylor, F.L., *The Art of War in Italy 1494–1529* (Cambridge, 1921)

25 Panipat 1526
Irvine, W., *The Army of the Indian Moghuls* (New Delhi, 1962)
Lane-Poole, S., *Bábar* (Oxford, 1999)
Powell-Price, J. C. *A History of India* (London, 1955)
Prasad, I., *The Mughal Empire* (Allahabad, 1974)
Richards, J. F., *The Mughal Empire* (Cambridge, 1993)

26 Mohács
Fodor, P., 'Ottoman policy towards Hungary, 1520–1541', *Acta Orientalia Academiae Scientiarum Hungaricae* 45, 2–3 (1991), 271–345
Murphey, R., 'Süleyman I and the conquest of Hungary: Ottoman manifest destiny or delayed reaction to Charles V's universal vision', *Journal of Early Modern History* 5, 3 (2001), 197–221
Perjés, G., 'The fall of the medieval kingdom of Hungary: Mohács 1526–Buda 1541', in *War and Society in East Central Europe*, vol. XXVI (Boulder, Co., 1989)
Szakály, F., 'Nándorfehérvár, 1521: the beginning of the end of the Medieval Hungarian kingdom', in Dávid G. & Fodor P. (eds), *Hungarian-Ottoman Military and Diplomatic Relations in the Age of Süleyman the Magnificent* (Budapest, 1994), 47–76
Veszprémy, L. & Király, B. K. (eds), *A Millennium of Hungarian Military History* (Boulder, Co., 2002)

27 Lepanto
Bicheno, H., *Crescent and Cross. The Battle of Lepanto 1571* (London, 2003)
Hess, A., 'The battle of Lepanto and its place in Mediterranean history', *Past and Present*, 57 (1972), 53–73
Imber, C., 'The reconstruction of the Ottoman fleet after the battle of Lepanto, 1571–1572', in idem, *Studies in Ottoman History and Law* (Istanbul, 1996), 85–101
Guilmartin, J. F., *Galleons and Galleys* (London, 2002)
Konstam, A., *Lepanto 1571: The Greatest Naval Battle of the Renaissance* (Oxford, 2003)

28 The Armada
Fernández-Armesto, F., *The Spanish Armada: The Experience of War in 1588* (Oxford, 1988)
Martin, C. & Parker, G., *The Spanish Armada* (London, 1988)
Mattingly, G., *The Defeat of the Spanish Armada* (London, 1959 and later editions)
Pierson, P., *Commander of the Armada: The Seventh Duke of Medina Sidonia* (New Haven & London, 1989)
Rodger, N. A. M., 'The development of broadside gunnery, 1450–1650', *The Mariner's Mirror*, vol. 82, no. 3 (1996), 301–24
Rodríguez-Salgado, M. J. & staff of the National Maritime Museum, *Armada 1588–1988: An International Exhibition to Commemorate the Spanish Armada* (London, 1988)

Seventeenth Century

29 Sekigahara
Bryant, A. J., *Sekigahara 1600. The Final Struggle for Power* (Oxford, 1995)
Friday, K. F., 'Beyond valor and bloodshed. The arts of war as a path to serenity', in Deist, R. (ed.), *Knight and Samurai* (Goeppingen, 2003), 1–13
Hurst III, G. C., *Armed Martial Arts of Japan. Swordsmanship and Archery* (New Haven, CT & London, 1998)
Scott Wilson, W. (trans.), *Ideals of the Samurai: Writings of Japanese Warriors* (Santa Clarita, 1982)

30 Breitenfeld & 31 Nördlingen (most overlap)
Asch, R. G., *The Thirty Years War. The Holy Roman Empire 1618–1648* (Basingstoke, 1997)
Guthrie, W. P., *Battles of the Thirty Years War from White Mountain to Nordlingen 1618–1635* (Westport, 2002)
Lundkvist, S., 'Slaget vid Breitenfeld 1631', *Historisk Tidskrift* 83 (1963), 1–38
Munro, R., *Munro: His Expedition with the Worthy Scots Regiment Called Mac-Keys* (ed. W. S. Brockington (Westport, 1999)
Parker, G. (ed.), *The Thirty Years War* (London, 1987)
Redlich, F., *The German Military Enterprizer and his Workforce*, vol. 1 (Wiesbaden, 1964)
Wedgwood, C. V., *The Thirty Years War* (London, 1938)

32 Shanhaiguan
Mote, F. W., *Imperial China, 900–1800* (Cambridge, MA, 1999)
Spence, J. & Wills J. (eds), *From Ming to Ch'ing: Conquest, Region and Continuity in Seventeenth Century China* (New Haven, 1979)
Wakeman, F., *The Great Enterprise* (Berkeley, Los Angeles & London, 1985)

33 Naseby
Carlton, C., *Going to the Wars: The Experience of the British Civil Wars, 1638–1651* (London, 1992)
Gentles, I., *The New Model Army: In England, Scotland and Ireland, 1645–1653* (Oxford & Malden, MA, 1991)
Kenyon, J. & Ohlmeyer, J. (eds), *The Civil Wars. A Military History of England, Scotland and Ireland, 1638–60* (Oxford, 1998)

34 Vienna
Kriegsarchiv [Vienna War Archive], *Das Kriegsjahr 1683* (Vienna, 1883)
Barker, T. M., *Double Eagle and Crescent: Vienna's Second Turkish Siege and its Historical Setting* (Albany, NY, 1967)
Broucek, P., Hillbrand, E. & Vesely, F., *Historischer Atlas zur Zweiten*

Türkenbelagerung: Wien 1683 (Vienna, 1983)
Kreutel, R. F. (ed.), *Kara Mustafa vor Wien* (Graz, 1982)
Parvev, I., *Habsburgs and Ottomans between Vienna and Belgrade 1683–1739* (Boulder, Co., 1995)
Stoye, J., *The Siege of Vienna*, new ed. (Edinburgh, 2000)

Eighteenth Century

35 Blenheim
Chandler, D., *Marlborough as Military Commander* (London, 1973)
Chandler, D., *The Art of Warfare in the Age of Marlborough* (London, 1976)
Jones, J. R., *Marlborough* (Cambridge, 1993)

36 Poltava
Duffy, C., *Russia's Military Way to the West. Origins and Nature of Russian Military Power 1700–1800* (London, 1981)
Englund, P., *The Battle of Poltava. The birth of the Russian Empire* (London, 1992)
Frost, R. I., *The Northern Wars 1558–1721* (Harlow, 2000)
Hatton, R. M., *Charles XII of Sweden* (London, 1968)
Massie, R. K., *Peter the Great. His life and world* (London, 1981)

37 Belgrade
Braubach, M., *Prinz Eugen von Savoyen. Eine Biographie. Band III, Zum Gipfel des Ruhmes* (München, 1964)
Gutkas, K., *Prinz Eugen und das barocke Österreich* (Salzburg & Wien, 1985)
Henderson, N., *Prince Eugen of Savoy* (New York, 1965)
Hochendlinger, M., *Austria's Wars of Emergence. War, State and Society in the Habsburg Monarchy, 1683–1797* (London & New York, 2003)
McKay, D., *Prince Eugene of Savoy* (London, 1977)
Mraz, G., *Prinz Eugen. Ein Leben in Bildern und Dokumenten* (München, 1985)
Parvev, I., *Habsburgs and Ottomans between Vienna and Belgrade 1683–1739* (Boulder, Co., 1995)

38 Rossbach
Duffy, C., *Frederick the Great. A Military Life* (London, 1985)
Duffy, C., *The Army of Frederick the Great* (2nd ed., Chicago, 1996)
Nosworthy, B., *The Anatomy of Victory. Battle Tactics 1689–1763* (New York, 1992)
Showalter, D., *The Wars of Frederick the Great* (Harlow, 1996)
Wilson, P. H., *German Armies: War and German Politics 1648–1806* (London, 1998)

39 Plassey
Edwardes, M., *The Battle of Plassey and the Conquest of Bengal* (London, 1963)
Spear, P., *Master of Bengal: Clive and his India* (London, 1976)

40 Quebec
Frégault, G., *La Guerre de la Conquête* (Montreal, 1955)
Stacey, C. P., *Quebec 1759: The Siege and the Battle* (Toronto, 1959)

41 Saratoga
Mintz, M., *The Generals of Saratoga. John Burgoyne and Horatio Gates* (New Haven, 1990)
Mackesy, P., *The War for America 1775–1783* (London, 1964)
Higginbotham, D., *George Washington and the American Military Tradition* (Athens, Georgia, 1985)

42 Yorktown
Black, J., *War for America. The Fight for Independence 1775–1783* (Stroud, 1991)
Black, J., *Britain as a Military Power, 1688–1815* (London, 1999)

Wickwire, F. B. & Wickwire M. B., *Cornwallis and the War of Independence* (London, 1971)

43 Jemappes
Blanning, T. C. W., *The French Revolutionary Wars 1787–1802* (London, 1996)
Forrest, A., *Soldiers of the French Revolution* (Durham, NC., 1990)
Griffith, P., *The Art of War of Revolutionary France 1789–1802* (London, 1998)
Lynn, J. A., *Bayonets of the Republic. Motivation and Tactics in the Army of Revolutionary France 1791–1794* (Boulder, Col., 1996)
Rothenberg, G. E., *Napoleon's Great Adversaries. The Archduke Charles and the Austrian Army 1792–1814* (London, 1982)
Scott, S. F., *The Response of the Royal Army to the French Revolution. The Role and Development of the Line Army 1787–1793* (Oxford, 1978)

Nineteenth Century

44 Trafalgar
Corbett, J. S., *The Campaign of Trafalgar* (London, 1910)
Desbrière, E., *The Naval Campaign of 1805: Trafalgar*, trans. and ed. C. Eastwick (Oxford, 1933)
Gardiner, R. (ed.), *The Campaign of Trafalgar, 1803–1805* (London, 1997)
Harbron, J. D., *Trafalgar and the Spanish Navy* (London, 1988)
Sturges Jackson, T. (ed.), *Logs of the Great Sea Fights 1794–1805, vol. 2* (London, 1900, reprinted 2004)
Tracy, N., *Nelson's Battles. The Art of Victory in the Age of Sail* (London, 1996)

45 Leipzig
Chandler, D., *The Campaigns of Napoleon* (London, 1966)
Esdaile, C., *The Wars of Napoleon* (London, 1995)
Leggiere, M. V. *Napoleon and Berlin: The Franco-Prussian War in North Germany, 1813* (Norman, 2002)
Nafziger, G., *Imperial Bayonets. Tactics of the Napoleonic Battery, Battalion and Brigade* (London, 1996)
Petre, F. L., *Napoleon's Last Campaign in Germany, 1813* (New York, 1974; 1st ed. 1912)
Rothenberg, G. E., *The Art of War in the Age of Napoleon* (London, 1978)

46 Waterloo
Britten Austin, P., *1815: The Return of Napoleon* (London, 2002)
Chandler, D. G., *Waterloo: The Hundred Days* (Oxford, 1980)
Chalfont, A. G. J., *Waterloo: Battle of the Three Armies* (London, 1979)
Hofschroer, P. *1815 – The Waterloo Campaign: Wellington, his German Allies and the Battles of Ligny and Quatre Bras* (London, 1998)
Hofschroer, P. *1815 – The Waterloo Campaign: The German Victory* (London, 1998)
Howarth, D., *A Near-Run Thing: The Day of Waterloo* (London, 1968)
Schom, A. *One Hundred Days: Napoleon's Road to Waterloo* (London, 1994)

47 Ayacucho
Anna, T., *The Fall of the Royal Government in Peru* (Lincoln, 1979)
Archer, C. (ed.), *The Wars of Independence in Spanish America* (Wilmington, Del., 2000)
Scheina, R., *Latin America's Wars: The Age of Caudillo, 1791–1899* (Dulles, Va., 2003)

48 Mexico City
DePalo Jr, W. A., *The Mexican National Army, 1822–1852* (College Station, 1997)
Johnson, T. D., *Winfield Scott: The Quest for Military Glory* (Lawrence, 1998)

Singletary, O. A., *The Mexican War* (Chicago, 1960)

Webster, C. L., *The Personal Memoirs of Ulysses S. Grant*, 2 vols (New York, 1885–86)

Winders, R. B., *Mr Polk's Army: The American Military Experience in the Mexican War* (College Station, 1997)

49 Inkerman

Baumgart, W., *The Crimean War 1853–1856* (London, 1999)

Hibbert, C., *The Destruction of Lord Raglan. A Tragedy of the Crimean War 1854–55* (London, 1961)

Kinglake, A. W., *The Invasion of the Crimea. Vol. III: Battle of Inkerman* (New York, 1875)

Massie, A., *The National Army Museum Book of the Crimean War. The Untold Stories* (London, 2004)

Royle, T., *Crimea. The Great Crimean War 1854–1856* (London, 1999)

Seaton, A., *The Crimean War. A Russian Chronicle* (London, 1977)

Warner, P., *The Crimean War. A Reappraisal* (London, 2001)

50 Antietam

Sears, S. W., *Landscape Turned Red: The Battle of Antietam* (New York, 1983)

Harsh, J. L., *Taken at the Flood: Robert E. Lee and Confederate Strategy in the Maryland Campaign of 1862* (Kent, OH, 1999)

Gallagher, G. W. (ed.), *The Antietam Campaign* (Chapel Hill, 1999)

51 Gettysburg

Coddington, E. B., *The Gettysburg Campaign: A Study in Command* (New York, 1984)

Hess, E. J., *Pickett's Charge: The Last Attack at Gettysburg* (Chapel Hill, 2001)

Pfanz, H. W., *Gettysburg: Culp's Hill and Cemetery Hill* (Chapel Hill, 1993)

Pfanz, H. W., *Gettysburg: The Second Day* (Chapel Hill, 1987)

Woodworth, S. E., *Beneath a Northern Sky: A Short History of the Gettysburg Campaign* (Wilmington, DE, 2003)

52 Sadowa

Addington, L., *The Blitzkrieg Era and the German General Staff, 1865–1941* (New Brunswick, 1971)

Craig, G., *The Battle of Königgrätz* (Philadelphia, 1964)

Showalter, D., *Railroads and Rifles: Soldiers, Technology, and the Unification of Germany* (Hamden, Conn., 1975)

Showalter, D., *The Wars of German Unification* (London, 2004)

Strachan, H., *European Armies and the Conduct of War* (London, 1983)

Wawro, G., *The Austro-Prussian War: Austria's War with Prussia and Italy in 1866* (Cambridge, 1996)

53 Omdurman

Steevens, G. W., *With Kitchener to Khartum* (London, 1898)

Churchill, W. S., *The River War: An Account of the Reconquest of the Sudan* (London, 1899)

Arthur, G., *Life of Lord Kitchener, vol. I* (London, 1920)

Pollock, J., *Kitchener. The Road to Omdurman* (London, 1998)

Spiers, E. M. (ed.), *Sudan. The Reconquest Reappraised* (London, 1998)

Modern Times

54 Tsushima

Evans, D. & Peattie, M., *Kaigun: Strategy, Tactics, and Technology in the Imperial Japanese Navy, 1887–1941* (Annapolis, 1997)

Hough, R., *The Fleet That Had To Die* (London, 1958)

Pleshakov, C., *The Tsar's Last Armada: The Epic Voyage to the Battle of Tsushima* (New York, 2002)

Watts, A., *The Imperial Russian Navy* (London, 1990)

Woodward, D., *The Russians at Sea: A History of the Russian Navy* (New York, 1966)

55 Tannenberg

Ironside, Edmund, *Tannenberg: The First Thirty Days in East Prussia* (London, 1928)

Showalter, Dennis, *Tannenberg: Clash of Empires* (original ed. 1991, reprinted Dulles, Va, 2003)

Stone, Norman, The Eastern Front (London, 1975)

56 Jutland

Fawcett, H. W. & Hooper, G. W. W. (eds), *The Fighting at Jutland: The Personal Experiences of Sixty Officers and Men of the British Fleet* (Annapolis, 2002)

Gordon, A. *The Rules of the Game: Jutland and British Naval Command* (Annapolis, MD, 1996)

Halpern, P. *A Naval History of World War I* (Annapolis, 1994)

Tarrant, V. E. *Jutland: The German Perspective* (Annapolis, MD, 1995)

Yates, K. *Flawed Victory: Jutland 1916* (London, 2000)

57 Verdun

Asprey, R., *The German High Command at War* (New York, 1991)

Audoin-Rouzeau, S., *Men at War, 1914–1918* (Oxford, 1992)

Brown, M., *Verdun, 1916* (London, 1999)

Horne, A., *The Price of Glory* (London, 1962)

Martin, W., *Verdun, 1916: They Shall Not Pass* (Oxford, 2001)

Ousby, I., *The Road to Verdun* (New York, 2002)

Whiting Halsey, F., *The Literary Digest History of the World War* (New York, 1919)

58 The Western Front

Doughty, R., *Pyrrhic Victory: French Strategy and Operations in the Great War* (Cambridge, MA, 2005)

Grotelueschen, M., *Doctrine Under Trial: American Artillery Employment in World War I* (Westport, Conn, 2001)

Terraine, J., *To Win A War: 1918, The Year of Victory* (London, 1978)

Travers, T., *How The War Was Won: Command and Technology in the British Army on the Western Front, 1917–1918* (London, 1992)

Travers, T., 'The Allied victories, 1918', in Strachan, H. (ed.), *The Oxford Illustrated History of the First World War* (Oxford, 1998)

59 Battle of Britain

Hough, R. & Richards, D., *The Battle of Britain: The Jubilee History* (London, 1989)

Murray, W., *Luftwaffe: Strategy for Defeat,* (London, 1985)

Overy, R., *The Battle of Britain: The Myth and the Reality* (London, 2001)

60 Battle for Moscow

Carell, P., *Hitler's War on Russia* (London & Boston, 1964)

Erickson, J., *The Road to Stalingrad* (London & New York, 1975)

Glantz, D. M., *When Titans Clashed: How the Red Army Stopped Hitler* (Lawrence, 1995)

Seaton, A., *The Russo-German War 1941–45* (London & New York, 1970)

61 Stalingrad

Beevor, A., *Stalingrad* (London & New York, 1998)

Craig, W., *Enemy at the Gates: The Battle for Stalingrad* (London & New York, 1973)

Erickson, J., *The Road to Stalingrad* (London & New York, 1975)

Glantz, D. M. (ed.), *From the Don to the Dnepr: Soviet Offensive Operations December 1942–August 1943* (London, 1990)

Goerlitz, W., *Paulus and Stalingrad* (London, 1963)

Kerr, W., *The Secret of Stalingrad* (New York, 1978; London, 1979)

62 Midway

Bicheno, H., *Midway* (London, 2001)

Fuchida, M. & Kkumiya, M., *Midway: The Japanese Story* (London, 2002)

Healy, M., *Midway 1942: Turning Point in the Pacific* (Oxford, 1993)

Prange, G., *et al.*, *Miracle At Midway* (New York, 1982)
Ugaki, M., *Fading Victory: The Diary of Admiral Matome Ugaki, 1941–1945*, trans. M. Chihaya (Pittsburgh, 1991)

63 Battle of the Atlantic
Buckley, J., *The RAF and Trade Defence 1919–1945* (Keele, 1995)
Hinsley, F. H., *Codebreakers: The Inside Story of Bletchley Park* (Oxford, 1993)
Milner, M., *The U-boat Hunters: The Royal Canadian Navy and the Offensive Against Germany's Submarines* (Annapolis, Maryland, 1994)
Milner, M., *The Battle of the Atlantic* (London, 2003)
Terraine, J., *Business in Great Waters: The U-boat Wars 1916–1945* (London, 1989)
van der Vat, D., *The Atlantic Campaign* (London,1988)

64 Battle for Normandy
Chandler, D. G. & Collins Jr, J. L., *The D-Day Encyclopedia* (Oxford & New York, 1994)
D'Este, C., *Decision in Normandy* (London & New York, 1983)
Keegan, J., *Six Armies in Normandy* (London & New York, 1982)
Messenger, C., *The D-Day Atlas: Anatomy of the Normandy Campaign* (London & New York, 2004)
Weigley, R. F., *Eisenhower's Lieutenants: The Campaigns of France and Germany 1944–1945* (London & Bloomington, 1981)
Wilmot, C., *The Struggle for Europe* (London & New York, 1952)

65 Operation Bagration
Adair, P., *Hitler's Greatest Defeat: The Collapse of Army Group Centre, June 1944* (London, 1994)
Erickson, J., *The Road to Berlin* (London & Boulder, Colorado, 1983)
Niepold, G., *The Battle for White Russia: The Destruction of Army Group Centre, June 1944* (London & Washington DC, 1987)

66 The American Air Attack on Japan
Alperovitz, G., *The Decision to Use the Atomic Bomb and the Architecture of an American Myth* (London, 1995)
Crane, C. C., *Bombs, Cities and Civilians: American Air Strategy in World War Two* (Kansas, 1993)
Hansell, H., *Strategic Air War Against Japan* (Maxwell, Alabama, 1980)
LeMay, C. with Kantor, M., *Mission with LeMay* (New York, 1965)
Schaffer, R., *Wings of Judgment*, (New York, 1985)
Sherry, M., *The Rise of American Air Power* (New Haven, Connecticut, 1987)
Werrell, K. P., *Blankets of Fire: US Bombers over Japan during World War Two*, (Washington, 1996)

67 Huai-Hai
Bjorge, G. J., *Moving the Enemy: Operational Art in the Chinese PLA's Huai Hai Campaign* (Kansas, 2004)
Chassin, L. M., *The Communist Conquest of China: A History of the Civil War, 1945–1949* (Cambridge, MA, 1965)
Dryer, E., *China at War, 1901–1949* (London, 1995)
Jowett, P. S., *Chinese Civil War Armies 1911–49* (New York, 1997)
Levine, S. I., *Anvil of Victory: The Communist Revolution in Manchuria, 1945–1948* (New York, 1987)
Morwood, W., *Duel for the Middle Kingdom: The Struggle Between Chiang Kai-shek and Mao Tse-tung for Control of China* (New York, 1980)
Pepper, S., *Civil War in China: The Political Struggle, 1945–1949* (Berkeley, 1978)
Westad, O. A., *Cold War and Revolution: Soviet-American Rivalry and the Origins of the Chinese Civil War, 1944–1946* (New York, 1993)
Yick, J. K. S., *Making Urban Revolution in China: The CCP-GMD Struggle for Beijing-Tianjin, 1945–1949* (Armonk, NY, 1995)

68 Dien Bien Phu
Fall, B. B., *Hell in a Very Small Place: The Siege of Dienbienphu* (Philadelphia, 1966)
Jules, R., *The Battle of Dienbienphu* (New York, 1965)
Simpson, H. R., *Dien Bien Phu: The Epic Battle America Forgot* (Washington, DC, 1994)

69 The Tet Offensive
Oberdorfer, D., *Tet!* (New York, 1971)
Smith, G. W., *The Siege at Hue* (Boulder, CO, 1999)
Westmoreland, W. C., *A Soldier Reports* (Garden City, NY, 1976)
Wirtz, J. J., *The Tet Offensive: Intelligence Failure in War* (Ithaca, NY, 1991)
Tucker, S. C. (ed.), *Encyclopedia of the Vietnam War: A Political, Social, and Military History, vol. 3* (Santa Barbara, CA, 1968), 1029–30

70 The Iraq War
Boyne, W., *Operation Iraqi Freedom: What Went Right, What Went Wrong and Why* (New York, 2003)
Cordesman, A. H., *The Iraq War: Strategy, Tactics, and Military Lessons* (New York, 2003)
Williamson, M. & Scales Jr, R. H., *The Iraq War* (Cambridge, MA, 2003)
Purdum, T. S., & staff of *The New York Times*, *A Time of Our Choosing: America's War in Iraq* (New York, 2003)
West, B. & Smith, R. L., *The March Up: Taking Baghdad with the 1st Marine Division* (New York, 2003)

Sources of Illustrations

a: above; b: below; c: centre; l: left; r: right;
CL = Cartographica Ltd; ML: ML Design
(any titles mentioned by author and date alone are detailed in full in Further Reading, p.291)

1 Photo akg-images; 2 V & A Picture Library; 4l © Peter Turnley/CORBIS; 4r Photo akg-images/Erich Lessing; 5l Bibliothèque Nationale, Paris, MS Fr. 2643, f. 165v; 5r V & A Picture Library; 6l Photo akg-images; 6r Photo akg-images; 7l Photo akg-images; 7r Peter Newark's Military Pictures; 10–11 ML; 12 Deutsche Historisches Museen, Berlin; 13 © National Maritime Museum, London; 14–15 Photo akg-images; 15 Getty Images; 16–17 Louvre, Paris. Photo RMN - Chuzeville; 18 © Mike Andrews/Ancient Art & Architecture Library; 19 Photo Will Pryce www.willpryce.com; 20a Staatliche Museen, Berlin; 20b & 21b CL; 22a Museum Narodowe, Warsaw; 22b Roger Wilson; 23 Archaeological Museum, Tehran; 24 Werner Forman Archive/Museo Ostia, Italy; 24–25 Photo akg-images/Peter Connolly; 26 ML; 27 Photo akg-images; 28 & 29b CL; 29a Photo akg-images/Peter Connolly; 30–31 Turkish National Museum, Istanbul; 32 Museo Nazionale Archaelogico, Naples; 33 Roger Wilson; 34a Ashmolean Museum, Oxford; 34b & 35 CL; 36a National Museum of Chinese History, Beijing; 36b ML after *Zhongguo gudai zhanzhong zhan li xuan bi'an* (1981) vol.1, pl.19; 37 National Museum of Chinese History, Beijing; 38 British Museum, London, GR1888.10-12.1; 39l The Bankes Collection, National Trust; 39r Staatliche Museen Antikensammlung, Berlin, 1976.10; 40a Staatliche Munzsammlungen, Munich; 40b Gregoriano Profano Museum, Vatican Museums, Vatican; 41 ML; 42a Photo akg-images/Museum Kalkriese; 42b Roger Wilson; 43a Photo akg-images/Museum Kalkriese; 43b & 44 ML; 45l British Museum, London; 45r Museo Nazionale in Palazzo Altemps, Rome; 46–47 Musée de la Tapisserie de Bayeux, France; 48 Stadtbibliothek, Trier Cod. 31, f.63; 49 Photo David Nicolle; 50 ML; 51l Photo akg-images/Schutze/Rodemann; 51r Magyar Nemzeti Museum, Budapest; 52 ML; 53 Wuttembergische Landesbibliothek, Cod. Bibl 2 23; 54 British Library, London Seal XXXIX.8; 55a The Board of Trustees of the Armouries; 55b ML after *Collins Atlas of Military History* (2004) p.41; 56–57 Musée de la Tapisserie de Bayeux, France; 58 Photo David Nicolle; 59 Werner Forman Archive/Biblioteca Nacional, Madrid; 60 ML; 61 British Library, London Yates Thompson 12 f.161; 62a The Masters and Fellows of Corpus Christi College, Cambridge, MS 26 279; 62b ML after *The Cambridge Illustrated Atlas of Warfare* (1996); 63 Musée Nationale, Damascus; 64 British Library, London Roy. 2 A XXII f.220; 65 The Master and Fellows of Corpus Christi College, Cambridge MS 16, f.166r; 66 Bibliothèque Nationale, Paris, MS lat 10136 Annales Geneunses f.141; 67 Topkapi Saray Museum, Istanbul; 68 ML after *The Cambridge Illustrated Atlas of Warfare* (1996) p.62; 69l Museum of the Imperial Collections (Sannomaru Shozokan) Photograph courtesy of the International Society for Educational Information, Inc; 69r © James P. Delgado; 70 ML; 71 Photo akg-images/Torquil Cramer; 72l Trumpington, Cambridgeshire; 72r Photo akg-images; 73 ML; 74 Bodleian Library, Oxford; 75 Christ Church Oxford, MS 92, f. 3; 76a The Board of Trustees of the Armouries; 76b ML; 77 British Library, London, MS. Cotton Nero E.II. f.152 v; 78 Reproduced with permission of Edinburgh University Library, Special Collections Department, Or Ms 20, f.119R; 79 ML after Alexandrescu-Dresca (1977); 80 British Library, London, Johnson Album 1, no 2; 81 Royal Collection, Windsor; 82a ML; 82b The Board of Trustees of the Armouries; 83 The Board of Trustees of the Armouries; 84 British Library, London, MS. Royal 14 E. IV, f.201v; 85 National Gallery, London; 86a Photo Heidi Grassley, © Thames & Hudson Ltd, London; 86b ML; 87 Bibliothèque Nationale, Paris, MS Fr 9087 f. 207v; 88 Private Collection; 89l V & A Picture Library; 89r The Society of Antiquaries of London; 90 ML after Foss (1990); 91 Photo courtesy of Leicestershire County Council; 92–93 Codex Duran, Chap. LXXV; 94 Photo akg-images/Erich Lessing; 95 Bridgeman Art Library/Archives Charmet; 96 ML after Hodgkin, T., 'The Battle of Flodden', *Archaeologia Aeliana* (1892) vol.16; 97a British Library, London; 97b The Board of Trustees of the Armouries; 98 © Archivo Iconografico, S. A./Corbis; 99 Newberry Library, Chicago; 100a & b ML after Sanders, Parsons & Santley, *The Basin of Mexico* (1979); 101 British Embassy, Mexico City/Bridgeman Art Library; 102 Codex Duran, Chap LXXV1; 103 Louvre, Paris; 104 ML after *Collins Atlas of Military History* (2004) p.47; 105 Bridgeman Art Library/National Museum, Stockholm; 106 Photo akg-images/Erich Lessing; 107 ML; 108 Photo akg-images; 109 The Board of Trustees of the Armouries; 110a Topkapi Saray Museum, Istanbul; 110b Photo akg-images/Erich Lessing; 111l & r ML after Perjés (1989) maps 6 & 9a; 112 Topkapi Saray Museum, Istanbul, f.219b–220a; 114–15 Photo akg-images/Cameraphoto; 116 ML after Davis, P. K., *100 Decisive Battles* (2001) p.197; 117 V & A Picture Library; 118 Museo del Prado, Madrid; 119 Private Collection; 120 ML after Martin & Parker (1988) and Pierson (1989) p.110; 121 Photo akg-images/Erich Lessing; 122–23 Photo akg-images/Erich Lessing; 124 Theatrum Europaeum; 125 Fukuoka Art Musuem, Fukuoka Prefecture, Japan; 126–27 Private collection; 126 Spencer Collection Japanese M553, New York Public Library; 128 ML after Sadler, A. L., *The Maker of Modern Japan* (1979) p.194; 129 Musée Historique de Strasbourg - Photo A. Plisson; 130a & b ML; 131 The Board of Trustees of the Armouries; 132 Photo akg-images; 133 Photo akg-images; 134 National Museum, Stockholm; 135a & b ML; 136 The Board of Trustees of the Armouries; 137a Ming Shilu; 137b ML after Wakeman (1985); 138 Her Majesty the Queen; 139a The Cromwell Museum, Huntingdon; 139b ML; 140 The Board of Trustees of the Armouries; 141 Anon, Battle of Naseby Purchased by Daventry District Council with assistance from the National Art Collection Fund and from the Purchase Grant Scheme administered by the Victoria & Albert Museum. Lent by Daventry District Council to Harborough Museum. Photo courtesy of Leicestershire County Council; 142a Historisches Museum der Stadt, Vienna. Inv. number 31.033; 142b Photo akg-images/Erich Lessing; 143 Rustkammer, Dresden; 144 ML after Barker (1967) p.331; 145 Photo akg-images/Erich Lessing; 146–47 Photo akg-images; 148 Bridgeman Art Library/Peterhof Palace, Petrodvorets, St Petersburg, Russia; 149 Courtesy of the Director, National Army Museum, London; 150 ML; 151 Courtesy of the Director, National Army Museum, London; 152 Courtesy Jeremy Whitaker; 153 Bridgeman Art Library/Tretyakov Gallery, Moscow; 154l & r ML; 155 The Board of Trustees of the Armouries; 156–57 Photo akg-images; 158a ML after Braubach (1964); 158b Private collection; 159 Photo akg-images/Erich Lessing; 160 Archiv Gerstenberg; 161a, bl & br ML; 162 Stadtmuseum Bautzen, Germany; 163 ML; 164a National Portrait Gallery, London; 164b The Board of Trustees of the Armouries; 165 National Archives of Canada, Toronto, Acc. No. 1991-209-1; 166a & b ML; 167 Library and Archives of Canada, Toronto, C-146340; 168 The Ashmolean Museum, Oxford; 169 Independence National Historical Park, Philadelphia; 170 Private collection; 171a & b ML after Bradford, J. C. (ed.), *Oxford Atlas of American Military History* (2003) p.22; 172 Yale University Art Gallery; 173 Courtesy of the Anne S. K. Brown Military Collection, Brown University Library; 174 Independence National Historical Park, Philadelphia; 174–75 Photo RMN - Philippe Bernard; 175 National Portrait Gallery, London; 176 ML after Bradford, J. C. (ed.), *Oxford Atlas of American Military History* (2003) p.30; 177 Photo akg-images; 178 Photo akg-images; 179 ML; 180–81 Photo akg-images; 182 Courtesy of the Director, National Army Museum, London; 183l © National Maritime Museum, London, Greenwich Hospital Collection; 183r © National Maritime Museum, London; 184 © National Maritime Museum, London; 185l & r ML after Taylor, A. H., *Mariner's Mirror* vol.36, no.4 (Oct 1940); 186 Private collection; 187 © National Maritime Museum, London; 188 Private collection; 190–91 Bibliothèque Marmotton, Boulogne-Billancourt, Paris, Photo Giraudon/Bridgeman Art Library; 192 Corbis/Archivo Iconografica; 193l National Gallery, London; 193c National Gallery of Art, Washington, Samuel H. Kress Collection; 193r Wellington Museum, Apsley House, London; 194a & b ML after Chandler, D. G., *Waterloo: The Hundred Days* (2001) p.129; 194–95 Bridgeman Art Library; 196–97 Photo akg-images; 198 ML; 199 The Art Archive/Museo Nacional de Historia Lime/Mireille Vautier; 200a Library of Congress, Washington; 200b Library of Congress, Washington; 201 Library of Congress, Washington; 202 ML after Bradford, J. C. (ed.), *Oxford Atlas of American Military History* (2003) p.59; 203 Library of Congress, Washington; 204 ML after Royle (1999) p.285; 205 Courtesy of the Director, National Army Museum, London; 206 Corbis; 207 Ridge Press, New York; 208 ML after McPherson, J., *Crossroads of Freedom: Antietam* (2002); 209 Library of Congress, Washington; 210 Library of Congress, Washington; 212 ML after Hess (2001) p.8; 213l Library of Congress, Washington, 213r Library of Congress, Washington; 213b Gettysburg Convention & Visitors Bureau. Photo Paul Witt; 214 Library of Congress, Washington; 215l Private collection; 215r Private collection; 216 ML; 217 Photo akg-images; 218 The Trustees of the Imperial War Museum, London; 219a from Black and White, 1 October 1898; 219b ML after Churchill (1899); 220–21 Bridgeman Art Library/Walker Art Gallery, Liverpool, Merseyside; 222 © Jacques Langevin/Corbis Sygma; 224 The Trustees of the Imperial War Museum, London; 225l from The War in the East by Repington, 1905, John Murray, London; 225r from With Togo by H. C. Seppings Wright, 1905, Hurst and Blackett Limited; 226 ML after Evans & Peattie (1997) p.123; 227 Peter Newark's Military Pictures; 228 Courtesy of Vickers Ltd; 229 Photo akg-images; 230a Ullstein Bilderdienst, Berlin, 00487531; 230b ML after *Collins Atlas of Military History* (2004) p.110; 231 The Art Archive/Bayer Army Museum Ingoldstadt; 232 The Trustees of the Imperial War Museum, London; 233 The Trustees of the Imperial War Museum, London; 234 Photo akg-images; 235l Collection Imperial War Museum; 235c&r ML; 236 Hulton Archive/Getty Images; 237a Hulton Archive/Getty Images; 237b ML; 238 Photo akg-images; 239 Roger-Viollet, Paris; 240 Photo akg-images; 241 © Bettmann/Corbis; 242 ML after Edmonds, J. E., *Military Operations, France and Belgium, 1918*, vols ii–v (1937–47) Endpaper A; 243l The Trustees of the Imperial War Museum, London; 243r Photo akg-images; 244 The Trustees of the Imperial War Museum, London; 245 Robert Hunt Library, London; 246 The Trustees of the Imperial War Museum, London; 247 The Trustees of the Imperial War Museum, London; 248 ML after *Collins Atlas of Military History* (2004) p.134; 249a The Trustees of the Imperial War Museum, London; 249b Hoover Institution on War, Revolution and Peace, Stanford University; 250 The Trustees of the Imperial War Museum, London; 251 ML after Messenger, C., *World War Two: Chronological Atlas* (1989) p.65; 252 © Bettmann/Corbis; 253 Photo akg-images; 254a Hoover Institution on War, Revolution and Peace, Stanford University; 254b The Trustees of the Imperial War Museum, London; 255 Photo akg-images; 256 Photo akg-images; 257 Photo akg-images; 258 ML after Newark, T., *Turning the Tide of War* (2001) p.117; 259 Photo akg-images; 260 US Naval Historical Centre; 261a ML after Bradford, J. C. (ed.), *Oxford Atlas of American Military History* (2003) p.138; 261b © Bettmann/ Corbis; 262 Naval Historical Foundation, Washington 88-188-AE; 263 Library of Congress, Washington; 264 The Mariners' Museum/Corbis; 265 Naval Historical Foundation, Washington 88-159ji; 266 ML after Bradford, J. C. (ed.), *Oxford Atlas of American Military History* (2003) p.159; 267l Naval Historical Foundation, Washington 88-159-jj; 267r © Corbis; 268 © Bettmann/Corbis; 269 © Bettmann/Corbis; 270a The Trustees of the Imperial War Museum, London, B6725; 270b & 271b ML after Messenger (2004); 271 The Trustees of the Imperial War Museum, London B6122; 272 Getty Images; 273 Photo akg-images; 274 ML after Messenger, C., *World War Two: Chronological Atlas* (1989) p.191; 275 Photo akg-images; 276 Hoover Institution on War, Revolution and Peace, Stanford University; 277 © Bettmann/Corbis; 278a ML after Bradford, J. C. (ed.), *Oxford Atlas of American Military History* (2003) p.155; 278b Photo akg-images; 279 Private collection; 280 ML after Davis, P. K., *100 Decisive Battles* (2001) p.418; 281 International Instituut voor Sociale Geschiedenis, Amsterdam Collection S. Landsberger; 282 ML after Newark, T., *Turning the Tide of War* (2001) p.171; 283 Rex Features; 284 Ullstein Bilderdienst, Berlin, 00054437; 285 Photo by John Olson/Time & Life Pictures/Getty Images; 286 ML after Newark, T., *Turning the Tide of War* (2001) p.177; 287 Defense Picture Library; 288 © Olivier Coret/In Visu/Corbis; 289 ML; 290 © Reuters/Corbis

Sources of Quotations

Bold numbers refer to the page showing a quotation; a: above; b: below; author's own translations unless specified

p. 19 Herodotus Book 5.105; **p. 30a** Plutarch *Alexander* 33.63; **p. 30b** Diodorus Siculus *Bibliotheca Historia* 17.60.1; **p. 33** Polybius 3.116; **p. 36** trans. ed. Nienhauser, Jr (Bloomington & Indianapolis, 1994, p. 202); **p. 38** trans. Day Lewis (Oxford, 1996, pp. 373–74); **p. 45** Ammianus Marcellinus 31.13; **pp. 85 & 86** Kritovoulos, *History of Mehmed the Conqueror*, trans. Riggs (Connecticut, 1954, p. 51); **p. 91** Polydore Vergil, *Three Books of Polydore Vergil's English History*, ed. H. Ellis (London, 1844, pp. 224–26); **p. 98** *Cortés: The Life of the Conqueror* by his secretary Francisco Lopez de Gomara, trans. Byrd Simpson (Berkeley & Los Angeles, 1964, p. 285); **p. 107** Lane-Poole, *Bábar* (Oxford, 1999, p. 165); **p. 118** Martin & Parker, *The Spanish Armada* (London, 1988, p. 268); **p. 136** Wakeman, *The Great Enterprise* (Berkeley, Los Angeles & London, 1985)/Kai-fu Tsao (1965 dissertation); **p. 156** McKay, *Prince Eugene of Savoy* (London, 1977, p. 164 after a contemporary source); **p. 169** taken from Schuyler's correspondence with Washington; **pp. 174 & 175** taken from Cornwallis's personal correspondence; **p. 179** Lefebvre, *The History of the French Revolution* (Paris, 1924); **p. 200** Webster, *The Personal Memoirs of Ulysses S. Grant* (New York, 1885–86, vol. I, p. 53); **p. 210** Woodworth, *Beneath a Northern Sky: a Short History of the Gettysburg Campaign* (Detroit, 2003); **p. 215** Wawro, *The Austro-Prussian War: Austria's War with Prussia and Italy in 1866* (Cambridge, 1996, p. 267); **pp. 218, 219 & 220** Churchill, *The River War: an Account of the Reconquest of the Sudan* (London, 1933 edition, p. 163, p. 273 & p. 300 respectively); **p. 236** Whiting Halsey, *The Literary Digest of the World War* (New York, 1919, vol. 3, p. 119); **p. 278** (factfile) *Army Air Forces Statistical Digest: World War Two* (1945); **p. 282** Navarre, *Agonie de l'Indochine* (Paris, 1956, pp. 199–200)

Index